ANATOMY OF A CONTROVERSY

ANATOMY OF A CONTROVERSY

The Question of a "Language" Among Bees

ADRIAN M. WENNER

PATRICK H. WELLS

Columbia University Press   New York

Columbia University Press
New York   Oxford
Copyright © 1990 Columbia University Press

Library of Congress Cataloging-in-Publication Data

Wenner, Adrian M.
Anatomy of a controversy:
the question of a "language" among bees
Adrian M. Wenner, Patrick H. Wells.
p.   cm.
Includes bibliographical references.
ISBN 0-231-06552-3
1. Honeybee—Behavior.
2. Animal communication.
I. Wells, Patrick H.
II. Title.
QL568.A6W46   1990
595.79'90459—dc20
90-30539
CIP

Casebound editions of
Columbia University Press books are Smyth-sewn
and printed on permanent and durable acid-free paper
∞

Printed in the United States of America

c 10 9 8 7 6 5 4 3 2 1

CONTENTS

PREFACE

During the mid-1960s we became embroiled in what has become one of this century's most important controversies in biology, a controversy that ostensibly revolves around the question of a "language" among honey bees. However, the topic of a honey bee "language" hardly qualifies as an important issue in science; something far more profound must have been the central concern in this particular dispute.

After a period of introspection and debate, we withdrew from the fray and spent more than twenty years studying the elements of scientific controversy; the last five of those years were spent writing this book. That study and writing led us into the areas of the philosophy, sociology, psychology, and politics of science, topics normally avoided by scientists.

The expression "scientific controversy" is for the most part a contradiction in terms, because everyone has a vague impression that scientific evidence is largely indisputable. How, then, can there be controversy? The net result of this confusion is that scientific controversy seems to be somewhat taboo whenever it is located too close to home. That is, scientists normally want nothing to do with controversy unless it is outside their immediate field.

Scientists also find scientific controversies embarassing; those episodes do not fit the public perception about their research. That is because both scientists and lay people fail to appreciate that such controversies center on *social* and *political* issues rather than on scientific results. Instead, when controversies erupt in their field, scientists tend to 1) pretend there is no controversy, 2) defer to the "authorities" in the field, and/or 3) insist that more evidence is needed.

Those factors together explain, in part, why there are so few accounts of what really happens behind the scenes during scientific controversy. Unfortunately, written histories of science eventually deemphasize the controversy and/or omit mention of such events altogether. One of the better examples of this "purification" of the scientific literature can be found in those biology textbooks that describe Louis Pasteur's contributions of the last century. Any mention of the various controversies Pasteur became embroiled in during his career has disappeared from most textbook accounts of his work.

While there is no question that science has benefited society immensely, the dearth of personal accounts written by scientists has made the task of scientific journalists, philosophers, and sociologists very difficult. Whereas a few successful scientists have written autobiographies, very few personal accounts have been written by scientists who have become involved in major scientific controversies.

Why participants on either side of a controversy fail to publish an account of their experiences is quite obvious. The "winners" (at least for the moment) in a controversy have no incentive to publish such an account, since they must continue on with their research programs. (A famous exception, in a few respects, was James Watson's 1968 book, *The Double Helix*.)

The temporary "losers" in a controversy end up in much more difficult straits. More often than not they become involved in a fight for their "professional lives." Funding sources may suddenly be no longer available, and publication outlets in journals may suddenly disappear (e.g., Feyerabend 1975). While many scientists deny that sociopolitical considerations are important in science (or that they even exist), the working scientist, again, may admit such events to be commonplace whenever such statements can be made under the cloak of anonymity.

Incipient scientists, especially biologists, thus generally enter graduate school remarkably unaware of the *process* of science; they usually receive no formal training in that subject. They are also remarkably naive about sociopolitical considerations, because biologists as a group tend to ignore the deliberations of philosophers, sociologists, and psychologists of science. Biologists usually feel that input from the social sciences is irrelevant to their research programs.

Thus it is that science as portrayed to the public appears to be very different from science as practiced; the real inner workings of science remain largely a mystery even to scientists. Within the past two decades this discrepancy between perception and practice among scientists has come under increasing scrutiny by sociologists and psychologists of science. More recently, journalists who deal with science have begun focusing on the fact that scientists actually often behave more like human beings than like methodological robots as they conduct their research.

For example, William Broad and Nicholas Wade, from their somewhat privileged position as science journalists, were able to write a revealing account of one rather unpleasant aspect of scientific activity. In the preface to their book, *Betrayers of the Truth: Fraud and Deceit in the Halls of Science*, they wrote:

> This book . . . is an attempt to understand better a system of knowledge that is regarded in Western societies as the ultimate arbiter of truth. We have written it in the belief that the real nature of science is widely misunderstood by both scientists and the public.
> According to the conventional wisdom, science is a strictly logical process, objectivity is the essence of the scientist's attitude to his work, and scientific claims are rigorously checked by peer scrutiny and the replication of experiments. From this self-verifying system, error of all sorts is speedily and inexorably cast out. (1982:7)

Broad and Wade then illustrated in their book, using a series of examples, just how vulnerable the scientific establishment can be. They also emphasized that scientists are often the last to recognize when violations of the ethical norm have occurred.

Despite the examples described by Broad and Wade, we believe that science runs rather smoothly, for the most part. However, we also recognize that scientists are quite unprepared for the importance and possible interruption of science when weaknesses of human character interfere with the conduct of that science. A recent and striking episode of self-delusion (and later mass delusion) concerned the "discovery" and demise of the "polywater" hypothesis in the field of physical chemistry (Franks 1981).

While Franks was writing his account of that episode, he received considerable input on whether it was wise to make public an account that would reveal just how much scientists could err (Franks 1981:vii). Concern was raised that honest accounts of scientific activity could damage the reputation of science as a whole; congressmen might seize on such an episode and insist on reduced funding for science. Fortunately, Franks ignored those reservations and wrote his book; he thereby provided a valuable contribution to the literature.

As with Franks, we pondered the wisdom of chronicling our experiences and wondered whether such a document might damage the scientific enterprise. After many discussions with people in diverse fields, however, we decided that, as scientists, we had no choice. Withholding information from those who study the process of science would hardly be in keeping with the freedom of information exchange that scientists pride themselves on.

The format we follow is quite direct as it relates to our personal experience. In the first two chapters (chapters 2 and 3) following the introduction we present some basic information about the philosophy of science and scientific method. Those who are well versed in those matters can move quickly beyond that material. In the next set of three chapters we begin (in chapter 4) with a brief summary of the rationale of bee "language" hypotheses in general and the course that notion has taken throughout history. We follow that historical treatment with a presentation of the contrast between a long-standing odor-search model (chapter 5) and the dance language model (chapter 6) of how naive honey bees might find food sources at which their hivemates have been successful.

The next several chapters (7–10), although not covering the material in strict chronological order, trace our disillusionment with the appealing honey bee dance language hypothesis formulated by the Nobel Prize winner Karl von Frisch. We recount our experiences as we uncovered a considerable amount of evidence that forced us back to an existing and previously embraced odor-search model (e.g., Maeterlinck 1901; von Frisch 1939).

After presenting the reasons for our disillusionment with the dance language hypothesis, we cover in the next three chapters various personal encounters as they relate to the sociology, psychology, and philosophy of science. There was a great deal of social interconnection among some very important biologists in the 1950s, 1960s, and 1970s (chapter 11), and a great deal of effort was expended to reaffirm the "truth" of the dance language hypothesis (chapters 12 and 13). Among other factors that arose during the controversy, the strong challenges by Rosin (chapter 13) were ignored, as the dance language hypothesis was shored up by the "scientific establishment."

In the last chapter of the main text, we summarize our impressions about the controversy, relate those impressions to what we have learned from studies in the sociology, psychology, and philosophy of science, and offer suggestions concerning the training of our undergraduate and graduate biology students.

The format of the remainder of the book deviates from what is normally found in scientific volumes. Early on in our writing of the main text, we found that we had to cover certain episodes critical to our treatment; however, inserting these accounts within the main body of the text would have disrupted the flow of the main message. To avoid confusion, we followed the lead of many books published in the social sciences and collected those diversions into a separate section, the Excursuses. Each of these excursuses elaborates on a point made in the main text itself.

Those excursuses are self-contained, semi-independent essays and are not meant to be read in sequence along with the text material. We expect that these topics will be explored when clarification of a point is desired. Perhaps the most efficient procedure would be to make note of the mention of excursuses as they arise and then refer to whichever of them is pertinent when that chapter has been completed.

A final small point: throughout the text we have written "honey bee" as two words rather than "honeybee" as prescribed by dictionaries. In doing so, we remain consistent with tradition in entomology (Wenner 1971a).

ACKNOWLEDGMENTS

Our first debt is to all of our colleagues who were involved, pro and con, in the "dance language" controversy. Through lively discussions, in and out of print, they articulated the essence of the various philosophies and group dynamics of science that form the basis of this volume. Our recognition of their input is implicit in the extensive use of specific citations and direct quotations throughout the text.

We appreciate Connie Veldink's efforts to document the various sociological aspects of this controversy, in that future students of science *as a process* will now have some of the necessary material for their deliberations on this issue. R. Rosin deserves a special note of thanks for persistence and insight into the fundamental issues at stake in the controversy. We also thank Thomas Kuhn for writing his book, *The Structure of Scientific Revolutions*, which early on provided us with stabilizing input; his analysis helped us to understand why our research received such negative response from the scientific community.

In our previous publications we acknowledged many people who helped us during experimentation and while we drafted manuscripts.

For this volume our special thanks go to Frederick Schram, Hilda E. Wenner, and two anonymous referees for their insightful editorial assistance on the entire manuscript, as well as to Jenifer Dugan, Mark Page, Martin Schein, and Harrington Wells, who read portions of the contribution. We thank Kim Vines for her extensive work in preparing figures and Larry Jon Friesen for his efforts in that same area. We also thank Pearl Wells and Hilda E. Wenner for their encouragement and patience during the five years we spent writing this volume.

The Biological Sciences Department of the University of California at Santa Barbara and the Department of Biology at Occidental College provided considerable help during these past twenty years. Besides logistical support, these departments furnished a suitable intellectual setting for work that did not fall within the "mainstream" of biology. Shanna Bowers, Juli Gotschalk, Mo Lovegreen, and Patti Thurston of the Marine Science Institute were most helpful; they provided extensive access to laser printing facilities during the final stages of manuscript preparation.

The editors and staff at Columbia University Press have been very supportive and helpful. Special mention goes to Susan Koscielniak, formerly executive editor at Columbia, for her willingness to consider publication of this contribution and to Edward Lugenbeel, current executive editor of Columbia, for his persistent support and insight into the honey bee dance language controversy. Both of these people recognized the need for "academic freedom" during the preparation of a treatise on a topic that some might consider "controversial." Even though they provided that freedom, we accept complete responsibility for any inadvertent errors, omissions, or other defects of scholarship our readers may discover.

Adrian M. Wenner
Patrick H. Wells

ANATOMY OF A CONTROVERSY

1

SCIENCE, CONTROVERSY, AND THE QUESTION OF A HONEY BEE LANGUAGE

REALISM VS. RELATIVISM

"Those who have treated of the sciences have been either empirics or dogmatical. The former like ants only heap up and use their store, the latter like spiders spin out their webs. The bee, a mean between both, extracts matter from the flowers of the garden and the field, but works and fashions it by its own efforts. The true labor of philosophy resembles hers, for it neither relies entirely nor principally on the powers of the mind, nor yet lays up in the memory the matter afforded by the experiments of natural history and mechanics in its raw state, but changes and works it in the understanding."

—*Sir Francis Bacon (1620)*

"The word science is often invoked as if it meant a particular 'thing' comprised of scientists, public and private laboratories, publications, and government agencies. For me; however, 'science' connotes a process or procedure for making inquiries about our world and for evaluating the hypotheses these inquiries generate."

—*Sigma Xi 1987:7*

"The production of scientific knowledge is simultaneously the production of scientific error."

—*Naomi Aronson 1986:630*

W̶hat is science? The words of Sir Francis Bacon (above) contain much of the essence of three possible scientific attitudes. At one extreme we find scientists who are primarily empirical, in that they are largely "ignorant of scientific principles and rely solely on practical experience." At another extreme are dogmatic scientists who rely heavily upon the "truth" of pronouncements made by fellow "authorities." In his figurative statement Bacon advocated instead a give-and-take approach within science, an approach some might like to describe as an ever-changing use of both inductive and deductive reasoning.

SCIENCE AS A PROCESS

Science is apparently a *process* (e.g., Hull 1988), not a "thing," and some scientists engage in science accordingly. Other scientists may treat science more as a career. These different perspectives naturally lead to the exacerbation of controversy when it arises in science, but working scientists may be quite unaware of the inevitability of controversy. In fact, scientists most often become puzzled and quite uncomfortable when controversy arises within their own research sphere, but that should not be so.

Judith Anderson recognized the dilemma posed: "To end controversies, scientists must first understand them; but scientists would rather do science than discuss it" (1988:18). Erich Bloch, director of the National Science Foundation, commented on that same point: "Science is all about new ideas, but when someone introduces them into the sociology of science, all the defensive mechanisms go up. Everyone favors new ideas, but not if it changes the way they are currently doing things" (Mervis 1988).

The reluctance of practicing scientists to dwell on the nature of the scientific process (despite what Bacon and others who followed him have said) is one reason science remains one of the least understood of all human activities (even though it is responsible for much of the success of modern technology). Equally puzzling is the fact that progressive science appears to exist only in some parts of the world. For example, some four thousand languages exist in the various cultures throughout the world; yet in only a few of those parent cultures has science been actively practiced (Kneller 1978).

Part of that poor understanding and limited scientific activity results from the fact that science as a process thrives only under special cultural circumstances (Harding 1986). Another reason for uncertainty about the nature of science stems from the fact that philosphers of science differ sharply with one another in their perception of how science works. Sociologists and psychologists of science fare little better in their deliberations.

That gap in understanding among scholars has apparently arisen from the lack of a clear and necessary distinction: how scientists *should* perform as scientists may be quite different from how scientists are *likely* to behave because of the fact that they are human beings first and scientists second.

Furthermore, philosophers and sociologists of science have usually focused their attention on the presumed reasons for successful careers of especially creative and/or controversial scientists whose work eventually became recognized. These scholars then extrapolated from their deliberations and advocated one approach or another; at the same time they have generally insisted that the approach they advocated could lead to "good" science.

The philosophical and sociological literature has thus relied on various *assumed* reasons for the success of scientists such as Boyle, Curie, Galileo, Jenner, Newton, and Pasteur. Unfortunately, most of the relevant material on the accomplishments and travails of the target scientists was lost long before philosophers and sociologists became interested in those specific success stories. Consequently, we lack enough essential documentation about how these people *really* functioned as scientists within their communities at the time they lived.

Only within the last few decades has the process of science come under both a broader and closer scrutiny. Most philosphers previously paid scant attention to factors other than those subscribed to by successful scientists themselves (see Feyerabend 1975). On the other hand, sociologists and psychologists of science have begun to scrutinize more carefully the day-to-day activities of scientists—both successful scientists and those who have encountered difficulties (e.g., Veldink 1989).

Much to the dismay of some scientists (the relatively few who pay attention to sociologists and psychologists), the findings and conclusions published by these more recent scholars all too often do not fit the public and self-image of scientists that one may find in textbooks. As Broad and Wade so succinctly wrote in the preface to their book:

> In the acquisition of new knowledge, scientists are not guided by logic and objectivity alone, but also by such nonrational factors as rhetoric, propaganda, and personal prejudice. Scientists do not depend solely on rational thought, and have no monopoly on it. Sci-

ence should not be considered the guardian of rationality in society, but merely one major form of its cultural expression. (1982:9)

If Broad and Wade are correct, there is a great discrepancy between the image scientists tend to portray of themselves and the actual behavior scientists exhibit during the course of their scientific careers. The philosophers of science and the public at large, in turn, apparently attend more to the *image* than to the *reality* of science.

In an effort to ascertain the attitudes of scientists toward their own discipline, Sigma Xi ("The Scientific Research Society") conducted a survey of its members in 1986, the year of its 100th anniversary (1987). Sigma Xi tried to determine which problems most concerned their membership by providing in a questionnaire certain statements about the process of science. The answers to the questions posed then revealed the degree to which its members could agree with the validity of those statements.

The epigraph above was one such example of statements used during the Sigma Xi survey, and it evoked the greatest degree of unanimity; more than 95 percent of the respondents agreed that science was more a "process" than a "thing." Authors of the report wrote:

> This degree of unanimity, far greater than was encountered in any of the other 35 questions in the Survey, is the more significant since it seems very probable that the view of science held by the non-scientific public is that science is much closer to being a "thing" or an "institution" than a process. This difference in perception or understanding may be the root of many other problems. (Sigma Xi 1987:7)

SOCIAL VERSUS SCIENTIFIC CONSIDERATIONS

In public, scientists generally deny that their work is influenced by social, psychological, and political considerations. Examples of such denial have repeatedly emerged in congressional hearings (Broad and Wade 1982). In unguarded moments, however, scientists often cite numerous examples in which sociological considerations have been more important than the scientific activity itself in their own personal experience. The current funding system in the United States, which implicitly includes rewards for conformity, has complicated relationships among scientists (e.g., Feyerabend 1975).

We cannot say that we were not forewarned; in 1967 Garrett Hardin published a provocative article, "Pop Research and the Seismic Market," in which he wrote:

> Ill-tended wealth has always a tendency to corrupt. More than one voice has been raised to cry out against the threat easy money poses to the honesty and integrity of science. A "realist" (in the uncomplimentary sense) might well say, "Here's all this federal money asking to be spent; what project can I dream up to get my share?" . . . Whether from venality or altruism, the result is the same: science is corrupted. The intrinsic worth of a proposal for investigation is replaced more and more by its saleability. Popularity with those who control the purse-strings becomes a prime consideration. Fundamental research gives way to what future historians may well call "Pop Research." (1967:19)

In that last connection, the Sigma Xi survey respondents were also asked to identify the two most important problems they faced in their own research programs. Eighty-five percent of the responses fell into only five of the available categories; the third most important was "over-politicization of research."

As an example, the respondents' concern with sociopolitical issues emerged most clearly in response to the following statement: "Procurement procedure for grants to do governmentally sponsored research depends on 'who you know.' Many requests seem to be funded primarily because the researchers are already known to and supported by the granting organizations" (1987:21).

Of the respondents, nearly 63 percent agreed with that statement. That is hardly the response one would expect from reading the deliberations of philosophers of science, from listening to scientists discussing the "objective" peer review system, or from reading textbook descriptions of scientific research.

We are thus left with a major discrepancy, as indicated above. Scientists often subscribe to an unrealistic image of their role in society and all too often portray that image to the public (an image that many laypeople subscribe to). That image closely matches an impression many philosophers of science seem to have relied upon. Broad and Wade (see above) expressed quite a different notion.

Kneller described scientists in a most favorable light, one commonly held by philosophers of science and often expressed by the scientists themselves, as follows:

> The scientist generally tries harder than the layman to screen out personal prejudice and check for possible error. He seeks to make his assumptions explicit and attends to the work of others in his

field. He reports his findings more accurately and makes predictions that can in principle be tested precisely. . . . As a rule he tests the predictions and publishes the hypotheses if he finds them confirmed. If they are refuted, he usually alters the hypothesis, or invents another one, and tries again. This process is self-corrective. By eliminating incorrect hypotheses, the scientist narrows the search for the correct one. (1978:117)

In most cases perhaps, Kneller's assessment fits the behavior of biologists as they proceed in their scientific investigations. Much research is routine, however, with little incentive for scientists to question the idealized norm. If an experiment "doesn't work" or if anomalous results emerge, chances are good that more information is needed.

Results and interpretations often form the initial assumptions for other projects. Scientists know that this is true, and they also know that a failure to pursue important leads may lead to trouble somewhere down the line for someone else who relies on the validity of experimental results. The original researcher, in turn, may also have to use those results and interpretations as the basis for another experiment.

A commonly held belief, as expressed by Kneller (above), is that science is "self-correcting," because others replicate experiments. Panem stressed the "self-correction" element as an essential operational difference between scientists and journalists when she wrote: "Science is often self-correcting; that is, the imperative for independent verification of facts forces accountability on scientific reports. In journalism, there is no comparable pressure for accountability" (1987:974).

That image is not universally shared, as Broad and Wade found:

> The notion of replication, in the sense of repeating an experiment in order to test its validity, is a myth, a theoretical construct dreamed up by the philosophers and sociologists of science. . . . By its very nature, a replication test . . . is seen as posing a direct challenge. The implication that there might be something amiss with a researcher's work arouses instant antagonism and defensiveness. (1982:77)

Clearly, another major discrepancy exists. If the scientific process itself were as cut-and-dried as is indicated in textbooks, one would think that progress would be uniform and would occur without stress. The history of science reveals otherwise. Controversies can erupt at any time in any of the subfields of science. When a controversy erupts, it may persist for decades, despite any stated adherence to "objectivity" or supposed reliance on "testing" of hypotheses or "replication" of experiments (Broad and Wade 1982). Also, social and political considerations enter into such controversies to a far greater extent than most philosophers of science have realized.

If scientists adhered strictly to the processes of objective reasoning, replication, and testing of hypotheses, why should controversies exist at all? Why should not replications that yield unexpected ("unwanted") results be welcomed? And, if controversies erupt, why should they persist? The philosophers of science have been remarkably silent on these issues, but the sociologists of science have begun addressing the problem. A serious handicap to their studies, however, has been the fact that they lack the raw material so necessary for their deliberations.

THE DANCE LANGUAGE CONTROVERSY

Few hypotheses in biology conceived during this century have gained more attention than the celebrated honey bee dance language hypothesis of Karl von Frisch (e.g., 1947, 1950, 1967a). That hypothesis was remarkable for its simplicity, and the supportive experiments were renowned for their repeatability.

Von Frisch's dance language hypothesis rested in part on the observation that returning successful foraging bees execute in the hive an apparently meaningful "waggle dance," a behavioral maneuver from which we can extract both direction and distance information about the location of a food source routinely visited by those foragers. In the mid-1940s von Frisch obtained experimental results which also indicated that potential recruit bees could *presumably* extract that same direction and distance information from waggle dances and fly directly out from the hive to the same site and exploit that food source.

Von Frisch apparently never provided a precise statement of his hypothesis; neither was it necessary, since acceptance was rapid and widespread (Rosin 1980a:797). Nor did anyone seem to notice that von Frisch's results did not correspond with the results he obtained earlier in support of his olfactory hypothesis (von Frisch 1939; see Rosin 1980a).

Despite the lack of a precise statement of the hypothesis itself, the claims made in the early years were precise enough to permit designs of experimental tests of the hypothesis, but no one did so; experiments that yielded supportive correlations substituted for tests (and were considered by many to be "tests"). Here we note the difference between *justifiability* and *acceptability* of hypotheses in a community. As an anonymous reviewer of our book manuscript wrote, "even widely accepted hypotheses may nonetheless be unjustified."

The dance language hypothesis thus remained untested and unchallenged for two decades. The claims of accuracy in use of information continued unabated. For example, early on von Frisch wrote: "We see that the majority of searching bees fanning out, moved within an angle deviating not more than 15 degrees each to the left and to the right from the direction leading towards the feeding place" (1948:10). Tinbergen echoed that claim when he wrote: "They fly in a definite direction over a definite distance (both communicated to them by the dancer) and begin to search for flowers" (1951:54).

Von Frisch never deviated from claiming great accuracy in "use" of "dance language" information by searching honey bee recruits. He later wrote, for example:

> For almost two decades my colleagues and I have been studying one of the most remarkable systems of communication that nature has evolved. This is the "language" of the bees; the dancing movements by which forager bees direct their hivemates, with great precision, to a source of food. (1962:78)

Even in his comprehensive review of experimental results, von Frisch remained steadfast: "This description of the location enables the newcomers to fly rapidly and with certainty to the indicated flowers, even when these are kilometers away—an accomplishment on the part of the bees that is without parallel elsewhere in the entire animal kingdom" (von Frisch 1967a:57), and "the persistent searching of a given insect at a definite distance shows that it is just here that she is expecting something" (von Frisch 1967a:86).

It should not be surprising that we initially agreed with von Frisch's assessment: "The language of bees is truly perfect, and their method of indicating the direction of food sources is one of the most remarkable mysteries of their complex social organization" (1950:75). Without the confidence engendered by such statements, we would not have begun our own research.

The anomalies we later uncovered arose out of our attempts to construct a "model" dancing bee, by which we had hoped to direct naive bees out to crops (see excursus VGR). Through a series of experiments we "rediscovered" the importance of learning and odor during honey bee recruitment to food crops. What we did not recognize at the time was that the reaction of biologists to our negative results would be perhaps more interesting than the results of our research.

Since the intellectual climate (in the sense described in part by Broad and Wade 1982) was hardly conducive to a new point of view at the time of our initial challenge to the dance language hypothesis, we bided our time for the next two decades. During the past several years the climate has been changing, and an account of our experiences should be of interest, as it relates to the deliberations of philosophers, sociologists, and psychologists of science.

This opportunity to provide raw materials for these other disciplines strikes us as a far more important issue than the rather trivial question of a possibility of a "dance language" among bees. (Although, as will be seen, the question of a language among bees has its own wide-ranging ramifications.)

Few biologists recognized the fact that a bee "language" hypothesis of one sort or another and an odor-search hypothesis can each explain virtually all of the experimental evidence that has been gathered on honey bee recruitment during the several decades. Neither do biologists seem to appreciate the fact that both explanations have been with us for centuries; there has been a vacillation between the two explanations as the sociopolitical climates have changed through time (see chapter 4).

How is it that a relatively simple issue, such as the possibility of a "language" among bees, could develop into a complex controversy? As we learned more about the history of both attempted explanations (odor-search versus language), we came to view any decision to accept one of those hypotheses over the other as more of a sociopolitical than a scientific issue.

A common theme during the controversy was the assertion that the scientific community needed more evidence to resolve the matter. We feel instead that the real problem has been the lack of ground rules on what constitutes valid scientific evidence. That is, when experimental results are evaluated without sufficient attention to basic assumptions or without regard to the suitability of the experimental approach used, issues cannot and will not be resolved.

From the perspective we eventually gained during our experience, it became evident that there were great differences in basic assumptions held by various participants during the four decades of inception and challenge of the most recent version of a bee language hypothesis. It also became evident to us that these differences were apparently irreconcilable.

An 1890 treatise by Thomas Chrowder Chamberlin had actually provided the basis for a perceptive attitude with respect to a choice among experimental approaches. Bee researchers and other biologists, by following Chamberlin's advice, could have resolved rather quickly the question that had arisen regarding a possible "language" among bees. However, Chamberlin's advice had become lost, as had Maurice Maeterlinck's (1901) considered judgment on the question of the presence or absence of such a "language."

Throughout the last portion of this book, we attempted to refrain from pressing others to accept our views regarding the possibility or lack of a "dance language" among bees, because that is no longer a burning question for us. We instead have become far more interested in how biologists reacted when we proposed an alternative interpretation to the dance language hypothesis, just as we stated earlier:

> We believe that experimentation does not "prove" or "disprove" hypotheses, but rather affects their credibility. If the credibility of a hypothesis at any given time is determined by the total body of relevant information available, then the [dance] language hypothesis of forager recruitment was very credible in 1946 when von Frisch proposed it. It is less so now, for the body of relevant information is quite different and includes much unfavourable evidence. . . . Do honey bees have a language? That is a question which may never be answered with certainty. It may be more useful to examine assumptions critically, state hypotheses and the consequences with precision, review the evidence objectively, and ask: can we now believe that honey bees have a language? Thus, it appears that the honey bee forager recruitment controversy is not about the nature of evidence but rather about the nature of hypotheses. It is not what investigators observe (the data) but what they believe (infer) that is at the heart of the controversy. (Wells and Wenner 1973:174)

We might add, in an anonymous reviewer's words: "This book is not only a documentation of the bee language controversy, it is also an implicit plea that acceptability of ideas in science should be based on justifiability."

If we have read the deliberations of philosophers, sociologists, and psychologists of science correctly, there is little need to change our basic attitude; we now appreciate more fully the sense of Bacon's words in the opening epigraph. We also feel confident that bees will go on behaving as they have for millions of years without regard for our theories.

2

PHILOSOPHERS
AND
PARADIGMS

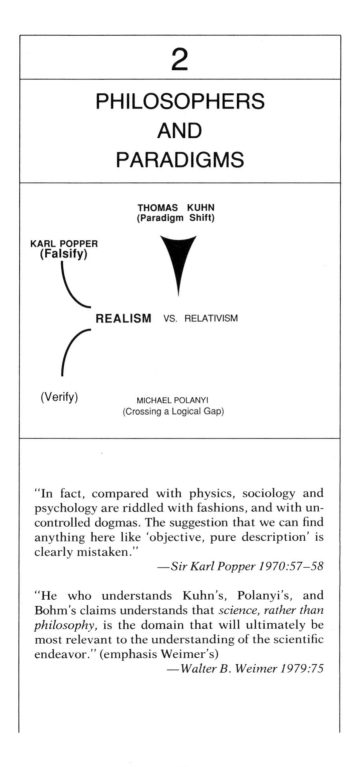

THOMAS KUHN
(Paradigm Shift)

KARL POPPER
(Falsify)

REALISM VS. RELATIVISM

(Verify)
MICHAEL POLANYI
(Crossing a Logical Gap)

"In fact, compared with physics, sociology and psychology are riddled with fashions, and with uncontrolled dogmas. The suggestion that we can find anything here like 'objective, pure description' is clearly mistaken."
—*Sir Karl Popper 1970:57–58*

"He who understands Kuhn's, Polanyi's, and Bohm's claims understands that *science, rather than philosophy*, is the domain that will ultimately be most relevant to the understanding of the scientific endeavor." (emphasis Weimer's)
—*Walter B. Weimer 1979:75*

S cience is one of the few human endeavors wherein we have collectively accumulated a body of quantitative knowledge that, in turn, has permitted an ever faster increase in understanding and the acquisition of further knowledge. However, philosophers of science currently disagree about the reasons for that success—that is, what science is and why it functions so well (e.g., Popper 1957, 1970; Kuhn 1962, 1970b; Lakatos and Musgrave 1970; Gutting 1980; Hacking 1983).

More recently, James Atkinson, while considering the possible reasons for that disagreement among philosophers, proposed a "crudely drawn model which requires additional supporting evidence drawn from both the history of science and the experience of active scientists" (1985:734). He elaborated:

> Perhaps we can summarize this model of science by defining science as a process whereby the human capacity for imagination creates and manipulates images in the mind producing concepts, theories, and ideas which incorporate and tie together shared human sensory experience and which are assimilated into human culture through a similar act of re-creation. These concepts, theories and ideas constitute a body of knowledge of that interaction of humans with nature which is accepted as reality. Since reality is a process of interaction and [since] the human experience and mind are both capable of generating an almost infinite array of images, scientific knowledge has changed and will continue to change, sometimes with revolutionary quickness and at other times with a slow gradual evolution. (1985:734)

For us, Atkinson's and Popper's attitudes stand in sharp contrast to one another. Popper suggested that "objectivity" can be attained in science and insisted that we can come ever closer to understanding "reality" (the "Realism" school; see excursus RE). Atkinson insisted that a knowledge of objective reality can never be fully achieved (the "Relativism" school; see Bernstein 1983; Hacking 1983; Latour 1987). Instead, he argued that what we accept as "reality" at any one time is based upon shared perceptions. He concluded that current teaching about science "fosters naive realism" in students and laypeople alike.

Apparently, a lack of comprehensive and accurate history of science, a lack of an inclusive and perceptive analysis of social relationships among scientists, and a scarcity of fully documented case histories have all contributed to the disagreements found among philosophers. In fact, all have acknowledged the need for more input in those areas. Atkinson stressed the need for his model (quoted above) "to be carefully evaluated through the study of the history of science."

Popper (in the above epigraph) had also acknowledged a possible role of social input in the practice of science (e.g., "sociology and psychology are riddled with fashions"), but he apparently felt that social input was of little importance in the "hard sciences," such as physics, chemistry, and (perhaps) biology.

RANKING THE BIOLOGICAL SCIENCES

As indicated by Popper, a hierarchy appears to exist among scientific disciplines, although perhaps not to the rigid degree expressed in his statement. In fact, scientists often jest about (and sometimes take seriously) the relative "respectability" of different scientific fields, thereby recognizing the existence of a "pecking order" analogous to that of various nonhuman animal species, as elucidated by studies in animal behavior. A physicist, for example, can deride research done in biology or psychology, but biologists and psychologists are unlikely, on those same grounds, to criticize research projects in physics.

Within the very diverse field of biology a similar hierarchy exists; the various disciplines vie for position in that "respectability" scale. One hears the expression "high-powered biology," and grant funds are much easier to obtain in some areas of research than in others (e.g., Whitley 1984). A biochemist or microbiologist may well question the "importance" of a field study of bird or lizard behavior, but the ornithologist or herpetologist would be less likely to question the importance of any study of biochemical processes in viruses or bacteria by someone in the former field (see also Zuckerman 1977; Schram 1979).

Karl Popper's statement conveys another important suggestion: the degree of objectivity in a researcher's scientific approach is often considered more a function of the discipline chosen while a fledgling scientist than a consequence of any specific training obtained in the methodology of science. Popper's implication is that a person, by becoming a physicist, automatically emerges a more objective scientist than by becoming, say, a sociologist.

Although philosophers and historians of science (e.g., Popper, Atkinson, and Kuhn) concern themselves with methodological, historical, and (sometimes) social problems, such as those alluded to in their statements, those same problems are rarely addressed or considered by people actively engaged in science. The scientists themselves are usually too involved in their research and in interchanges with colleagues to be especially introspective (or retrospective) about their particular roles in science. Nor have they seemed too concerned about understanding the process of science itself.

Karl Popper omitted the field of biology in his very brief example, which is probably just as well; as indicated above, that field is very diverse and the experimental approaches used are quite varied. In this book, however, we cannot avoid the problem of ranking within the biological sciences. Neither can we avoid treating social relationships and "objectivity" among biologists, since those factors are essential components of the topic under consideration (scientific controversies in general and the honey bee dance language controversy in particular).

As an example, we next present the history of a sociopolitical "resolution" of a little-known controversial issue during the nineteenth century.

THE THOMPSON AND WESTWOOD CONTROVERSY

The expectation we can get from Popper—that reality exists in the world and that science can reveal that reality—is widely shared and subscribed to. Not all agree; the case of John V. Thompson's (1835a, 1835b) studies on the natural history of crabs and their life cycle illustrates how difficult it may be for scientists to engage in the "objective, pure description" advocated by Popper, even in one of the "hard" sciences.

Thompson's experience (Coffin 1960)—a rejection of his findings on crustacean metamorphosis, which later were found valid—illustrates what can happen when results obtained do not mesh with "known" facts and current interpretation. The scientific community was ill prepared for what arose out of his research, and consequently scientists "settled the issue" (for a time) in a sociopolitical rather than in a scientific manner.

Some background information is necessary to understand Thompson's contribution. Most crustaceans, including decapods (e.g., shrimps, crabs, and lobsters) have a complex life cycle, with some of their growth patterns bordering on the unbelievable (see Wenner 1985). For example, a transparent larva, known as a *zoea* in crabs, hatches from the egg after embryonic development and begins life as a member of the oceanic plankton (figure 2.1). The transparent larval crab, which passes through several molts and which may pass through different larval forms, most often bears no resemblance to the pigmented and calcified adult it becomes.

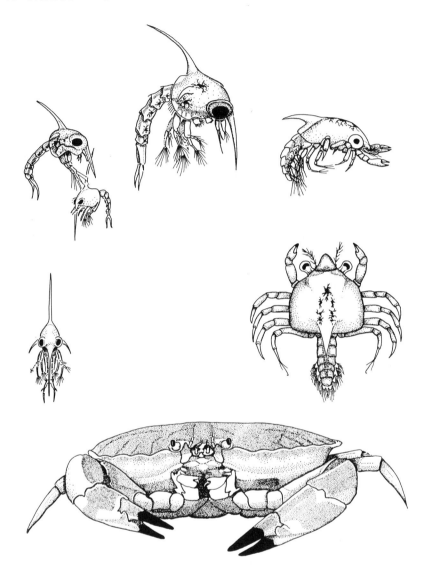

FIGURE 2.1. Life cycle of a crab (read clockwise from middle left). The first four larval stages shown as very small transparent "zoeae" are part of the ocean plankton (zooplankton). After many molts during those zoeal stages, the animal molts into a translucent settling form (megalopa, middle right on the diagram) before metamorphosing into a juvenile crab. After many more molts, the crab attains sexual maturity (bottom illustration).

Marine biologists prior to Thompson had no suitable seawater facilities where they could maintain those larvae and raise them through larval and juvenile stages to adulthood. Thus they had no direct means by which they could establish the identity of larvae, even if they had been aware that they were dealing with larvae and not with adults of some undescribed species.

Early zoologists worked under an even greater handicap; they were not even certain about the proper placement of these zoeae (the plural of zoea) into phyla. For convenience in identification, those crab larvae most similar to each other were placed in a new genus, *Zoea*. Thompson was the first person to recognize, by direct observation, that a larva eventually metamorphosed into a familiar crustacean. His observations were thus the "objective, pure description" of Popper. We also recognize that Thompson "created an image" different from that which others had seen before him; this is the sense of Atkinson's comments (above).

Harold Coffin summarized what transpired when Thompson published his results:

> The different stages in the life cycle of decapods were known and described in the early years of the nineteenth century, but they were not recognized as larvae of known animals and were assigned to new genera and placed in wrong suborders. . . . The suspicion that the genus *Zoea*, admittedly containing some of the most remarkable members of the class, was composed of larval forms was first expressed by J. V. Thompson (1828, 1829, 1831). Despite personal observations and excellent illustrations, his claim that the genus *Zoea* consisted (of) the larvae of decapods was not taken seriously. . . . [However], old established concepts die hard, as was evidenced by the many strong contradictions to the remarks of Thompson. Westwood (1835) reviewed Thompson's work point by point and showed how his observations were contrary to the known methods of metamorphosis and ecdysis and therefore impossible. He even went so far as to suggest that the zoeae Thompson saw hatch from crabs confined in the laboratory were parasites which had emerged subsequent to earlier penetration of the crab eggs. (1960:1)

Note in that passage Westwood's indirect challenge to Thompson's methodology. Note also how Coffin brought out the influence of other social forces in science pertinent to that controversy: "Westwood drew to his support the statements of several important men of his period, including Latreille (1830) and H. Milne-Edwards (1830). He received a gold medal from the Royal Society of London for completely refuting Thompson's theory of crustacean metamorphosis (Bate,

1878)" (1960:1). Coffin then concluded that portion of his passage with a comment: "Apparently Thompson knew the difference between reality and optical illusion and continued with his research" (1960:2).

One rarely finds an account such as Coffin's in the biological sciences journals or textbooks, perhaps because biologists may feel that "objectivity" reigns supreme, perhaps because biologists feel that science is "self-correcting" and such incidents rarely occur, and/or perhaps because of lack of space in journals for "nonessential matter."

Coffin himself introduced the above passage by the qualifying statement: "A *peculiar circumstance* in the history of investigations on Crustacea delayed the development of the correct concept of complete metamorphosis of Decapoda" (1960:1; emphasis ours). Scientists today may ask: Was that circumstance really so peculiar?

If the incidents as described by Coffin are not permitted to be related in scientific journals or in serious publications, for whatever expressed reason, how is one to know for certain just how common these incidents might be? Are philosophers and historians of science thereby routinely denied an important source of information for their deliberations? A lack of sufficient input might also account for the current division within the ranks of science philosophers, at least some of whom have split into two recognizable schools of thought (see Lakatos and Musgrave 1970; see also our chapter 3).

One school has been led for a considerable period of time by Sir Karl Popper (e.g., 1957), who insisted that science progresses rapidly *because* scientists readily yield to new interpretation when better evidence becomes available. The possibility of the existence of different approaches was entertained by Thomas Kuhn (1962), who felt that the issue was far more complex than related by Popper. He proposed that unwritten rules of behavior dictate the degree of acceptability of new interpretation within the social community of scientists.

More recently, other sociologists and philosophers of science have indicated that any new and better results and interpretation, which one gains through experimentation, may count for little unless the "climate" is right for acceptance (e.g., Griffith and Mullins 1972; Feyerabend 1975, 1978; Schram 1979; Whitley 1984). For example, Thompson's "objective description" of crab larvae and his accurate interpretation concerning their metamorphosis into crabs would deserve a high ranking in Popper's criteria relative to the hierarchy of scientific "acceptability."

Happily, today Thompson is given credit for his important contributions toward our understanding of crustacean development, one of the most complex processes in natural history. An example of the recognition Thompson ultimately received is as follows:

> From the beginning of any zoological system the barnacles had been classified among the Mollusca or their subdivision, the Testacea. It created a sensation when John Vaughan Thompson observed on May 8, 1826, a crustacean larva attached to the bottom of a glass vessel change into a young barnacle (Winsor 1969). Further studies left no doubt that the barnacles were sessile crustaceans. Thompson and other students of marine life found, furthermore, that many plankton organisms are nothing but the larval stages of well-known invertebrates, and that even the free-living crustaceans may metamorphose through several larval stages (nauplius, zoea, cypris). (Mayr 1982:204)

Mayr's account implied that the unfolding of a crustacean's life history was a very straightforward and "scientific" process; he even pinpointed a moment of "discovery." However, Thompson did not receive in his day the acclaim he deserved. We feel that, if our present grant award system had been in effect during his lifetime, he probably would not have been able to obtain grant support for his future research (see Muller 1980).

It would thus appear that the behavior of the scientific community in Thompson's day was more in line with what Kuhn would have predicted than with what Popper would have expected (see the treatment below of Popper and Kuhn).

Westwood, on the other hand, despite the support provided by the scientific community in his time and despite the gold medal he received, slipped into obscurity. Charles Singer's 1959 volume, *A Short History of Scientific Ideas to 1900*, for example, contains no mention of Westwood. Unfortunately, the true account of the initial rejection of Thompson's work and the resultant controversy have also nearly vanished from recent accounts of his contributions (as in the example passage above from Mayr).

Perhaps it is history rather than science that is the "self-correcting" discipline.

THE NEO-POPPERIAN SCHOOL

The position Sir Karl Popper adopted is adhered to by many biologists today; the "null hypothesis approach" is an example. One of the more lucid expressions of that position by Popper himself is contained in what some of us believe to be a classic contribution: "Philosophy of science: A personal report." A slightly shortened version of Popper's conclusions follows:

1. It is easy to obtain confirmations, or verifications, for nearly every theory—if we look for confirmations.
2. Confirmations should count only if they are the result of *risky predictions;* that is to say, if, unenlightened by the theory in question, we should have expected an event which was incompatible with the theory—an event which, had it happened, would have refuted the theory.
3. Every "good" scientific theory is one which forbids certain things to happen; the more a theory forbids, the better it is.
4. A theory which is not refutable by any conceivable event is nonscientific. Irrefutability is not a virtue of a theory (as people often think) but a vice.
5. Every genuine *test* of a theory is an attempt to falsify it, or to refute it. Testability is falsifiability; but there are degrees of testability: some theories are more testable, more exposed to refutation, than others; they take, as it were, greater risks.
6. Confirming evidence does not count *except when it is the result of a genuine test of the theory;* and this means that it can be presented as an unsuccessful but serious attempt to falsify the theory.
7. Some genuinely testable theories, when found to be false, are still upheld by their admirers—for example, by introducing *ad hoc* some auxiliary assumption, or by re-interpreting the theory *ad hoc* in such a way that it escapes refutation. Such a procedure is always possible, but it rescues the theory from refutation only at the price of destroying or at least lowering its scientific status.

   One can sum up all this by saying that *falsifiability, or refutability, is a criterion of the scientific status of a theory.* (1957:159–160; emphasis Popper's)

However, Popper also recognized that human beings would not necessarily behave in accordance with those conclusions. He wrote:

Our propensity to look out for regularities, and to impose laws upon nature, leads to the psychological phenomenon of *dogmatic thinking* or, more generally, dogmatic behaviour; we expect regularities everywhere and attempt to find them even where there are none; events which don't yield to these attempts we are inclined to treat as a kind of *"background noise";* and we stick to our expectations even when they are inadequate, and when we ought to accept defeat. This dogmatism is, to some extent, necessary. It is demanded by a situation which can only be dealt with by forcing our anticipations upon the world. (1957:175)

The principles stated by Popper in 1919 (Popper 1957) are still adhered to by many. Atkinson acknowledged Popper's eminence in that regard (1985:728):

> Perhaps the most widely known and influential view of this portion of science is that of Karl Popper. Building on the model of the hypothetical-deductive system of rationality, Popper placed great emphasis on the quality of falsifiability. Hypotheses are proposed, their consequences deduced and experimental tests carried out in an attempt to prove the hypothesis false (Popper 1968). Since we seek understanding of nature in terms of universals, we cannot prove our hypothesis true because universals are beyond our experience. Thus we should strive to eliminate incorrect hypotheses through empirical tests. This, of course, is envisioned as a thoroughly rational process; in ideal situations, the process adheres to the rigor of mathematical logic and the appearance of experimental results which do not fit the predictions of theory culminated in either a reformulation of the deductions or a rejection of the original hypothesis. Popper realized that the process of falsification was never so simple in practice. Nevertheless falsifiability is for Popper and his followers the major point of demarcation between science and non-science. (1985:728)

THE ONSET OF THE KUHNIAN REVOLUTION

Thomas Kuhn was one of the first to recognize and successfully stress the importance of social input in the scientific processes. He proposed in 1962 that scientific inquiry proceeded in a different manner than that advocated or believed to be the case by earlier philosophers of science (including Popper) and by the scientific community.

Prior to the publication of Kuhn's book, *The Structure of Scientific Revolutions*, scientists generally adhered to a "gradualism" concept. That is, the common belief before Kuhn was that scientific progress is cumulative and that the scientific community readily yields when confronted with new and better evidence (in the Popperian sense). Kuhn challenged that belief; his premise in some ways thus contrasted sharply with ideas expounded earlier by Popper and others.

The previous view has often been expressed by the phrase "On the shoulders of giants we stand" (attributed to Newton), which refers to the debt we owe the great scientists who have gone before us. The present-day implication is that most of those findings will stand indefinitely and provide the basis for future research; however, that was not the original intent of the phrase (Merton 1973).

THE "PARADIGM" NOTION

Kuhn's small book, which many now consider a classic, presented the argument that major advances in science have occurred in a sudden manner (a "punctuated" process) rather than in a gradual fashion. He further advanced the "paradigm" notion, which was an essential component of his "nongradual" hypothesis dealing with the manner in which science progresses.

Within each scientific community, Kuhn (1962) reasoned, individuals work within certain doctrinal and social constraints and become "locked in" to given explanations and attitudes as they proceed with their work; the current body of acceptable thought then dictates the spectrum of approaches open to them. Kuhn wrote: "paradigms [are] universally recognized scientific achievements that for a time provide model problems and solutions to a community of practitioners" (1962:viii).

As simple and apparently innocuous as his statements may seem to some (scientists readily accept the idea of "scientific breakthroughs" brought about by advances in technology), Kuhn's conclusions produced a considerable ripple among philosophers of science. His statements (the one above and others) apparently conveyed a considerable amount of hidden meaning and implication and seemed to lack precise definition. These very issues were to be raised in later years by other philosophers who were unhappy with Kuhn's "revolutionary" viewpoint (see, e.g., Masterson 1970).

Kuhn's earliest adoption of the paradigm notion included, among other implications, the concept of a "gestalt." He felt that scientists working within the constraints of a paradigm actually view their research problems and possible approaches from a very limited perspective, as shaped by a prevailing viewpoint (world view) in their particular scientific community (see also Griffith and Mullins 1972). As Kuhn later stated: "Paradigms may be prior to, more binding, and more complete than any set of rules for research that could be unequivocally abstracted from them" (1962:46).

Stated more simply, Kuhn felt that scientists might well be completely committed to a certain approach or viewpoint (a "gestalt" commitment or "paradigm hold") during the study of a particular problem. Under that circumstance, it is conceivable that completely inexplicable results (results not fitting within existing interpretation) could arise during their study (perhaps supplemented with results of studies by close colleagues). When that happens, they and other established scientists would be unable to appreciate an emerging alternative explanation that could account for both the earlier results and the newly observed results.

However, Kuhn indicated that such a commitment to a paradigm did not necessarily inhibit high-quality research. He felt that much can be accomplished when one need not constantly question the starting position (basic assumptions). He termed the acceptance of a given paradigm, as well as research conducted within that paradigm, a "normal science" approach. He then illustrated the necessity and value of that approach throughout the third and fourth chapters of his book and concluded: "Normal science . . . is a highly cumulative enterprise, eminently successful in its aim, the steady extension of the scope and precision of scientific knowledge" (1962:52).

Kuhn also outlined inherent shortcomings in the practice of normal science. Among other problems, he discussed what often occurs when a scientist or a small group of scientists discovers a totally different interpretation for the existing body of knowledge in a particular area. Thompson's observation that the earlier crustacean "genus" *Zoea* was actually a variety of larvae of well-known crabs in many genera is an excellent example.

Social constraints (at times unconscious), Kuhn argued, may prevent recognition and/or acceptance of any alternative interpretations which may be superior to earlier explanations. As research proceeds, however, the failure of "establishment science" to acknowledge the existence of a possibly more suitable alternative interpretation leads to a crisis. Kuhn considered the development of that crisis a necessary precondition for the acceptance of the new interpretation. He expressed his views about the initial reaction to crisis as follows:

> Let us then assume that crises are a necessary precondition for the emergence of novel theories and ask next how scientists respond to their existence. Part of the answer, as obvious as it is important, can be discovered by noting first what scientists never do when confronted by even severe and prolonged anomalies. Though they may begin to lose faith and then to consider alternatives, they do not renounce the paradigm that has led them into crisis. (1962:77)

Kuhn concluded that historical controversies usually arise as a consequence of this inability of scientific communities to appreciate the potential validity of a new idea while they are working within their earlier gestalt perspective (i.e., they are under a paradigm hold).

The *quality* of existing evidence would then be less of a factor in "resolving" conflict than would be the influence of the paradigm hold (basic assumptions) of the scientific community.

Kuhn's examples of difficulties encountered in the history of progress by physicists and chemists were supplemented by examples of resistance to new ideas encountered by scientists such as Lavoisier, Galileo, and Pasteur. (Within biology we could add Darwin, Thompson, and others to that list.)

SOCIAL STRUCTURE, SCIENCE, AND PROGRESS

The disparity between the Popper and Kuhn views was seen by many as a confrontation between the traditional or "logical empiricism" view (the Realism school) and the as yet undefined pragmatic view (e.g., the Relativism school; see Bernstein 1983). The confrontation, in that sense, was misdirected (see Lakatos and Musgrave 1970); Popper and Kuhn were apparently not really in direct opposition to one another (see excursus RE).

Whereas Popper insisted that great men of science succeeded by the rigorous and persistent application of logic (and advocated that approach), Kuhn concluded that scientific progress proceeded instead by fits and starts (figure 2.2). At the same time Kuhn did not really advocate any one approach; he was describing, not advocating. Paul Feyerabend recognized that distinction as follows: "Whenever I read Kuhn, I am troubled by the following question: are we here presented with *methodological prescriptions* which tell the scientist how to proceed; or are we given a *description*, void of any evaluative element, of those activities which are generally called 'scientific'?" (1970:198).

One might consider Popper's position a "noncontroversial" approach and something to be striven for (the public image of science). Its proponents apparently believe that truth (or "true" reality) exists and that it can be found (known) or closely approximated by rigorous experimentation. Any controversies arising in science can then be ascribed to the weaknesses of the methods used by the scientists involved (for an example see excursus GT).

By contrast, Kuhn attempted to describe what he felt actually happens (an occasional forced move to the pragmatic approach, later labeled "relativism," "antirealism," or some other term). That is, he felt that controversies may be expected to arise whenever totally unexpected experimental results lead to a drastic reinterpretation of

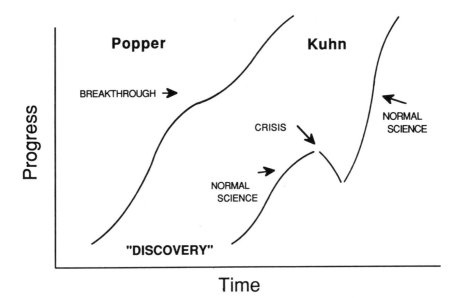

FIGURE 2.2. Schematic diagram of presumed progress in science as a function of time, according to: a) a stepwise function *(left)*, as such progress might be perceived within the Realism school and as exemplified by Popper, and b) an interrupted or sawtooth function *(right)* as progress might be viewed by Kuhn. (See text of chapter 3 and excursus RE for further explanation.)

existing evidence. Emergent controversies are not due all that much to a failure of the individual scientists involved to agree on the quality of the evidence. Controversies arise instead when a new way of viewing evidence cannot be reconciled with the currently accepted views adhered to by the established scientific community.

To illustrate our view of the confrontation between Popper and Kuhn, we include here a partial diagram (figure 2.3). It is evident from his writings that Popper *advocated* the falsification approach because of his belief that earlier great scientists had succeeded by applying that approach. Up until the time of Kuhn, Popper's stand had remained relatively unchallenged; "logical empiricism," as it was called, dominated the thinking of philosophers of science and was generally accepted as an appropriate methodology by the scientific community (see excursus SCI).

Perhaps the most profound idea proposed by Kuhn was his emphasis on the important role of attitude in the "scientific community" within the larger research establishment (see also Griffith and Mullins

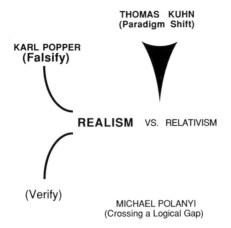

FIGURE 2.3. (same as theme diagram 2.0). Relationship between Karl Popper and Thomas Kuhn, who were not in direct opposition to one another. Michael Polanyi had actually preempted Kuhn on one point; a sudden switch in interpretation may occur whenever conflicting evidence permits new perspective. The Relativism school was not well defined when the Popper-Kuhn controversy erupted.

1972; Atkinson 1985). Although everyone is aware that no scientist works in a vacuum, Kuhn stressed the importance of "peer group" pressure from within that scientific community and how it related to his paradigm notion. He wrote:

> Normal science, the activity in which most scientists inevitably spend almost all their time, is predicated on the assumption that the scientific community knows what the world is like. Much of the success of the enterprise derives from the community's willingness to defend that assumption, if necessary at considerable cost (1970a:5). . . . The study of paradigms . . . is what mainly prepares the student for membership in the particular scientific community with which he will later practice. . . . Men whose research is based on shared paradigms are committed to the same rules and standards for scientific practice. That commitment and the apparent consensus it produces are prerequisites for normal science. (1962:11)

Kuhn's statements contrast markedly with the self-image of scientists and thus have far-reaching and perhaps somewhat disturbing implications. A host of questions arises beyond those points that are obvious within the statements themselves. Does a scientist have freedom of thought or must conclusions meet with the approval of others in the community? Do those with greater standing in the community hierarchy have more freedom of expression and opportunity for adventure than others due to social rather than scientific reasons? Is "scientific objectivity" somewhat ephemeral, changing along with prevailing attitude, or is scientific objectivity more absolute? Does the long-held and cherished notion that all views are welcome really hold true?

Kuhn's advocacy of the paradigm notion became an interesting example of his own thesis, as clearly stated by Margaret Masterson: "Kuhn's paradigm, in my view, [is] a fundamental idea and a new one in the philosophy of science" (1970:61).

The previous and well-established "realism" paradigm in the philosophy of science rested on the premise that one could understand how science progresses by reviewing recorded historical events (e.g., the accomplishments of Lavoisier, Galileo, Pasteur, and Darwin). That older paradigm also relied on the assumption that new and better evidence would result in rapid change. Kuhn's paradigm, by contrast, included the concept that an abrupt "paradigm shift" would occur not merely because of the appearance of new and conflicting evidence. He felt that assumptions would change only when the scientific community (as a social institution) could no longer hold on to an older and more emotionally satisfying paradigm.

Few scientists realize that Michael Polanyi (1958) preempted Kuhn by a few years on the matter of a "paradigm shift" or "gestalt switch." Polanyi, however, assigned a different term, "crossing a logical gap," to that phenomenon (see figure 2.3) in his perception of the sudden appearance of new insight on a long-standing problem.

The conflict between those two philosophical views (the "realism" of Popper and the revolutionary uncertainty of Kuhn) soon led to an international colloquium on the matter (Lakatos and Musgrave 1970). At that time various participants had the opportunity to exchange views concerning the contrast between what Kuhn recognized as divergent schools of philosophy. Apparently no consensus was reached during that symposium, as exemplified in a statement by Kuhn:

> I conclude that a gestalt switch divides readers of my book into two or more groups. What one of these sees as striking parallelism (between Kuhn and Popper) is virtually invisible to the others. . . . How am I to persuade Sir Karl . . . that what he calls a duck can be seen as a rabbit? How am I to show him what it would be like to wear my spectacles when he has already learned to look at everything I can point to through his own? (1970b:3)

SCIENCE: A SELF-CORRECTING ENTERPRISE?

As indicated above, scientists actively engaged in research (particularly those engaged in "Normal Science") usually do not concern themselves with questions regarding the *process* of science itself. Normally they do not need to do so, even though they may include mention of some classic controversies in the classes they may teach. Part of this security rests on the premise that science *is* "self-correcting" and that any disagreements will shortly be resolved as the quantity and quality of evidence increase and improve (an adherence to the Popper position).

Several elements complicate this rather relaxed position. Textbooks rarely include any detail about the time span of controversies, the emotional stress and possible ostracism of individuals by the community, or the basic unfairness that might prevail under those conditions. What might seem an instant in time in the textbook account may actually have represented several years of trauma for individual scientists, as was the case for Pasteur (see Duclaux [1896] 1920 and DuBos 1950).

Yes, science is perhaps "self-correcting" in the long run, but that is not necessarily true in individual cases during short time spans. One of the more revealing examples we found of the unfairness that can prevail is the 1960 Coffin account of Thompson's experience with his interpretation that zoeae were crab larvae, not a discrete genus (see above). Consider the trauma Thompson must have experienced.

Thompson's long-unheralded success leads one to wonder, "How often do such events occur?" Unfortunately, no statistics are available, since those who become embroiled in a controversy and "lose their case" all too often leave science, change fields within science, or move away from an active role, even if it later turns out that they were right. As such, the troubles they have faced never become recorded; their personal experiences during controversies are thus never considered by philosophers of science.

Thompson's subsequent experience (continuing to pursue his studies) appears to be more the exception than the rule. He continued to do important research in his field and eventually gained the credit and recognition he deserved, although he received no gold medal, as Westwood did. Coffin mentioned one such episode of Thompson's success; "In the same volume with Westwood's work is Thompson's paper which shows extensive metamorphosis in the Cirripedia (barnacles) and places them in the Crustacea rather than the Mollusca (Thompson 1835b)" (1960:1).

PARADIGMS AS CONTROLLING FACTORS

Paradigms, those controlling impressions that scientists unconsciously adhere to and work under, permit an essential agreement about basic assumptions for the narrow scientific community in which they apply (Kuhn 1962). While doing research in the "normal science" mode, scientists need not question these basic assumptions. Neither do others in the community expect them to, because they accept the same assumptions. Kuhn, in fact, stressed the value of this basic agreement about assumptions; acceptance can lead to rapid progress in the conduct of "normal science."

Unfortunately, every coin has its opposite side. As Duclaux wrote: "However broad-minded one may be, he is always to some extent the slave of his education and of his past" ([1896] 1920:272). If scientists were more aware that they nearly always worked under the control of a set of paradigms and recognized them as such, those paradigms and the assumptions underlying them could be examined periodically for their validity. Instead, Kuhn stressed the existence of that particular weakness in scientific activity, the controlling "paradigm hold." He suggested that the scientific community experienced unnecessary limitations because of those unwritten paradigms. Bohm and Peat reiterated that message: "[A paradigm] exacts a price in that the mind is kept within certain fixed channels that deepen with time until an individual scientist is no longer aware of his or her limited position" (1987:53).

As a consequence, anomalies often accumulate during research until basic assumptions held within one of the paradigms may no longer be tenable. That accretion of negative evidence, in turn, precipitates a "crisis" stage in a research project and later in the scientific community. Eventually, perhaps, a single scientist (or a few at most) recognizes the discrepancies and suddenly gains new insight.

For those who recognize anomalies when they arise and then pursue those leads, however, research may proceed very haphazardly for a while; a series of poorly designed preliminary experiments is run before one is once again able to conduct an experiment within the traditional accepted framework. The "expected" result more often than not may fail to appear, or may not appear at the expected time or in the expected manner. It is only the last experiment or two that can be written up in a form acceptable to most journals.

After (and if) the wider community becomes "converted" to the importance of the negative evidence, there develops a "paradigm shift," as described by Kuhn (1962). A paradigm shift can be rather abrupt, as in Kuhn's examples, but the form of the paradigm can also change incrementally over time. The latter is especially true for those cases where assumptions are ill-defined to begin with.

Other questions arise as well. Do all new paradigms meet the same fate (i.e., difficulty of acceptance), or is degree of acceptance of a new paradigm an inverse function of the importance of the question asked? Can a new paradigm be accepted more readily when proposed by a "giant" in the field? Should a novice with a new paradigm attempt to "convert" the "giants" in the field to the new viewpoint before publishing the results? Would the "giants" then take possession of (credit for) the new paradigm if they have experienced the same creative process, by "conversion," before publication by the original discoverer?

One can readily find answers to these questions, some of which arise in each scientist's career; it should be obvious to many that Kuhn may be correct. The role of the community may be far more important than is indicated in textbook accounts of scientific advancement.

3

RELATIVISM
AND
STRONG INFERENCE

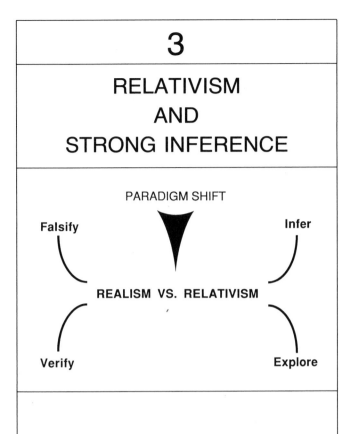

"Do the comrades who flock to the treasure only follow the bee that first made the discovery, or have they been sent on by her, and do they find it through following her indications, her description of the place where it lies? Between these two hypotheses, that refer directly to the extent and working of the bee's intellect, there is obviously an enormous difference."

—*Maurice Maeterlinck 1901:167*

"The controversy between the von Frisch group's 'language' hypothesis ... and Wenner's group's olfactory hypothesis ... for the arrival of honey bee recruits at field sources, is essentially a controversy between a human-level hypothesis for an insect and an insect-level hypothesis for an insect."

—*R. Rosin 1978:589*

A ristotle is sometimes credited with publication of the first account of the means by which honey bees may be recruited to
food sources (e.g., von Frisch 1967a; Gould 1976). Exactly what Aristotle meant, however, is open to question, since translations of his
work have been known to differ according to the intellectual climate
of the times and according to the desired ends of researchers (David
Young, University of California at Santa Barbara, personal communication).

Professor Young translated for us the only passage in Aristotle's
writings that directly pertains to honey bee recruitment (see excursus
AR). Professor Young concluded, on the basis of what is usually intended in such ancient Greek phrases, that Aristotle meant that the
three or four bees referred to in that passage actually "followed" each
forager bee back out to the food source in the field.

The first description of what might be construed as the waggle
dance of bees appeared in 1609. At that time Butler wrote, in reference
to the behavior of bees in swarms:

> All swarms, if the morrow be fair, will desire to be abroad betimes,
> and knowing their want, will bestir themselves more lustily in their
> labor than other bees.
>
> But if the foul weather keep them in the first day, then are they
> much discouraged; the next day being indifferent, when other bees
> work hard, they will scarce look out of the door, not daring to
> commit their [empty] and thin bodies to the cold air. And if they be
> shut in the second day also, then will they not waggle . . . until the
> weather be very pleasant. ([1609] 1969: ch. 5, sec. 62)

Wildman (1768) also may have appreciated the existence of "dancing" bees. He wrote: "They *understand* one another likewise, *when*, by
a motion of their wings, they ask, as it were, to be unloaded of the
wax, which they have gathered in the country; likewise *when* in the
morning they rouse each other to go out to work" (1768:30; emphasis
Wildman's).

Only twenty years later a German scientist, Ernst Spitzner (1788),
wrote a flowery account of the "dance" of the bees:

> When a bee finds a good source of honey somewhere, after her
> return home she makes this known to the others in a remarkable
> way. Full of joy she waltzes around among them in circles, without
> doubt in order that they shall notice the smell of honey which has
> attached itself to her; then when she goes out again they soon follow
> her in crowds. I noticed this in a glass-walled hive when I put some
> honey on the grass not far away and brought to it only two bees
> from the hive. Within a few minutes, these two made this known to

the others in this way, and they came to the place in a crowd. (translation from Ribbands 1953:147)

More than fifty years later, John Burroughs was more specific about how bees might recruit others. He described the practice of "bee hunting," a procedure used to locate feral bee colonies in the woods ("wild" bees in "bee trees"). Bee hunters placed bees from flowers in a special box which also held a piece of honeycomb. After these bees had filled themselves with honey, they returned to their colony; some eventually came back for other loads. Burroughs wrote:

> A bee will usually make three or four trips from the hunter's box before it brings back a companion. I suspect the bee does not tell its fellows what it has found, but that they smell out the secret; it doubtless bears some evidence with it upon its feet or proboscis that it has been upon honey-comb and not upon flowers, and its companions take the hint and follow, arriving always many seconds behind. (1875:53)

Maurice Maeterlinck, a 1911 Nobel Prize winner (in literature), was perhaps the first to distinguish clearly between the possibilities of an odor-search pattern and some type of "verbal or magnetic communication" (as he termed it) during the recruitment of naive bees to food sources. In his investigations Maeterlinck marked individual bees as they fed upon honey in his second-story office (his study) and kept records of how often other bees arrived; he wrote:

> I will frankly confess ... that the marked bee often returns alone. ... A friend who stood by and watched my experiment declared that it was evidently mere selfishness or vanity that caused so many of the bees to refrain from sharing the source of their wealth. ... it will also happen that the bee ... will return to the honey accompanied by two or three friends. (1901:164)

Maeterlinck then related his observations to those made previously by Lubbock:

> I am aware that Sir John Lubbock ... records the results of his investigations in long and minute tables; and from these we are to infer that it is a matter of rarest occurrence for a single bee to follow the one who has made the discovery. ... my own tables, compiled with great care—and every possible precaution having been taken that the bees should not be directly attracted by the odour of the honey—establish that on an average one bee will bring others four times out of ten. (1901:162)

Maeterlinck and his predecessors had obviously pondered the question of how bees might recruit hivemates to a food source in the field and wondered whether a "following" or a use of odor were somehow involved.

In his review volume, von Frisch included a short historical treatment of some of these early accounts (excluding Maeterlinck), and concluded with the statement: "None of the observers named pursued his discovery further. Thus they remained in ignorance of what will now fill the pages of this book" (1967a:6).

In the body of his 1967 review volume, von Frisch did not cite Maeterlinck's contributions; neither did he mention an important "strong inference" experiment (as defined by Platt in 1964; see below) that had been conducted by Maeterlinck. Von Frisch thereby avoided the problem that Maeterlinck had already obtained negative results on the question of a bee "language" by his use of that "strong inference" approach. A point which escaped the readers of von Frisch's volume was that there was no incentive for Maeterlinck to have gone "further" on that question at the time.

To illustrate why Maeterlinck need *not* have proceeded along the course von Frisch later followed, the notion of "strong inference" has to be explained more fully. We will return to Maeterlinck's experiment after describing the nature of that particular experimental approach. In doing so, we will also fit the honey bee dance language controversy into the larger context of the philosophy of science.

STRONG INFERENCE: CHAMBERLIN'S "GREAT INTELLECTUAL INVENTION"

In the epigraph at the beginning of this chapter (and as indicated in the paragraphs above), Maeterlinck evidently appreciated the advantage of pitting one hypothesis against another. That quotation is an excellent example of the application of what John Platt labeled the "strong inference" approach in his paper with that same title published in the journal *Science* (Platt 1964).

Platt wrote his article in response to a question he had posed to himself (paraphrased here): "Why should [scientific] advances be so much faster (perhaps by an order of magnitude) in some fields (such as in molecular biology and high-energy physics) than in others?" He suggested that the reasons for that success were twofold: 1) application of the Karl Popper "falsifiability" approach (Popper 1957), *con-*

current with 2) "a second great intellectual invention, 'the method of multiple [working] hypotheses' " (emphasis ours), as proposed in 1890 by Thomas Chrowder Chamberlin (co-originator of a hypothesis on the origin of the solar system).

Platt felt that Popper's "falsifiability" approach (outlined in chapter 2) was "[too] hard [a] doctrine" to follow. He wrote: "If you have a hypothesis and I have another hypothesis, evidently one of them must be eliminated. The scientist seems to have no choice but to be either soft-headed or disputatious. Perhaps this is why so many tend to resist the strong analytic approach—and why some great scientists are so disputatious" (1964:350).

As an alternative to "disputatious" behavior, Chamberlin had advocated "The Method of Multiple Working Hypotheses" in 1890, wherein:

> The effort is to bring up into view every rational explanation of new phenomena, and to develop every tenable hypothesis respecting their cause and history. The investigator thus becomes the parent of a family of hypotheses: and, by his parental relation to all, he is forbidden to fasten his affections unduly upon any one. ([1890] 1965:756)

Actually, Chamberlin espoused many ideas in his paper that have application even today. So much so, in fact, that Platt later (in 1965) convinced the editors of *Science* to reprint Chamberlin's paper in its entirety. Platt admonished in his 1964 paper: "[Chamberlin's article] should be required reading for every graduate student—and for every professor." Some of Chamberlin's more important points are worth repeating here, particularly as they pertain to the honey bee dance language hypothesis and to Maeterlinck's 1901 account.

The Theme Diagram

It is not easy to understand how science functions. Indeed, disagreements among the philosophers of science often reflect the confusion within science itself. In that connection, Kuhn commented: "We simply no longer have any useful notion of how science evolves, or what scientific progress is" (Kuhn, in Winkler 1985).

We found that a rather straightforward diagram (see figure 3.1) could encompass the various philosophical approaches and schools. Furthermore, it appears that various participants in any scientific controversy exhibit a complex polarity of thought that fits within that diagram, according to which school of philosophy they embrace.

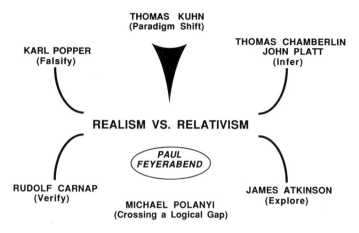

FIGURE 3.1. Diagram of our understanding of the relationship among different views of how science might operate. Whereas Popper and Carnap (the "Realism school") both indicated that "truth" exists and can be ascertained, they differed in their views about the means that "should" be employed in the search for that "truth." For Popper, repeated failures at sincere attempts to falsify an hypothesis can be recognized as reason to accept the probable truth of that hypothesis. Carnap accepted the presence of overwhelming supportive evidence as a sufficient basis for belief that truth has been "discovered" (i.e., proven to exist).

"Relativists" do not search for *ultimate* truth but still recognize the usefulness of acquired knowledge. Both Chamberlin and Platt insisted that acquisition of that knowledge can be accelerated by rapid testing and rejection of unsuitable explanations. Kuhn highlighted the problem; he recognized the hindrance posed by unwitting social commitment to explanations within accepted notions (paradigms). Progress would then be resultantly spasmodic, rather than steady (see figure 2.2).

Atkinson moved beyond the thinking of other relativists. He suggested that the process of science is a creative experience; we actually "create" phenomena ("truth") by generating support for our hypotheses and winning (i.e., "converting") others in the scientific community to our cause.

In that diagram (presented in greater detail in Wenner 1989) Karl Popper and Rudolf Carnap, although often at odds with respect to certain features of philosophy, actually remained close in principle (Hacking 1983). Both belonged to the "Realism school" (i.e., they believe that truth exists and can be discovered or proved).

Whereas Popper insisted upon hypothesis testing, Carnap felt that strong supportive evidence can suffice for "proof" of a hypothesis. Popper's school used the label "falsifiability" for the approach he advocated. We use the term "verifiability" here with the approach advocated by Carnap.

At an opposite pole in the philosophical scheme we find Chamber-

lin, Platt, and Atkinson. The first two advocated an alternating inductive-deductive approach, which consisted of simultaneously rejecting
one hypothesis while retaining the other(s). Atkinson (1985) stressed
how "image creating" was involved during the generation of an hypothesis.

Neither Michael Polanyi (1958) nor Thomas Kuhn (1962) *advocated*
any particular research approach. That point was not at all obvious
to us during the first few years of our shift away from the dance
language hypothesis. We were not alone in that matter; others felt
that Kuhn advocated one or another approach, but we later realized
that that was not the case.

Hull recognized Kuhn's silence on that point, and wrote:

> Looking back on the reception of his brainchild, Kuhn (1970a) him-
> self was dismayed. All the wrong people seemed attracted to his
> book for all the wrong reasons. Social scientists in particular read
> him as advocating a relativist view of scientific knowledge, as if
> truth were nothing more than what the scientists say it is. He
> intended no such conclusion. (1988:112)

Rather, Polanyi and Kuhn described what they perceived about philosophical attitudes; that is, we do not have as much control of our
destiny as we would like, due to our "paradigm holds" (the *idols* of
thought that preoccupied Bacon). Whereas Polanyi exerted a great
influence on nonscientists, Kuhn's writings appealed to scientists and
helped break the dominance in thought previously held by realist
philosophers such as Popper and Carnap (see Lakatos and Musgrave
1970).

Atkinson even suggested that much of what we consider to be
"discovered truth" may actually be nothing more than ideas generated or created in our minds. In 1986 Atkinson (in a personal communication) used the term "exploration" for this process. That is, all of
us may begin a research project in the exploration mode, without any
preconceived notions of what might be "truth." Later, if a sufficient
number of high-ranking scientists (in the ever-present social "pecking" order; see chapter 11) becomes converted to any notion that has
been generated or created, that notion may become accepted as "truth"
and form the basis for more research.

The acceptance of a new idea in science, accordingly, is not auto-
matic. Keller pre-empted Atkinson somewhat on that score: "A new
idea, a new conception, is born in the privacy of one man's or one
woman's dreams. But for that conception to become part of the body

of scientific theory, it must be acknowledged by the society of which the individual is a member" (1983:xii).

Paul Feyerabend (1970, 1975, 1978) treated these last points quite forcefully, and we included his name in the diagram in a special place, since he appears not to agree with other philosophers of science on most issues. He militantly insisted that no one approach should be advocated in scientific research (see our chapter 14 and Wenner 1989). Regarding theory acceptance, he wrote:

> [The] appearance of success [of an endorsed theory] *cannot in the least be regarded as a sign of truth and correspondence with nature. . . . the suspicion arises that this alleged success is due to the fact that the theory, when extended beyond its starting point, was turned into rigid ideology. . . .* Its "success" *is entirely man-made.* (1975:43; emphasis Feyerabend's)

Chamberlin's Input

Chamberlin distinguished between: 1) those who attempted "to follow by close imitation the processes of previous thinkers, or to acquire by memorizing the results of their investigations," and 2) those who engage in primary or creative study and who "think independently, or at least individually, in the endeavor to discover new truth."

In ranking intellectual approaches, Chamberlin postulated that there had been three phases of scientific advances up to 1890. He wrote: "These three methods may be designated, first, the method of the ruling theory; second, the method of the working hypothesis, and, third, the method of multiple working hypotheses" ([1890] 1965:754).

Some of Chamberlin's writing would perhaps be considered "quaint" by today's standards; for example: "As in the earlier days, so still, it is the habit of some to hastily conjure up an explanation for every new phenomenon that presents itself. Interpretation rushes to the forefront as the chief obligation pressing upon the putative wise man" ([1890] 1965:754).

Note in this last passage the inherent caution against a too ready acceptance of teleological implications (see excursus TEL). Chamberlin continued: "Laudable as the effort at explanation is in itself, it is to be condemned when it runs before a serious inquiry into the phenomenon itself" ([1890] 1965:754).

If one equates Chamberlin's "ruling theory" with Kuhn's "paradigm hold" (Kuhn 1962; see also our chapter 2), it appears that Kuhn was anticipated by Chamberlin seventy years earlier, at least in terms of attitude about the pitfalls of adhering too strongly to a prevailing (ruling) theory. We see here also a strong correspondence between "ruling theory" and the verification approach advocated by Carnap (see our figure 3.1).

Chamberlin warned against self-deception when working within the confines of a general theory:

> For a time [a general theory] is likely to be held in a tentative way with a measure of candor. With this tentative spirit and measurable candor, the mind satisfies its moral sense, and deceives itself with the thought that it is proceeding cautiously and impartially toward the goal of ultimate truth. It fails to recognize that no amount of provisional holding of a theory, so long as the view is limited and the investigation partial, justifies an ultimate conviction. ([1890] 1965:754)

Chamberlin also wrote of "parental affection" for an hypothesis— that is, those circumstances in which one may have only a single hypothesis (theory) under consideration. He summarized: "the evolution is this: a premature explanation passes into a tentative theory, then into an adopted theory, and into a ruling theory. When the last stage has been reached, unless the theory happens, perchance, to be the true one, all hope of the best results is gone" ([1890] 1965:755)

With the above as background, we can return to Maeterlinck's contribution to the seemingly ever-present conflict between the concepts of "bee language" (of one sort or another) and odor search during honey bee recruitment to food sources.

The Maeterlinck "Strong Inference" Experiment

Chamberlin's concern about the matter of hypothesis testing barely preceded Maeterlinck's apparently independent recognition of the same problem: that is, investigators may become "locked in" to an hypothesis due to "parental affection," as Chamberlin worded it.

Maeterlinck's awareness of the problem of a bias favoring a single explanation, which Kuhn later termed "paradigm hold," was vividly illustrated in a footnote appearing in a 1939 French language edition of his classic 1901 book. In that footnote Maeterlinck described a response he obtained from a beekeeper after he had reported to that friend the negative results of an experiment he had done with regard to the possibility of bee communication (described below). Maeterlinck wrote:

On the other hand, one of my beekeeper friends, a very skilled and sincere observer to whom I submitted the problem, wrote to me that he obtained four unquestionable communications [favorable results], using the same experimental protocol. The facts must be verified and the question is not resolved. But I am convinced that my friend was misled by his desire, a very natural one, to see the experiment succeed. ([1901] 1939:129; translation from the French by Yann Ricard)

Maeterlinck's desire to avoid bias led him to design and conduct an experiment with a mutually exclusive format (a "crucial" or "strong inference" experiment, as illustrated in chapter 10). He marked the bee that collected honey from a table in his second-floor study and later observed it after it had returned to its hive. He then captured the bee before it could again leave the hive. At the same time, he permitted other bees in attendance (potential recruits) to leave the hive; that way he would be able to determine whether they could find the same source of honey on their own. Maeterlinck wrote: "When satisfied, she flew away and returned to the hive. I followed, saw her pass over the surface of the crowd, plunge her head into an empty cell, disgorge her honey, and prepare to set forth again. At the door of the hive I had placed a glass box; . . . I imprisoned her and left her there" (1901:170).

Maeterlinck also recognized the need for replication during experimentation, as well as the need to mark bees that had contacted the successful bee within the hive, and wrote:

> I then repeated the experiment on twenty marked bees in succession. When the marked bee reappeared alone, I imprisoned her as I had imprisoned the first. But eight of them came to the threshold of the hive and entered the box, accompanied by two or three friends. By means of the trap I was able to separate the marked bee from her companions, and to keep her a prisoner in the first compartment. Then, having marked these companions with a different colour, I threw open the second compartment and set them at liberty, myself returning quickly to my study to await their arrival. (1901:170–71; emphasis ours)

Maeterlinck provided a statement about procedure that would today be interpreted as a "falsifiability approach." He also included predictions relative to possible outcomes of the experiment. Together those comments constituted a (null) hypothesis approach, which we phrase as follows: "Naive bees cannot find a source of food without a successful forager 'leading' them." Maeterlinck wrote:

Now it is evident that *if a verbal or magnetic communication had passed*, indicating the place, describing the way, etc., a certain number of bees, having been furnished with this information, should have found their way to my room. *I am compelled to admit that there came but a single one.* Was this mere chance, or had she followed instructions received? (1901:167; emphasis ours)

The requisite scientific caution about interpretation was also present in Maeterlinck's account when he wrote: "The experiment was insufficient, but circumstances prevented me from carrying it further." Maeterlinck, however, later repeated that experiment "in the first few sunny days of this unpleasant spring." He added: "It gave the same negative result" ([1901] 1939:129; translation by Yann Ricard).

Note an important distinction here (shared by Chamberlin). It is clear that Maeterlinck did not consider that he had the "answer" to exactly *how* the foragers recruited naive bees. He merely felt that naive bees were successful *only* if the experienced foragers were free to travel back and forth between the hive and food place, as he indicated by his statement: "I released the 'baited' bees, and my study soon was besieged by the buzzing crowd to whom they had taught the way to the treasure" (1901:167).

In that sense, Maeterlinck had been using two powerful approaches. He had used the "falsifiability" approach later advocated by Popper in 1920–1921 (Popper 1957) and as shown in the upper left corner of our diagram (see figure 3.1). He had also used the "strong inference" approach of Chamberlin (see the upper right corner of our diagram), an approach that was later formalized by Platt (1964).

THE ATTITUDE OF VON FRISCH AND OTHERS TOWARD THE MAETERLINCK EXPERIMENT

Von Frisch was clearly aware of Maeterlinck's book (e.g., von Frisch 1954), but he must have either ignored its content or must not have studied the appropriate passages. He consequently later totally dismissed Maeterlinck's contribution as follows: "There is the famous book by Maeterlinck, *The Life of the Bee*, . . . [an excellent piece] of natural history observation and a joy to the knowledgeable; but the unscientific reader will find it hard to tell where the observation ends and the poetic fancy begins" (1967a:vii).

Robert Ardrey (1963) dealt more harshly with Maeterlinck by resurrecting a long-ignored assertion that Maeterlinck was a plagiarist.

The original charge against Maeterlinck by Marais, however, was apparently unfounded (see excursus MM).

We have found only one other person who has referred to Maeterlinck's experiment: James Gould. In his doctoral dissertation (1975a), in a later review article (1976), and in a popular book (Gould and Gould 1988) Gould interpreted Maeterlinck's results as providing support for the dance language hypothesis, and wrote:

> Maeterlinck (1901) tested this explanation by letting a forager find the food and return to the hive. He then caught the forager on its way back out of the hive. Even though recruited bees had no forager to follow, *some* of them nevertheless found the food. *A forager must communicate to recruits enough information for them to find the food by themselves.* Maeterlinck speculated that some *"tactile language or magnetic intuition"* might be involved. (1976:211; emphasis ours)

There is, of course, the possibility that Gould's misinterpretation of Maeterlinck's results and conclusion (and error in the quoted passage) might have been due to youthful exuberance occasioned by studies done in support of an hypothesis while still a graduate student (see chapter 11). A more recent treatment by Gould and his wife, however, further diminished the importance of Maeterlinck's contribution by warping the account even more into the "ruling theory" format; their account is even further altered from what was contained in Maeterlinck's original passage. They wrote:

> The idea that the forager leads the recruits to the food received a blow in 1901 when Maurice Maeterlinck . . . was doing research for his book, *The Life of the Bee.* Maeterlinck captured a forager and, while she was feeding on a drop of honey, carried her from the hive entrance to another location. After marking the forager with a paint drop, he went back to the hive and watched her return. When she reemerged Maeterlinck captured her, and then he rushed back to the food in time to see a recruit arrive without having followed the forager. (Gould and Gould 1988:55)

It would have been an easy matter for von Frisch and/or his disciples to have repeated Maeterlinck's experiment. The fact that no one did so may hinge greatly on the question of philosophy. Those who work within the Realism school and who employ the verification approach in their research programs give greater credence to evidence that supports "ruling theory," as described by Chamberlin ([1890] 1965).

A fuller understanding of why neither von Frisch nor his followers (including us) repeated Maeterlinck's experiment may also become more evident from the material presented in the chapters that follow.

A FORTY-FIVE-YEAR HIATUS

When very definitive, but negative, results are obtained and published, they often dampen further research on the relevant hypothesis. In the case of honey bee recruitment, very little research directed toward "proving" the existence of a "language" among honey bees seems to have occurred during the forty-five years after the publication of Maeterlinck's 1901 book.

Von Frisch did publish some papers just before and after 1920. In those papers he recognized the existence of waggle dances and of a correlation between the presence of bee dances and the exploitation of nectar and/or pollen sources in the field. However, he clearly felt at that time that odor search was the mechanism involved in honey bee recruitment (von Frisch 1939). He apparently did not yet recognize the full range of possibilities in such a dance maneuver, including possible recruitment by means of a "dance language" (i.e., a complex and "unbelievable information code," as it came to be known). More than two decades passed after von Frisch recognized the existence of the waggle dance maneuver before he proposed his dance language hypothesis of honey bee recruitment to food sources (Lindauer 1985:130).

During the intervening time, von Frisch's studies were largely in an area that would then have been labeled "sensory physiology" rather than in the area of honey bee recruitment, per se. Also, it is evident that von Frisch later apparently did not distinguish between rerecruitment of experienced bees and recruitment of bees that had never before been to the food source (e.g., Wenner 1962, 1974). That lack of awareness led to further difficulties with regard to the interpretation of his experimental results, a point that will be covered in chapter 7.

PLATT'S ADMONITION: PHILOSOPHICAL IMPLICATIONS

In a brilliant essay, Chamberlin ([1890] 1965) emphasized the utility of his "multiple working hypotheses" approach (Chamberlin's "Great Intellectual Invention," as Platt labeled it). Chamberlin also dwelt on what he considered to be two less fruitful approaches. The next step down from "multiple working hypotheses" was "the method of the working hypothesis" (which is perhaps equivalent to the contemporary "null hypothesis" approach or the falsification approach, as shown in figure 3.1). Chamberlin felt that the least productive of the three was "the method of the ruling theory" (which we equate with the verification approach, as shown in figure 3.1).

The three approaches described by Chamberlin could today be considered different levels of effectiveness in scientific approach. The least effective would be the "ruling theory" approach, by which one attempts to gather evidence in support of a hypothesis. The next level (the null hypothesis approach, the mainstay approach in several sub-fields of biology) is not as free from error as is commonly believed (e.g., Mahoney 1976:100–103). The most effective of the three, Chamberlin felt, would be the "strong inference" or "multiple inference" approach that Platt felt was responsible for the rapid advances in fields such as nuclear physics and molecular biology.

Chamberlin's concept of the three levels can also be related to two subjects broached in chapter 2; the distinction between "realism" and "relativism" as well as the distinction between "discover," "prove," and "hypothesize."

Within the Realism school, truth is considered an absolute which can be either discovered or "proved" (established beyond doubt). That approach also readily permits one to become committed to a particular viewpoint, which is what Chamberlin meant by his "ruling theory" concept and what Kuhn proposed as a "paradigm hold." Under the Relativism school's approach, however, the scientist recognizes the ephemeral nature of knowledge and plans research accordingly. That is what both Chamberlin and Platt advocated.

Mahoney (1976) also dealt with the artificiality of the scientific paper format imposed on the authors by referees and editors (to conform to journal procedure). Manuscripts are prepared to fit a theoretical "scientific method" (see excursus SCI) presumably used during the research project.

Sir Francis Bacon expressed the same notion somewhat differently in 1620: "never any knowledge was delivered in the same order [in which] it was invented" (in Blissett 1972:50). Bacon's use of the word "invented" indicates that he did not accept the ruling theory approach. One can also readily recognize that "discover" and "prove" were not as important to Bacon as "hypothesize." Atkinson's "image creation" also appears to match Bacon's use of the word "invented."

Blissett added to the above: "Beneath this placid exterior, however, is a subterranean scientific world of conflict and movement, a world characterized not by abstract and dispassionate discussion, but by activities that are both selfish and aggressive—a world victimized by the *idols* of thought Bacon hoped he could erase" (1972:50, 51). He clarified the matter further in a footnote: "Bacon's use of the word *idol* refers to conceptual 'prejudices' that are characteristic of the human condition" (1972:51).

If the foregoing analyses are correct, it should be apparent why so much controversy exists in science. If scientists belong to different philosophical schools and thereby start their research programs with different assumptions about the fundamental approach to be used, they will not be able to communicate effectively with one another. Atkinson recognized this gulf in communication in his "allusion to the ancient legend of the blindmen and the elephant":

> Each of the men having hold of a portion of the elephant proclaims knowledge of the whole; each is partially right but all are wrong. So, too, the various historians of science, philosophers of science, sociologists of science, and psychologists of science seem to have grasped some part of the intellectual pachyderm we call science yet none of the various schools or "isms" seems entirely satisfactory. (1985:727; see also excursus RE)

Perhaps it was for the above reasons that Platt wrote his paper on strong inference and later convinced the editors of *Science* to republish the 1890 Chamberlin paper. Chamberlin's paper covered the essential points. Platt moved forward with examples not available to Chamberlin and made specific suggestions:

> It seems to me that Chamberlin has hit on the explanation—and the cure—for many of our problems in the sciences. The conflict and exclusion of alternatives that is necessary to sharp inductive inference has been all too often a conflict between men, each with his single Ruling Theory. But whenever each man begins to have multiple working hypotheses, it becomes purely a conflict between ideas. It becomes much easier then for each of us to aim every day at conclusive disproofs—at *strong* inference—without either reluctance or combativeness. (1964:350)

Platt went further by formalizing the procedure as follows:

Strong inference consists of applying the following steps to every problem in science, formally and explicitly and regularly:

1. Devising alternative hypotheses;
2. Devising a crucial experiment (or several of them), with alternative possible outcomes, each of which will, as nearly as possible, exclude one or more of the hypotheses;
3. Carrying out the experiment so as to get a clean result;
   1') Recycling the procedure, making subhypotheses or sequen-

tial hypotheses to refine the possibilities that remain, and so on. (Platt 1964:347)

Platt also emphasized both that the method *can* be taught (as it apparently is done in nuclear physics and molecular biology) and that the method is already included in many first-year chemistry books, as a "conditional inductive tree" or "logical tree" approach for the quantitative analysis of an unknown sample. The dichotomous keys used by field biologists could be added to those examples; the identification of an unknown organism can be ascertained quite efficiently.

There is good reason for pursuing science via this method, according to Platt: "It is clear why this makes for rapid and powerful progress. For exploring the unknown, there is no faster method; this is the minimum sequence of steps. Any conclusion that is not an exclusion is insecure and must be re-checked. Any delay in recycling to the next set of hypotheses is only a delay" (1964:347).

The above rationale seems simple in principle, but scientists do not necessarily follow such a straightforward methodology. Their own divergent backgrounds (different prior exposures) may interfere with their protocol, as expressed by Atkinson: "the concept of science presented by scientists themselves is made up from their own experience and reflections from various philosophers, sociologists, or historians of science" (1985:731).

POLYWATER

An excellent example of an episode that illustrates the sociological aspect of science was the "discovery" and research on "polywater" (Franks 1981). In 1962 an obscure Russian physicist reported the "discovery" of a polymerized form of water. A Soviet Academy of Science physical chemist appropriated (became "converted" to) the idea and embarked on a massive study of the new compound. On a 1966 visit to Britain, this eminent Russian physical chemist converted others to the notion.

A United States representative of the Office of Naval Research, reacting to the "gentle cloak of silence" exhibited by the British scientists on this issue during the subsequent two years, extracted the idea from them and sent that idea home in his reports. American scientists, not to be beaten in a repeat of the Sputnik affair, launched their own investigation of "polywater" properties, beginning in 1969. With the massive federal funding available, they soon dominated the research field. It was not until late in 1971 that polywater began to be perceived as an artifact of experimental technique (contamination of glassware).

In the polywater episode, social considerations obviously played an important role in the conduct of that research. Philosophers and historians of science, however, have too often ignored such considerations in their deliberations.

OTHER PROBLEMS WITH PHILOSOPHY

Atkinson perceived yet another problem with the philosophy of science. He stated:

> The philosophy of science seems to have a split personality, sometimes claiming to be merely descriptive and at other times clearly attempting to be legislative—telling scientists how they ought to proceed. . . . sometimes philosophers of science let their formalism and their tendency toward legislation combine to generate a picture of an ideal to which they wished scientists would conform rather than a description of how science is actually done. (1985:731)

We are thus left with a seemingly bewildering set of attitudes on how science functions and/or on how it should function. Yet there remains a common thread among all of the possibilities covered in this and in the preceding chapter. Much of that thread was spun into a framework by Chamberlin in 1890. It appears that Chamberlin belonged to Atkinson's "legislative" category when he proposed what techniques would advance science fastest. However, Chamberlin was in the descriptive mode when he advanced his thesis that research could be practiced at three levels of effectiveness: use of the "ruling theory," the "working hypothesis," and "multiple inference."

All of the "characters" and concepts in this book seem to fit in well with these three levels as described by Chamberlin and outlined here:

1. *The ruling theory.* Controversy within a field is most likely to occur when scientists adhere strongly to a prevailing hypothesis (Kuhn's "paradigm hold" or Chamberlin's "ruling theory") as they conduct their research. Kuhn's "paradigm shift" or Polanyi's "crossing a logical gap" can only apply in those cases where Chamberlin's "ruling theory" prevails.
2. *Chamberlin's concept of the "working hypothesis"* (which, as indicated above, may well be synonymous with the "null hypothesis" approach) fits Popper's "falsifiability" doctrine.

The "falsifiability" doctrine advocated by Popper is also a critical element of the "multiple inference" approach of Chamberlin or the "strong inference" approach of Platt.

3. *Multiple inference.* Advances in science seem to be most rapid when Platt's "strong inference" (a simple version of Chamberlin's "multiple inference") approach has been applied. Strong inference involves a choice between alternative hypotheses.

Scientists who belong to the Realism school often have a philosophical perspective that leads to predictable behavior, that of rejecting hypotheses that might compete with prevailing thought. The basis for that attitude can be illustrated in another diagram (see figure 3.2). One may live under the assumption that truth exists and can be ascertained, either by verification or falsification (null hypothesis) approaches. Ever more experimentation, in those approaches, will lead one closer to what is believed to be an approximation of that truth. When sufficient supporting evidence has been gathered, such scientists often reach a point of no return (see the shaded area in

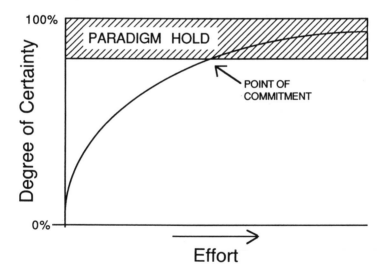

FIGURE 3.2. Progress as viewed by the Realism school. Under either the verification or the falsification (null hypothesis) approaches, continued experimentation leads to an ever greater appreciation of what might be "true" in the system under study. While working on any one project, scientists may reach a point of no return. That is, they may then assume that there is no longer any doubt about the truth of a given hypothesis; that attitude locks them into the "paradigm hold" described by Kuhn ([1962] 1970a).

figure 3.2). They have then reached the "paradigm hold" of Kuhn (1962).

THE NONUNIVERSALITY OF COMMITMENT

The philosophical approaches outlined in the previous pages are not an "all-in-one" situation for any one scientist at any one time. During experimentation on a single project, for example, one can move from exploration to verification to falsification. Perhaps one can even entertain a host of alternative hypotheses during an early stage of work on that project. The foregoing is especially true when the project poses no particular threat to existing paradigms (the "normal science" of Kuhn).

However, the very same person who can use a strong inference approach on one project may merely seek verification on another project; that happens when that person is bound by a paradigm hold. In such a case, the basic assumptions may include the "truth" of existing theories. The stronger such ties, the greater the "crisis" (Kuhn 1962) when ever more negative evidence accumulates in opposition to a favored hypothesis.

THE THEME AND THREAD OF THIS VOLUME

The material in this chapter has provided some essential background for the main theme of this volume, the interplay of attitude, evidence, and social relationships during scientific research. If we have made some of these points clear enough, the reader may begin to understand how the relatively simple issue of a "dance language" among bees could develop into a complex controversy (the thread of our volume). The differences in the basic assumptions held by the participants during the relevant four decades was far too great to permit a coordinated and concerted attack on the problem. This point will be far more evident in the material presented in the last few chapters of this book.

SUMMARY

Chamberlin's 1890 treatise had actually provided the basis for an effective set of approaches which could have resolved rather quickly the question that had arisen regarding a possible "language" among bees. In 1901, in fact, Maeterlinck described an experimental design that admirably fit the approach described by Chamberlin. When Maeterlinck applied that approach, a "language" hypothesis failed to account for the results. That hypothesis was also "falsified" in the same sense as advocated by Karl Popper nearly twenty years later.

Perhaps because of Maeterlinck's report, no serious consideration was given to the possibility of a "language" among bees until decades later. After Maeterlinck's contribution was either forgotten or ignored, von Frisch gradually "created an image" that recruited bees might find the food by following the forager's "description of the place where it lies," as previously negated by Maeterlinck (1901:167). In any event, and despite Maeterlinck's earlier negative results, von Frisch formally proposed his complex "dance language" hypothesis for bees in 1945 (Lindauer 1985).

However, a very important fact was overlooked during the rather rapid and overwhelming acceptance of the language hypothesis. Maeterlinck's experiment and von Frisch's hypothesis were actually only the most recent of many such episodes in the history of the study of this problem—the manner by which honey bees might become recruited to food sources (part of the thread of this volume).

What few people appreciate is that the two paradigms, odor search versus "language," have actually been with us for centuries, albeit often in more of a romantic than in a scientific sense. The next chapter will more fully review some of that history.

4

TWO HUNDRED YEARS OF UNCERTAINTY

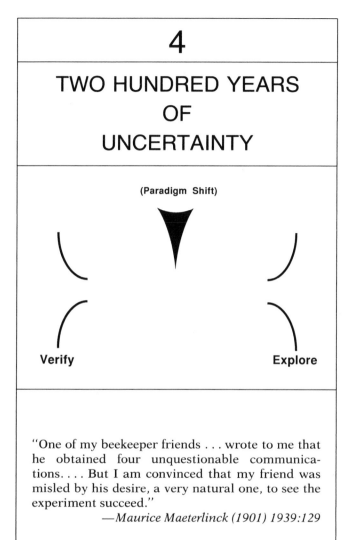

(Paradigm Shift)

Verify

Explore

"One of my beekeeper friends . . . wrote to me that he obtained four unquestionable communications. . . . But I am convinced that my friend was misled by his desire, a very natural one, to see the experiment succeed."
——*Maurice Maeterlinck (1901) 1939:129*

"It appears that the discoverer of [nectar or pollen] produces a scented trail through the air, thus enabling other bees to follow it. So fantastic is such a theory that one hesitates to announce it, were it not that the facts observed are of such a nature as well-nigh to establish such a theory as a fact."
——*Bruce Lineburg 1924:531*

"The bees communicate with each other, and are even capable of transmitting instructions with a precision that is sometimes astounding." (emphasis Francon's)
——*Julien Francon 1939:107*

55

'To-day, after two years of experimenting, I have come to realise that these wonderful beings can, in a manner hitherto undreamt of, give each other exact data about the source of food."

—*Karl von Frisch 1947:5*

The question of a language among bees, although with us intermittently for a very long time, was certainly not an important issue until the mid-1940s. What happened then? Why should there be controversy on this topic at all?

The answer to those questions hinges on several fundamental issues intertwined at various levels, not the least of which is the problem of social interaction among scientists (e.g., Mahoney 1976; Veldink 1989; see also our chapter 11). A lack of clarity of definitions and expectations of hypotheses may follow closely behind.

As an example of the latter point, it is highly unlikely that biologists of today can provide, out of memory, either 1) a precise statement of von Frisch's dance language hypothesis, 2) the evidence in support of that hypothesis, or 3) a set of testable predictions that can be made, even though they may believe that a "dance language" exists. Although biologists in the 1940s could recount the substance of those points (see chapter 1), the accumulation of negative evidence through subsequent years led to a clouding of the issue (see chapter 13), along with reduced expectations.

Neither is it likely that the average biologist knows the history of pre–von Frisch attempts to establish a "language" hypothesis of one sort or another or of the history of the simple and competing odor-search hypothesis that the dance language hypothesis replaced so precipitously. That competing odor-search hypothesis nevertheless has survived and flourished in research on the food-searching and mate-locating behavior of other insects as well as other species of animals (see chapter 5 and excursus OS).

Before proceeding with a full coverage of the two competing hypotheses and some coverage of the evidence that supports each of them, fundamental issues have to be addressed. These items include a treatment of some early history, a few definitions, a formal statement of the dance language hypothesis, a contrasting of some of the sets of competing paradigms we have recognized, and mention of von Frisch's own paradigm shift on this issue.

EARLIER INTEREST IN THE POSSIBLE EXISTENCE OF A BEE "LANGUAGE"

Much of the research done prior to von Frisch on the notion of a "language" among bees was conducted within the confines of the verification approach. Ribbands (1953) provided a short summary of several such attempts to demonstrate a "language" among bees, beginning with the previously quoted 1788 account by Spitzner (see our chapter 3). Ribbands also mentioned other observations, including those published by Dujardin in 1852, Emery in 1875, Bonnier in 1906, and Root in 1908, all of whom had either experimented in that area or had observed the waggle dance and concluded that there might be a "language" among bees.

By contrast, negative evidence relevant to various language hypotheses existed before von Frisch's time. Ribbands, for example, mentioned Lubbock's 1874 account and described those efforts as "unsuccessful in similar attempts to demonstrate communication" (1953:147). However, Ribbands unaccountably omitted Maeterlinck's 1901 contribution, which was admittedly an unsuccessful attempt to establish the presence of a language among bees (see chapter 3). Neither did Ribbands include Lineburg's 1924 theory of recruitment by means of odor-search behavior (see the epigraph and chapter 5), even though he cited other papers written by Lineburg.

As with the 1901 Maeterlinck experiment and Lineburg's theory, Ribbands also failed to mention Lubbock's considerable insight into the matter of honey bee recruitment, an insight best illustrated in Lubbock's own words:

> Every one knows that if an ant or a bee in the course of her rambles has found a supply of food, a number of others will soon make their way to the store. This, however, does not necessarily imply any power of describing localities. A very simple sign would suffice, and very little intelligence is implied, if the other ants merely accompany their friend to the treasure which she has discovered. On the other hand, if the ant or bee can describe the locality, and send her friends to the food, the case is very different. (1882:160)

During the early 1920s von Frisch first broached the notion of a "speech" *(Sprache)* among bees. At that time he mistakenly interpreted the "round dance" as a stimulus to gather nectar and the "waggle dance" as a stimulus to gather pollen. Even in the late 1930s, however, he still insisted that recruited bees use odor alone in their search for whatever food was being collected at the time by experienced foragers (von Frisch 1939).

THE FIRST REBIRTH OF A COMPLEX "LANGUAGE" HYPOTHESIS: JULIEN FRANCON

Maurice Maeterlinck (see the epigraph) was very popular and his 1901 book, *The Life of the Bee,* very readable. Subsequently, no serious consideration was given to the possibility that a "language" or so-phisticated mode of honey bee communication could exist among honey bees. For example, Burroughs wrote in 1921; "that bees tell one another of the store of honey they have found is absurd (1921: 158).

Eventually, however, nearly four decades after Maeterlinck's publication of negative evidence, his contribution was no longer considered relevant by those who studied the question of honey bee recruitment to food sources—or perhaps his message faded out of memory. His experiment and results were then largely ignored (e.g., Francon 1939), dismissed (e.g., von Frisch 1954), or misinterpreted (e.g., Gould 1976:211). Curiously, Burroughs (1921:158) had also misinterpreted the results of Maeterlinck's experiment.

In any event, the way became open for Julien Francon in France to "create his image" (Atkinson 1985) of how honey bees might be recruited to food sources; that is, he concluded that recruited bees might find the food by following the forager's "description of the place where it lies" (in Maeterlinck's words, 1901:167).

Francon (1939) proposed his sophisticated communication hypothesis for honey bees in 1938, but those efforts seem to have been set aside during World War II. During a series of experiments, he noticed that foraging bees recruited others to the same site when the food could be collected easily but did not do so when the task was difficult. He felt that a simple odor-vision hypothesis, by which hivemates could somehow follow a forager out to the food, would not clear up the mystery of the success of his searching recruits. Bees in Francon's experiments appeared to perform better than that, leading him to conclude that foraging bees must have an ability to somehow communicate information to their hivemates about the location and physical characteristics of food sources (see the above epigraph).

Francon did not "convert" (in the sense of Atkinson 1985) very many others to a belief in his hypothesis. That may have been due in part to the fact that his claims about the ability of bees were greatly exaggerated relative to the evidence at hand. That is, he felt that foragers could communicate information about feeding dish characteristics, including information about color, the presence of dry or wet sugar, and the mode of entry into a box. He also preempted von Frisch on the proposal that foragers could indicate to hivemates the distance of a food source from the hive.

Francon did have one important "convert" to his hypothesis. H. Eltringham, a noted entomologist and fellow of the Royal Society, translated Francon's book, *The Mind of the Bees*, from the original

French and wrote the preface to the English edition. In that preface Eltringham wrote of Francon's experimental results:

> Reinforcements do not necessarily *follow* the original pioneer, but frequently arrive at the scene of operations quite independently. Having arrived, they show complete knowledge of the position and means of access. . . . It seems . . . impossible to suggest how such achievements can be attained unless the original bee can, in some way unknown to us, give to the assistant bees the most precise and accurate instructions. (Francon [1938] 1939:V)

Von Frisch did not cite Francon's book in his research papers, but finally did so in his 1967 review volume. There he summarily dismissed Francon's results and ignored Francon's priority in the idea that bees could communicate distance information. Instead, he criticized Francon's experimental technique, as follows:

> When feeding dishes and other pieces of equipment are reused, one must realize that the bees leave behind persistent traces of odors that are attractive to their comrades. If Julian Francon (1938, 1939) had noted this source of error he would not have adorned his affectionate descriptions of the "sagacity of the bees" with such fantastic statements. . . . Actually the newcomers doubtless smelled the places where their predecessor had been. (1967a:22)

Francon's contribution was later either forgotten or ignored during the rather rapid and overwhelming acceptance of von Frisch's dance language hypothesis in the mid-1940s. One of the reasons for the difference in the fortunes of the two men revolves around one of the important distinctions between the concepts of "paradigm" and "hypothesis." In regard to the former, Bohm and Peat wrote: "Paradigms clearly involve, in a key way, the process of taking ideas and concepts for granted, without realizing that this is in fact going on" (1987:52).

Thus, there are those who work under the assumption that a "language" can be (or has been) "discovered" or can be (or has been) "proved to exist." Such an assumption then suffices for a starting point, without the need for formal definition. Francon, for example, worked within a "language" paradigm and assumed that it would be present.

By contrast, others of us recognize that von Frisch *generated* the honey bee dance language "hypothesis," a relatively narrow interpretation for the combined set of results from his experimentation. Von Frisch clearly had the edge over Francon on that matter. The narrower concept of hypothesis, as used here in contrast to the paradigm notion, however, requires a careful statement of assumptions, clear definitions of terms, and a suitably precise statement (at the time) of the hypothesis itself (see chapter 1).

We turn first to a treatment of a few of the problems that have contributed to some of the past confusion in the dance language controversy. Among these is the fact that there has always been considerable confusion about what constitutes "communication" among organisms. As an example, Lewis wrote: "We all believe we intuitively know what is meant by 'communication,' yet many conflicting definitions have been proposed. . . . Burghardt (1970) concluded that the concept of communication in animals must involve intent and thus be adaptive" (1984:1–2).

Unfortunately, Burghardt's attitude includes a strong teleological component (see excursus TEL). Can one *ever* know the "intent" of another animal?

We followed quite a different procedure in our research. We recognized that, prior to von Frisch, any "language" and odor-search paradigms were vague; definitions kept shifting. The von Frisch era overlapped with an adoption of a more precise terminology in behavioral studies, a terminology that did not require any evaluation of an animal's "intent" (table 1 in Wenner 1969; see also Wenner 1971a).

The honey bee dance language hypothesis as proposed by von Frisch fit the notion of an "instinctive language." The results he obtained appeared to indicate that recruited bees could obtain discrete information from the waggle dance of a successful bee, decode that information, and then fly directly out to the same site visited by that forager (see chapter 1 and below). Both von Frisch and those who followed him then gathered a considerable body of evidence in support of that hypothesis by exploiting the verification approach.

Furthermore, scientists throughout the world followed von Frisch's verification lead, repeated his experiments in the same manner as done initially, and gained additional support for the dance language hypothesis. Unfortunately, no one ever thought to *test* the dance language hypothesis during the first two decades of its existence.

SOPHISTICATION: THE VON FRISCH DANCE LANGUAGE HYPOTHESIS

As mentioned above, in the late 1930s Julien Francon of France became convinced that bees had a "language" of sorts on the basis of his experimental results. However, Francon could not fathom any possible mechanism for that communication, and wrote:

We have established the certainty that the bees communicate between themselves, and have disclosed the whole extent of the instructions they are capable of transmitting. . . . But we have no idea
by what mechanism, auditory, or vibratory, these communications
are established. (1939:143)

Von Frisch eventually pursued the possibility of a language among
bees far more diligently than did his predecessors, despite the negative results obtained by Lubbock (1882), despite the results of Maeterlinck's "crucial" experiment (1901), despite the existence of Lineburg's 1924 odor-search theory, and despite his own earlier and firm
commitment to an odor-search hypothesis (von Frisch 1939).

Historically, von Frisch's substantive contributions to the dance
language hypothesis itself occurred in three stages. First, he proposed
an ill-defined *"Sprache"* of bees in the early 1920s. Second, in the fall
of 1944, von Frisch discovered a mechanism by which forager bees
might transmit direction and distance information to potential recruit bees; that is, he "decoded" the waggle dance maneuver performed in the hive by returning foragers (von Frisch 1947). That
insight permitted him to generate his "dance language" hypothesis
("create the image"; see Atkinson 1985).

The dance maneuver correlations von Frisch described would later
come to be accepted as the "established" mechanism by which foraging bees direct hivemates out to a crop (in the teleological sense). That
is, most biologists came to believe that recruited bees would be able
to fly from the hive in a given direction and to a specific distance on
their way to the food by using information gained from the dance
maneuver before they left the hive (see chapter 1).

In the third phase, during the early 1950s, von Frisch conducted a
series of experiments to determine the *precision* of the "dance language" use by newly recruited (naive) bees. The conclusion that *naive*
bees could *efficiently* "use" the distance and direction information
present in the dance maneuver was an essential component of the
language hypothesis. Von Frisch did not realize, however, that the
very design of his precision experiments could bias the experimental
results (see excursus PN).

Despite the existing negative evidence relative to a language hypothesis of any kind, and despite von Frisch's earlier published argument in support of an odor-search mechanism during recruitment,
social attitudes in the biological community had changed; its members had become receptive to a renewed generation of some sort of
bee "language" hypothesis after the mid-1930s.

There were similarities and differences between the "bee communication" hypothesis of Francon and the "dance language" hypothesis of von Frisch. Both of them presumed that honey bees were capable of anthropomorphic, human-level behavior (see Rosin 1978 and our chapter 13). Both researchers used the verification approach during their experiments; that is, they searched for confirming evidence. Their experimental "tests" were also designed to obtain additional confirming evidence for their hypotheses. Both concluded from their results that bees could communicate abstract information (such as the distance of a food source from the hive).

One major difference between Francon's and von Frisch's hypotheses and approaches was that von Frisch also studied the behavior of bees in the hive. That study led him to recognize the presence of correlations between elements in the celebrated waggle dance and the location visited by foragers in the field. Von Frisch found that he could "decode" the pattern of that dance maneuver and deduce the geographic location of a food source previously visited by that forager; Francon had found no such correlations.

A second major difference between the Francon and von Frisch experiments was one of numbers. Francon had provided a sequence of increasingly difficult tasks for each single forager to "master." From those experiments he obtained only *qualitative* evidence as confirmation for his communication hypothesis. Von Frisch, on the other hand, conducted experiments that yielded *quantitative* results (relative numbers of recruits arriving at various stations) in support of his dance language hypothesis.

Furthermore, whereas Francon's experiments were not especially repeatable, von Frisch's experiments were eminently repeatable. Other scientists could readily gather additional confirming data; such replication is one of the cornerstones of science (see chapter 4 in Broad and Wade 1982). As Donald Griffin wrote: "I confess without embarrassment that until I performed these simple experiments myself, I too retained a residue of skepticism" (in von Frisch 1950:vi). The fact that the rationale of the waggle dance ("dance language") hypothesis was quite straightforward and simple in principle also contributed to its rapid acceptance.

THE HONEY BEE DANCE LANGUAGE HYPOTHESIS

We turn now to a formal statement of the honey bee dance language hypothesis as we feel it was originally intended by von Frisch and as distinct from the vague notion of a honey bee "dance language" paradigm. A condensation of that rationale was published earlier, as follows:

Postulates

1. A bee successful at exploiting a source of food in the field succeeds in stimulating other bees (recruits) to leave the hive and search for the same source.
2. The successful forager, while stimulating others to leave the hive, executes a 'dance" upon the surface of the comb. This dance contains quantitative direction and distance information. A human being can "read" the dance maneuver and deduce the field location exploited by the forager.
3. "Recruits" soon arrive at or near that site exploited by the bee they contacted before leaving the hive.

Conclusion

Recruits can *use* the direction and distance information provided by successful "dancing" bees and fly straight out to the appropriate location. (Wenner 1971a:30)

The von Frisch experiments were also *testable* in a rigorous sense (e.g., Popper 1957; Platt 1964).

Unfortunately, no one attempted "to find out if the hypothesis will stand up to critical evaluation." That is, no one did so until we did just that more than twenty years after von Frisch first proposed his hypothesis (Johnson 1967a; Wenner 1967; Wenner, Wells, and Johnson 1969).

Neither did others appreciate the fact that von Frisch's new interpretation was a conclusion based upon circumstantial evidence. Their displeasure with our tests of that hypothesis, the first real tests ever run, was thus quite understandable and probably inevitable.

VON FRISCH'S EARLIER PARADIGM SHIFT

Those who credited von Frisch with "discovering" *the* "dance language" of bees or with "proving" that bees have a language were thus apparently neither fully aware of the philosophical basis of the concept nor of the history of earlier attempts to develop that sort of hypothesis. They also may not have been aware of alternative hy-

potheses on honey bee recruitment to food sources, either those proposed by others (e.g., Francon) or by von Frisch himself (von Frisch
1939; see also Rosin 1980b). The earlier contributions of Lubbock,
Maeterlinck, Lineburg, and Francon and the later von Frisch contributions are actually only a few of many such episodes in the history
of this problem—the manner by which honey bees might become
recruited to food sources.

Historical accounts often omit important episodes. For example,
and as indicated above, after the rapid acceptance of the von Frisch
dance language hypothesis, nearly everyone seems to have forgotten
that von Frisch had earlier been convinced that recruited bees used
odor exclusively in their search. In 1939 he described the general and
nondirectional search pattern of recruited bees as follows:

> I fed some of the numbered bees of the observation hive at a feeding-
> place 40 feet to the west of the hive. . . . If the dancer bee dancing in
> the hive reported where the feeding-place was, the new bees would
> all fly to the west feeding-place. As a matter of fact, a few minutes
> after the commencement of the dance new bees appeared at the
> same time at all the little dishes to the north and south, to the west
> and east. They did not know where the food was. They flew out in
> all directions and looked for it. . . .
>
> But not only in the neighborhood! . . . It is clear from a long
> series of experiments that after the commencement of the dances
> the bees first seek in the neighborhood, and then go farther away,
> and finally search the whole flying district.
>
> So the language of bees seemed to be very simple. (1939:428)

Von Frisch thus did not experience "creation of an image" and formally propose his more complex "dance language" hypothesis until
1945 (Lindauer 1985), seven years after Francon had already proposed
a similar idea.

The well-defined dance language hypothesis, as stated above, lost
its distinctive limits soon after its inception; the scientific community
instead veered away from its earlier recognition of the honey bee
"dance language" as a hypothesis. Instead, scientists worked within
the dance language concept as a full-fledged paradigm. By the time
we began to examine the significance of the anomalies we uncovered,
the pendulum had swung even further toward the notion that honey
bees could have a "language." By that time the dance language hypothesis was being treated as a fact.

Why test a "fact"?

AT ISSUE: MULTIPLE SETS OF COMPETING PARADIGMS

Although anyone may recognize and/or may be working primarily within a single paradigm during any particular project, several paradigms actually control the course of our research efforts at any one time. Thomas Kuhn spoke of research under any such umbrella of circumstances as "normal science." He devoted considerable space to describe the utility of that restriction; that is: "When the individual scientist can take a paradigm for granted, he need no longer, in his major works, attempt to build his field anew, starting from first principles and justifying the use of each concept introduced" (1962:19–20).

However, when Kuhn first introduced the notion of "paradigm," he actually used that term in two different senses:

> On the one hand, it stands for the entire constellation of beliefs, values, techniques, and so on shared by the members of a given community. On the other, it denotes one sort of element in that constellation, the concrete puzzle-solutions which, employed as models or examples, can replace explicit rules as a basis for the solution of the remaining puzzles of normal science. (1962:175)

The fact that Kuhn's use of the term "paradigm" was deliberately vague led to considerable debate within the philosophical community (see Lakatos and Musgrave 1970). However, those of us who are not philosophers were more comfortable with Kuhn's intent. Bohm and Peat, for example, emphasized the essence of the "paradigm" concept in their statement:

> The tacit infrastructure [of science], mostly unconsciously, pervades the whole work and thought of a community of scientists.... it must also be realized that a paradigm has the power to keep a whole community of scientists working on a more or less common area. In a sense, it could be taken as an unconscious or tacit form of consent. (1987:52–53)

As for Bohm and Peat, the above statement by Kuhn fits our experience quite well and serves as a sufficiently clear definition for our purposes.

Whereas many have concluded that our challenge of the honey bee dance language hypothesis was ill-conceived, others have recognized a fundamental question here—that is: "How does one go about doing scientific research?" Yet others became hopelessly confused by what transpired, partly because they were unaware of the distinction between "hypothesis" and "paradigm" and partly because they could not follow the intricacies of the argument.

In order to focus attention on the issues we believe to be most important in honey bee recruitment, we use the phrases "dance language paradigm" and "odor-search paradigm" as shorthand. Those who work within the dance language paradigm certainly share an "entire constellation of beliefs, values, techniques, and so on." However, those who study the odor-searching behavior of flying or swimming animals likewise share a constellation of beliefs, etc., a constellation that might have elements considerably different from those used by workers within the other paradigm.

We turn now to a brief summary of three sets of paradigms central to the dance language controversy.

Odor-Search Versus Dance Language Paradigms

Although we began research within the accepted dance language paradigm and were initially a secure part of that community, the experimental results we obtained as we began and continued to test the dance language hypothesis led us ever more toward a position of uncertainty, ever more into the Relativism school (see excursus RE), and ever further away from a consensus that had been reached by that segment of the scientific community interested in studies of non-human communication.

Inevitably, we gravitated toward the position that it *was* conceivable that no animals other than human beings had a "language." Our willingness to question the basic assumptions underlying the "constellation of beliefs, values, techniques, and so on" isolated us from the other members of that community (Veldink 1989).

The paradigm hold, as in Kuhn's expression, was very strong (and remains so today) for proponents of the dance language hypothesis. Those in that area of research readily accepted supportive evidence; negative evidence was no longer considered relevant once that "ruling theory" (Chamberlin [1890] 1965) took hold.

Insect-Level Versus Human-Level Paradigms

Rosin (1978, 1980a, 1980b, 1988b) was the first to emphasize the importance of this distinction. "Discovering" or "proving" the existence of a language in a nonhuman species does not hinge only on evidence. One first of all has to be able to "believe" that such a capability can be possible. Prior to the mid-1930s there was an abundant literature on either side of that fence. For the dance language hypothesis to succeed as well as it did, there had to be a sizable number in the scientific community who considered bees capable of such a feat. The resistance to the dance language hypothesis elicited initially among psychologists stemmed from their membership in a different community (the Schneirla-Lehrman school; see Rosin 1980a), a community that worked within quite a different paradigm than that within which the dance language paradigm developed.

In brief, the question at issue here is: "Can one really believe that the small honey bee visiting a flower has language capability?" (See Gould and Gould 1988 for descriptions of other presumed powers of honey bees.) The same social situation that permitted the rise of "New Age" thinking in the public at large had apparently spilled over into the biological community.

Realism School Versus Relativism School Paradigms

As indicated earlier, Thomas Kuhn is primarily responsible for pointing out the discrepancy between what philosophers of science advocated prior to 1962 (the date of first publication of his classic book) and the actual process of science as it is practiced. The terms "realism" ("objectivism") and "relativism" ("antirealism") became popular after that time. Those terms served as labels for those philosophers and scientists who shared one or the other of the two sets of "entire constellation of beliefs, values, techniques, and so on" in their pursuit of explanations applicable to the natural world.

We have concluded that proponents of the dance language hypothesis apparently belong to the Realism school (a school that included us, initially) and have worked within that paradigm ever since the inception of that hypothesis. That position permits a consensus that bee language was either "discovered" or "proved." Once that "language" has been established as a fact, in their view, it is time to move on and no longer question that basic assumption.

THE IMPLICATIONS OF A "LANGUAGE" AMONG BEES

The history of recent research on honey bee recruitment to food sources (after the rebirth of a "language" hypothesis) was fully reviewed in von Frisch (1967a) and in other sources (e.g., Wilson 1971; Wenner 1974; Gould 1976, Rosin 1980a, 1980b; Lindauer 1985) and will not be repeated here. Hundreds of bee researchers followed von Frisch's lead and published the results of a great many experiments on this apparently unique phenomenon, namely a "language" capability in a nonhuman species. The fields of ethology and sociobiology gained a firm foundation, as expressed by Brian Smith: "it was not until the systematic inquiry of Karl von Frisch in this century that the potential implications of honey-bee behavior for behavior theory in general were realized" (1988:250).

The apparent breakthrough, that is, the "establishment" of a "language" capability in a nonhuman species ("discovery" or "proof" of that "fact"), permitted others to do equivalent types of research on dolphins, apes, and other animals. Moreover, nearly all of that research was also initially accomplished under the "method of the ruling theory," which is exactly what Chamberlin warned against.

When we began our research on honey bee recruitment, we were ignorant of the rich history and extent of interest in the two opposing hypotheses and worked intensively only within a "dance language" paradigm, and primarily exploited the verification approach. Little did we realize that we would eventually obtain evidence contradicting that dance language hypothesis, just as Maeterlinck had obtained it sixty-five years earlier. Nor were we aware of von Frisch's earlier staunch adherence to the odor-search paradigm (von Frisch 1939; Rosin 1980a), largely because that earlier commitment of his was not alluded to, either by him or by others once the dance language hypothesis caught hold.

The issue is thus actually more complex than was appreciated earlier by any of those involved in the controversy. There is not only the problem of which hypothesis might better explain any existing set of experimental results. There is also the problem of fundamental assumptions about what an insect is capable of doing and the problem of the research approach used during experimentation, as advocated and practiced in the Realism and Relativism schools.

In the chapters that follow (and in the excursuses), we will provide specific examples of the way in which adherence to paradigms (or the failure to adhere to them) directs research efforts.

5

THE
ODOR-SEARCH PARADIGM:
HISTORY AND REVISION

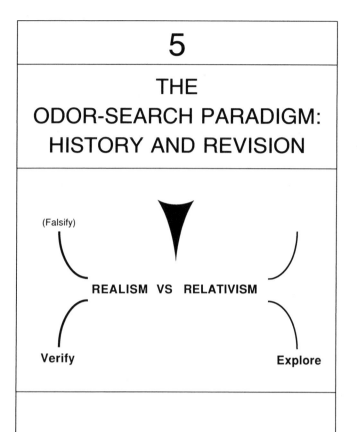

"For all insects as a class, have, thanks to the species of odour correlated with nutrition, a keen olfactory sense of their proper food from a distance, even when they are very far away from it; such is the case with the bees."

—*Aristotle (330* B.C.*) 1931:vol. 4, passage 444*

"Their smelling is excellent, whereby, when they fly aloft in the air, they will quickly perceive anything under them that they like, as honey, or tar, though it be covered; as soon as the honeydew is fallen, they presently [take wind of] it, though the oaks that receive it be afar off."

—*Charles Butler (1609) 1969:ch. 1, passage 42*

"The theory of a scented trail is strengthened by the apparent elimination of other theories which have been proposed, that is, the sight theory and the theory of a general search."

—*Bruce Lineburg 1924:536*

"It is clear from a long series of experiments that after the commencement of the dances the bees first seek in the neighborhood, and then go farther away, and finally search the whole flying district. . . . It is thus seen that there is a biological function of flower scent not known before. The dancing bee can communicate a message about all kinds of scented flowers by means of the scent adhering to its body."

—*Karl von Frisch 1939:428, 429*

"The way in which a bee which has found a rich source of nectar communicates this information to her sisters has puzzled beekeepers and naturalists for a long time. The explanation, however, is really quite simple; and any fairy tales about one bee telling the others, or leading the others to a locality, can be discounted. When a bee returns to the hive with her stomach filled with honey or nectar, she starts dancing on the combs in a characteristic way, beating her wings and thus spreading the smell of the flower which clings to her body. The other bees become interested by the dance and go searching for that particular smell."

—*Hans Kalmus 1960:96*

"We are now at a stage in the controversy where supporters of the 'dance language' hypothesis concede that honey-bees normally use odor alone."

—*R. Rosin 1980a:798*

"[That] the principal mechanism of 'long-distance' flying orientation to an airborne chemical stimulus in the wind is an optomotor-guided, chemically-induced, upwind orientation (or *anemotaxis*) has gained wide acceptance as a considerable body of experimental evidence in support of this mechanism has accumulated."

—*Ring Carde 1984:111*

The idea that honey bees depend on odor for recruitment to food sources has apparently existed for centuries (see chapter 4). It is quite surprising, then, that nearly all biologists embraced von Frisch's dance language hypothesis so quickly after its inception in the mid-1940s (see chapter 6). That ready acceptance occurred even though many of those same scientists had earlier accepted his olfactory hypothesis (e.g., von Frisch 1939), complete with *its* supportive evidence.

That general acceptance of von Frisch's earlier hypothesis was largely forgotten or ignored during and after World War II, perhaps due to disruption in scientific communication during that war. Another factor was that von Frisch generated the language hypothesis during the war years and reported it immediately after that long period of scientific inactivity. The new hypothesis filled a relative vacuum.

Examples of acceptance of von Frisch's earlier views on odor-search behavior, however, can be found in writings based upon materials written before the acceptance of the dance language hypothesis. One such example is provided by Buzzard, who wrote:

> It was Von Frisch, a Bavarian investigator, who, some years ago, discovered that bees scouting for nectar return to their hives with some of this [nectar] found on a particular plant, say borage, and perform a kind of dance among the inmates of the hive, attracting their attention. Immediately bees, who have clustered round and recognised the nectar, go forth in *every direction* from the hive seeking borage. (1946:58; emphasis ours)

Buzzard, in referring to the previously mentioned book written by the Frenchman, Julien Francon (*The Mind of the Bees* [1939]; see our chapter 4), elaborated upon why he thought von Frisch's odor-search explanation was better than the mechanism proposed by Francon, who had attributed a "language" of sorts to bees. Buzzard wrote:

> Francon, after elaborate and prolonged experiments covering a period of eight years or more, was quite persuaded that bees not only inform their comrades of the presence of booty, but tell them exactly how to reach it . . . readers of this book, where the interesting experiments are described at full length, will be astonished at the results obtained, and will probably at first agree with the author's conclusions that bees can describe to their comrades the positions of sites most difficult to find, with the greatest accuracy. (1946:155)

Buzzard, however, would have nothing to do with Francon's conclusions but chose, instead, to accept von Frisch's insistence that bees relied solely upon odor after starting their search. He explained why he rejected Francon's "language" hypothesis:

> I gather that Francon was not aware of the proved results of Von Frisch's experiments, which Baldensperger saw and described to me, nor of the experiments made by Dr. Michaud and myself independently, and confirmed by Rothamsted [an experimental station in England]. . . . Francon's trials were conducted in the open air, and if the first bee gave the discovery of honey in the hive, the air would soon be full of bees radiating in every direction. Moreover, those that found no honey would circle in ever-increasing circles in an attempt to find it. Again, no wonder that numbers of bees saw Francon's first bee returning to her booty. (1946:166)

Under the circumstances, the rather rapid and nearly complete reversal of attitude by scientists was puzzling; they turned from acceptance of von Frisch's first conviction and embraced his later diametrically opposed conviction. In order to accept the more recent dance language hypothesis, then, biologists simultaneously and suddenly had to ignore a considerable body of existing evidence at variance with the dance language hypothesis but supportive of the earlier olfactory paradigm (see Rosin 1980a, 1980b).

Such reversals normally cannot be readily accommodated by those working within the verification approach of the Realism school (see chapter 3). A trend toward a return to teleology by the scientific community may have been responsible for the speed of that "conversion" (see excursus TEL and below).

Hans Kalmus at University College in London was one of the prominent holdouts in the biological community (above epigraph), and for good reason. Two factors weighed heavily against acceptance of the dance language hypothesis at the outset. One was a strong movement among some students of animal behavior at the time to describe behavioral acts in quantitative or mechanistic terms (the mechanistic paradigm, still embraced by many today). The dance language hypothesis did not mesh well with that movement (Rosin 1980b).

The other factor contributing to slight hesitancy, with regard to acceptance of the dance language hypothesis, was a general but ill-defined acceptance of the fact, during the 1930s and 1940s, that animals always move upwind ("exhibit positive anemotaxis") while searching for an odor source. In other words, a newly described ability of bees to locate an odor source irrespective of wind direction violated the law of parsimony under the mechanistic anemotaxis hypothesis.

THE MECHANISM SCHOOL

During the decades prior to von Frisch's introduction of the language hypothesis, then, insect behavior was described primarily in mechanistic terms. That approach was the result of an attempt to move away from an undue influence of anthropomorphism and teleology during the design of experiments and the interpretation of experimental results (Loeb [1918] 1973; Fraenkel and Gunn [1940] 1961; see also excursus TEL).

In those days behavioral acts were described as "taxes" or "kineses" and were considered "instinctive" responses to discrete and immediate stimuli. The goal was to describe behavior in simple, objective terms so that it could be studied with less of the human bias used earlier. The term "positive phototaxis," for example, was used to describe the behavior of an animal traveling (walking, swimming, or flying) toward a light source. In the example used above, "positive anemotaxis" would describe the behavior of an animal traveling upwind (or upcurrent).

The advent of the "ethology" school, led largely by K. S. Lashley and Konrad Lorenz, stimulated some investigators to focus more on "the internal system of co-ordination of special behaviour patterns on the one hand and the special receptive sensory mechanisms on the other" (Thorpe 1963:20; see also Burkhardt 1988). Thorpe summarized the climate of the times as follows:

> The psychologists . . . fastened on the psychological aspects of instinctive behaviour as fundamental. The mechanist-physiological school, on the other hand, . . . became obsessed by the extreme fixity of much instinctive behaviour. . . . they tended to ignore perception and the releaser problem and concentrated instead on the apparently more tractable problems of the stereotyped fixed-action pattern of instinctive behavior, and so tried to fit everything into a system of chain reflexes. (1963:21)

While the dance language hypothesis was gaining acceptance in some spheres, the previous diligence in favor of noninterpretive terminology was being eroded in other quarters. What later came to be known as the ethology group turned their attention increasingly toward an analysis of "purposive" behavior (excursus TEL). And bees, if they had a "language," certainly seemed capable of behaving in a purposeful manner. Lindauer later summarized that attitude as follows:

> One of the most fruitful guiding principles of biology has been that each morphological structure and behavioral act is associated with a special function. On this basis alone, it would seem highly unlikely that the information contained in the waggle dance of a honeybee is not transmitted to her nest mates. (1971:89)

The first of those sentences often serves as a starting point for research. However, the second statement is a non sequitur, because the presumed function embraced by the scientist may not be the actual function of the structure or act.

Chamberlin ([1890] 1965) probably would have recognized therein the influence of his concept of the "ruling theory" (see our chapter 3). Under the multiple inference approach advocated by Chamberlin, one would immediately seek to consider all *possible* "functions" and explanations for the existence of information in the dance maneuver, rather than the single one embraced by Lindauer.

In one of the final attempts to accommodate the language hypothesis within the older chain reflex vocabulary, Leppik (1953) proposed the term "melittolexis" (honey bee mode of expression) for "the sign language of bees." The term never caught on.

At the same time that many students of animal behavior were yielding to the spell of teleology and anthropomorphism, biochemistry was moving in the opposite direction. Keller described that move: "Jacques Monod, . . . who said of himself, 'I have to stick to a linear, logical thread—otherwise I am lost,' . . . took upon himself the task of ridding biochemistry of its teleological language" (1983:175).

Monod largely succeeded, and biochemistry subsequently experienced an acceleration in rate of progress.

THE EARLIER ODOR-SEARCH PARADIGM

The other major factor that caused people, such as Kalmus, to hesitate in their acceptance of the dance language hypothesis was the universality of an ill-defined odor-search paradigm that had persisted since Aristotle's time (330 B.C.). In one place Aristotle wrote:

> The mollusc, the crustacean, and the insect have all the senses: at all events, they have sight, smell, and taste. As for the insects, both winged and wingless, they can detect the presence of scented objects afar off, as for instance bees and cnipes [ants] detect honey at a distance; and they do so recognizing it by smell. ([330 B.C.] 1931:vol. 3, passage 534)

In another volume (vol. 4, passage 444), as in our epigraph, Aristotle reiterated the same message.

Two thousand years later others recognized the same principle, as stated quite simply by Butler (see the epigraph) and Wildman, 160 years after Butler, as follows: "Nature hath endued the bees with an exquisite smell, for they scent at a great distance the honey and wax" (1768:26).

As an aside, Butler's mention of "honey, or tar" and Wildman's mention of "honey and wax," as being material gathered by bees from flowers deserves special treatment. Butler ([1609] 1969) knew that beeswax used in the production of honeycomb, was produced by glands on the underside of the abdomen of worker bees (Ribbands 1953). However, both later and earlier investigators felt that beeswax was gathered from flowers, because the pollen pellets carried on the hind legs of forager bees felt somewhat greasy when pressed between the fingers. In addition, bees gather pitch from pine trees and other sources, which they mix with beeswax to form glue that helps seal the cavity in which they live. Butler's and Wildman's use of the terms "tar" and "wax" become understandable in that context.

Knowing the propensity of bees to odor search had a practical twist. Before the days of parcel post shipping of package bees to beekeepers in northern climates in North America, anyone wishing to start new colonies often had to resort to "bee hunting," a specialized procedure used to find feral colonies of bees (usually located in "bee trees"). Such people were referred to as "bee hunters" (Root et al. 1947:55–58). Burroughs, in his account of bee hunting, described his impression of the importance of odor in that process:

> A bee will usually make three or four trips from the [bee] hunter's box before it brings back a companion. I suspect the bee does not tell its fellows what it has found, but that they smell out the secret; it doubtless bears some evidence with it upon its feet or proboscis that it has been upon honey-comb and not upon flowers, and its companions take the hint and follow, arriving always many seconds behind. (1875:53)

Von Frisch and others worked within that same paradigm for more than twenty-five years (see the above epigraphs and chapter 4; see also Lineburg 1924; von Frisch 1939; Rosin 1980a). Lineburg, in fact, developed an odor-search model that resembled the one we developed many years later (see below and excursus OS). In our view Lineburg was prevented from developing the full model by two circumstances: 1) his adherence to the Nasanov scent gland attraction hypothesis (which we later found wanting; see excursus NG) and 2) his focus on scent traveling downwind from an *individual* flying forager (rather than from the many foragers traveling along an "aerial pathway"; see excursus OS).

Lineburg listed "four conditions which must obtain in order that one animal may follow another by scent" (1924:531). These four are worth comparing with what occurs in nature as foragers travel between hive and feeding place, as follows:

1. "The creature followed must possess a scent." With regard to that condition Lineburg wrote: "Not only does [the bee] possess a body-scent, as do many other creatures, but it also possesses a special scent-producing organ" (1924:532).
2. "This scent must be of such strength and character as to be perceptible to the individual which is following." Here Lineburg did not recognize the utility of odor emanating from the *many* foragers that would simultaneously travel between the parent hive and the target food place (and the "aerial pathway" so produced).
3. "The scent must possess sufficient permanence to enable the pursuer to pick it up after the pursued has passed." Again, the permanence would not be very great for an individual forager, but would be great for the body of foragers traveling the same path.
4. "Such a trail, although it may be broken, must possess a degree of continuity sufficient to enable the pursuer to cross such breaks." Once again, a body of foragers traversing the same path would fulfill this condition.

Lineburg continued and discussed examples of odor use by bloodhounds and the movement of a column of smoke from a train traveling in a path at right angles to the wind direction. He wrote: "In hunting, game sometimes passes within clear view of the hunters so that its path may be seen. Not infrequently is it observed that the dogs run in a course parallel to that taken by the quarry and at a distance of a hundred or more yards to [the leeward] side of it" (1924:533).

This last statement has particular relevance to results obtained by Friesen (1973), who found that a concentration of searching recruits existed downwind from the aerial pathway of foragers (see our chapter 8).

In March 1937 von Frisch summarized his earlier research (a summary that did not contradict the model proposed by Lineburg) during a lecture at University College in London (the same institution where Kalmus later taught; see the epigraph). Von Frisch's lecture text was published in *Science Progress* ([1937], vol. 32, no. 125) and later reprinted in the 1938 Annual Report of the Board of Regents of the Smithsonian Institution (1939).

Apart from Rosin's citation (1980a), that 1939 von Frisch contribution seems to have been ignored subsequent to the acceptance of the dance language hypothesis, even by von Frisch himself (e.g., von Frisch 1967a). Lineburg's contribution was apparently also subsequently ignored by all but von Frisch, who finally treated that work on pages 222 and 223 of his 1967 review volume.

Von Frisch dismissed Lineburg's proposal by referring to the results he himself had obtained in his September 17–20, 1944 experiments. Unwittingly, however, von Frisch failed to realize even then that his own results were internally inconsistent (see chapter 6). Von Frisch also erred both in not recognizing the importance of locality odors that might adhere to the body of bees and in considering only the path of single foragers rather than the concept of an aerial pathway.

It is important to keep in mind, however, that von Frisch's earlier view (recruits use only odor while searching for a food place) was held by others right up to the time that he proposed his revolutionary dance language hypothesis. One example of the acceptance of that odor-search explanation was provided in the first pages of this chapter (Buzzard 1946), but the impression was general. In the standard manual for beekeepers *(The ABC and XYZ of Bee Culture)*, Root and coauthors wrote:

> There seems to be some question whether the bees that follow the dancers go straight to the find or whether they wander around until they do locate it. [We incline] to the latter opinion. In a bad case of robbing, the bees that follow the dancers will wander all over the apiary; hunt over the ground, inspect buildings and objects of all sorts, and increase the circles of flight until the coveted sweets are located. (1947:49)

The last phrase, "increase the circles of flight until the coveted sweets are located" is interesting. That expression is significant for our odor-search model (see excursus OS).

THE "LAW" OF ODOR-SEARCH BEHAVIOR

One of the tenets inherent in the mechanistic approach to the study of behavior is that the movements of animals searching for odor sources conform to the laws of physics. Both light and sound travel in straight lines in all directions from the point of origin; those stimuli can also be readily perceived and measured. In earlier times the phrases "positive phototaxis" and "negative phonotaxis," for example, were used when referring to a directed movement of animals toward a light source or away from a sound source, respectively.

Odor perception is quite a different matter than sound or light perception, but we found that a rather common misconception existed among ethologists and physiologists when we first suggested our odor-search hypothesis as an alternative to the dance language hypothesis. We were often challenged during discussions or seminars. Dance language proponents claimed that bees could not be using odor; they believed that the perception of faint odors from a great distance is not possible.

The thinking of these scientists apparently relied somehow on assumptions relevant to principles of diffusion theory. Under that model, odor concentration would decrease as the square of the distance from its source (just as light and sound intensities do). Under that theory, bees while searching for odors would somehow have to exploit changes in odor concentration and alter their course in response to the concentration of odor molecules.

It is indeed true that, in a completely calm atmosphere (a rare event), odors (strong or otherwise) cannot be used for directional orientation from any great distance. The diffusion of odor molecules is much too slow, and perception (and then use) of an odor gradient by itself would hardly be feasible.

Those scientists who argued against long-distance perception of odors erred because they failed to appreciate the relevance of wind. At the time that we proposed our odor-search model, they failed to recognize the fact that odors are physical particles, molecules that drift downcurrent from their source. Even though an animal can often perceive the direction of either a source of sound or light, no animal can actually perceive an odor from a distance. The molecules must be physically transported by a current before they can be intercepted by one of the animal's odor receptors.

After perceiving an odor, an animal can locate the parent source of that scent only by heading upcurrent (e.g., Kennedy 1983). When air turbulence is at a minimum and breezes minimal, these odor molecules travel a considerable distance. That was the sense of long-distance perception of odors referred to by Aristotle, Butler, Wildman, and Burroughs (above). It was for those same reasons that early animal behavior mechanists did not use a Greek term (such as "ozotaxis") when writing about orientation to odors. Instead, they selected the terms *anemotaxis* (wind) and *rheotaxis* (water) when referring to directional movements of animals in an odor field. They thus recognized the primary importance of the *medium* that transports those odor molecules rather than the stimulus itself.

The truth of the matter ("law," as it were) is that animals searching for an odor source normally fly across a current, usually in a zigzag manner, and gradually work their way upwind (e.g., Kennedy 1983; see also excursus OS). Zigzagging means that they continually reverse their flight direction as they proceed slowly upwind, turning at slightly less than 180 degrees while they are still within the odor plume. This reversal procedure occurs more frequently as they approach the odor source, both because the odor plume narrows and because the odor becomes more concentrated and more well defined as the animal travels further upstream.

Von Frisch himself had noticed this odor-search behavior and wrote:

> The behavior of the bees toward the scent cards is very expressive. They come flying slowly along near the ground and against the wind, searching in short zigzags, and hover over the card. . . . As a rule they then settle on it and run about over the card, displaying unequivocally their interest in the source of scent. (1967a:85)

Although most of the more recent odor-search studies have been done on moth orientation (Carde 1984), the principles elucidated would apply to any animal orienting toward an odor source. Carde expressed that generality as follows (as in part in the epigraph):

> The [proposal] that the principal mechanism of "long-distance" flying orientation to an airborne chemical stimulus in the wind is an optomotor-guided, chemically-induced, upwind orientation (or *anemotaxis*) has gained wide acceptance as a considerable body of experimental evidence in support of this mechanism has accumulated. . . . our current understanding of the "instantaneous" structure of a chemical stimulus emanating from a point source in continual or intermittent wind is imperfectly developed and this limits our ability to hypothesize intelligently on alternatives to the upwind anemotaxis paradigm. (1984:111)

ODORS AS INVISIBLE AND SILENT STIMULI

Experiments that examine the role of odor stimuli are far more diffi-cult to conduct than those that involve light or sound stimuli; one can neither hear nor see what is happening. Also, one cannot capture a variety of odor stimuli in the same manner as one can, for example, capture visual images (patterns) with a camera or sounds with a tape recorder. If a sound is too faint or a light too dim to perceive with our limited senses, we can amplify or intensify the image. If a sound or light frequency is too high or too low for us to hear or see, we can electronically alter their frequencies into our own range of percep-tion.

In the case of experiments with odor, by contrast, one must rely almost entirely upon how animals *appear* to behave during the course of an experiment. That behavior itself, however, can be open to wide differences in interpretation. For example, a bee apparently using "dance language" information can actually be responding to odor; nothing we see or hear tells us otherwise. Also, we human beings may not be able to perceive whatever odors are important to a bee while it orients in flight, just as some people cannot taste certain chemicals that others find bitter.

Human sensitivity to odors appears to be quite limited in compar-ison to reports of insect perception. As Carde and Charlton wrote, "the maximum distances of communication attributed to moths are legendary" (1984:245). No one makes anywhere near such a claim with regard to human perception of odors. In fact, we only rarely attempt to locate an odor source by moving upwind toward that source; other mammals, such as dogs, do very well by comparison.

Flight has advantages over slower travel during chemo-orientation (Carde 1984). By rapidly flying across the wind ("casting"), an insect can sample the odor mix from vast areas upwind of its flight path (figure 5.1); only a relatively few molecules of an appropriate odor may alter that flight path.

Winds, especially when they are light, also shift direction fre-quently. A flying insect that has flown outside an odor plume during its zigzagging can begin casting, increasing the chances that it can reenter the odor plume. Another interception of that odor plume permits it to "lock-on" and gradually travel upwind by once again zigzagging toward the parent odor source (e.g., Kennedy 1983).

Two other easily observable flight behaviors of honey bees are important for understanding any mechanism of recruitment to food

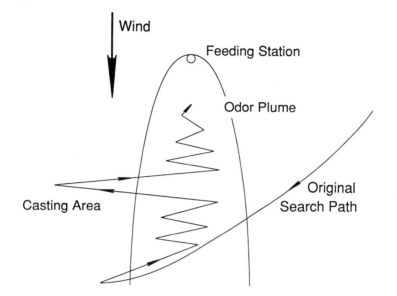

FIGURE 5.1. Odor molecules emanating from a source drift downwind just above the ground under gentle wind conditions. Since wind direction always varies somewhat, the resultant odor plume meanders (Carde 1984). After entering an odor plume, insects searching for an odor orient upwind toward the odor source in a zigzag manner (slow back-and-forth upwind flight). They switch into a casting flight (rapid back-and-forth flight) if they no longer encounter familiar odor molecules. That casting flight may again bring them back into the odor plume, at which time they can resume the zigzagging flight.

sources. One is the circling "orientation flights" of bees as they leave their hive (mentioned earlier). The other is a looping up into the air once bees have lost an odor track while in flight, a maneuver that permits them to be carried downwind by the prevailing wind. All four of these behaviors—zigzagging, casting, near-hive circling orientation, and looping up and traveling downwind—are important components of our odor-search model (see excursus OS).

Our suggestion that available evidence indicates that bees use only odor as they search for a food source was often later countered by use of a non sequitur during the interpretation of experimental results. The reasoning was that, if one can conclude that bees had not used the *experimental* odor while orienting, then they must have used *their* "language." That line of reasoning (the use of a non sequitur) avoided consideration of the possibility that searching bees had perhaps used odors *other than* those altered during the experiment.

Actually, odors in the food, in the locality, and in the hive may each play a role in the success of searching bees (our chapter 8; Wenner 1974). Experimental results can be most easily altered in a repeatable manner by changing the quality and quantity of one or more of those odors in or near the food. By contrast, control against extraneous locality odors in the field and the interpretation of their importance during recruitment can be quite difficult; such extraneous odors can actually alter results (Wenner 1974). Finally, one can only draw inferences about what may happen during odor transmission among bees in the colony.

One must also distinguish between the behavior of regular foragers (experienced bees) and searching recruits (inexperienced bees). Von Frisch failed to do so in his classic 1950 volume and also during the interpretation of results in many of his early "dance language" experiments (von Frisch 1947; see also Wenner 1971a; Gould 1976; and below). Every example von Frisch provided in his 1950 volume as conclusive evidence for use of "language," for example, could be interpreted equally well as evidence of communication by means of conditioned response (Johnson and Wenner 1966; see also our chapter 7).

THE ODOR ORIENTATION OF RECRUITED BEES: PERTINENT EVIDENCE

The following treatment is a summary and interpretation of much of the available knowledge concerning honey bee recruitment, not in terms of "dance language" use but in terms of olfaction and learning. That evidence, which will be covered rather fully in our chapters 7 through 10, provides a basis for the revised odor-search model of recruitment to food sources presented in excursus OS.

Experienced Bees

During each day, foragers (experienced bees that had routinely collected nectar the previous day) intermittently leave the hive on inspection trips and visit those sources at which they had had success before. Some degree of time sense may determine when a forager leaves for its first trip out of the hive, but that does not seem to be an essential factor in honey bee recruitment (see chapter 7).

Once successful (after blossoms first begin secreting nectar during the day), the first loaded foragers return to the hive but normally do not dance there until they have made several round trips. The recruitment of other foragers occurs nevertheless by means of conditioned response (chapter 7). Foragers previously successful at visiting *any* site with the same odor leave the hive immediately after perceiving that odor and travel directly to the location at which they had been successful a day earlier, whether or not such sites are the same ones frequented by the first successful foragers on the new day (Johnson and Wenner 1966; Wells and Wenner 1971; Wells 1973). The flight pattern of all of these re-recruited foragers is the famous "beeline" of foraging bees; landmarks suffice for orientation.

Communication by means of conditioned response has confounded the issue of whether bees have a "language." The flight behavior of forager bees, who are once again recruited by a simple odor stimulus, is strikingly suggestive of what was considered a true "language" use (e.g., von Frisch 1950). The net result of this type of communication by conditioned response is a logarithmic buildup of foragers, even in the absence of dancing (see chapter 7). Hundreds or thousands of foragers can become recruited quickly to sources in all directions and at all distances from standard hives, once a few of the experienced foragers have been successful on the new day.

Many statements in print appear to apply to this conditioned response behavior rather than to an hypothesis of communication by means of a "language." Consider again Spitzner's statement: "When a bee finds a good source of honey somewhere, after her return home she . . . waltzes around among them in circles, without doubt in order that they shall notice the smell of honey [nectar] which has attached itself to her; then when she goes out again they soon follow her in crowds" (Ribbands 1953:147).

Both Ribbands (1953) and von Frisch (1967a) used that passage as evidence that an investigator (Spitzner in this case) had earlier recognized "language" use by recruited bees. However, Spitzner's statement actually indicates that odor could well have been the sole stimulus used by recruits in their search.

It should be evident from the above treatment (as covered more fully in chapter 7) that one does not *need* the dance language hypothesis to explain the recruitment of *experienced* forager bees to sources where they had previously been successful. That mechanism of "communication by means of conditioned response" was actually described earlier by von Frisch, even though he may not have been aware of the implication of his statement: "It follows further that a communication can be transmitted from the returning bee to other bees by touch alone, without the necessity for any dance" (1947:13; see also our chapter 7).

Ribbands also noticed the same phenomenon at a later date: "the mere presence of the training scent in the hive, in the absence of either food-sharing or dancing, can encourage crop-attached bees to go to their crop" (1954:13).

Neither scientist, however, pursued that alternative possibility after that time, and the possibility of recruitment by odor and conditioned response became lost until we again stumbled onto the same behavior and recognized its implications in the mid-1960s (see our chapter 7).

Inexperienced Bees (Recruits)

Proponents of the dance language hypothesis, during the interpretation of their experimental results, focused primarily on evidence that "verified" that hypothesis. Accordingly, they focused on the performance of "successful" recruits, even though the percentage of searching bees that arrived at the "correct" station was always very low (e.g., Gould, Henerey, and MacLeod 1970; see also excursus NEG).

Results obtained both from the experiments run by the dance language proponents and from the experiments we conducted provided considerable evidence on the flight behavior of newly recruited bees. Whereas language proponents have paid scant attention to the implications of that evidence (peripheral to them), we see it as a solid basis for our odor-search model of honeybee recruitment (see excursus OS). In the following paragraphs we summarize and interpret some of that relevant evidence, evidence that indicates that recruited bees obviously must search diligently for an odor source exploited by foragers from the same parent hive.

1. *Distant perception of odors emanating from food sources.* Anyone who wishes to do so can easily verify the fact that recruits approaching a feeding station in the field always arrive from downwind. Dance language proponents claim that such a searching behavior does not begin until after recruits have used the distance and direction information obtained from the dance maneuver and arrived near the "target." However, if one looks in a direction downwind from a feeding station (as we have done with the aid of binoculars), recruits can be observed displaying the typical zigzag odor-search flight upwind toward stations, even when those searching recruits are still well beyond the limits of the area supposedly specified by the dance maneuver.

Furthermore, searching recruits can be siphoned off from stations by placement of the training food odor at test sites even when they are downwind of the stations (Wenner 1971a; see our chapter 8). That fact, coupled with the results of field research by Friesen (1973), reveal the existence of a pool of searching recruits downwind from the "bee-lines" of experienced foragers (Wenner 1974).

2. *Dependence on odor.* As Aristotle indicated and as Butler ([1609] 1969) stressed, odor is a very important factor in the life of honey bees. It is the odor of a food source to which newly recruited bees orient and land (von Frisch 1915; see also our chapter 8), but in their subsequent harvesting activity they remain constant to the recruitment odor and/or the visual image of the reward source (e.g., Wells, Wells, and Smith 1983; Wells and Wells 1983, 1985, 1986).

If one eliminates all odor cues, recruits cannot find a feeding station visited by foragers (Wenner, Wells, and Johnson 1969; Wells and Wenner 1971; Friesen 1973). In addition, recruits attending disoriented dances (dances without direction information) still managed to find the "correct" odor-marked site in the field (Wells and Wenner 1973), even without the supposedly requisite direction information.

Conversely, the failure of recruitment to cease, after Gould, Henerey, and MacLeod switched to unscented sucrose in their experiments (see table 3 in Gould, Henerey, and MacLeod 1970), may indicate no more than that an odor contamination occurred in their experimental protocol.

3. *Inefficiency of recruitment.* Under the best of circumstances, the flight performance of searching recruits is remarkably poor. Most recruits fail to find the feeding station visited by foragers (Esch and Bastian 1970; Gould, Henerey, and MacLeod 1970; Johnson and Wenner 1970; see also excursus NEG). For those successful recruits that find the station, several flights out from the hive may be necessary before success (Esch and Bastian 1970; Gould, Henerey, and MacLeod 1970; Friesen 1973).

4. *Flight times.* Most recruits are in the air many times longer than necessary for a direct flight out from the hive (Esch and Bastian 1970; Gould, Henerey, and MacLeod 1970; Friesen 1973; see also excursus NEG).

On the repeated trips out from their hive, searching recruits that are eventually successful can obviously cover a considerable amount of territory during the extended search times before (and/or *if*) they locate the station visited by foragers from their hive. Those results are also consistent with earlier statements made by von Frisch (1939), prior to his announcement of the full-fledged dance language hypothesis in 1945 (von Frisch 1947), and cannot be reconciled with implicit predictions of the dance language hypothesis.

5. *Recruitment as a population phenomenon.* Proponents of the lan-

guage hypothesis appear to focus on encounters between foragers and recruits only as interactions between individuals (human-level interaction; see Rosin 1978). In that approach each recruit is believed to obtain direction and distance information from the dance maneuver of a forager and travel independently and directly toward the precise location of a food source.

Recruits that found the food dish in our experiments were always killed or caged upon landing; hence, they could not recruit others. However, recruits do not begin arriving in quantity until almost an hour after foragers begin making regular trips (Wenner, Wells, and Johnson 1969; Friesen 1973). Neither do recruits arrive at a constant rate, as would be expected as a consequence of the constant rate of round trips by the set number of foragers and as predicted by the language hypothesis.

Instead, the number of recruits *per unit time* increases steadily with time (figure 1 in Wenner, Wells, and Johnson 1969). Data gathered by Friesen (1973) suggested that such a steady increase in the success rate of recruits was due to a cumulative number of *forager trips* rather than being due to a one-on-one interaction between forager and recruit. It is also apparent that recruits interact in the field while in flight and perhaps in the hive as well (Wells and Wenner 1971; Friesen 1973).

In addition, data on recruit arrival at an array of stations often fit a mathematical model (binomial distribution), with the number of recruit arrivals at each station being inversely proportional to the distance of each station from the center of all stations (Johnson 1967a; Wenner 1967; Johnson and Wenner 1970; Gould 1975a). Finally, the search times of a population of successful recruit bees nearly perfectly fits a lognormal distribution (see excursus NEG), a result totally inconsistent with the dance language hypothesis.

All of these points indicated to us that the recruitment of honey bees to food sources could parsimoniously be interpreted as a population phenomenon (Wenner 1974). As a result, once again we find the existence of two opposing paradigms (Rosin 1978). Those who take a human-level approach to studies of insect behavior often do not recognize the applicability of mathematical models to a *population* of searching bees. They focus instead only on interactions between individual bees in the hive.

6. *Success dependence on odor but not on dances or scent gland exposure.* Finally, and perhaps most puzzling of all, recruit success at finding feeding stations is apparently independent of the rate of forager scent gland (Nasanov gland) secretions at the dish; it is also

independent of the frequency of performance of dance maneuvers in the hive (Wells and Wenner 1971; see also excursus NG).

The odor mix and odor concentrations at the food site thus appear to us to be the primary (if not the only) factor responsible for success in recruitment. How can these facts be accommodated in an odor-search model? For that we provide excursus OS.

Research projects in science are very much like situations where crimes must be solved and criminals convicted. Various bits of evidence can be marshaled in support of a particular interpretation with respect to what might have gone on during the commission of a crime. The defense marshals other evidence, including alibis, in an effort to counter the prosecution's interpretation. When all of the evidence and interpretation has been presented, the jury begins deliberations.

In this chapter we have presented an opening statement concerning the odor-search model we came to embrace with respect to honey bee behavior during the recruitment of naive bees to food sources. We will next provide a summary of the von Frisch dance language hypothesis and some behind-the-scenes information about the initial reception of von Frisch's hypothesis by the scientific community. In the chapters that follow we will present some of the evidence that led us to propose our alternative model for the method by which honey bees might become recruited to food sources.

6

THE DANCE LANGUAGE PARADIGM: EVOLUTION AND ACCEPTANCE

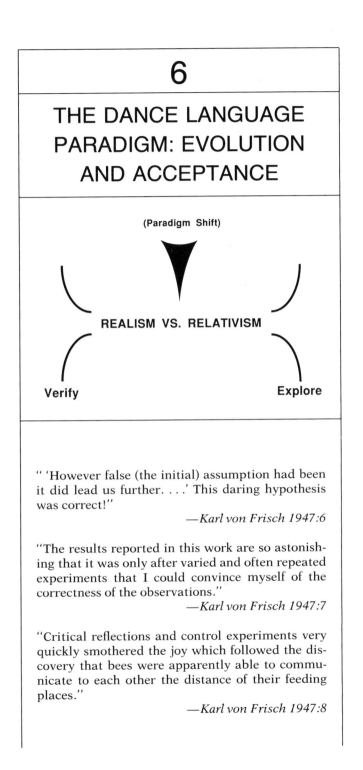

(Paradigm Shift)

REALISM VS. RELATIVISM

Verify   Explore

" 'However false (the initial) assumption had been it did lead us further. . . .' This daring hypothesis was correct!"

—*Karl von Frisch 1947:6*

"The results reported in this work are so astonishing that it was only after varied and often repeated experiments that I could convince myself of the correctness of the observations."

—*Karl von Frisch 1947:7*

"Critical reflections and control experiments very quickly smothered the joy which followed the discovery that bees were apparently able to communicate to each other the distance of their feeding places."

—*Karl von Frisch 1947:8*

"I therefore considered the idea that bees could communicate distances to each other, as nothing but a very beautiful dream—without knowing at that time that they showed each other also the direction and *therefore* paid little attention to places situated in other directions. . . . Then I opened the hive, hardly daring to hope that there might be a difference recognisable by the human eye between the dances of the 'near' and 'far' bees."

—*Karl von Frisch 1947:10*

As indicated earlier, von Frisch's dance language hypothesis swept the world by storm shortly after its inception in 1944. That "conversion" of the scientific community (Chamberlin [1890] 1965; Kuhn 1962; Atkinson 1985) occurred in a remarkably short span of time, despite the fact that no one had rigorously tested the new hypothesis. It also occurred even though his "dance language" experiments had lacked adequate controls against the odor-search interpretation advocated earlier by von Frisch himself (1939; see also our chapters 7–10).

DIE "SPRACHE" DER BIENEN

Von Frisch first recognized the possible implications of the honey bee dance maneuvers in experiments during the 1920s. He then distinguished between a "round dance" (for nectar foragers) and a "waggle dance" or "figure-eight dance" (for pollen foragers). These were both executed by successful forager bees after their return to the hive. He later summarized the results of that earlier work:

> In my previous studies concerning the "language" of bees (1923) I had arrived at the following results: when a bee discovers a source of nectar . . . she informs the inmates of the hive of her find by performing a round dance on the comb after her return. . . . The pollen collectors also dance when they have found abundant food. I described the waggle dance as characteristic of these. In a later piece of work with Rosch [published in 1926] we concerned ourselves with the question whether the round dance and the waggle dance could be two different 'words' in bee language, one meaning the exhortation to collect nectar and the other to collect pollen; and whether they were understood in this sense by the inmates of their hive. (1947:5)

Later, Henkel (1938, as cited in von Frisch 1947) noticed that foraging bees that visited natural nectar sources also sometimes performed waggle dances "indistinguishable in form from those of the collectors of pollen" (von Frisch 1947:5). The implication was that the round dances von Frisch had observed earlier were only performed after visits to extra rich food sources (such as concentrated sugar solution). This apparent discrepancy was resolved in von Frisch's mind in a manner typical of the Carnap approach within the Realism school: "But on further examination (1942) I also saw round dances performed by bees who were foraging in the open under natural conditions, and waggle dances by collectors of pollen; in this way I verified my former conclusions" (1947:5).

Von Frisch later recognized that his earlier distinction between round and waggle dances was an artifact of his experimental procedure and wrote: "I discovered a serious error in my previous interpretation of my observations. I confess it immediately. . . . The two forms of the dance in fact indicate different distances of the food source. I made this mistake through always offering sugar-water and nectar near the hive" (1947:5).

Even though von Frisch used the word *Sprache* in his earlier publications, we now recognize that a nectar dance/pollen dance distinction relative to the recruitment of bees, even if it had been true, would have represented no more than different forms of a stimulus-response situation. Linguists of today would not consider such an interaction as evidence of a "language" use. Furthermore, by the end of the 1930s von Frisch himself still insisted that recruited bees use odor alone as they search for nectar (von Frisch 1939).

THE PRESUMED ATTRACTIVENESS OF THE SCENT GLAND

Von Frisch proposed a second major hypothesis, one on the presumed attractiveness of scent gland (Nasanov gland) secretions, during his early 1920s period of research. While worker honey bees are imbibing sugar solution from a feeding dish, they often open a gland near the tip of the abdomen and exude a fragrant chemical (but do not do so when visiting flowers).

In a rather limited series of experiments in those years, von Frisch found that more recruits had arrived at stations where foragers had their glands open than at competing stations where those glands had been sealed shut with shellac. Again, under the verification approach (the Realism school), those positive results led von Frisch to conclude that the scent exuded by the gland had attracted searching foragers.

In his mid-1940s experiments, while "decoding" the dance language information von Frisch obtained results relative to Nasanov gland exposure which contradicted those obtained twenty years earlier (Wenner 1971a); recruits often came in greater numbers to stations where bees had their scent glands closed by shellac than to stations where the glands were left open (see excursus NG). Although von Frisch recognized that contradiction, he evaded treating its significance, as follows:

Although there is no doubt about the existence of an attraction exerted by the scent organ (c.f. von Frisch 1923: 155ff), which has also been confirmed in further experiments into which I do not want to go here, it has now become clear that another factor must be acting as a guide for direction at a greater distance. (1947:22)

An important point which emerges here is the permissibility of thought implicit in the verification approach (the Realism school): initial experiments may suggest an hypothesis, experiments are run that provide supportive data, and the conclusions derived provide the basis for further research. A true test of the hypothesis, such as advocated by Karl Popper (see, e.g., our chapter 2—the falsification approach), is neither executed nor considered necessary. Also, once "better" supportive data are gained by subsequent experimentation, workers can admit the fact that earlier experimental designs were flawed.

DECODING THE "DANCE LANGUAGE": FORMALIZING THE HYPOTHESIS

As indicated before (in chapter 4), three points must be considered while evaluating the validity of the dance language hypothesis:

1. Does the dance maneuver as executed in the hive contain distance and direction information about a food source in the field?
2. Do recruited bees arrive at the same site in the field as the successful foragers they had earlier attended in the hive?
3. Do searching recruits actually *use* the distance and direction information which is present in the dance maneuver and then fly *directly* out to the food source?

The answer to the first question is quite straightforward. The dance maneuver in the hive *does* contain distance and direction information (see figure 6.1). A dancing bee heads in a particular direction on the comb in the hive while it waggles its abdomen. The angle of that heading with respect to the top of the comb is correlated with the direction of the food source being exploited outside the hive, with respect to the direction of the sun at that time.

More than one element of the dance maneuver is correlated with the distance a bee has traveled before returning and executing its dance in the hive; in fact, many correlations exist between dance

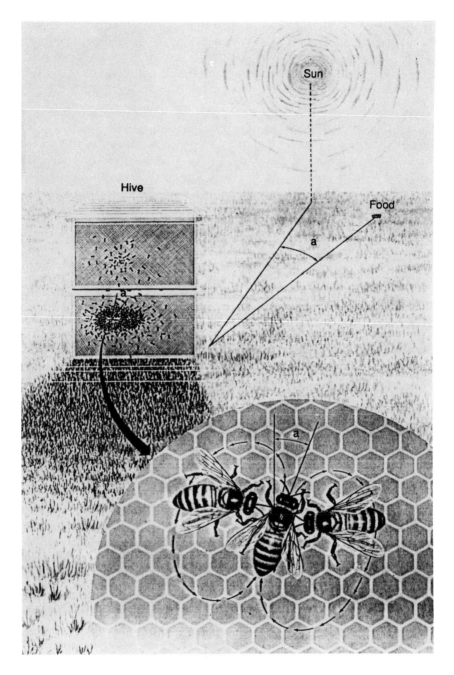

elements and environmental factors (Wenner, Wells, and Rohlf 1967).

Initially, von Frisch found an inverse correlation between the frequency of straight run portions of the dance and the distance of the food source (the more waggle runs per minute, the closer the food). He wrote: "The distance is indicated in a rather exact manner by the number of turns in the wagging dance that are made in a given time" (von Frisch 1950:72).

Later, he and Jander (1957) reported a positive correlation between the length of time spent waggling (straight run portion) and the distance of food from the hive. Even later one of us (Wenner 1962) found another correlation: the duration of sound production during each cycle is correlated with the distance of food from the hive (see chapter 7).

The answers to the second and third of the above questions are much less clear and are responsible for the controversy that ensued. Von Frisch's approach to those two questions (the Carnap-realism verification approach) is evident throughout the text of the 1947 Grossfield-Thorpe English translation of the original 1946 German version *(Osterreichische Zoologische Zeitschrift)*.

A large section of that paper (Section 3) treated the evidence in favor of communication of distance information, and another large section (Section 4) covered the evidence supporting the thesis that bees could communicate direction information. The evidence that did not fit was either not included or was not stressed.

However, the distinction among the above three questions was never clarified within the text of that original and classic account of von Frisch's hypothesis; his account is more descriptive than concise. We expand on that point here.

Von Frisch began each of the two main sections of his paper (3 and 4) by presenting the results of his experiments on the disposition of searching bees (that is, evidence relative to question 2, above). In each of those two sections von Frisch also described the procedure by which he obtained the relevant correlations between dance maneuver elements and the location of the feeding station with respect to the distance and direction traveled by experienced foragers (evidence

FIGURE 6.1. A successful foraging bee executes a waggle dance on the surface of a comb in the hive after its return from the field. The duration of the straight-run (waggle) portion of the dance (bottom) is correlated with the distance flown to the food source. The angle of that straight run relative to the top of the comb is correlated with the angle of the outgoing flight path relative to the direction of the sun. Potential recruits are most often nearly at right angles to the dancing bee.

relative to question 1, above). That is, he documented the fact that the dance configuration varied in a predictable manner as a function of the distance and direction of the food source in the field.

The results provided by von Frisch relate to the second of the above questions and the answer to that question. Did recruits end up at or near the site visited by successful foragers? Yes, it is evident from his data that bees *often* ended up at or near the site visited by previously successful foragers. The results obtained in those early experiments, however, were not consistent (see below). We treat his research on these two locational components in the dance maneuver separately here, just as he did.

Distance Experiments

Besides reporting results that confirmed the fact that the dance maneuver actually contains distance information, von Frisch reported the results of two types of distance experiments designed to reveal the possible *use* of distance information in his 1947 paper (relevant to questions 2 and 3, above).

In the first set of four experiments illustrated in figures 1–4 of that paper, newly recruited bees had arrived more often at a test station at the same distance from the hive as the feeding station (see table 6.1), compared to a test station placed at a different distance. Super-

TABLE 6.1. Results obtained by von Frisch for a series of five experiments dealing with the recruitment of honey bees at a feeding station and at two test stations.

Date	Feeding Station (meters)	Recruit Arrivals	Test Site #1 (meters)	Recruit Arrivals	Test Site #2 (meters)	Recruit Arrivals
August 11	10	?	10	340	150	8
August 11	15	49	10	267	140	8
August 12	150	?	15	29	140[a]	38
August 13	300	?	15	8	300[b]	61
August 14	10	?	10	174	300	12

SOURCE: Adapted from von Frisch 1947, figures 1–4.

NOTE; The second line in the table represents results from the fifth experiment (adapted from the text of the same papewr).

[a] Test station placed 90 meters laterally from the forager station but at an equal distance from the hive.

[b] Test station placed 100 meters laterally from the forager station but at an equal distance from the hive.

ficially, given the results provided, there seems to have been a relatively good success rate; bees appeared to arrive at a station situated at the same distance as the feeding place.

Von Frisch provided neither wind conditions nor the number of arrivals at the feeding station itself for those four experiments. However, he did reveal what happened on the day following the first of those four experiments, as follows:

> We obtained a similar result when repeating the experiment on the following day with minor alterations in direction and distance: on the feeding place, 15 m. from the hive, 49 newcomers; on an observation place at the same distance, 267 visits; on an observation place at 140 m., 8 visits. (1947:8)

That result was surprising. More recruits should have arrived at the feeding station itself than at one laterally displaced from it at an equal distance from the hive! Von Frisch himself recognized that all was not well, as was apparent from his comment on that same page:

> Could not the scent organ of collecting bees provide the sole reason for the fact that an excess of newcomers arrived at the observation place near the feeding place? But if the scent organ was the decisive factor, most of the newcomers would arrive on the very feeding place itself—*as a rule, however, this was not the case.* (von Frisch 1947:8; emphasis ours)

Clearly, the arrival of more recruits at stations other than where the scent gland was exposed contradicted earlier results reported by von Frisch (1923) on supposed scent gland attractiveness (see above and excursus NG). In those earlier experiments, ten times as many bees had arrived at stations where the scent gland of foragers was open than at another station where the scent gland had been sealed shut.

Second, the arrival of more newcomers at the test station than at the foraging place itself (90 or 100 meters away in experiments 174 and 175) would indicate that newcomers had failed to arrive at a station in the appropriate *direction*, as supposedly indicated in the dance maneuver. (James Gould later encountered the same dilemma; see our chapter 13.)

The second major type of distance experiment performed by von Frisch also dealt with the purported use of dance language information by searching bees. Those results were summarized in his tables 1 and 2. A study of the data and protocol reveals, however, that the recruitment in those cases was clearly that of *experienced* bees; that is, bees that had been out to the two competing stations earlier had been *re-recruited* to the same sites at which they had been successful previously (see chapter 7).

Direction Experiments

In his section dealing with the presumed use of *direction* information (section 4), von Frisch began the presentation by describing the experiments he did to test whether searching bees could *use* direction information. That is, whether recruits would appear more frequently at a station in the field located in the same direction as that visited by the successful foragers. He first reported the results of three experiments (nos. 180, 181, and 182, which were conducted on August 16, 17, and 18, 1944, respectively) and included diagrams of the experimental arrangement of hive, feeding station, and control stations. We include here diagrams of all three of those experiments (figure 6.2A, B, and C).

The results shown in those diagrams, particularly in figure 6.2A, can be interpreted as support for von Frisch's conclusion that re-

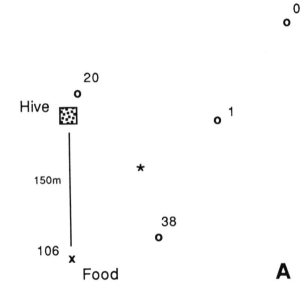

FIGURE 6.2. The results of three of von Frisch's original experiments run on consecutive days (after figures 9, 10, and 11 of von Frisch 1947). On the first two days (Figures 6.2A and 6.2B), nine bees regularly foraged at a food dish located in one direction from the hive. On the third day (figure 6.2C), nine bees foraged at a food dish located in the opposite direction from the hive. The small circles denote positions of the scent plates,

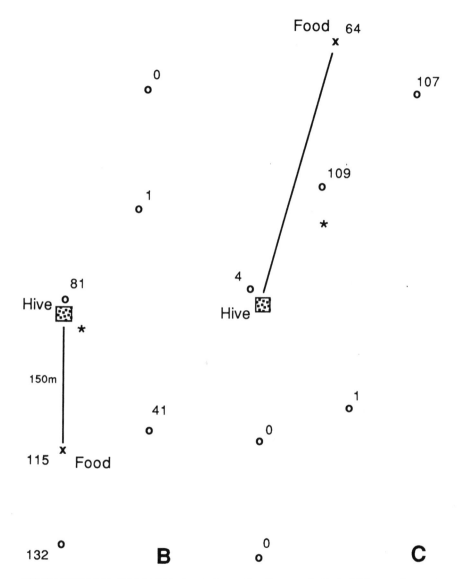

with the number of unmarked bees seen inspecting them, as indicated. The number next to the small *x* indicates the number of new recruits that arrived at the food place itself. We have placed an asterisk at the geometric center of all stations, exclusive of the hive. (Von Frisch provided no information about wind direction.)

cruited bees had traveled in the same direction as that indicated in the dance maneuver. However, a closer inspection of the other two diagrams reveals that the results given there indicate that, at the same time, bees failed to use the *distance* information contained in the dances. In figure 6.2B, for instance, more bees arrived at a control station at nearly twice the distance of the feeding station than at a station located at the same distance from the hive as the feeding station.

The data shown in figure 6.2C contradicted the expectations of the language hypothesis even more. It is evident that many more bees arrived at a control station only halfway to the feeding station than at the feeding station itself, for which distance information had supposedly been provided in the dance maneuver. That result constituted another negative result with regard to *distance* communication.

It is also obvious that the 107 arrivals at a control station 100 meters distant from the feeding station far outnumbered the 64 that arrived where they should have arrived if they had been using *direction* information. In fact, overall, in the experiment illustrated in figure 6.2C, less than a quarter of the total number of recruits tallied had arrived at the location "indicated" by the dance.

In addition to the results shown in those three diagrams, von Frisch executed a similar set of four experiments in which the scent gland was open on two days but sealed shut on two subsequent days. Once again, his results were not internally consistent (see table 6.2). In experiments 1 and 3, more recruits had arrived at a station equidistant but 30 meters removed from the goal than at the goal itself. The reverse should have occurred if recruits had used direction information obtained from the dance maneuver.

It is also significant that the results for experiments 1 and 3 in that series (see table 6.2) were essentially identical to one another. That result is not compatible with the hypothesis that the scent gland attracts recruits (see also excursus NG). If the scent gland had attracted recruits, the ratio of successful recruits, as shown in the results of experiments 1 and 3, should have more closely approximated the results obtained in experiments 2 and 4.

Now consider again a statement by von Frisch on this matter, which illustrates the attitude he held on the basis of work he published in 1923: "there is no doubt about the existence of an attraction exerted by the scent organ" (von Frisch 1947:22). Once again we see the expression of one committed to the Carnap-realism approach. There is also a tone in that quotation of the attitude warned against

TABLE 6.2. Summary of results from four experiments, showing the number of recruits arriving at a feeding station and at a test station a short lateral distance from it.

| Date | Food in One Direction from Hive | | Food in Opposite Direction from Hive | |
	Food Place at 300m	Station 30m from Food Place	Food Place at 250m	Station 25m from Food Place
	Scent Gland Open			
Sept. 17	178	257	—	—
Sept. 18	—	—	362	39
	Scent Gland Closed			
Sept. 19	190	228	—	—
Sept. 20	—	—	80	25

SOURCE: Adapted from information on pp. 21 and 22 of von Frisch 1947.

NOTE: On two days regular foragers had their scent glands open; on the other two days the glands were sealed shut.

by Chamberlin (see figure 3.1 and chapter 3); he labeled that attitude "parental affection" for a hypothesis.

Another set of apparently negative results arises with respect to the language hypothesis, particularly when one compares two of von Frisch's statements to one another. The first deals with procedure, as follows: "If (a recruited bee) appears on her feeding place within five minutes after her contact with the dancer, we can assume on the grounds of our previous experience, that she has been induced to do so by the dance" (von Frisch 1947:12).

The second quotation deals with von Frisch's analysis of his results, after he noticed that some bees succeeded *without* having attended a dancing bee in the hive: "It follows further that a communication can be transmitted from the returning bee to other bees by touch alone, without the necessity for any dance" (von Frisch 1947:13).

First of all, one can wonder why von Frisch allowed an entire five-minute period as evidence that a recruit bee had *used* dance information. The direct flight time in his experiments would have been much less than a minute (Park 1929; Wenner 1963); five minutes of flying at 7.5 meters per second would have permitted a recruit to search a vast area (see excursus NEG).

Secondly, we did not appreciate the significance of the contradiction inherent in the above two comments by von Frisch until we at first inadvertently (and later deliberately) conducted conditioned-response experiments in the mid-1960s (see chapter 7). A careful reading of von Frisch's 1950 book reveals his recognition of such contradictions but a lack of concern for the implications of those discrepancies.

In von Frisch's book, many cases of "proof" that bees had *used* language information appear to be no more than examples of *conditioned-response* behavior by experienced foragers. However, the requirement for demonstrating *use* of language information necessarily involves the demonstration that *naive* bees (those not conditioned to feed at the station), which supposedly acquire direction and distance information from a dancing bee while still within the hive, fly directly out to the feeding station.

Section 4 of von Frisch's 1947 paper contains a description of the correlation between the direction of the food source in the field and the angle of the straight-run portion of the dance on the comb in the hive. It was through noticing that bees altered the direction of their dances on the surface of the comb during the course of the day that von Frisch recognized that the dances contained direction information:

> Another surprise followed. . . . Our numbered bees altered their direction of dancing in the course of the day, although the feeding place remained the same. We soon recognised from more accurate notes that within a few hours the direction of the waggle dance changed by approximately the same angle through which the sun had meantime moved in the sky. (1947:22)

For clarification, we repeat here that the dance maneuver unarguably contains direction and distance information by which we human beings can determine the location of food sources visited by successful foragers. However, von Frisch's experiments clearly fell short of demonstrating that other bees could "decode" and *use* the information contained therein.

REALISM, REPEATABILITY, AND RELIABILITY

The verification approach (the Realism school) that von Frisch used apparently "proved" to many the existence of a "language" among bees. For anyone who has a relativist perspective, however, that research fell short on five counts, as follows:

1. *Ignoring negative results.* As can be seen from the above analysis,

searching bees, while apparently using distance information, failed to perform well in using direction information. The same was true in the converse situation; bees supposedly flying directly out to a station in the proper direction often failed to arrive at the proper distance.

Those inconsistencies were ignored by both von Frisch and those who championed him later. Such serious discrepancies, however, would have dictated the use of new experimental designs under either the Popper "falsification" approach (still within the Realism school) or under the Chamberlin multiple inference approach (see chapter 3).

2. *A failure to recognize the importance of conditioning.* In many of the experimental results included in von Frisch's (1947) classic paper, it is evident that his recruited bees had been out to the station before. Those bees thus could have used familiar landmarks on their way out once having been stimulated to leave the hive. Von Frisch admitted that possibility but ignored its implications.

We rediscovered that conditioned response phenomenon (Wenner and Johnson 1966; Johnson and Wenner 1966) after the dance maneuver and its purported "use" had already become known as an instinctual signaling system. Gould (1976:216), who initially objected to our challenge of von Frisch, later also acknowledged the importance of learning in the recruitment of honey bees.

3. *The lack of adequate controls in experimental design.* In all of the experiments described in his classic 1947 paper, von Frisch failed to control against any undue influence on recruits of wind or flight paths of experienced foragers. That left open the possibility that recruited bees had intermittently and indirectly "followed" one or more of the foragers that regularly traveled between the hive and feeding station (described as an "aerial pathway" in Wenner 1974). The results Maeterlinck (1901) had obtained, if attended to, could have alerted von Frisch to that possibility (see chapter 4).

Gould later conceded this lack of adequate controls in all of von Frisch's experiments when he wrote: "Von Frisch's controls do not exclude the possibility of olfactory recruitment alone" (1976:241). However, Gould apparently did not realize that the lack of adequate controls in von Frisch's experiments undermined the basis for his own experimental protocol (see our chapter 13).

4. *Excessive faith in the "successful" repetition of experiments.* In the "verification" approach, as advocated by Carnap, an overwhelming amount of supportive evidence would suffice to confirm the "truth" of a hypothesis. This approach was evident throughout von Frisch's career and was especially evident in his 1967 review volume.

After we had stressed that point, Gould also conceded that such an approach would not necessarily provide greater confidence in an hypothesis when he wrote: "Wenner is certainly correct in saying that an endless repetition of ambiguous experiments does not add anything to the evidence" (1976:241).

5. *A failure to test the hypothesis.* Von Frisch came remarkably close to conducting a true test of his hypothesis in those early years. He wrote:

> [Earlier results] had made the existence of a corresponding communication in this respect seem very likely, and the observation of the different conduct in the hive of those bees foraging near and far had brought confirmation with unexpected clarity. *It did not seem advisable to check this by following up the behavior of newcomers. We should hardly have found out anything more than we knew already.* (1947:11; emphasis ours)

In summary, if von Frisch had "followed up the behavior of the newcomers," as Maeterlinck had done earlier (Maeterlinck 1901; see also excursus MM), he might have obtained valuable information on the poor performance of searching bees (too long in transit and too few successful). Gould and others later obtained data consistent with Maeterlinck's results (Esch and Bastian 1970; Gould, Henerey, and MacLeod 1970; Johnson and Wenner 1970; Friesen 1973; see also excursus NEG).

That contrary evidence, in turn, might have forced von Frisch to abandon the language hypothesis before he had formed the Chamberlin-type "parental affection" for it. In fact, the test he dismissed as unnecessary was remarkably similar in principle to Maeterlinck's experiment. Instead, von Frisch wrote: "But there seemed a better way of making a critical test" (1947:11).

However, by use of the word "test," von Frisch apparently meant that he had thought of a better way to obtain *confirming* evidence (see excursus SCI). It was at this point that he went on to describe the experiments he had done on "rerecruitment" of *experienced* foragers, a recruitment process that he failed to recognize as a conditioned response phenomenon (see Johnson and Wenner 1966). He instead interpreted his results as a demonstration of "language" use.

Eventually, it apparently became evident even to von Frisch that his earliest experiments had not "established" the existence of a language among bees. Perhaps that is why he omitted all results from those "classic" mid-1940s experiments when he compiled his 1967 review volume.

THE "CONVERSION" OF THE SCIENTIFIC COMMUNITY

Early reaction in the scientific community to von Frisch's assertion that bees had a "language" was often initially one of sheer disbelief. After others had successfully repeated his experiments but not really tested his hypothesis, however, the "conversion" from the earlier odor-search model of von Frisch (1939) and others became complete in a remarkably short period of time.

As indicated earlier (see chapter 4), that rapid acceptance seems to have hinged in part on the fact that experimental "demonstration" of a "language" in a nonhuman species legitimized the fledgling fields of ethology and sociobiology. It may also be evident, in the sections and chapters that follow, that in one sense that conversion was more a sociological than a scientific matter.

A few of those who challenged the notion of a language, in fact, retained their skepticism, despite advocacy of that new hypothesis by eminent members of what was to become the sociobiology community. As indicated earlier, H. Kalmus of University College, London, for example, wrote as late as 1960: "any fairy tales about one bee telling the others, or leading the others to a locality, can be discounted" (1960:96).

Kalmus then described a simple experiment reminiscent of von Frisch's earlier work (pre-1940). Kalmus considered that such an experiment showed "that it is mainly the smell which serves as a principal means of orientation" (Kalmus 1960). By 1960, however, the larger scientific community was already firmly committed to the dance language hypothesis, and statements such as those by Kalmus had little impact.

What actually transpired in the early years after von Frisch's discovery of the correlation between dance elements and food location in the field appears to fit the notion of a "conversion" phenomenon in the scientific process (e.g., Chamberlin [1890] 1965:754; Kuhn 1962:150; Griffith and Mullins 1972; Atkinson 1985). That is, von Frisch became converted to his hypothesis in the "ruling theory" sense (see our chapter 2) and gained a local following. Other notables within the incipient fields of ethology and sociobiology themselves became converted when they repeated von Frisch's experiments and obtained the same results (the verification approach in the Carnap-Realism school). They then championed the cause, and the dance language hypothesis gained widespread acceptance.

One of the first prominent people in the English-speaking world to play a role in the acceptance of von Frisch's hypothesis was W. H. Thorpe, one of the foremost zoologists in the field of learning and instinct (see Thorpe 1963). Thorpe published a preface to the 1947 English version of von Frisch's classic 1946 paper, with the following comment:

> The recent remarkable work of Professor Karl von Frisch has such significance for biologists and students of animal behaviour and such interest for the scientifically-minded bee-keeper that we feel there is no apology needed for offering to English readers a translation of "Die Tanze der Bienen" published in 1946. (in von Frisch 1947:3)

August Krogh, a Danish physiologist who was awarded the 1920 Nobel Prize in medicine, followed Thorpe soon after. He provided an article in English for *Scientific American* (August 1948), "The Language of the Bees." In his concluding comments, he wrote:

> This series of experiments constitutes a most beautiful example of what the human mind can accomplish by tireless effort on a very high level of intelligence. But I would ask you to give some thought also to the mind of the bees. I have no doubt that some will attempt to "explain" the performances of the bees as the result of reflexes and instincts. . . . for my part I find it difficult to assume that such perfection and flexibility in behavior can be reached without some kind of mental processes going on in the small heads of the bees. (1948:21)

Donald R. Griffin, then at Cornell University, was another such person who was "converted" to the dance language hypothesis after an initial reluctance; see his foreword in von Frisch's 1950 book. He also later followed in Krogh's footsteps by crediting "lower animals" with higher levels of intelligence than permitted by prevailing theory (e.g., Griffin 1984).

Griffin played a major role in getting the dance language hypothesis accepted in the United States, as well as a major role in assuring its continued life later (see chapter 11). Griffin arranged a three-month lecture tour for von Frisch in the United States during the spring of 1949. The classic 1950 book, written by von Frisch, was the substance of the three lectures delivered at three of the seventeen universities visited during that trip (von Frisch 1950:viii). Griffin also assisted with the translation and wrote the foreword to that book.

In that foreword, Griffin wrote of the "independent confirmation" of von Frisch's experiments, including the " 'repeats' of certain of the

most crucial experiments" by Thorpe. Griffin then added an account
of his own experience:

I confess without embarrassment that until I performed these simple experiments myself, I too retained a residue of skepticism. But a
few weeks' work with an observation beehive . . . led me to the same
degree of conviction as that which Thorpe reports. (in von Frisch
1950:vi)

There is, of course, confusion here with respect to the phrase "crucial experiments." In today's sense (as well as in Chamberlin's 1890
sense), use of that phrase implies a true test involving mutually exclusive predictions of two competing hypotheses, a procedure routinely
employed in molecular biology or genetics (see the account of Chamberlin and Platt in chapter 3). Both Thorpe and Griffin, however, were
apparently satisfied with a simple repetition of von Frisch's experiments.

Considering the degree of skepticism normally prevalent in the
social sciences, it is somewhat surprising that acceptance of the dance
language hypothesis spread rapidly through those fields as well. For
example, the noted anthropologist A. Kroeber endorsed von Frisch's
conclusions. A year after von Frisch was elected as a foreign member
of the U.S. National Academy of Sciences, Kroeber discussed the
implications of the dance language hypothesis in the proceedings of
that academy, and wrote:

Von Frisch's classic studies of the "language" of honey bees deal
with communications among the members of a species which—like
all other subhuman species—has been believed to be wholly non-
symbolizing. However, he has shown conclusively that these inter-
communications of bees successfully convey information. . . . On
their face, the von Frisch observations and experiments thus seem
to establish a phenomenon of revolutionary novelty. (1952:753–754)

The Griffith and Mullins (1972) notion of "coherent social groups
in scientific change" apparently manifested itself further in 1955. In
that year von Frisch was awarded the Magellanic Premium of the
American Philosophical Society (von Frisch 1956). A footnote in the
acceptance paper reads, in part: "On November 11, 1955, the Society
in Executive Session voted to [give the award] . . . to Dr. von Frisch in
recognition of his studies of animal sense organs and his analysis of
the dances of the bees."

That premium is awarded at times: "to the author of the best
discovery or most useful invention relating to navigation, astronomy,

or natural philosophy (mere natural history only excepted)" (*American Philosophical Society Yearbook* [1955], p. 420). Donald Griffin, by then at Harvard University, read the acceptance address for von Frisch during the presentation of that award (von Frisch 1956).

By 1955, the notion of a "language" among bees had evolved from an hypothesis into a paradigm in the sense of Kuhn. The awarding of the Magellanic Premium to von Frisch by the American Philosophical Society, "in recognition of his rather sensational work on the 'mathematics' and navigation of bees" (*American Philosophical Society Yearbook* [1955], p. 75) assured the dance language hypothesis its place in history.

The rapid acceptance of the dance language hypothesis as a replacement for the odor-search hypothesis (von Frisch 1939) was remarkable; that hypothesis appealed to members of many fields, scientific and nonscientific. What few realized at the time was that the dance language hypothesis was actually too alluring; that sort of hypothesis can easily evolve too quickly from an untested hypothesis into an accepted paradigm (the ruling theory of Chamberlin). The novelist John Steinbeck had earlier recognized the same complication that a fascinating hypothesis can lead to when he wrote:

> There is one great difficulty with a good hypothesis. When it is completed and rounded, the corners smooth and the content cohesive and coherent, it is likely to become a thing in itself, a work of art. It is then like a finished sonnet or a painting completed. One hates to disturb it. Even if subsequent information should shoot a hole in it, one hates to tear it down because it once was beautiful and whole. [1941] 1962:180)

The relatively complete and rapid conversion of the scientific world to the dance language hypothesis is the more remarkable when one considers the long-term earlier satisfaction with the extant odor-search paradigm, problems with experimental designs (outlined above), numerous inherent contradictions in the results obtained by von Frisch and others, and the lack of a true experimental test of the hypothesis (e.g., Wenner 1971a). All further research by the "coherent social group" (e.g., Griffith and Mullins 1972) of dance language proponents, including us initially, thereafter began with the relatively untested assumption that a "language" of bees had finally been "discovered" or "proven" to exist.

7

A PARADE
OF ANOMALIES:
LEARNING

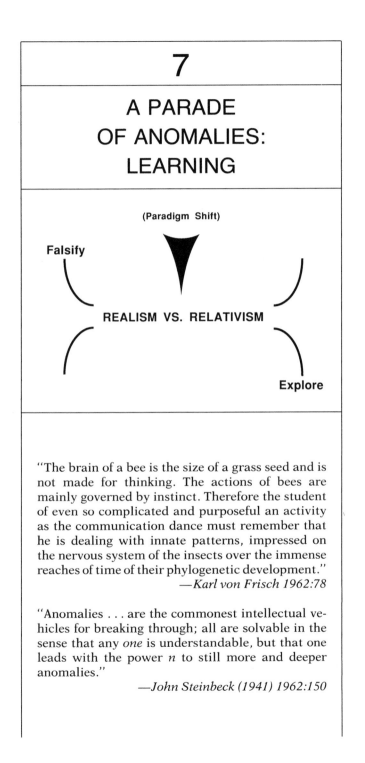

(Paradigm Shift)

Falsify

REALISM VS. RELATIVISM

Explore

"The brain of a bee is the size of a grass seed and is not made for thinking. The actions of bees are mainly governed by instinct. Therefore the student of even so complicated and purposeful an activity as the communication dance must remember that he is dealing with innate patterns, impressed on the nervous system of the insects over the immense reaches of time of their phylogenetic development."
—*Karl von Frisch 1962:78*

"Anomalies . . . are the commonest intellectual vehicles for breaking through; all are solvable in the sense that any *one* is understandable, but that one leads with the power *n* to still more and deeper anomalies."
—*John Steinbeck (1941) 1962:150*

A nomalies encountered during scientific research, although most often ignored due to paradigm hold, at other times provide a basis for solid research. However, even though anomalies are common and valuable during the conduct of research, anomalies and their impact can quickly fade from consciousness as more solid evidence gains priority; what is anomalous under one paradigm becomes the expected after a "conversion" to another paradigm (gestalt switch).

In this and in the following chapter, we include anecdotes from our own experience as examples of the importance of anomaly and how it directed the course of our own research. The recognition of the existence of those anomalies and the consideration of various interpretations led to changes in our subsequent experimental designs. Augmentation of our own experiences by the input of even a single anecdote from other people often helped create new images in our minds.

Edward Jenner's account of studies of the link between cowpox and smallpox is a significant example of what would now be considered an unacceptable inclusion of anecdotes in a published paper. That research, however, led to the eventual worldwide eradication of smallpox (see excursus JNR). Jenner included a series of anecdotes in order to augment his case, but (as indicated above) a single anecdote may help "create an image" and lead one to new interpretation.

"LEARNING" VERSUS "INSTINCT" AMONG INSECTS

In the 1940s and 1950s only a few students of insect behavior explained behavioral patterns in terms of learning. Most others proceeded strictly within an "instinct" paradigm while interpreting behavioral patterns (see the von Frisch epigraph, above). The "spirit of the times" was permissive; either explanation could be used for a given behavioral act, despite the lack of experimental tests.

Earlier, Loeb ([1918] 1973) and Fraenkel and Gunn ([1940] 1961) had advocated the use of a more quantitative approach to descriptions of animal behavior, including a series of terms that persist today (e.g., "taxes" and "kineses" for animals and "tropisms" for plants). Since 1950, however, the prevailing thought in ethology has shifted gradually toward ever less well-defined terminology and assumptions. The "instinct" versus "learning" issue remains obscure and largely ignored in the animal behavior community (Rosin 1980a, 1980b; see also our chapter 13).

THE "INSTINCTIVE LANGUAGE" OF BEES

Research on honey bee communication during the 1940s and 1950s, then, still relied heavily upon the notion that the behavior of these small animals was largely "innate" or "instinctive" (see the von Frisch epigraph). Thorpe summarized that attitude as follows:

> Much of the recent work on insects and other arthropods seems to fit in very well with the hierarchy concept of instinctive behaviour of Tinbergen. Perhaps this fact . . . receives some further elucidation from recent researches on the mode of action of the insect nervous system. Thus Vowles (1961) points out that the properties of the insect neurone, which are very different from that of the vertebrates, and the small size of the insect nervous system, render necessary a functional organisation of behaviour far simpler than is often supposed. (1963:231)

The attitude that insect behavior was fundamentally more simple than that of vertebrates would seem to exclude the possibility of a "language" among bees (Rosin 1978). However, if one pursues research within the verification approach (the Carnap arm of the Realism school), it is possible to retain both notions; a simple system can permit the existence of "language" if one considers the more complex behavior to be merely a fixed sequence of simple steps. Tinbergen verbalized that amalgamation as follows:

> When "unemployed" honey bees, waiting in the hive for a messenger, are at last activated by one performing the "honey dance," . . . the stimulus delivered by the dancer bee stimulates them to leave the hive. They fly in a definite direction over a definite distance (both communicated to them by the dancer) and begin to search for flowers, selecting only those that emanate the scent carried by the messenger. They suck honey [sic], and after having made a "locality study," they fly home. In this latter case the stimulus given by the messenger [dancing bee] releases a complicated behaviour pattern. (1951:54, 55)

The "chain reflex" explanation of behavior, as used by Tinbergen and others at that time, permitted the phenomenon of honey bee recruitment to food sources to be known eventually as an "instinctual signaling system." The teleological notion of "purposefulness," which later came to be so fundamental in ecology and sociobiology, also was relied upon in those early days. Thorpe, for example, invoked that concept in describing honey bee recruitment to food sources, as follows:

> An insect with such a high degree of organisation of labour, and having only a limited period of the year in which to forage, needs some means of communication by which a scout which has discovered a rich source of food can quickly recruit a body of workers large enough to fetch the available booty but not so great as to waste the worker strength of the hive in unprofitable foraging. . . . In other words, bees need a language; and von Frisch . . . did not hesitate in his earlier papers to speak of "the language of bees." (1963:268)

The above summary provides only a sketch of the attitude prevalent in insect behavior research when we began work in the late 1950s. However, at that time we agreed completely with both the notion that bees were bound to simple behavioral patterns (i.e., that they exhibited "instinctive" behavior) and to the notion that honey bees had a 'language." In that sense we accepted the essence of Tinbergen's above expression, that the "dance language" of bees was little more than a fixed sequence of simple behavioral acts ("chain reflex" behavior). That positive attitude was possible because we had also used the same verification approach (the Realism school in the Carnap sense) in our research that other researchers in animal behavior had used in theirs.

The first several years of our research were thus conducted well within the limitations of the verification approach; our goal was to verify ("prove") the existence of a language already "known" to exist. We concurred wholeheartedly with von Frisch's statement: "The language of bees is truly perfect, and their method of indicating the direction of food sources is one of the most remarkable mysteries of their complex social organization" (1950:75).

A Verification Approach: Sound Waves as a Language Element?

The first nine-year period (1957–1966) of our research was thus conducted under the premise that honey bees *had* a "language" and that they behaved as outlined in the passages quoted above. There was no reason to suspect otherwise at the time. However, as indicated above and in chapter 2, it was already apparent to us by 1965 that the von Frisch dance language hypothesis, appealing as it was, rested entirely on circumstantial evidence. Even though we worked within the verification approach, we felt that a more direct type of supportive evidence was needed (as opposed to the existing circumstantial evidence).

By the mid-1960s, then, several years of research had been spent pursuing the possibility that bees somehow made direct use of the sounds they made during their waggle dance (e.g., Wenner 1959, 1962, 1964; Esch 1961), *"while* communicating the location" of food sources. The discovery that sounds existed within the dance maneuver had provided an entirely new set of possibilities regarding communication among bees (Wenner 1964).

Admittedly, this research activity was not altogether a detached scientific pursuit (Wenner 1971a); "discovery" and "proof" are essential elements leading to success within any scientific community, particularly when it functions primarily within the verification approach. Encouragement at that time came from all quarters; other scientists were quite receptive to the possibility that honey bees were perhaps capable of an even more complex behavior (anthropomorphically, an "acoustic speech") than had been reported earlier.

The spectrographic pattern obtained from an analysis of sounds produced by dancing bees (see figure 7.1) differed markedly from sounds made by bees engaged in other behavioral acts (Wenner 1964). Most bee sounds are continuous tones, but during each straight-run

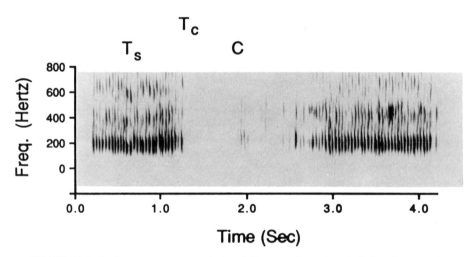

FIGURE 7.1. Audiospectrogram analysis of the sound produced during the waggle dance. Sound pulses produced during the two straight runs (T_s) appear as dark areas. The large blank between straight runs (C) represents the turnaround time between straight runs. An inverse of the total of those two (T_c) indicates the number of dances per minute (after Wenner 1962).

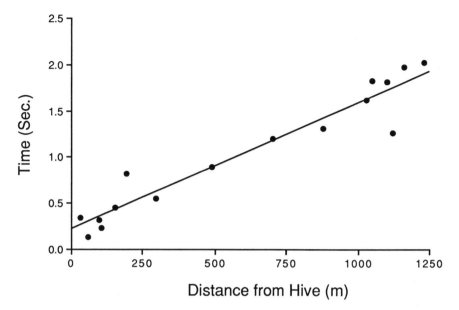

FIGURE 7.2. Time spent producing sound (T_s of figure 7.1), as a function of distance a forager has traveled on its way to the food source (after Wenner 1962). Each point is an average for several dancing bees.

portion of the waggle dance (see figure 7.1) foragers produce a burst of pulsed sound (amplitude modulation). The duration of that train of pulses is correlated with the distance a forager has traveled between hive and feeding place in the field (see figure 7.2).

It is tempting to examine the foregoing correlation in a teleological context. One could argue that a correlation between sounds produced in the hive and distance traveled in the field would not exist unless it had a purpose. One could also argue that amplitude modulation in a "sound signal" also would not exist unless it were somehow "useful" to recruit bees. Phrased teleologically: "Bees would not waste that much energy in a purposeless act" (see excursus TE).

Moreover, the location in the hive where the dance is conducted is often exceedingly dark. That is because the hive entrance is normally very small, and there are a great number of bees with an abundance of hair on their bodies between the entrance and surface of the comb; both of these factors would restrict the amount of light that could penetrate in as far as the dance area on the combs.

There is also the problem of dance attendants and their orientation on the comb relative to the position of the dancing bee. Virtually all early diagrams and their legends indicated that potential recruits "followed" or "tripped after" the dancing bee (e.g., figure 46 in von Frisch 1967a). However, we have noticed that recruits are most often positioned at right angles to the dancer during the straight-run portion of the dance (see figure 6.11).

The antennae, which contain sound-sensing units, of those recruits are also in intimate contact with the body of the dancer when sound is being produced (see figure 7.1). Under all of the above circumstances, one could reasonably conclude that sound signals were an important constituent of *the* "dance language" of bees.

While von Frisch was "decoding the dance language of bees," he was unaware that dancing bees made those peculiar sounds during the straight-run portion of the waggle dance. He therefore had researched only *some* of the possibilities by which communication of food location could occur, if indeed bees had a "language." Several years later von Frisch recognized the potential importance of sounds during the waggle dance when he wrote: "Taking all . . . facts into account, we regard the acoustically emphasized duration of waggling as the index of distance" (1967a:104).

The discovery of sound production during the dance represented to us the first of many anomalies that arose during our research program. More important to us (in retrospect) was the fact that we began to become more aware of the multiplicity of explanations and approaches that could be important during any investigation of a problem in science.

Conditioned Responses: Another Anomaly

A major and drastic turning point in our research occurred when it abruptly became apparent to us that bees could learn very rapidly in the classic conditioning sense. Our surprise (gestalt switch) was due to the fact that most of the earlier von Frisch results (1947, 1950) that he had submitted as evidence of "language" use could be interpreted instead as merely the result of conditioned responses to stimuli (Johnson and Wenner 1966). One then no longer needed to postulate an elaborate "instinctual signaling system" to explain the von Frisch results—a simple conditioned-response explanation would suffice.

It had long been known that honey bees can be "trained" to visit a feeding station (e.g., Maeterlinck 1901; von Frisch 1950). However, prior to 1965 that particular behavioral pattern had not been placed within the context of various theories of learning behavior. That training phenomenon is now recognized as a form of "choice discrimination conditioning" or "simple conditioning" (Wenner and Johnson 1966); bees can be trained to visit blue rather than yellow flowers or to visit a square design rather than a circle (see Wells 1973).

Each bee will, in fact, essentially *train itself* upon first visit to a colored and/or scented food source. From then on it will be a constant forager on sources of that type, as long as sufficient reward remains available (Wells, Wells, and Smith 1983; Wells, Wells, and Contreras 1986). Neither these well-known abilities nor the interpretation of their roles in behavior have ever been challenged.

Evidence that insects could also perform "simple discrimination conditioning" was quite inadequate before the 1960s (see Thorpe 1963 for a complete review of literature up to that time). This type of conditioning involves a pairing of some apparently "neutral" stimulus with the presentation of a reward. Later, when one presents that same stimulus in the absence of a reward, the animal nevertheless proceeds to behave as if a reward were imminent. One of the more famous examples is that of Pavlov's dog being conditioned to salivate at the ringing of a bell.

We found quite accidentally that honey bees could learn in the classical "simple discrimination conditioning" sense (Wenner and Johnson 1966; Wenner 1971a). That incident occurred during a "normal science" (e.g., Kuhn 1962) sequence of experiments. Inadvertently, during laboratory studies, a "reward" of sugar solution had been provided each time a neutral stimulus (a draft of air) had been administered. Later, when an air draft was provided while the reward was momentarily delayed, the experienced bees rushed out to the empty food dish as if the sugar solution had already been provided.

When the bees thereby demonstrated that they could learn in the classical conditioning sense, the "My God!" reaction of Bruner and Postman (1949) followed immediately. First there was disbelief. Then there emerged a strong desire to dismantle the apparatus and tell no one about this apparent anomaly. However, the urge to learn more about what bees really do in nature prevailed over that temptation.

We had first learned of the Bruner and Postman experiments from Kuhn, who wrote:

In a psychological experiment that deserves to be far better known outside the trade, Bruner and Postman asked experimental subjects to identify . . . a series of playing cards. Many of the cards were normal, but some were made anomalous, e.g., a red six of spades and a black four of hearts. . . . After each exposure the subject was asked what he had seen. ([1962] 1970a:62–64)

These psychologists had thus altered some of the playing cards in an otherwise standard deck; the new reality did not conform with any earlier experience the subjects had had with playing cards. When subjects first viewed altered cards, they initially did not recognize them as other than normal and continued to record a number and/or color they expected to see. They consequently erred whenever one of the altered cards was shown to them. Only when an inordinate amount of time was allowed for viewing each false card did they begin to perceive that their earlier identifications had been in error. A common expression among these experimental subjects when they first realized the fact that they had earlier erred was "My God!"

The experience we had when bees clearly demonstrated that they were capable of learning in the classic manner paralleled the playing card experience studied by Bruner and Postman. All common preconceived notions, such as the instinct-versus-learning distinction between insects and vertebrates, were suddenly open to question. The immediate reaction of shock when bees demonstrated their ability to learn was soon replaced by a need for us to return to reality. It became evident that it was no long possible to ignore either what had transpired or what adverse reactions might be ahead in the scientific community (see chapter 12).

We had thereby been propelled from an exercise in normal science (Kuhn 1962) into the "image creation" experience of Atkinson (1985). Unwittingly we proceeded thereafter under the mistaken belief (see chapter 9) that the results of more tightly controlled experiments would be welcomed by the same community that had welcomed our research on analysis of honey bee sounds. We also felt that we could succeed in "converting" others to the important role of learning in honey bee recruitment.

However, studies of learning remained a side issue. We still believed that honey bees had a "dance language," albeit one of reduced importance in foraging behavior, that functioned during the first recruitment of naive bees to a food source. After several experiments on simple conditioning, we again returned to the question of what might constitute "vigor" in the waggle dance in order to attempt to construct an imitation bee (see excursus VGR). That approach would permit us to gather "direct" evidence in support of the notion that sound signals were an essential component of dance language (the verification approach once again).

While our intent was clear, the approach instead led (inadvertently at first and deliberately later) to a sequence of experiments that further clarified the role of learning in the recruitment of honey bees to food sources in the field (e.g., Johnson and Wenner 1966).

The first stage in subsequent research included experiments that actually extended our understanding of the "simple conditioning" phenomenon. We first confirmed, as others had found earlier (e.g., von Frisch 1950), that foragers accustomed to visiting a station at which they have previously been successful will continue to visit that site, even if food is no longer available. In fact, their visits, on average, are remarkably regular (see figure 7.3). That result agreed fully with von Frisch's perception:

> We then stopped supplying sugar at both places, and allowed the dishes to remain empty for an hour or two. After this time most of the bees from both groups were sitting inactive in the hive; only from time to time would one of them fly out to the feeding place to see if anything was to be had. (1950:72)

However, neither observation agreed with a later statement by von Frisch:

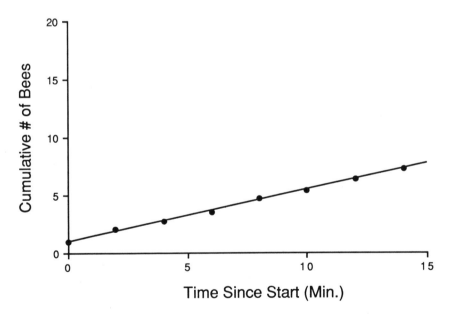

FIGURE 7.3. Routine inspection pattern by foraging bees (cumulative number of visits by different foragers) at an empty dish (after Johnson and Wenner 1966). Before a site begins yielding nectar each day, experienced foragers regularly visit the site at which they had had success the previous day.

> Suppose we remove the little sugar-water dish from our feeding table, so that our marked bees find that there is no food in the usual place? They will behave exactly as they would if their natural food, the honey flow, had dried up owing to bad weather, when their usual flowers temporarily cease to provide them with nectar. The bees will stay at home, and stop dancing. From then on the little honey dishes laid out round the hive may have to wait on the lawn for hours or even days on end before a single bee will visit them again. (1954:105)

Nor with yet another of his comments:

> There still remains one factor that plays a part in the frequenting of flowers by bees: their pronounced time sense. . . . I know of no other living creature that learns so easily as the bee when, according to its "internal clock," to come to the table. . . .These relations are easily imitated experimentally. If at an artificial feeding station one offers sugar water at a set time of day, within a day or two the visitors adjust themselves to the schedule. Thenceforth they come at the designated time, whereas before and after the hour of feeding even informational flights are almost entirely omitted. The foragers remain sitting at home, saving their strength and risking no unnecessary flights. (1967a:253–253)

Von Frisch apparently did not realize that his statements were not consistent with one another (the appearance of anomaly, once again).

Peter Craig at the University of California, Santa Barbara (unpublished results), repeated a 1929 experiment performed by Beling (figure 35 in Ribbands 1953). He had thirty-five individual bees trained to visit a feeding station at which food had been provided for several days only between 4 and 5 p.m. Craig then tallied all visits by each of the thirty-five bees; he found that some of them inspected the dish more than once during the day. That was the same result found by others (summarized in chapter 7 of Ribbands 1953).

Craig then recognized a problem with data display in earlier studies. The repeated tallying of the same bee visiting a station provided an impression of greater precision in "time sense" than was merited by the results. That is, a forager in the general area of the feeding dish could periodically reinspect the dish without returning to the hive. Each such visit was counted as an additional point in Beling's display.

Figure 7.4 presents Beling's results in a different manner. The data are now included for only the *first* visit of the day by each of the foragers. By the beginning of the training period (2:30 p.m.) more than half of the foragers had already inspected the dish.

Craig's data are shown in the same figure for comparison. By 4

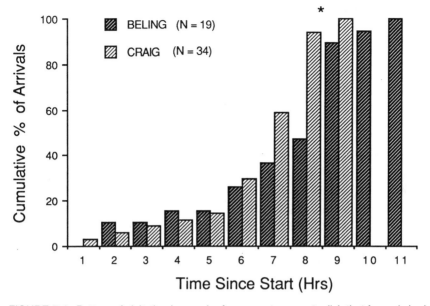

FIGURE 7.4. Pattern of visitation by regular foragers at an empty dish that formerly had sugar solution provided in midafternoon for several days prior to the 1st day. The time at which food had been provided on earlier days is designated with an asterisk (*). Beling (in Ribbands 1953, dark bars here) tested visitation for bees that had previously only been provided food after 2:30 p.m. Craig (unpublished data, used with permission) did the same for bees that had not received food before a 4 p.m. training time.

p.m. (the start of the training time) 95 percent of the experienced bees in Craig's study had already inspected the empty dish at least once during the day. More than half of them had done so at least an hour and a half early, and a tenth of them had already inspected the dish five hours before the training time.

In both experiments, it is apparent that foragers did not "remain sitting at home" (von Frisch 1967a:254). The "pronounced time sense" was certainly not impressive.

"LEARNING" AND THE EVIDENCE FOR "LANGUAGE"

The second stage of our experimental program was an attempt to repeat von Frisch's experiments in order to clarify his comments about what he meant by differences in dance "vigor." That is, he had indicated that bees visiting a rich food source dance more "vigorously" than those visiting a poorer food source.

It should be possible to elucidate this "vigor" effect by altering sugar concentration at a dish in the field while simultaneously observing the foragers upon their return as they danced in the hive. In conducting such an experiment, one must first observe dancing bees carefully to ascertain just what features of the dance might vary. During the first attempt at such a study, we used a hive and feeding station that were already in operation. One of us was to observe dancing bees in the hive while another person added a sugar solution of known concentration to the dish that had been empty since the previous day.

Initially all went as planned. Whereas the visitation of experienced foragers was linear and regular when no food was present in the dish (see figure 7.3), the cumulative number of arrivals became exponential once food was again provided (see figure 7.5). That result is exactly what one would expect if successful bees had recruited others. The result, however, was anomalous, in that an exponential rise in visitation occurred at the dish *even though no dancing had occurred in*

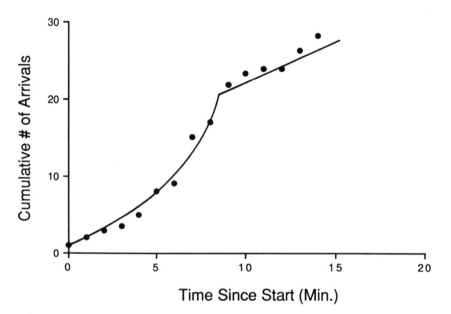

FIGURE 7.5. Increase in recruitment of experienced foragers at a site once food was again provided (after Johnson and Wenner 1966). Foragers apparently communicated by means of conditioned response; that is, they recruited one another by means of odor stimuli without dancing. Compare to shape of curve in figure 7.3 during regular inspection trips at an empty dish.

the hive. Clearly, bees had been recruited by successful foragers *despite* the lack of dancing during that initial fifteen-minute period.

Many experiments later we could interpret those anomalous results. One can associate a stimulus, such as odor, with the reward to be provided. When that is done, one can later inject odor into the hive without providing a reward. We then did just that by injecting odor into the hive by using a turkey-basting syringe. Experienced bees then immediately left the hive and flew directly to the familiar, but empty, dish in the field (Johnson and Wenner 1966).

In nature the same condition can hold true. Experienced bees will occasionally inspect the empty food dish (or blossoms not yet producing nectar). Once foragers can again fill up, they will return to the hive and unload. While there, the odor emanating from their bodies can alert other experienced bees that food is again available. Recruitment can then occur even in the absence of dancing.

When that interpretation became evident from the experimental results, we passed through another "conversion" sequence, as described by Kuhn:

> Initially, only the anticipated and usual are experienced even under circumstances where anomaly is later to be observed. Further acquaintance, however, does result in awareness of something wrong or does relate the effect to something that has gone wrong before. That awareness of anomaly opens a period in which conceptual categories are adjusted until the initially anomalous has become the anticipated. At this point the discovery has been completed. (1962: 64)

The first sentence of that quotation is particularly significant with regard to the conditioned-response phenomenon we observed. Earlier workers must have observed the same "communication by means of conditioned response" behavior among recruited bees but had apparently failed to recognize its potential significance during the recruitment of experienced foragers to food sources. In that connection, consider a series of earlier quotations relevant to conditioning and recruitment.

One significant sentence can be found in the initial report of von Frisch's experiments with honey bee recruitment. He wrote: "It follows further that a communication can be transmitted from the returning bee to other bees by touch alone, without the necessity for any dance" (1947:13). However, that qualification was absent from a later summary of his 1946 results:

> The dances are apparently understood by the bees in the hive, as could be shown by the following experiment. . . . If we now refilled

the dish at [a] distant site, then the wagging dances of the first gatherers to return with full stomachs aroused chiefly bees from the group which had previously visited the distant feeding place. But when we offered sugar-water at [a] nearer site, then the resulting round dances aroused mostly bees which had previously been feeding there. (1950:72)

On the basis of results from the experiments on conditioned responses described above, (e.g., Wenner and Johnson 1966; Johnson and Wenner 1966), it would appear that the von Frisch results, which supposedly had demonstrated the use of "language," agreed equally well with the interpretation that conditioned bees had responded to some simple stimulus (odor?) provided by a returning bee.

Ribbands (1954) had also obtained results earlier than we, results that indicated that experienced foragers could be recruited to their food site by means of odor alone. He published a paper to that effect: "Communication between honeybees, part 1: The response of crop-attached bees to the scent of their crop."

However, Ribbands apparently functioned within the paradigm hold described by Kuhn; that is, "only the anticipated and usual are experienced where anomaly is later to be observed." In fact, a year later Ribbands published the second paper of the series, "The recruitment of trained bees, and their response to improvement of the crop." An inspection of some of his data and one of his conclusions reveals that he came very close to recognizing what we published a little more than a decade later. He wrote:

In favourable conditions recruitment is very rapid. For instance, on the afternoon of 20th August dish b was put down at 13.20 hours G.M.T. and the first trained bee arrived at 13.36 hrs. Two others came at 13.38, and another one at 13.39—the absence of bees [at another dish] indicates the probability that these bees were recruited by the first bee on its first return to the hive; it returned itself at 13.39. Another bee arrived at 13.41, two at 13.42, two at 13.43, four at 13.44, one at 13.45, one at 13.46, one at 13.48, one at 13.49, two at 13.51, one at 13.52, one at 13.54. One other did not come until 15.15 (perhaps alerted by vigorous dancing after the increase in syrup concentration at 14.00 hrs.). (1955a:27)

Just how close Ribbands came to our notion of "communication by means of conditioned response" is evident in one of his conclusions in that same paper (1955:31): "Lindauer reported that bees did not dance until they had paid several visits to a food source (at or near threshold syrup concentrations). The arrival times of the recruited trained bees

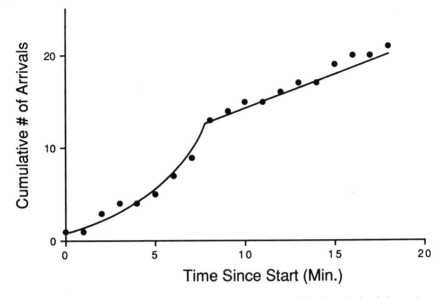

FIGURE 7.6. A similar pattern to that shown in figure 7.5A but derived from data published much earlier by Ribbands (1955:27).

... are *only* consistent with the supposition that the first arrival danced on her first return to the hive" (1955:31; emphasis ours).

The data published by Ribbands (above) escaped our attention at the time when we began our experiments. That was partly because we were unprepared for a conditioned-response behavior in bees and partly because Ribbands' results were in the form of a paragraph rather than a figure. By expressing his data in the form of a graph (see figure 7.6), however, it is evident that our results were essentially identical to his. The main difference was that we were observing the foragers in the hive and knew that they were, indeed, *not* dancing upon their return (just as Lindauer had observed). The conditioned-response explanation was sufficient to explain our results, but Ribbands did not recognize the implications of his earlier statement: "the mere presence of the training scent in the hive, in the absence of either food sharing or dancing, can encourage crop-attached bees to go to their crop" (1954:143).

A concise statement of the alternative hypothesis for the recruitment of experienced bees was now possible.

Foragers routinely monitor known sources of food even after those sources become empty. (That statement agrees with one but not with another of von Frisch's statements, above.) If food again becomes available, returning loaded bees enter their hive, bearing the characteristic odor of the food source and/or of the location on their bodies. Other foragers that have visited those same sources are stimulated to leave the hive by the odor stimulus carried in by the first successful forager(s) and travel to whatever site at which they had earlier had success (Johnson 1967b).

One very important fact had emerged from our studies of conditioned responses. In his classic little Cornell University Press book (1950) von Frisch made a number of claims with respect to what he felt was the conclusive nature of experiments purporting to demonstrate the use of "language" by bees. Yet the results of every one of those experiments could also be interpreted as an example of the behavior of bees during a conditioned response to an odor stimulus.

Increasingly we had come to appreciate also the importance of odor in the recruitment of naive honey bees to those food crops visited by their more experienced hivemates. That increasing awareness of ours is the subject of the next chapter.

8

A PARADE OF
ANOMALIES: ODOR
("Back to Exploration")

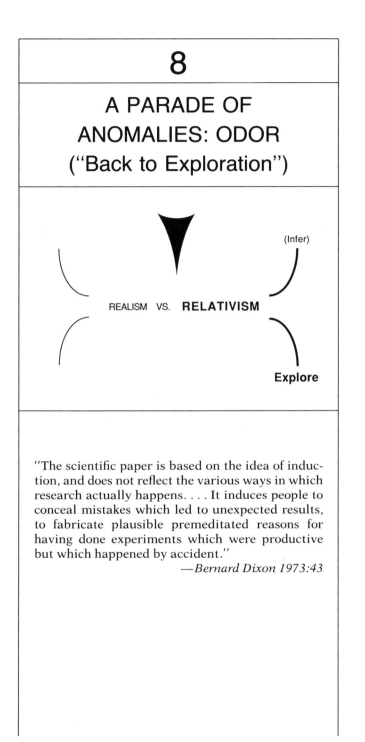

REALISM VS. **RELATIVISM**

(Infer)

Explore

"The scientific paper is based on the idea of induction, and does not reflect the various ways in which research actually happens. . . . It induces people to conceal mistakes which led to unexpected results, to fabricate plausible premeditated reasons for having done experiments which were productive but which happened by accident."
—*Bernard Dixon 1973:43*

The typical journal article in biology starts with an introduction, which is followed by sections on methods, results, discussion, and (perhaps) conclusions. The introduction is often completed after the body of the paper has been written, since it is imperative (under the dictates of the traditional format) that the research reported upon be placed into a "proper" perspective with regard to what has gone on before. The implication is that one "stands on the shoulders of giants" and extends the limits of knowledge in a very deliberate manner. Mahoney (1976:129) described that traditional approach in detail.

The description of science as an inductive process is almost always based upon necessarily inadequate information; that is, researchers rarely publish accounts of what really happened. Mahoney wrote: "Despite the fact that David Hume recognized the impossibility of an 'inductive logic' almost two centuries ago, many philosophers of science have continued unsuccessful salvage attempts" (1976:135).

Moreover, some philosophers of science have concurred. Putnam clearly recognized the weakness of the inductive approach, as follows: "Today, a host of negative results, including some powerful considerations due to Nelson Goodman, have indicated that there *cannot* be a completely *formal* inductive logic" (1981:125).

Mahoney (1976:129) also listed and discussed the inadequacy of claims made by those who present the traditional explanation of the process by which science supposedly operates (he called it a "caricature"). One can also recognize in that traditional treatment elements of an adherence to the verification approach within the Realism school (see chapter 3). In the "normal science" procedure as described by Kuhn (1962: our chapters 2 and 3), however, research following the verification approach could well be commonplace, particularly within the strictures of the grant award system.

Clarifying the role of learning in bees during recruitment to crops (see chapter 7) facilitated our later experimental designs in that line of research, but the anomalies we found with respect to odor use by searching recruits were ultimately far more important. Each of the incidents by itself was not especially compelling. However, the composite impression gained during a given experimental sequence provided insight and led to new experimental design. The experience we had was strikingly similar to the description of science as a process, furnished by Atkinson and quoted in the second chapter: "[Science is] a process whereby the human capacity for imagination creates and manipulates images in the mind[,] producing concepts, theories, and ideas which incorporate and tie together shared human sensory experience" (1985:734).

That expression also indicates the importance of the laboratory setting (i.e., a community of scholars) in biological research. Early in our experimental program we came to perceive and accept the significance of anomalies and anecdotes (ours and others) in the later design of experiments. That was especially true in the case of research on the role of learning and odors in bee recruitment.

THE IMPORTANCE OF LOCALITY ODORS IN THE RECRUITMENT OF NAIVE BEES

According to the dance language hypothesis, recruited bees that supposedly have obtained direction and distance information from dancing foragers should fly directly out (in the same direction and to the same distance) to that food source exploited earlier by the forager they contacted within the hive (e.g., von Frisch 1950; see also our chapter 1).

If bees had a language, then, and if recruits flew directly out to the site specified in the dance maneuver, the odor concentration in the food should be important only during the final approach flight of those recruited bees and then only for that proportion of searchers ending up downwind from its source (see chapter 5 and excursus OS). Searching bees arriving from any direction other than downwind should not be able to perceive *any* of the characteristic odor and would have to rely entirely on the direction and distance information contained in the dance.

However, we found that varying odor concentrations in the food and in the field (even at sites remote from the experiment) mattered a great deal in terms of searching recruit success (see also Friesen 1973). We received many anomalous results during routine experiments before we became aware of the overriding importance of odor during the recruitment process. Each of these incidents enhanced our understanding of searching bee behavior; several examples follow.

Fortunately, the Santa Barbara area normally has no rain between the months of April and October. Most of the vegetation either dies or becomes dormant during that time if it is not irrigated. Dead vegetation soon loses much of its odor. However, at one time during our experiments, an unseasonal shower wet the leaf litter and produced a characteristic "wet vegetation" odor near one but not near the other of our two dishes, each of which contained the same lightly scented sugar solution.

Immediately after the rain, the site near wet vegetation was overwhelmed by new recruits; the same sudden influx of recruitment did not happen at the other site, which had been sheltered from the rain. Since the number of regular (marked) foragers had remained constant and equal for both sites, it appeared that the odor of wet vegetation had adhered to the bodies of regular foragers and later served as an odor cue for searching recruits.

At several other times, isolated incidences of a similar increase in the arrival of new recruits coincided with a sudden marked increase in locality odor near one station, even though the number of regular foragers remained constant. For example, when an assistant at one of the food dishes applied scented suntan lotion, the influx of recruits continued high until the suntan lotion odor dissipated.

During another experiment in a different locality, gardeners sprayed some bushes with pungent insecticide near one of the stations. When that happened, the number of new recruits increased only at that station. An application of chicken manure fertilizer to the field between the hive and feeding station on another occasion forced us to abandon that locality for the remainder of the season. The use of laboratory paper towels under the feeding dish in early experiments imparted a characteristic "paper" odor to the station; a switch to filter paper excluded problems associated with the "paper factor" (Wenner 1971a:67).

One incident actually constituted a controlled experiment. Regular foragers collected unscented sugar solution from either one of two dishes in opposite directions from the hive. (Earlier it had become apparent that unscented food resulted in no recruitment or an extremely low level of recruitment.) However, a gardener mowed the lawn near one of the stations, which then experienced an immediate surge in arrival of new recruits. As the grass dried, recruit success diminished until it reached the low level recorded throughout the morning at the other station (see figure 8.1). The next morning the gardener mowed the lawn near the other station, and a repeat of the results was obtained; the second station now received a sudden large influx of unmarked recruits which declined with time.

A more amusing episode (although annoying at the time) occurred when an assistant chewed clove-flavored gum at one of the food dishes during the course of the experiment. Whereas that may not have been a problem in other circumstances, clove oil had been added as a marker to the sugar solution for that experimental series. The number of new recruits that arrived (with many recruits attracted to his face) completely overwhelmed the assistant. The experiment was terminated for the day.

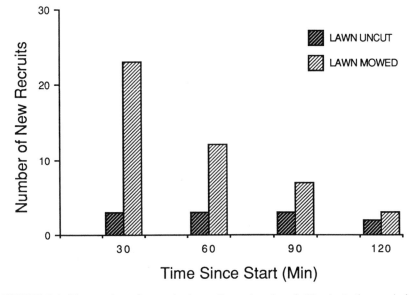

FIGURE 8.1. The number of unmarked recruits captured each 30-minute time period at two stations furnished with unscented sucrose solution. At one station (light bars), lawn mowing in the area contributed a characteristic cut-grass odor, which disappeared as the grass dried. Recruitment declined steadily as the odor of cut grass dissipated. At a control station located in the opposite direction from the hive (dark bars), recruitment showed no such pattern.

Eventually, it became apparent to us that a total lack of odor in the food or near the stations resulted in a near absence of recruit arrivals. In fact, if we obtained *any* recruitment when we used unscented sucrose solution, we concluded that such recruitment was likely due to locality odor. One of the more convincing examples occurred during some sessions prior to the conduct of our "crucial" experiment (see chapter 10). We wrote:

> That bees locate a food source by olfaction is especially possible in view of the extremely low recruitment rate of regular foragers collecting unscented sucrose at an unscented site. On 25 July 1968, for instance, in the absence of a major nectar source for the colony, we received only five recruits from a hive of approximately 60,000 bees after ten bees had foraged at each of four stations for a total of 1374 round trips during a 3-hour period. (Wenner, Wells, and Johnson 1969:84)

RECRUIT BUILDUP OVER TIME

The normal procedure during an experimental series of studies of honey bee recruitment is to have a fixed number of regular foragers visiting a dish day after day. One succeeds in maintaining that constant number by killing all newcomers immediately upon their arrival. Experienced foragers know the way, however, and travel back and forth by means of landmarks.

At the beginning of each day, a dish newly filled with sugar solution is normally visited soon thereafter by one of the marked bees that had been there the day before. Shortly thereafter all other experienced foragers begin regular trips, apparently as a manifestation of a stimulus-response behavior (see chapter 7). If one of the marked bees from the group does not show up as expected, a new recruit is marked as a replacement, rather than killed. This procedure keeps the number of foragers constant.

Under the dance language hypothesis, one would expect that the recruitment of *new* bees would begin immediately after the first experienced bee once again became successful at the start of each day and after it danced upon its return to the hive. That does not happen, however, even though dancing may begin within half an hour after foragers begin making regular trips. Very few recruits ever arrived at our stations within the first forty-five minutes of each day's experiment (see figure 8.2). Another anomaly had become apparent.

One would also expect that a fixed number of experienced foragers would recruit a given number of recruits per unit time. That did not happen either; recruit success built up steadily during each three-hour period (see figure 8.2). On the basis of that evidence we concluded that the odor provided in the food and collected by the foragers had accumulated in the hive during each experiment. The regular pattern displayed in figure 8.2 would thus reflect the *cumulative number* of round trips by the foragers rather than a constant number of bees that could be recruited per unit time by use of any "dance language" information (Wenner, Wells, and Johnson 1969).

It became apparent to us that newly recruited bees must leave the hive and search for a considerable period of time before they are successful (see also Esch and Bastian 1970; Gould, Henerey, and MacLeod 1970; excursus NEG). A body of searching recruits would thus accumulate in the air (and in the general area) somewhere between the hive and food sources (Friesen 1973; Wenner 1974; see also

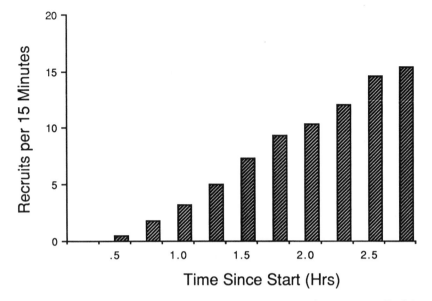

FIGURE 8.2. Average daily pattern of recruitment during a 26-day sequence. Each bar represents the mean number of recruits captured each 15-minute period during the course of nearly three hours, while only 20 foragers made regular round trips between hive and feeding dishes. The bar heights should have been nearly equal (i.e., constant rate of recruitment) if searching recruits had *used* dance language information.

chapter 10). We had moved one step closer to an experimental design that could test predictions of the language hypothesis.

REMOTE INTERFERENCE WITH BEE RECRUITMENT

Surprises became apparent more frequently (but disturbed us less often) once we knew that anomalies *could* exist. One of the more dramatic events occurred when we altered recruitment at two stations placed in nearly opposite directions from one hive by providing the standard scented sucrose simultaneously at a second hive located 280 meters from the first hive, as well as 360 meters and 390 meters downwind from the two experimental sites (see figure 8.3).

That unplanned experimental design included the use of two hives. The experimental hive contained normal European bees (dark-colored bees), and the other contained European bees genetically different only in color (bees without black pigment). The color difference enabled us to identify the hive from which recruits had come. Dark-

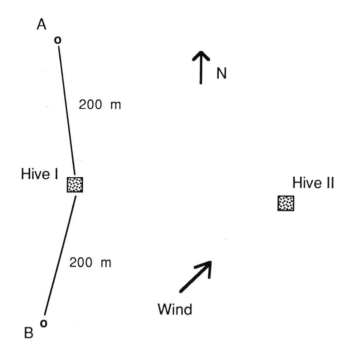

FIGURE 8.3. Arrangement of hives (each with its own color of bees) and dishes in a two-hive experiment (after Wenner 1971). Ten dark-colored foragers from one colony (Hive I) collected clove-scented sugar solution from each of two stations placed 200 meters from that hive (at Stations A and B). Light-colored bees from a second colony (Hive II), located 280 meters downwind from that system, visited only natural nectar sources in the area.

The sudden addition of clove-scented solution to that second hive (containing light-colored bees) markedly reduced the recruitment of new bees from *the first hive* (containing dark-colored bees) at stations A and B, even though regular foragers from the first hive continued making round trips to those stations. If those dark-colored recruits had been using "dance language' information, the presence of this odor in the second hive should not have interfered with the first system (Hive I, Stations A and B).

colored bees from the experimental hive (Hive I in Figure 8.3) collected clove-scented sugar solution from each of two dishes located in nearly opposite directions from their hive. Light-colored bees from the other hive visited only natural sources in the area.

On one day in an experimental series, after the first hive and its two stations had shown the normal daily increase in recruitment at a clove-scented sugar solution, we attempted to recruit bees from the second hive (with light-colored bees) to the two experimental feeding stations without any formal training procedure (see excursus GT). We merely lifted the lid of the hive containing light-colored bees and liberally sprinkled clove-scented sugar solution onto the combs. However, recruitment of light-colored bees to the two stations from the downwind hive did not occur. (The technique may work if one injects odor into the hive for several days before setting out a station.)

Instead of the recruitment of light-colored bees to the experimental stations, both observers at the two feeding stations reported an almost immediate and unexpected cessation in the recruitment of unmarked dark-colored bees at those sites, despite the continuing round trips executed by regular foragers. At the same time, unmarked dark bees from the experimental hive began arriving at the second hive containing light-colored bees and attempted to collect the sugar solution from among the occupants of that hive instead of at the experimental dishes. That result surprised us, since dark bees should have been searching only near the experimental sites, as one would expect from the dance language hypothesis. The intruders were attacked.

Those results were completely anomalous. According to the expectations of the dance language hypothesis, the locations of the two experimental sites were supposedly indicated by the dance maneuver in the first hive; searching dark-colored recruits from that hive should not have been anywhere near the area of the second hive. That is, recruits should not have been there unless they had left their hive and flown somewhere downwind of the food sources (see chapter 5 and excursus OS). The results thus directly contradicted the "flying directly out" prediction for the behavior of searching bees, as expected under the prevailing dance language hypothesis.

We concluded from this unplanned experiment that newly recruited bees begin their search pattern in earnest when they are downwind from food and/or odor sources. They could then perceive the odor of the food to which they have been recruited and work their way upwind in the characteristic odor-search manner executed by other animals (see excursus OS).

RECRUITMENT BY DISORIENTED DANCES

Recruitment experiments can be run in a situation in which foragers execute their dances on a horizontal surface rather than on the vertical surface of the comb in the hive (e.g., von Frisch 1950:87). When foragers can see the sky, dances on a horizontal surface contain direction information for *us*. That is, the straight-run portion of the dance is directed toward the food site previously visited.

When foragers cannot see the sky, on the other hand, horizontal dances are disoriented and lack any direction information. By running a set of experiments in which foragers perform such "disoriented" dances, one can eliminate any appreciable transmission of direction information between forager and attendant recruit. The recruit thus cannot exploit any knowledge about direction during its search behavior.

We ran a series of such experiments (three hours a day for eleven days), during which experienced bees danced on a specially designed horizontal surface after re-entering the hive. While outside the hive, those same foragers had visited one or another of different sugar solution concentrations provided at the two sites (Wells and Wenner 1973). That is, on any given day a rich solution (1.8M) was offered at one station, and a not-so-rich solution (1.3M) was offered at the other. (The use of richer solutions results in more recruits than does the use of solutions of lower sugar concentration [e.g., Gould, Henerey, and MacLeod 1970].)

In all, fewer than 3 percent (50) of the dances by our marked bees were oriented on the surface of the comb (see figure 8.4A), while 97 percent (1,743) of the dances by our marked bees were disoriented on the dance platform (see figure 8.4B). There was thus virtually no direction information provided to the group of potential recruits by dancing bees. If locality odors had played only a minor part in the success of recruited bees (during the final approach phase), we reasoned that the distribution of recruited bees at the two stations should have been nearly identical to one another.

The two stations with different molarities did not have equal recruitment; whichever station had the highest molarity always received the most recruits (see figure 8.5). The outcome was quite clear; recruits arrived primarily at whichever site had the richest food, despite there being essentially no direction information provided in the hive by experienced foragers.

The results also indicated that recruited bees had apparently used some obscure (to us) but distinctive odor (to them) during their search. Lacking any other explanation, we felt that the odor cue must have been an odor characteristic of the environment near each of the stations (see the above anecdotes).

All of the above indicated to us that recruited bees, after receiving an odor stimulus from experienced foragers, begin some sort of a

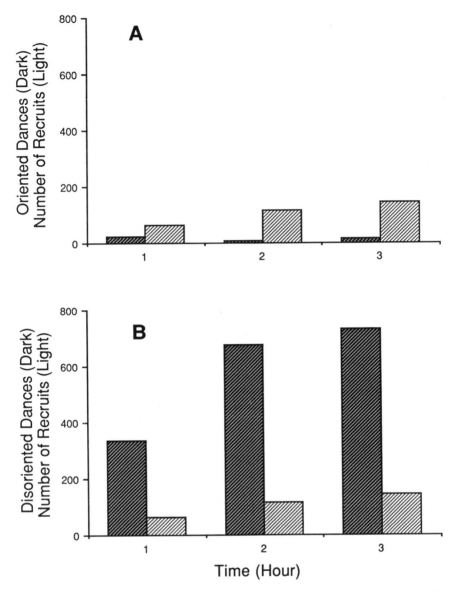

FIGURE 8.4. Incidence of oriented and disoriented dances compared to recruit arrivals at feeding stations (based on data from table 1 of Wells and Wenner 1973). A) Oriented dances (dark bars) occurred seldom under conditions of the experiment, and recruit arrival frequency (light bars) was not correlated with that incidence. B) Disoriented dances (dark bars) were frequent; odor buildup and the pattern of recruit arrivals (light bars) paralleled that incidence, even though no direction information was provided in waggle dances.

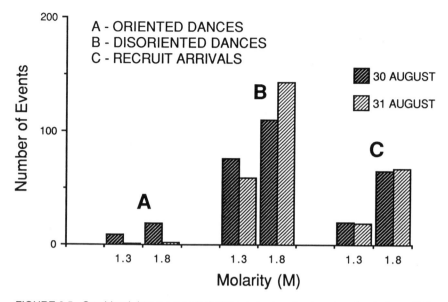

FIGURE 8.5. Combined data on events that transpired on the two days (as in figure 8.4) with the greatest number of oriented dances and the greatest number of disoriented dances (based on data from table 2 of Wells and Wenner 1973). A) Number of oriented dances observed in the hive at two molarities of sucrose solution (1.3 molar and 1.8 molar). B) Incidence of disoriented dances at the two molarities. C) Recruit success at the two stations, each with its own sugar concentration. Note that the recruitment pattern (C) did not change on the two days, even though oriented dance frequency diminished to near zero on the second day (as in A).

distinctive search pattern that does not involve a direct flight out from the hive to the feeding site (see excursus OS). Friesen (1973) took up the challenge of that discrepancy and studied the possible flight behavior of searching recruits. We provide some of his results next.

THE SPATIAL DISTRIBUTION OF SEARCHING BEES

If bees are not "flying directly out," where might they be? In experiments conducted with the use of a single hive and with bees trained to visit a single feeding station, Friesen (1973) found that a reduction in the number of foragers to half of what was normal led to a reduction of successful recruits to less than a quarter of what was normal. That result was clearly anomalous to what one might expect within the dance language hypothesis. If only a certain number of foragers can make round trips per unit time, they can only provide just so many dances in the hive per unit time, and such a set number of dances should result in a given number of recruits per unit time.

Friesen began to suspect that searching recruits somehow relied more on odor(s) and/or on the density of foragers in the field (at the dish and/or on their flight paths) than on the frequency of dancing in their hive.

During one four-hour period, Friesen carefully monitored the total number of forager trips in each fifteen-minute period. He also tallied the number of recruit arrivals during each time period. At the end of the first two hours, Friesen suddenly replaced the scented solution with unscented solution. Recruit arrivals then virtually ceased (see the arrow in figure 8.6A), following the usual customary buildup (see e.g., figure 8.2).

However, forager visitation in the meantime had continued much as before, with only a slight decrease in round-trip frequency (figure 8.6B). This anomalous result occurred despite the fact that dance frequencies in the hive have been found to be higher for unscented food than for scented food (Wells and Wenner 1971).

To find the whereabouts of searching bees present in the area (since they obviously were not "flying directly out from their hive") Friesen placed two hives, each with its own color of bees, 600 meters apart in an open field such that one was downwind of the other (see figure 8.7). He then placed his feeding station (one only) sequentially at each of five locations between those two hives (a preset 75 meters apart). That procedure permitted him to determine the relative success of recruits from each of the hives at specific distances under different wind conditions.

Friesen's results in that experimental series did not fit the expectations of the dance language hypothesis, either. That is, the direction in which a feeding station is located relative to wind conditions should not alter flight patterns appreciably for recruits using "dance language" information. Instead, the composite recruitment patterns he found for the two hives differed markedly. On the one hand, the distance between hive and food mattered little for those recruits that succeeded in finding a station upwind from their hive (see figure 8.8). The by now familiar increase in rate of success with time (see figure 8.2) appeared once again.

Friesen obtained a very different set of results for recruits that eventually found the downwind station. Recruits searching for stations located at increasing distances downwind from the hive had an ever more difficult time finding those stations (see figure 8.9). It would appear that recruits might not even be able to find a station located

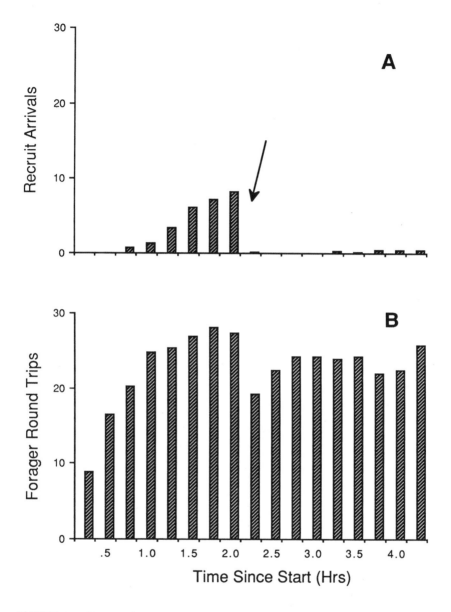

FIGURE 8.6. Pattern of recruit arrivals and regular forager visitation before and after removal of scent from the food, two hours into the experiment (from Wells and Wenner 1971). A) Scent was removed from the food after two hours (arrow). Recruit success then plummeted to near zero, despite steady visitation by regular foragers (B) and despite the likelihood of increased dancing in the hive with removal of scent from the food.

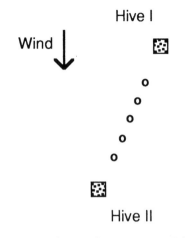

FIGURE 8.7. A two-hive and feeding station arrangement for an upwind, downwind experiment (after Friesen 1973). Foragers from the two hives (each with its own color of bees) simultaneously visited only one station at a time at varying distances (between 150 and 450 meters from the hives, 75 meters apart), either upwind or downwind from their hive.

The pattern of recruit success through time under those circumstances for the two end stations is shown in figures 8.8 and 8.9 (complete set of data in Freisen 1973). Under expectations of the dance language hypothesis, the patterns of success rate, as shown in those two figures, should have been nearly identical.

1,000 meters or more downwind from a hive with so few regular foragers, either with or without "dance language" information.

There were noticeable exceptions in the pattern of results for stations located close to the hive. There were actually many arrivals per unit time at the two stations (I and II) closest downwind from the upwind hive (Hive I) during the course of the experiment (see figure 8.9). The recruit success rate was actually better for stations immediately downwind from the hive than it was for bees searching for a site immediately upwind from their hive (see figure 8.8; see also excursus OS and chapter 12).

Friesen's crosswind-versus-downwind experiments cast further light on the nature of recruit search behavior. For those experiments, Friesen (1973) used two stations simultaneously for recruitment from a single hive; one was 360 meters in a direction perpendicular to the prevailing wind direction, and the other was 360 meters downwind from the hive (see figure 8.10). Under the predictions of the dance language hypothesis, the two stations should have had equal recruitment per unit time, since the same number of foragers traveled the route between the parent hive and each of those two feeding stations.

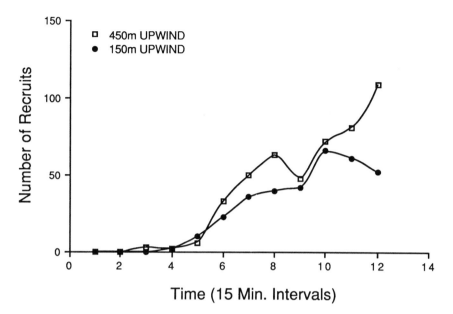

FIGURE 8.8.   The relative success rate for recruits that had arrived at stations at different distances *upwind* from Hive II. Having two stations 300 meters apart did not appreciably alter the recruitment pattern.

The actual results were quite different from those one would expect under the predictions of the dance language hypothesis. The station located downwind from the hive had very little increase in rate of recruitment with time (see figure 8.11A). However, recruits readily found a station located in a direction crosswind from the hive (see figure 8.11B); the familiar recruitment pattern seen in figure 8.2 was again evident there.

Friesen found another discrepancy when he examined the influence of wind speed on the success of recruits searching for a point source of food. Recruits coming to a downwind station (as for Hive I in figure 8.7) arrived in the greatest number just after each slight temporary increase in wind speed. Upwind sites (such as for Hive II in figure 8.7), on the other hand, showed little such variation with slight changes in wind.

Friesen exploited yet another technique to determine the amount of time recruits spent searching for the food source. Unloaded bees fly at an average speed of 7.5 meters per second (Wenner 1963; see also excursus NEG). A flight from the hive to a 300-meter site thus would require less than a minute if bees were "flying directly out," as ex-

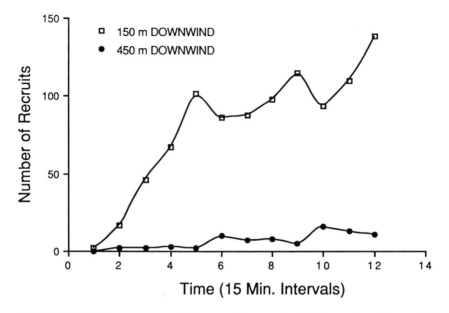

FIGURE 8.9. Relative success rate for searching recruits at stations placed *downwind* from Hive I (figure 8.7). Now the distance factor influenced the success rate of recruits greatly. While a station only 150 meters from the hive fared well, recruits could find a station 300 meters further downwind (at 450 meters) only with difficulty. Differences such as those shown in these two figures should not exist if recruits could use dance language information.

pected from the dance language hypothesis (see chapters 1 and 4 on this point). He intermittently closed one hive at a time and thereby occasionally prevented recruits from leaving for a short duration. Friesen was then able to determine both the minimum and maximum flight times for recruited bees that had arrived at either the upwind or downwind 300-meter site (that site intermediate between the two hives).

The data on minimum search times were obtained by opening a previously closed hive. Friesen then noted the time of first departure of regular foragers and measured the elapsed time before the first recruit arrived. No surprises were found in that series.

The data on maximum search times for recruits were obtained by noting the time of arrival of the last recruit after closure of the hive. (Regular foragers cease round trips immediately upon closure, since they cannot dispose of their load of sugar solution when the entrance to their hive is blocked.)

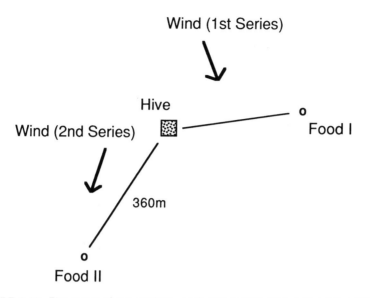

FIGURE 8.10. Placement of two stations, each 360 meters from a hive (after Friesen 1973). In the first series of experiments, foragers collected sugar solution at a station *crosswind* from the hive. In a second series, foragers visited a *downwind* station. If recruits could use "dance language" information, the recruitment pattern for new bees should not differ much at the two stations. For the results of those two series of experiments see figure 8.11.

The maximum flight times obtained for recruits at downwind versus upwind stations were very different for searchers from the two hives. In Friesen's four experiments, maximum search times were 24.3 minutes for those unmarked recruits that managed to find the site downwind from their hive. However, maximum search times were only 8.8 minutes for a site situated upwind from a hive. In either case, the times were far too long for bees to have "flown directly out" in response to dance language information.

A direct flight out from the hive should have required only a small fraction of these measured times at the distance involved if bees had been using dance language information. Newly recruited bees obviously had been searching over a vast area of terrain before they were successful, if they arrived at all. The above and other experimental results led Friesen to conclude:

An hypothesis consistent with the data from the previous experiments suggests that a population of searching bees accumulates within an area under the influence of bee and bee-carried odors. A

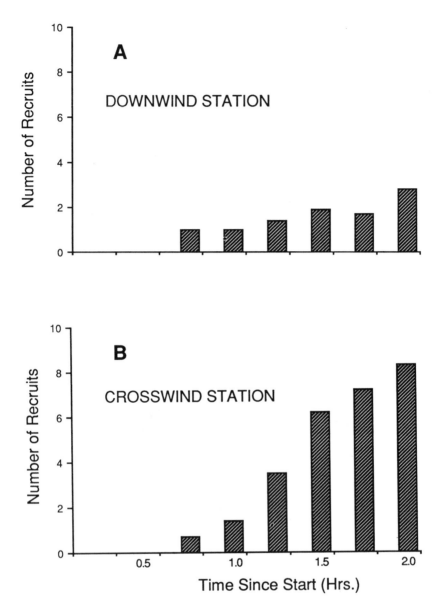

FIGURE 8.11. Recruitment patterns for stations placed in two directions from the hive (after Friesen 1973). A) Arrivals per unit time at a *downwind* site. B) Recruit arrival pattern at a *crosswind* site (compare to the pattern shown in figure 8.2). The two patterns should have been nearly identical if recruits had used "dance language" information.

monitoring station placed in this population of searching bees will receive recruits in numbers and times dependent on the odor of the station and the density of bees searching in that area for the same odor. (1973:121)

Throughout all of the previous experiments (both Friesen's and ours), we had also noticed anomalies with respect to use of the Nasanov gland (scent gland) by successful foragers. Our observations did not fit what might be expected from earlier hypotheses with respect to any possible "function" for that gland (see excursus NG). Once again, expectations did not hold up to reality.

The anomalies we encountered during those years influenced us greatly. Repeatedly we had been led, by the behavior of the bees themselves, to the fact that the prevailing hypotheses that had formed the basis for our original research program were inadequate. It also became increasingly clear to us that the basic concepts underlying research on honey bee recruitment to food sources had slipped out of the realm of scientific hypotheses. Researchers (including us) had instead been trapped by a paradigm hold (the "ruling theory" of Chamberlin [1890] 1965). These concepts were thus "no longer open to question" in the minds of the scientific community.

Disregarding the perils associated with going against conventional wisdom, we moved ahead with our next step: an experimental test of the dance language hypothesis. By now we realized that this would be the first test ever run of that hypothesis, fully twenty years after its inception. That material is the subject of the next two chapters.

9

TRANSITION IN APPROACHES: TESTING THE DANCE LANGUAGE HYPOTHESIS

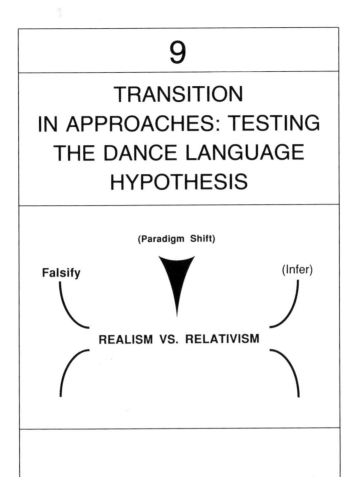

(Paradigm Shift)

Falsify   (Infer)

REALISM VS. RELATIVISM

"How am I to persuade Sir Karl . . . that what he calls a duck can be seen as a rabbit? How am I to show him what it would be like to wear my spectacles when he has already learned to look at everything I can point to through his own?"
—Thomas Kuhn 1970b:3

"Under the method of the ruling theory, the stimulus was directed to the finding of facts for the support of the theory. Under the working hypothesis, the facts are sought for the purpose of ultimate induction and demonstration, the hypothesis being but a means."
—Thomas Chrowder Chamberlin (1890) 1965:755

B iologists generally dismiss deliberations by sociologists, psychologists, and philosophers of science; they apparently feel that
such studies are irrelevant to their research programs. At most they
may endorse a portion of one philosophy when justifying a particular
approach in common use. One of the more evident examples is an
endorsement of Karl Popper's "falsification" approach during hypothesis evaluation, as is done in "null hypothesis" testing.

However, if Atkinson's view that scientists "create images" and
later "convert" others to that image (see our chapter 3) has any merit,
broader input from research done by sociologists, psychologists, and
philosophers could be exploited to facilitate research in biology. Increased self-awareness of the degree to which human involvement
influences research efforts could only be beneficial to the participants.

Teachings from these other fields indicate that traditions followed
in a given field and interpersonal relationships experienced during
one's scientific career largely dictate what approach one uses in research. That means that the basic assumptions relied upon during
experimentation may vary to a far greater degree than biologists have
been willing to admit.

Early on during the honey bee dance language controversy, it became evident to us that the actual experimental evidence obtained by
von Frisch and by us was not a major factor in debates during that
dispute (see Veldink 1989). The challenges we encountered centered
instead on whether the dance language hypothesis and the related sun
compass hypothesis were even open to question. From our current
perspective, each of those hypotheses had evolved from the status of a
hypothesis to one of a ruling paradigm.

Our experimental challenge of the dance language hypothesis, then,
was simply inappropriate behavior on our part in the minds of those
committed to the dance language paradigm. Our situation was similar to the essence of what Kuhn wrote by way of introduction to the
above epigraph:

> Sir Karl [Popper] and I do appeal to the same data; to an uncom-
> mon extent we are seeing the same lines on the same paper; asked
> about those lines and those data, we often give virtually identical
> responses, or at least responses that inevitably seem identical. . . .
> Nevertheless, experiences . . . convince me that our intentions are
> often quite different when we say the same things. Though the lines
> are the same, the figures which emerge from them are not. That is
> why I call what separates us a gestalt switch rather than a disagree-
> ment and also why I am at once perplexed and intrigued about how
> best to explore the separation. (1970b:3)

Much scientific research is simply unplanned, because unexpected results often lead to new insights and experimental protocol. Any shift from one of the major approaches to another, as from one position to another in the theme diagram of this book (see figure 3.1), may well constitute a "gestalt switch," as described by Kuhn. Such a switch by only one or a few members of the scientific community may in turn lead to controversy (if the sociologists, psychologists, and philosophers of science are correct). In that perspective, scientific controversies arise primarily because of fundamental differences in approach and/or attitude.

An emergent controversy thus may well be the result of one laboratory (or research group) suddenly donning "a different pair of spectacles" than had been customarily used in that research field. Those in the wider scientific community may not be able to follow the lead so opened up by one segment of its constituency. The broader community has no access to the same spectacles, because its members remain constrained by traditional attitudes and approaches. On the other hand, the controversies that erupt in science are viewed most often *by the participants* as due either to discrepancies in experimental protocol or to differing interpretations of data.

One of the more recent (and by now well known) examples of difference in perspective by scientists was the work of Nobel Prize–winner Barbara McClintock (on genetic transposition in maize plants). She understood the process she studied long before others could "visualize" the implications of her findings (Keller 1983).

OUR MOVE AROUND THE DIAGRAM

When we shifted from the "verification" approach to a "falsification" approach and actually tested the dance language hypothesis for the first time (Johnson 1967a; Wenner 1967; see also chapter 8 and this chapter, below), we had apparently experienced a "gestalt switch" and adopted another mode of thinking. We had put on a new pair of spectacles.

Scientists have the reputation of welcoming any opinions that differ from theirs. When we submitted articles to journals, however, the hostility expressed by the anonymous reviewers (see, e.g., excursus EXC) cannot be reasonably explained in any way other than that we "wore new spectacles" and now had a totally different perspective than that embraced by the broader community.

The reaction we experienced more closely matched the reaction encountered by Mahoney (1976), who studied referee reaction to manuscripts that did not fit the prevailing paradigm. The heated response generated by his study even included requests for his expulsion from the American Psychological Association (reported in *Science* [1986], p. 1333).

However, one cannot go back to wearing old spectacles once one has donned a better pair. Stated otherwise, one cannot go back and embrace old ideas once new and more adequate perspectives have been gained. As a consequence of our new vision, we no longer could ask the teleological question, "Why do bees dance?" We now saw the problem as an earlier and more fundamental question: how do recruited bees find the food visited by successful foragers? It was that new attitude of ours that permitted us to test the dance language hypothesis for the first time.

Others in our research field, those locked into the dance language paradigm and adhering to the verification approach, could see no reason even to ask the question we now saw as the more important one.

The anomalies we had uncovered (see chapters 5, 7, and 8) altogether constituted strong support for the null hypothesis: "Honey bees do 'not' use the distance and direction information contained in their dance maneuver." That means, in the jargon used in that research approach, that the null hypothesis had not been falsified. Nevertheless, the dance language hypothesis itself remained intact largely because of its acceptance by the scientific community and by its continued repetition in journal articles, in books, and in the popular media.

From our new perspective, those scientists thoroughly entrenched in the verification approach and locked into the dance language paradigm could not appreciate the significance of the anomalies we had uncovered. Apparently, in the minds of members of the scientific community (the Realism school) the anomalies we had found simply did not weaken the honey bee "dance language" hypothesis. Von Frisch had either "discovered" or "proved" that bees have a "language"; a paradigm had replaced the hypothesis.

SINGLE-CONTROL EXPERIMENTS, "POSITIVE" RESULTS, AND DIRECT EVIDENCE

The single-control design is the common scientific method for those scientists who work within the verification approach. Von Frisch and all subsequent proponents of the dance language hypothesis, for example, relied almost entirely on the single-control design in their experimentation. In the early phase of our research, when we were attempting to establish the role of sound waves in "the dance language," we had also used the verification approach almost exclusively (e.g., Wenner 1971a:52).

Within the realm of single-control experiments, one can further distinguish between *indirect* evidence (simple correlations) and *direct* evidence (correlations with some *apparent* degree of cause and effect). As indicated above, essentially all of von Frisch's experiments were single-control experiments that yielded indirect evidence (see also chapters 2 and 4). Once we recognized the weakness of that approach in the face of contradictory evidence, we attempted to design an experiment that would leave less room for alternative interpretation.

In our research program (while still functioning within the Realism school and adhering to the dance language paradigm), we attempted to obtain "direct" evidence in support of a bee language. We had planned to send bees out from the hive to a site in a given direction at a given distance by means of an "imitation" dancing bee. While doing so, we planned to either include or not include sound during the artificial dance maneuvers of that imitation bee. Success at sending real bees to a point source in the field when using sound, coupled with failure to do so when not using sound (direct evidence), would implicate the use of that stimulus in a "dance language" of bees.

(Gould, as covered in chapter 13, claimed that he had obtained such direct evidence with the use of a single-control design in his "misdirection" experiments. That interpretation is debatable; see Rosin 1978, 1980a, 1980b; see also our chapters 12 and 13 and excursus NEG.)

THE FALSIFICATION APPROACH AND A SEARCH FOR RIGOR

"Positive" results from single-control experiments, which we now recognize as lacking rigor, still suffice for many of those interested in the outcomes of experiments. Our impression (though new to us at the time) is not new in the annals of science. In 1620 Sir Francis Bacon wrote:

> Besides ... it is the peculiar and perpetual error of the human understanding to be more moved and excited by affirmatives than negatives, whereas it ought duly and regularly to be impartial; nay,

in establishing any true axiom the negative instance is the more powerful. ([1620] 1952: book 1, passage 46)

While the first part of that passage explains the appeal of the single-control design, it is the last thought in that quotation that forms the basis for the null hypothesis and "strong inference" approaches.

Neither is the null hypothesis experimental design any longer considered a panacea, as it was once believed to be and as deeply entrenched as it is in some treatments of methodology (e.g., Mahoney 1976:100–103, 147). That is because an unconscious bias on the part of the experimenter can lead to an experimental design that evades a true test of the null hypothesis. To the uncritical eye, though, the design then may *appear* to "settle the issue" in favor of the hypothesis supposedly being "tested" (by only appearing to be a "negation" of the null hypothesis).

Our own introduction into use of a more effective experimental design had a large sociological component and an important accidental component. The social input occurred while one of us (Wenner) was serving as a discussant at a talk given by Harald Esch at the Salk Institute in 1966 (see excursus SI). Apparently, a group of influential biologists at that event (led by mathematician-theorist Jacob Bronowski) were about to embark on a rather exotic research program to study the brain function. One of the phenomena considered for emphasis in research was the "dance language" of bees. For their research to work, it would have been necessary that bees indeed had a language, that it was precise, and that its use was instinctual.

By the time of that meeting, however, it was already apparent to our research group that learning played an important role in the recruitment of experienced bees (e.g., Johnson and Wenner 1966; see also our chapter 7). However, when our new experimental results ("a relationship between conditioning and communication in honeybees") were described, the audience did not take kindly to the new information. That adverse reaction, in turn, stimulated us to examine critically the experimental designs used by von Frisch to see if his results had truly "proved" that bees have a "language" (see excursus SI).

We could no longer merely insist that von Frisch needed better controls; we had to demonstrate that a need for such controls existed. Once we suspected that basic flaws *could* exist in the foundations of the bee language hypothesis (that is the most difficult part), however, it didn't take us long to find what those flaws might be. Our new spectacles were in place.

Our first task included a careful analysis of the design of von Frisch's "step" and "fan" experiments. We were led to realize fully (for the first time) that the dance language hypothesis was based solely upon circumstantial evidence provided by single-control experiments and, hence, was not "proof" after all (see chapters 2 and 3). Even though our claim to that effect was roundly rejected for many years, there now seems to be general acceptance of that fact (e.g., Gould 1976:241).

As in many single-control designs, there was also a problem with the control stations used in von Frisch's experiments; the control stations, by their geometrical placement, were not equal to one another or to the experimental station, as they must be for adequate control of the experiment (Wenner 1962). That is because each of them would necessarily have an unequal number of stations on either side of it compared to the others (see excursus PN).

Despite the obvious (by now) weaknesses of the experimental design in von Frisch's step and fan experiments, that design has continued to be a mainstay in experiments run by dance language proponents (e.g., Gould 1974, 1975a, 1975b, 1975c).

FAILURE OF THE SINGLE-CONTROL DESIGN

Learning the "ins and outs" of methodology is a slow procedure in the game of science, especially when one learns primarily by trial and error.

As indicated above, it became evident to us that the peculiar experimental design of von Frisch's "step" and "fan" experiments could have been responsible for the "precision" observed by him in his experiments (Wenner 1962; see also excursus PN). Much later we realized that finding positive correlations was quite a different matter from establishing cause and effect (Wenner, Wells, and Rohlf 1967). Finally, we became aware that the time had come, and was actually long overdue, to truly test the dance language hypothesis.

Our first task involved repeating von Frisch's original step and fan experiments, while paying particular attention to the behavior of incoming unmarked recruit bees. We asked, "Were recruits flying directly out from the hive?" as described in print and as believed to be true under the dance language hypothesis.

REPEATING THE STEP EXPERIMENTS
("STUFENVERSUCHEN")

In 1962 von Frisch had stated:

> For almost two decades my colleagues and I have been studying one
> of the most remarkable systems of communication that nature has
> evolved. This is the "language" of the bees; the dancing movements
> by which forager bees direct their hivemates, with great precision,
> to a source of food. . . . When [the recruited bees] fly out, they search
> only in the neighborhood of the indicated range, ignoring dishes set
> closer in or farther away. (1962:78)

Since the above statements are both simple and unequivocal, they
provide the basis for a test of the hypothesis. By this time we were
also aware of the importance of locality odor (see chapter 8), and set
up our experiment in a relatively dry, open grassy area. In the absence
of rain for several months, this area apparently had few volatile odors
that could serve as cues for searching bees. In addition, the wind blew
lightly from the southwest each day of the experimental series. We
exploited this constancy of wind and set up a line of stations across
the wind direction (see figure 9.1), effectively neutralizing any effect
of wind while testing the hypothesis.

At the end of the training period, only forty-three marked bees
regularly foraged at the 400-meter distance (all unmarked arrivals
had been killed in the several days preceding any data gathering).
That meant that those forty-three regular foragers would travel only
between the 400-meter site and the hive and could presumably execute a dance maneuver in the parent hive that would provide "precise" location information (direction and distance) to their hivemates.
The three other sites had dishes of scented sugar solution and served
as controls; no bees were permitted to return to the hive from those
sites.

The experimental design, as described here and as conducted by
von Frisch, constitutes a single-control experiment. *If* each of the
experimental and control stations were equal in attractiveness *and if*
recruits flew out only in the proper direction and to the proper distance, as could be read by us from the dance maneuver, *then* one
could suspect that they had *used* the information contained in the
dance.

The three control dishes, *if* equal in attractiveness to each other

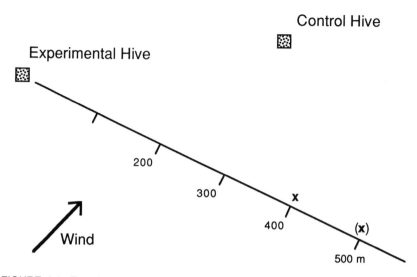

FIGURE 9.1. Experimental arrangement for the double-control experiment, a test of recruit ability to *use* distance information (after figure 1 in Wenner 1967). Dark-colored foragers from the "experimental hive" collected sugar solution only *either* at the 400-meter site (marked by an x) *or* at the 500-meter site (marked by an x in parentheses) in different experiments. Light-colored bees from the "control hive" collected solution at dishes located at all four marked sites.

Predictions of the dance language hypothesis would necessitate greatly different results in recruitment patterns for the two hives if searching recruits could *use* distance information.

and to the experimental dish, could collect any recruits that had "read" the dance incorrectly or that had "used" the information incorrectly after leaving the hive.

Our first runs with this experimental design yielded results consistent with the predictions of the language hypothesis (see figure 9.2). Almost 80 percent of the successful unmarked recruits arrived at the 400-meter site, while apparently "ignoring dishes set closer in or farther away" as stated by von Frisch. Our successful repeat of von Frisch's step experiment also indicated clearly: 1) that our training method could not be faulted (see excursus GT) and 2) that the wind apparently did not influence recruit distribution (see von Frisch 1967b). On the surface, it appeared that the unmarked recruits had "used" the direction and distance information contained in the dance maneuver, which they had attended before leaving the hive.

As was true in the von Frisch results, though, the recruits did *too* well. Almost 80 percent arrived at the 400-meter station, but at most

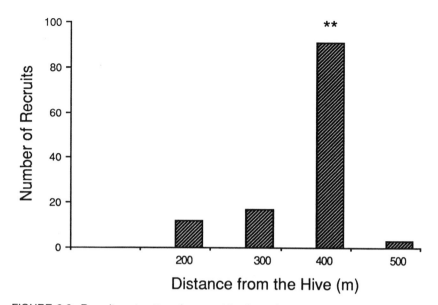

FIGURE 9.2. Recruitment pattern for searching bees from the experimental hive. Recruits ended up primarily at the 400-meter station (double asterisk) when foragers from the other hive were not permitted to travel between their hive and feeding stations (derived from data obtained in experiment 1, table 1 of Wenner 1967). The results matched those obtained earlier by von Frisch (e.g., 1954, his figure 42).

only 40 percent should have done so on the basis of the information contained in the dance maneuver. That is because forager bees will perform differently from one another and will even perform differently between runs themselves; the result will be an increased error with respect to expected performance (Wenner 1962).

Several repeats of the von Frisch experimental protocol, along with careful observations of approaching unmarked recruits, provided new insight into the problem. With binoculars we could observe recruits coming into the station from downwind in the zigzag pattern characteristic of animals traveling upwind to an odor source (see excursus OS).

That direct observation meant that recruits were obviously approaching along a path perpendicular to the line of flight between hive and station (instead of "flying directly out"). Furthermore, they approached the stations from a distance downwind that was much greater than the search area expected. If these recruits had been using direction and distance information obtained from a dancing bee, they should have started their odor-search pattern from only a fraction of the distance downwind that was actually observed.

While watching these recruits as they came close to the stations, we also noticed that the flight behavior of these searchers differed markedly according to whether they were coming into the experimental station or toward the control stations. That should not have been the case if the latter were true "controls." Recruits arriving at the control stations also behaved more erratically and most often did not land at all (one of our requisite conditions for their being tallied as arrivals).

By contrast, recruits heading toward the experimental station almost always flew directly in after their earlier zigzag flight. They then landed alongside a regular forager and began imbibing the sugar solution.

After those direct (and anomalous) observations, we installed several visual and odor markers that might permit recruits to land more readily at the control sites (since the sight and odor of feeding bees were already present at the feeding station). Brown and yellow pipe-cleaner segments (the length of a bee) twisted together resulted in less hesitation on the part of approaching recruits; some propolis (bee gum) from the parent hive made an even greater difference.

Reruns of the von Frisch–type experiments with these additional visual and odor cues provided results far different (Wenner 1967) than those obtained when the same experiments were run as von Frisch had done them (as in figure 9.2). One lack of a necessary control in the von Frisch design thus became apparent. The experimental station always had bees landing at the dish, but the control stations had no such visual or odor cues.

There still remained the possibility (as is so often true in single-control experiments) that there might be something special about the 400-meter site. Was some unknown odor cue present at or near the 400-meter site but not near the others? Or, as suggested by von Frisch (1967b) later, do the two rows of trees deflect the wind (or bees)?

We began again with a new set of thirty-eight foragers trained to travel only to the 500-meter station and set up an intermediate control station at 350 meters. The results were even more dramatic. At the end of a three-hour period, 96 percent of the recruits had arrived at the 500-meter station (see figure 9.3); the novice recruits had certainly not "been misled" by the dish set in closer to the hive and had not been "diverted by wind."

FIGURE 9.3. A repeat of the experiment shown in figure 9.2, after foragers visited food provided only at the 500-meter location (double asterisk). This time a single control station was placed at 350 meters. The recruitment was again compatible with results obtained by von Frisch earlier and in accord with expectations of the dance language hypothesis.

STRONG INFERENCE: DOUBLE-CONTROL EXPERIMENTS

Although widely used in sociology and psychology, the double-control experimental design is rarely employed by biologists who work within the Realism school format, regardless of whether they practice the verification approach or the falsification approach in their research. Neither could we claim real insight into the need for that experimental protocol during our early years in bee research; instead, the Salk Institute experience (see excursus SI) led us to use double-control experiments, largely by trial and error.

We finally fully recognized the nature of the design flaw exposed during the Salk Institute episode, while later repeating von Frisch's classic experiments (both with and without additional controls). Anomalous results kept arising (see chapter 8). After deciding that we had to repeat von Frisch's experiments with even tighter controls, we wondered how we could make control stations more nearly identical to the experimental station.

Once again, we did not rely upon any training in methodology, but upon happenstance. Quite by chance we had a second hive in the area (the "Control Hive" in figure 9.1). That hive differed from what we considered our "experimental" hive at the time only in that its bees were light-colored instead of dark-colored. Those light-colored bees were genetically marked by their lack of black pigment; their biology and behavior were not different from those in the other hive.

The availability of light-colored bees in that remote hive (downwind from the forager flight line, which passed between the first hive and one of the stations) permitted us to train a few bees from that second hive (designated here as a "control" hive) to *each* of the four stations (control *as well as* experimental stations). At the same time we allowed foragers from the experimental hive to visit only one experimental station.

We later realized that each hive and its set of foragers at one or at all four stations then actually served as a control against what happened with the other one. That is, dark-colored foragers could only provide dance information in their hive about one of the stations. Light-colored foragers could provide dance information in their hive about all four of the stations. Furthermore (and as part of our original goal), there would be foragers from at least one of the hives routinely visiting all four of the sites, not just the one experimental station as in the von Frisch experiments.

The unexpected development ultimately most important to us, then, was that we no longer had to "prove" or "disprove" a hypothesis in which we might have a vested interest (consciously or unconsciously). The ultimate distribution of searching bees would reveal whether they behaved according to the expectations of the "dance language" hypothesis or in some other manner. We could not inadvertently alter the results.

The experiment was ready to run. If a vast majority of the dark recruits again arrived at the 500-meter station visited by foragers from their hive (as in figure 9.3), while ignoring stations set closer to their parent hive, the dance language hypothesis would remain intact. That conclusion would be reinforced if a nearly equal number of light-colored recruits arrived at *each* of the four stations visited by foragers from their hive; the dance language hypothesis would also survive.

Under the dance language hypothesis, then, different distributions were predicted for recruit arrivals from the two hives. To repeat: each hive and its population of searching bees thus served as a control for the other system. Each of the two hives was both experimental and control, in that sense.

When the experiment had been run, and after the results had all been tallied, it was evident that the recruit bees from *both* hives had ignored any "dance language" information they may have obtained while contacting foragers in their parent hives. It was immediately evident that recruits were *neither* using "dance language" information *nor* searching strictly at random! There was another component in the undescribed pattern of their search behavior.

We ran three experiments in the series; the design and protocol of the second and third experiments were tightened up ever more as we became increasingly aware of the degree to which odor influenced the behavior of searching bees. The third experiment of the series (run for three hours) was designed to put the dance language hypothesis to its most severe test to that date. In that experiment we allowed fourteen dark foragers to regularly visit only the 500-meter station (see the double asterisks in figure 9.4), since we already knew that recruits

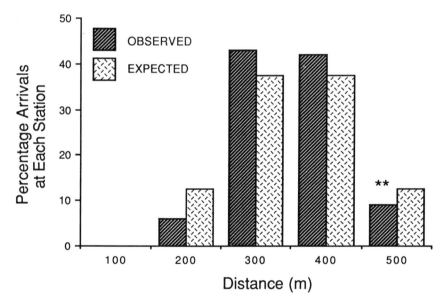

FIGURE 9.4. A test of the dance language hypothesis, when foragers from the experimental hive visited only the 500-meter site (double asterisks) and when foragers from control hives were free to visit all four stations (derived from data of experiment 3, table 1 of Wenner 1967). The arrival pattern for recruits from the experimental hive (dark bars; compare to results shown in figure 9.2) no longer supported the dance language hypothesis. Insertion of a new control had altered the experimental results.

The recruitment pattern now closely approximated a theoretical binomial distribution (speckled bars), a result that correlated with the distance of each station from the center of all stations.

from the parent hive could easily find that station (as shown in figure 9.3). Foragers from the other hive visited all four stations.

The results were striking. During that three-hour test period, sixty-seven unmarked recruits from the parent hive arrived at the four stations. In contrast to the results shown in figure 9.3 (in which 96 percent of the recruits had arrived at the 500-meter station), however, 85 percent of the recruits had now arrived at the two central stations (see figure 9.4). Only six dark-colored recruits (9 percent of the total) were collected at the 500-meter station to which they had presumably been directed by dance language information. That outcome thus negated the von Frisch–type results that we had obtained earlier when we ran the single-control design experiment.

The recruitment pattern for recruits from the hive containing light-colored bees mirrored that of the first hive, even though foragers from that hive routinely visited *each* of the feeding stations in equal numbers (as indicated by the single asterisks in figure 9.5). Of the 409 light-colored recruits caught and killed, 92 percent had arrived at the two central stations (see figure 9.5). This result thereby also differed markedly from that expected by the dance language hypothesis; only about 50 percent of the light-colored recruits should have arrived at the central stations if they had been using information obtained from waggle dances.

The recruitment pattern surprised us, even though we no longer expected data consistent with the dance language hypothesis. We had still expected a nearly equal distribution at all four of the stations for recruits from each hive (a uniform random pattern) once we had made the stations nearly equal in "attractiveness" (an equal number of foragers feeding at each station). That is because we still had no concept of what type of recruit search pattern could replace the dance language hypothesis (see excursus OS).

The results we had obtained (see figures 9.4 and 9.5) actually formed a multinomial distribution, a mathematical pattern often obtained in genetics experiments. The implication was that the population of searching recruits was sorting itself out in a probabilistic manner, based on the distance of each station from the center of all stations. That line of reasoning led us to suspect that the body of searching recruits was heading toward the center of all odor from some indeterminate point far downwind from the line of stations (Johnson 1967a; Wenner 1967, 1974; see also excursus OS).

To illustrate that last point, figures 9.4 and 9.5 each have a set of speckled bars alongside the data bars themselves. Those bars represent the recruit distributions one would expect to get from a *popula-*

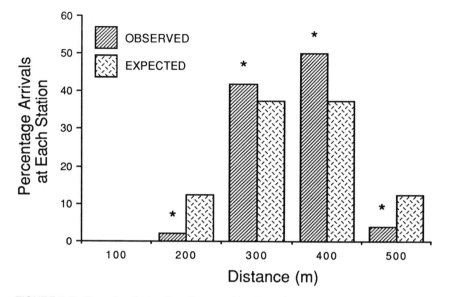

FIGURE 9.5. Recruit arrival pattern for searching bees from the "control hive." All four stations were visited by foragers from that hive, as indicated by single asterisks. Instead of near equal recruitment at all four stations, as expected from the dance language hypothesis, the pattern again fit a mathematical model (as shown by speckled bars). The searching recruits from both hives thus merely ended up at stations according to the distance of each from the center of them all (compare to figure 9.4).

tion of searching bees that had merely sorted itself out according to the distance of each station from the center of them all.

INSERTING BETTER CONTROLS INTO THE FAN EXPERIMENTS

Elsewhere in this volume we illustrated how the placement of feeding stations in the von Frisch step and fan experiments (e.g., von Frisch 1954) could dictate the distribution of recruit arrivals (see chapter 6 and excursus PN). We concluded in that chapter and excursus (and earlier, in Wenner 1962) that the very design of the experiment could enhance the apparent "precision" of "dance language" use.

In addition to a symmetrical design, von Frisch also conducted some fan experiments that lacked symmetry on either side of the line of flight between hive and feeding station (see, e.g., figure 6.2A). In that design the results could not be ascribed merely to a search for the center of all odor sources.

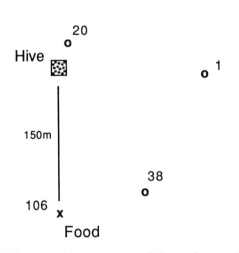

FIGURE 9.6. Experimental arrangement of hive and scent stations (as in figure 6.2A) for one of von Frisch's direction experiments (after von Frisch 1947, figure 9–actually a variation of the "fan" design, with feeding station at x). The number near each scent post represents the number of searching bees counted there.

Figure 9.6 (a repeat of figure 6.2A) shows one such example; re-cruited bees apparently "flew with great precision" to the same station frequented by the foragers and apparently ignored stations located in a different direction or set closer to the hive. As seen above, though, control stations again lacked the presence of feeding bees and were thus not equivalent to the feeding station, as they should have been if they were to serve as proper controls.

Dennis Johnson (1967a) repeated the von Frisch half-fan experiment. He set up an arc of three control stations and one (experimental) feeding station beyond a control station at one end of the array. He initially obtained results (see figure 9.7) similar to those reported by von Frisch (as in figure 9.6). For clarity and to permit better comparisons, we also present Johnson's results as a histogram (see figure 9.8A).

Then, by moving the hive containing light-colored bees, which had been used as a "control" in the earlier experiments, adjacent to his experimental hive, Johnson could train light-colored foragers to visit each of the four stations. At the same time, foragers from the experi-

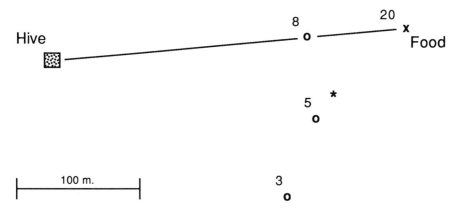

FIGURE 9.7. Experimental arrangement of hive and feeding stations for Dennis John-son's repeat of von Frisch's direction experiment (after Johnson 1967a, figure 1, second series). The numbers beside each station (*Feeding Station, North, Middle,* and *South,* respectively) represent numbers of recruit arrivals at each.

mental hive (dark bees) could visit *only* the experimental feeding station.

Johnson then found that the distribution of recruit arrivals from the "experimental" hive (dark-colored bees) had shifted dramatically with the introduction of regular visitation by light-colored foragers at each of the stations (see figure 9.8B). Dark-colored bees had now ended up primarily at or near the station nearest to the center of all stations (the "center of moment"); he wrote: "most recruits [were] collected at the middle site when all stations became more similar in attractiveness" (Johnson 1967a:845).

Furthermore, light-colored recruits from the "control" hive again exhibited the same distribution pattern as those recruit arrivals from the "experimental" hive. It was evident that most recruits from both hives had arrived at the station closest to the "center of moment" of all four stations. In doing so, they had obviously ignored any infor-mation presumably obtained from the waggle dance before leaving the parent hive.

One can also calculate the number of recruits that should have arrived at the four stations if each had been heading somewhat toward the center of all stations and if the body of them had then randomly ended up in a multinomial distribution. One need only measure the distance of each station from the center of all stations (the center of moment), calculate its inverse, and compute the expected percentage

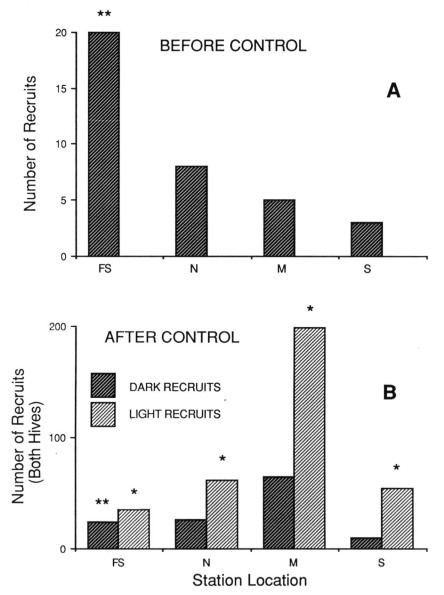

FIGURE 9.8. Results obtained by Johnson at the four feeding stations both before (A) and after (B) insertion of the new control, the new control being visitation at all four stations by foragers from the "control hive" (dervied from data in Johnson 1967b, experiment 2B in his table 1). The double asterisk denotes the station visited by regular foragers from the experimental hive. Single asterisks indicate vision by foragers from the control hive. A) Johnson's results corresponded with those obtained by von Frisch before insertion of the new control. B) After insertion of the new control, recruits from both hives ended up primarily at or near the station closest to the center of all four stations.

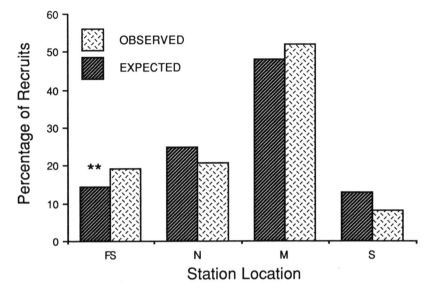

FIGURE 9.9. Results actually obtained (dark bars) compared with the mathematical model of expected results from an odor-search hypothesis (speckled bars). It is clear that the searching recruits in Johnson's experiments had become distributed at the four stations as a function of their distance from the center of all stations.

The population of searching bees from the "experimental hive" (dark-colored bees) was not using direction information obtained from dancing bees, or they would have arrived primarily at the feeding station (FS, as they had done earlier, as shown in figure 9.8A).

of searching bees on the basis of the distance of any one site from the center of all sites. The closest station to the center of all stations should get the most recruits under that model.

We computed the expected distribution under those assumptions; the body of searching recruits had evidently performed remarkably close to that model (see figure 9.9). In fact, the distribution of searching dark bees did not differ significantly from that predicted by the multinomial distribution model (chi-square n.s.; n = 125). The distribution of searching recruits, however, differed strikingly from any results one might predict on the basis of the dance language hypothesis.

It was at about this time that we fully recognized a paradox in the von Frisch step and fan experimental designs. A station at the end of an array physically cannot have a station on either side of it, as the other control stations do. For that reason, end stations can never be considered equivalent to the other control stations. Therefore, experiments of this design cannot be expected to yield an equal number of recruits at each station, even if all stations were "equal in attractiveness." (Despite that paradoxical flaw in the experimental design, dance language proponents such as Gould and Schricker continued to use the fan design; see chapters 12 and 13.)

The most important outcome from all of these experiments for us was that we were moving into a position to appreciate more fully the 1890 Chamberlin statement quoted in chapter 3:

> Intellectual methods have taken three phases in the history of progress thus far. . . . These three methods may be designated, first, the method of the ruling theory; second, the method of the working hypothesis; and, third, the method of multiple working hypotheses. ([1890] 1965:754)

That is, through a several-year period in our research program we had moved from "the method of the ruling theory" (single-control experiments) to "the method of the working hypothesis" (double-control experiments). We were now ready to explore more fully "the method of multiple working hypotheses" (see chapter 10). Our clockwise movement around the theme diagram (see figure 3.1) had continued.

10

MULTIPLE INFERENCE
AND
"CRUCIAL" EXPERIMENTS

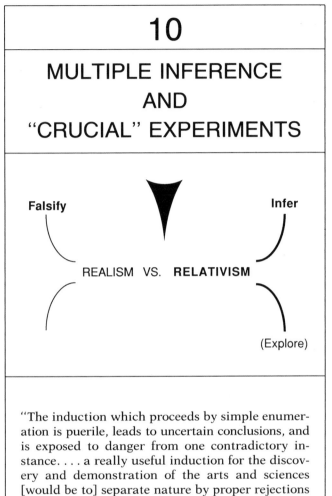

Falsify

Infer

REALISM VS. **RELATIVISM**

(Explore)

"The induction which proceeds by simple enumeration is puerile, leads to uncertain conclusions, and is exposed to danger from one contradictory instance. . . . a really useful induction for the discovery and demonstration of the arts and sciences [would be to] separate nature by proper rejections and exclusions, and then conclude for the affirmative, after collecting a sufficient number of negatives.

—Sir Francis Bacon (1620) 1952:book 1,
passage 105

"Conscientiously followed, the method of the working hypothesis [e.g., the null hypothesis approach] is a marked improvement upon the method of the ruling theory; but it has its defects—defects which are perhaps best expressed by the ease with which the hypothesis becomes a controlling idea. To guard against this, the method of the multiple working hypotheses is urged."

—Thomas Chrowder Chamberlin (1890) 1965:756

"It is clear why [strong inference] makes for rapid and powerful progress. . . . Any conclusion that is not an exclusion is insecure and must be re-checked. Any delay in recycling to the next set of hypotheses is only a delay."

—*John R. Platt 1964:347*

John Platt (1964) published "Strong Inference" two years before we ran our double-control experiments, (see, e.g., our chapter 9; Johnson 1967a; Wenner 1967). A year later (1965) Platt persuaded the editor of *Science* to reprint "The Method of Multiple Working Hypotheses," written by Thomas Chrowder Chamberlin in 1890. Platt's interest in the subject grew out of his concern for the striking difference he noticed in the rate of progress that existed between various fields of science (see chapter 3).

Our own appreciation of how bees might be recruited to crops by means of odor would have been greatly expedited if we had known at the inception of our research program the implications of the writings of Chamberlin and Platt. Instead, we were only beginning to appreciate the utility of attempting to "falsify" hypotheses. Our attitude at the time did not conform so much to the null hypothesis approach (as advocated by Popper) as it did with Chamberlin's views (see the above epigraph).

We were also only beginning to recognize the social and psychological impact of our findings on the scientific community, as recognized by Kuhn ([1962] 1970a). Gestalt switches were now possible for us, although apparently not for others in our field, but we had learned the hard way. Our design of a crucial (strong inference) experiment thus had to emerge through a trial-and-error process rather than by benefit of an earlier education in the essence of science.

CRUCIAL EXPERIMENTS

Unfortunately, the phrases "crucial experiment" and "critical experiment" have both generic and specific meanings in science. Under the verification approach (see chapter 3), "crucial" or "critical" may merely mean "decisive" in a generic sense (e.g., von Frisch 1947:11, 1973:630). That is particularly true when the evidence obtained from experimentation convinces key members of the scientific community that the hypothesis under consideration has received *compelling* support during experiments. However, compelling evidence to one person may not be convincing to another.

By contrast, the *strong inference* or "crucial" approach involves an *a priori* experimental design that permits the validation of only one of two or more predetermined and mutually exclusive interpretations for any forthcoming set of results. That is, one set of results from an experiment would validate one of the hypotheses while simultaneously negating the other(s). The converse would also be true. The true "crucial experiment" thus precludes ad hoc rationalizations at the conclusion of the experiment about any "unfavorable" results that might have been obtained.

Von Frisch had earlier (1920) embraced the possibility that recruits use only odor and spend much time searching for an odor source after leaving the hive (see our chapter 4). In fact, he held that view until the late 1930s (von Frisch 1939) and probably until 1944, when he "created the image" of a "dance language" among bees (see our chapter 6). Both interpretations (dance language and odor search) were thus available to von Frisch when he proposed the dance language hypothesis.

As indicated in chapter 4, von Frisch (1947) and many other dance language supporters (including us initially) all missed an opportunity to follow up on a lead Maeterlinck (1901) had provided in his earlier account of the behavior of searching recruits (see also our chapter 3). Von Frisch's adherence to the verification approach instead altered the course his experimentation could have taken. He was unwittingly at the threshold of designing a true "crucial experiment" when he wrote (as quoted in chapter 6):

> The observation of the different conduct in the hive of those bees foraging near and far had brought confirmation with unexpected clarity. It did not seem advisable to check this by following up the behaviour of the newcomers. . . . there seemed a better way of making a critical test. (1947:11)

Von Frisch's notion of "a critical test," however, was generic in the above sense, rather than in the specific sense; he merely wished to seek further supportive evidence. If von Frisch had been more sensitive to the inference approach, he could, for instance, have designed an experiment that measured flight time for searching recruits as they traveled between hive and feeding station (as Gould, his co-workers, and Esch and Bastian did later; see our chapter 12). Two of the possible mutually exclusive hypotheses then would have been:

1. the flying time of searching recruits matches closely that of experienced foragers; or
2. the flying time of searching recruits is very long compared to the "beeline" flight time of experienced foragers.

It was more than twenty years after von Frisch formulated his dance language hypothesis that several groups gathered evidence that indicated that the second of the two above hypotheses is the better one (Esch and Bastian 1970; Gould, Henerey, and MacLeod 1970; Friesen 1973; see also excursus NEG). Recruits obviously search for a considerable length of time before they find a station (if they succeed at all).

As indicated in chapter 3, von Frisch also could have repeated Maeterlinck's experiment (a crucial design). Instead, von Frisch "concluded for the affirmative" (Bacon [1620] 1952) and went on to search for additional verification for the image he had created: "Bees have a symbolic 'dance language.' "

RECRUIT BUILDUP WITH TIME

Once we recognized that the use of odor alone could be the basis for a viable alternative to the dance language hypothesis of von Frisch, we were ever on the alert for other evidence that might help us understand the behavior of searching recruits. One of the more striking anomalies we had found earlier was that of remote interference with the distribution of new recruits (see figure 8.3 and chapter 8).

Another anomaly found was that of the very peculiar pattern of recruit arrival during each three-hour run of our experiments (see figure 10.1, which is a repeat of figure 8.2); the number of successful recruits *per unit time* had increased uniformly during each day, even with a constant number of round trips per unit time by regular foragers. As indicated in our discussion of odor in chapter 8, under the dance language hypothesis one would expect instead a *constant number* of new arrivals per unit time whenever a constant number of foragers made round trips between hive and feeding station.

Odor accumulation in the system, of course, was one explanation for the anomalous pattern observed, since the recruit arrival pattern paralleled the *cumulative* number of trips made by experienced foragers; the pattern certainly did not correspond to the constant number of round trips made per unit time. Our experience led us to suspect that the odor in the food collected by experienced foragers apparently accumulated in the hive, both within a day and between days.

Any such odor accumulation, in turn, could lead to an increase in the efficiency of odor search by recruited bees. That is, an increase in odor stimulus in the hive with time, due to repeated forager trips, would provide an ever more powerful cue for recruits before they left the hive. An ever higher percentage of recruits would then be able to locate the food source visited by foragers in the field. We felt that this

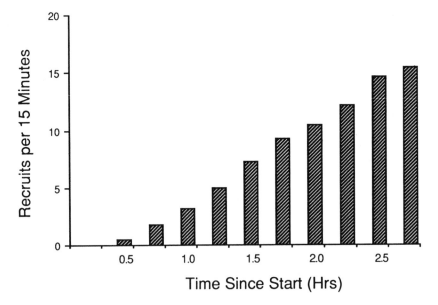

FIGURE 10.1. Observed pattern of recruit buildup with time (same as figure 8.2). The number of recruits caught per 15-minute period increased steadily through time, on average, even though the number of foragers making round trips remained constant.

odor accumulation phenomenon could be exploited in an experimental design; that line of thought eventually led to the next step, the design of a "crucial" experiment.

OUR "CRUCIAL" EXPERIMENT

It seemed obvious to us that potential recruits do not "fly directly out" from their hive (see excursus NEG). Searching recruits instead somehow get into a position from which they can head upwind toward a familiar odor that they had encountered while still in their parent hive (see excursus OS). They then apparently rely on odor cues and begin their *oriented* search pattern from downwind of the food sources to which they have been recruited.

With that knowledge at hand, we reasoned that any odor accumulation in the system (as indicated above and in chapter 8) should enhance success in the field. A greater amount of odor in the hive would expedite search behavior.

These points taken all together (along with the other information reviewed in chapters 5–9) suggested to us that a simple odor-search hypothesis was sufficient and parsimonious; it eliminated the need for the more complicated dance language hypothesis (application of Occam's razor). Eventually, we thought of a mutually exclusive experimental design that involved the direct pitting of those two hypotheses against one another.

Our idea was to run a twenty-four day experimental sequence of three hours each day, with recruit bees placed in a position whereby they could use *either* "dance language" information *or* odor information. That experiment would then be a specific, rather than a generic, "crucial" design.

On most days we would predict results similar to those von Frisch published, since the basic protocol (single-control design) would be the same as the one that he used. On preset experimental days interspersed among those control days, however, we would provide conditions under which each of the two hypotheses would *exclusively* predict results. That is, if recruit bees used "dance language" information they would largely ignore odor information, and vice versa. These experimental days would then test which of the two hypotheses best corresponded to the results obtained, relative to the presumed search pattern of potential recruits.

We set up a hive and three potential feeding stations on a relatively level open grassland (dry annual grasses), with no trees nearby (see figure 10.2). The stations were placed far enough apart that the middle control site was well outside the area supposedly indicated by dances of foragers feeding at the two outside stations.

We then allowed ten experienced bees (numbered foragers) to visit each of the two outside stations for more than two weeks, in order to eliminate any unmarked strays left over from the training period (see excursus GT). During that time and later, these experienced foragers never visited the intermediate station. All recruits (unmarked visitors) were captured and killed. According to the dance language hypothesis, regular foragers could thus perform oriented dance maneuvers in the hive, dances that supposedly indicated only the location of the two outside stations.

The mutually exclusive feature of the experimental design hinged upon the fact that we never provided the standard marking odor (clove oil scent) at all three sites on the same day. That is, clove oil–scented sugar solution was *either* placed at the two outside stations *or* at the central station (or a few times at neither). Also, as indicated above, experienced foragers visited only the two outside stations throughout the twenty-four day period.

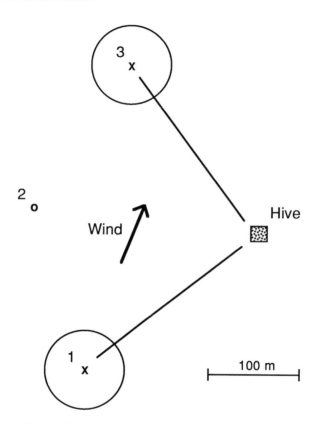

FIGURE 10.2. Hive and feeding station arrangement for the "crucial experiment" (after Wenner, Wells, and Johnson 1969). Foragers were permitted to collect food at sites 1 and 3 but never at 2. They could thus presumably provide direction and distance information in their hive for the outer sites but not for the middle site. The circles denote the predicted area of language effectiveness if searching bees *used* information obtained from dancing bees in the hive.

Predictions were then straightforward. If recruits used dance language information, they should always arrive at the two outside stations, regardless of odor location. On the other hand, if odor was the guiding factor in their search pattern, they should arrive at the central station when odor was present exclusively at that station (thereby ignoring "dance language" information).

(A third outcome was also possible and is often mentioned in informal discussions, a posteriori, without regard for the results actually obtained. That rationalization is that *some* recruits use odor and/or language *some of the time*. If such an ad hoc explanation were true,

TABLE 10.1. Total number of recruits received per day and the experimental procedure at the three sites.

| Day | Procedure | Recruitment (No. at each site) | | | Nasanov Gland Exposure |
		Site 1	Site 2	Site 3	
1	Scent at 1 and 3	42		71	31.0
2	No scent at 1 and 3, scent at 2	15	38	3	134.5
3	Scent at 1 and 3	89		76	71.5
4	No scent at 1 and 3	20		7	182.0
5	Scent at 1 and 3	87		90	94.5
6	Scent at 1 and 3	70		55	82.0
7	No scent at 1 and 3, scent at 2	4	51	0	139.5
8	Scent at 1 and 3	111		101	136.5
9	No scent at 1, 2, or 3	0	3	17	223.0
10	Scent at 1 and 3	44		90	149.0
11	Scent at 1 and 3	159		89	160.0
12	No scent at 1 and 3, scent at 2	4	91	5	253.0
13	Scent at 1 and 3	102		61	92.0
14	No scent at 1, 2, or 3	6	2	5	161.5
15	Scent at 1 and 3	93		87	87.5
16	2d scent at 1 and 3, 1st scent at 2	2	44	0	82.0
17	Scent at 1 and 3	71		29	55.5
18–22	[Separate experimental series, scent at 1 and (or) 3]				
23	Scent at 1 and 3	68		32	168.5
24	Scent, but no bees at 1, 2, and 3	1	0	0	0.0

SOURCE; Table 1 in Wenner, Wells, and Johnson 1969.

NOTE: Foragers never visited the control site (no. 2), and ten bees made a relatively constant number of trips per unit time to the experimental sites (nos. 1 and 3). On day 7 only five of the regular foragers arrived at site 3. On day 16 a second scent (0.13 ml of oil of peppermint per liter of 1.5 molar sucrose solution) was used at each experimental site (no peppermint scent had accumulated in the hive previous to this time). The number of times the Nasanov gland was exposed is the average for sites 1 and 3.

however, then recruits should have arrived at all three stations in an unpredictable manner. That did not happen; results were remarkably consistent; see table 10.1.)

As indicated, the experimental sequence was varied throughout the twenty-four-day period (see table 10.1), with the fourteenth and twenty-fourth days serving as special controls. On the twenty-fourth day all foragers were killed, so that none of them could return and recruit others; only one recruit arrived. That control thus revealed that regular forager trips were necessary for recruitment.

The converse control was run on day 14. On that day no scent was provided at any of the three stations. When we provided no scent anywhere, very few recruits were successful, despite a high level of Nasanov gland exposure (see table 10.1 and below) and a predictable higher level of dancing in the hive (Wells and Wenner 1971; see also our chapter 8, above).

The stage was now set. One or two days' use of scented solution at the two outside stations preceded a day on which the same scented solution was furnished only at the central test station (see table 10.1). The two mutually exclusive sets of results could now reveal which information searching recruits had used as they traveled between hive and feeding place.

Some of the results did not surprise us. Recruits performed as expected by both the dance language hypothesis and the odor-search hypothesis on control days (1, 3, 5, 6, 8, 10, 11, 13, 15, 17, and 23), when the language was *not* put to a test.

Results obtained on experimental days, on the other hand, contrasted sharply with predictions of the dance language hypothesis (when odor cues *of the day before* competed with presumed "use" of dance language information). If searching recruits had used their "dance language" information on those experimental days (2, 4, 7, 9, 12, and 16) they should have arrived only at the two outside stations. If they had used the odor *of the day before* on those days, they would have arrived primarily at the central station.

The arrival of recruits predominantly at the central station during experimental days (see table 10.1) indicated to us that recruits, while conducting their search, had ignored any "dance language" information they might have obtained before leaving the hive.

In summary, on the various days when the two outside stations had scent in the food, recruitment was prevalent at those two stations (see figure 10.3), as expected both by the odor search hypothesis and by the dance language hypothesis. The cumulative nature of the pattern of success during each three-hour period, however, differed from that expected by the implied predictions of the language hypothesis (see above). Recruitment was not uniform throughout the three-hour period as one would expect to be the case for a set number of round trips made per unit time by regular foragers.

However, when only the central station had odor in the food, the searching recruits primarily ended up there (see figure 10.4B). By contrast, they failed to arrive at the same time in appreciable num-

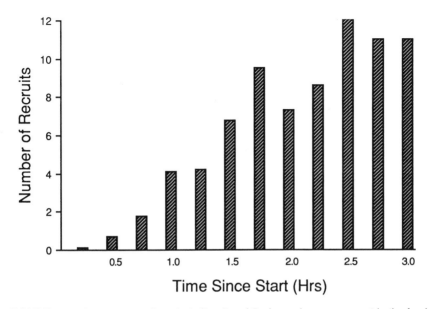

FIGURE 10.3. Average recruitment at sites 1 and 3 when odor was present in the food and when no station 2 was in place. (Note similarity to results shown in figure 10.1 for another experiment.)

bers at the two outside stations, stations to which they had presumably been directed by the "dance language" information (see figure 10.4A). The results on those control days thereby supported an odor-search hypothesis while simultaneously contradicting the predictions of the dance language hypothesis. (Hence the terms "mutually exclusive" or "crucial" design.)

Results obtained during a particular three-day sequence (days 15–17 in table 10.1) were especially revealing. On the first and third of those three days, the marking scent (clove oil) was provided at the outside stations; recruitment was then heavy. On the intervening day, however, while the clove scent was provided at the central (test) station, peppermint scent was added to the food at the two outside stations routinely visited by foragers.

Regular foragers now returned to their hive *with* an odor stimulus *and* could also presumably indicate by their dances the location of the two outside stations. However, no appreciable peppermint odor accumulation would have occurred in the hive during such a short span of time.

That new condition did not alter the results. Recruits again arrived

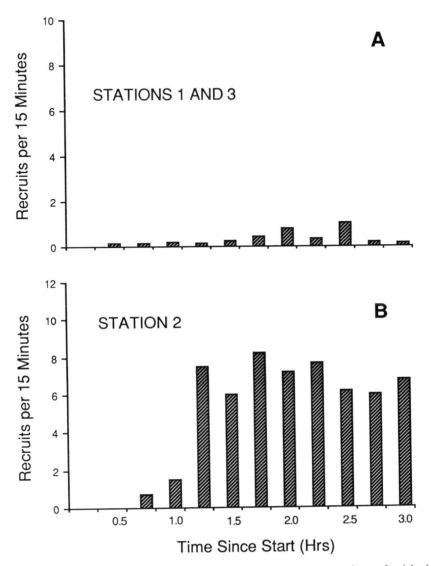

FIGURE 10.4. Average recruitment at all three sites when odor was no longer furnished in the food at stations 1 and 3. A) Although the dance maneuvers of experienced foragers continued to contain information about the presence of sites 1 and 3, and even though Nasanov gland use was very high (see table 10.1), recruits generally could not find those two stations supposedly indicated to them by the dance. B) Instead, recruits arrived at site 2 (not indicated by forager dances) in great numbers when the type of odor that had been provided *the day before* was furnished there instead of at sites 1 and 3. Contrast the pattern obtained with results shown in figure 10.1; here odor accumulation could not occur in the hive since none was being brought in.

preferentially at the central station that was marked by the *odor used in the food the day before* during the intervening day (day 16), rather than at the two outside stations. That happened despite the fact that dances presumably indicated those two outside stations *and* despite the fact that both outside stations were now marked with a specific odor as well.

In all, the evidence obtained during this twenty-four-day sequence provided strong support for an as yet ill-defined odor-search model of honey bee recruitment. That same evidence had also simultaneously "falsified" the dance language hypothesis, just as results from the double-control experiments had done earlier (see chapter 9).

THE NASANOV GLAND ATTRACTION ANOMALY

Experiments run with certain questions in mind almost always yield unexpected results, results that sometimes apply to other hypotheses not under consideration at the moment. The scent gland attraction hypothesis is a case in point. Our full awareness of the failure of the scent gland (Nasanov gland) attraction hypothesis occurred during these experiments (see excursus NG) and led to a series of studies of that problem.

We also puzzled over the fact that bees do not expose those glands when visiting natural food sources such as flowers (e.g., Ribbands 1953). At experimental feeding stations, however, the percentage of bees exposing those glands increases when less odor is added to the food (Wells and Wenner 1971). The inverse pattern between Nasanov gland exposure and recruitment is also obvious from a perusal of the data contained in table 10.1, which can be shown as a contingency table containing mean values for the two relevant variables (see table 10.2):

TABLE 10.2

	Nasanov Gland Exposures	Number of Recruits
Scented food	103	78
Unscented food	182	7

Clearly, the results we obtained directly contradicted expectations of the scent gland hypothesis; higher levels of gland exposure did not attract a greater number of searching recruits (see excursus NG).

We were now in a position to "create an image" of the means by which bees stimulated to leave their hive could locate the food source in the field that had already been visited by foragers from their own hive. The dance language hypothesis had failed repeated tests. The scent gland hypothesis had likewise failed such tests. Searching recruits seemed to use nothing more than odor.

The results we had obtained and published, however, fell on deaf ears. Neither could we get others to repeat our experiments. We did not understand why that was so at the time, because we still underestimated the power of social control (peer group pressure) in the scientific community. That material is the topic of the next chapter.

11

THE SOCIAL NETWORK

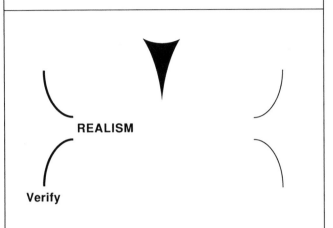

REALISM

Verify

"As in political revolutions, so in paradigm choice —there is no standard higher than the assent of the relevant community."

—Thomas Kuhn 1962:94

"To be acceptable, the new material must appear to be a natural extension of the old. Novel observations and hypotheses that are discontinuous with the thought style are usually discounted, at least temporarily." (emphasis Grinnell's)

—Frederick Grinnell 1987:45, 46

"To examine communication *only* within a discipline or a department is to miss a large part of the crucial network of informal contacts."

—Nicholas C. Mullins 1968:796

"Like any other profession, science is ridden with clannishness and clubbiness. This would be in no way surprising, except that scientists deny it to be the case. . . . In fact, researchers tend to organize themselves into clusters of overlapping clubs."

—William Broad and Nicholas Wade 1982:180

The honey bee dance language controversy episode is perhaps un-precedented in the number and diversity of people (biologists as well as others) who became personally involved with a scientific par-adigm. It should also be noted that many of them were "outsiders" and did none of the relevant experiments themselves. Most of the principals in the controversy, in fact, knew very little about honey bees.

Frederick Grinnell coined a term, "scientific thought collective," for a group of scientists who are unwittingly locked into the same paradigm hold; he wrote:

> One interesting feature of scientific thought collectives is their ano-nymity. Most investigators do not think of themselves as partici-pants in a thought collective. This anonymity vanishes, however, whenever conflicts arise. Then the battle lines ... are drawn be-tween different "schools of thought." (1987:46)

In contrast to the "outsiders," there are many bee researchers and ethologists who *had* the necessary expertise and who *could have* re-peated our various experiments (or those of Gould) and manipulated controls while doing so. They could have thereby gained understand-ing on their own. However, those qualified individuals remained on the sidelines and relied on the consensus of notables in the field.

Louis Pasteur encountered that same sort of reticence when it came to other scientists repeating his experiments during his controversial period. He implored at the time: "Repeat [the experiments] with the details which I give you and you will succeed just as I have done" (in Duclaux [1896] 1920:97).

That reticence of bee researchers and animal behaviorists to be-come involved in the dance language controversy stands in sharp contrast to what normally happens in the more rapidly moving fields of biology. In those fields, the principals in controversies: 1) have the necessary expertise, 2) conduct various interesting experiments, and 3) become involved first hand in the issue(s). Workers in those fast-moving fields are thereby more likely to relish the challenge of new results and interpretation.

That striking contrast between researchers in slow- and in fast-moving fields of science parallels the contrast between attitudes held by scientists who belong to the Realism school and by those who belong to the Relativism school (see chapter 3). Logical positivists (those who practice logical empiricism) can "rest on their laurels," so to speak; they can be content when they manage to gain additional supportive evidence or fail to falsify their hypotheses.

Those who conscientiously use the inference approach, on the other hand (by definition), recognize that new experimental results mean only that they have gained enough information for another experimental design. They have climbed just one more rung on the infinite ladder toward fuller understanding.

What *is* surprising, in the case of the honey bee dance language controversy, is the fact that many famous biologists from other fields, who may have used the inference approach in their own research, behaved as confirmationists when they discussed the dance language hypothesis. They focused only on evidence that was supportive of that hypothesis; apparently that was because they assumed that the dance language hypothesis had been tested early in the history of its success.

As suggested in one of the above epigraphs, well-known scientists in one field also tend to be respected by well-known scientists in other fields (the broader social network), even if they are unfamiliar with the research (or methods) of luminaries in those other fields. That trust sometimes leads to a false impression about the validity of advances in other fields. As one molecular biologist remarked to us at a national meeting, "I had always assumed that the honey bee dance language hypothesis had been tested by the same experimental rigor we use."

The *social network* phenomenon is not only largely ignored by most scientists; most scientists often publicly even deny the existence of such a force (as indicated in the epigraph by Broad and Wade). In the biologists' equivalent of "smoke-filled rooms" during national meetings, however, one finds a considerable amount of "politicking" and jockeying for position in the scientific social structure.

To illustrate these last points, we can examine some facets of the "social network" that we encountered during the course of the dance language controversy. In turn, we will illustrate how that network functioned as a controlling force in the controversy. First, however, we provide some sociological background.

THE "MATTHEW EFFECT"

One of the more prominent manifestations of social networks in science was termed the "Matthew effect" by Robert Merton (1968), after the biblical verse in Matthew:

> For unto every one that hath shall be given, and he shall have abundance: but from him that hath not shall be taken away even that which he hath. (Matthew 13:12 and 25:29)

Merton applied the essence of that quotation to the misallocation of credit for scientific work accomplished. "Giants" in the field receive a disproportionate amount of credit for research conducted in their sphere, even if that work has been done primarily by colleagues and even if research done by giants in their later years is no longer of high quality.

That last point might raise the hackles of those scientists who would insist that reviewers and referees of manuscripts and grant proposals are objective and base their decisions strictly on the merits of the material submitted. However, Michael Mahoney studied review practices and found:

> Who you are does make a difference. . . . the influence of prestige appears to be greatest when the manuscript is mediocre in quality. . . . There is a sad irony to the fact that eminence eases publication. Analogous to the Matthew Effect and accumulative advantage, eminence begets eminence. (1976:87)

Peters and Ceci (1982) went one step further by resubmitting twelve published articles as manuscripts to the very same journals that had published them just eighteen to thirty-two months earlier. The difference was that, in the original publications, those same articles had been published by investigators from prestigious universities, while the second time around fictitious names and institutions were used. (These journals were noted for their high rejection rates of 80 percent.) In all, even though thirty-eight editors and reviewers were involved, only three of the resubmitted articles were recognized by the referees as having appeared in print before. Of the twelve articles, nine thus made it all the way through the review process again, but eight of the nine were rejected by the referees as being substandard.

A NEW LOOK AT THE MATTHEW EFFECT: THE FIRST PART

"For unto every one that hath shall be given, and he shall have abundance." Merton's assessment of the biblical passage applied mostly to that first part of the excerpt. However, that portion of the biblical passage from Matthew can be interpreted in another sense, one that reveals a fundamentally different aspect of the problem. That is, there is a tendency in science (as in other areas of human relationships) to elevate certain individuals to a position of authority.

In perhaps few cases in biology has the application of the Matthew effect been more obvious than during both the promotion of the dance language hypothesis and the subsequent controversy. A chronology of events that occurred during the emergence, challenge, and "rescue" of that hypothesis when it was challenged should make this point clear. We start here with the first portion of the Matthew effect.

As documented in chapter 4, the question of language versus odor use by searching bees has been with us for centuries. In the late 1930s Julien Francon had followed a line of reasoning that was remarkably close to that proposed later by von Frisch, at the time when von Frisch still insisted that searching bees use odor. However, Francon failed to "convert" (Atkinson 1985) a sufficient number of other biologists to his interpretation (see our chapter 4).

Von Frisch also proposed the concept of "speech," in principle, more than twenty years before Francon, but his proposal at that time had no great impact during the subsequent decades.

Curiously, the acceptance of the von Frisch dance language hypothesis during the mid-1940s did not rely on the rigor of the experiments he ran; everyone now seems to agree that those early experiments of von Frisch (those done during the mid-1940s) lacked necessary controls. Rather, it would seem that the rapid acceptance of the von Frisch dance language hypothesis stemmed more from the strong endorsement it received from the relevant scientific community at the time (see the Kuhn epigraph).

Bennett addressed the question of why innovative ideas become accepted at one time but not at another:

> Why should some new ideas be acceptable to scientific fraternities while others are rejected on *non-scientific* grounds? . . . The following distinctions [apply]. . . . Innovation, by its very nature, is compatible, while creativity is antithetical to commonly held beliefs. Innovation results from research in accordance with accepted rules and evaluative standards. It is new knowledge. . . . it springs from boundary-maintaining research and sustains established theoretical frameworks—a fulfilment of expectations in compliance with accepted formulations. (1968:237; emphasis Bennett's)

In other words, the von Frisch dance language hypothesis was accepted in the 1940s only because the "climate" had become favorable by then. His "language" proposal fit in well with a growing romanticism in the incipient fields of sociobiology and ethology. His experimental protocol was innovative and provided supportive material to a receptive audience at the time.

We cannot provide a full chronology of the events that transpired during that period, but we can provide sufficient documentation to illustrate the degree to which social influence played a role in the acceptance, promotion, and defense of the dance language hypothesis. Others, such as sociologists of science, have found the full story worth pursuing further (e.g., Veldink 1989).

When von Frisch's revolutionary 1945 paper first appeared in the German language, his conclusions were initially greeted with a wave of skepticism (see Thorpe 1949). However, none other than W. H. Thorpe himself, a "giant" in the field of animal behavior at the time, later saw to it that von Frisch's paper got translated (von Frisch 1947) and wrote a preface endorsing that research. Thorpe provided even more enthusiastic support when he wrote:

> By this latest work . . . [von Frisch] poses tremendous problems for the neurophysiologist and psychologist and shows that the foraging and orientation behaviour of bees is such as to require a reconsideration of some of the most fundamental concepts used in our explanations of the behaviour of insects and other animals. The day of Loeb and the tropism theory now seems far away indeed. (1949:14; see also our chapters 7 and 13)

Shortly thereafter (as indicated in chapter 6), the dance language hypothesis received an even more powerful endorsement by a Nobel laureate, August Krogh, who had received the Nobel Prize in 1920 for his research on the physiology of gas exchange and osmoregulation in various animals.

Krogh (1948) described von Frisch and his research in an article for *Scientific American*. While that magazine is not considered a "refereed journal" by scientists, publication therein carries with it considerable prestige. In addition, those articles are written in simple language; Krogh was thus able to provide a convincing account of von Frisch's experiments and their purported significance to a very wide audience. Krogh's endorsement, as given in chapter 6, bears repeating in this context: "This series of experiments constitutes a most beautiful example of what the human mind can accomplish by tireless effort on a very high level of intelligence" (1948:21).

In the final paragraphs of Krogh's article we also find one of the first deliberations about the conflict between insect-level and human-level capabilities (see chapters 7 and 13).

Donald Griffin, who later became famous for his work with bat "sonar," was one of the next to press for acceptance of the dance language hypothesis; as indicated in chapter 6, he arranged for von Frisch to visit the United States in 1949. Griffin was then at Cornell, initially one of three universities von Frisch was to visit. Shortly thereafter, arrangements were made for visits to thirteen other universities, with one or more of three lectures to be given at each place (von Frisch 1950) during a three-month period.

That trip also led to the publication of von Frisch 's three lectures in a small book, *Bees: Their Vision, Chemical Senses, and Language* (Cornell University Press). His book soon became highly popular; the message was appealing, and it was written in very understandable language. One can recognize in this episode, in the acceptance of the dance language hypothesis, the strong dependence on the verification (confirmation) approach in that type of research (see chapter 3). In an earlier passage, Griffin emphasized the reliance on that approach more succinctly: "Indeed, independent confirmation has already been accomplished in the United States, in England, and on the continent of Europe" (Griffin, in von Frisch 1950:v).

Shortly after the publication of that book in 1951, von Frisch was made a foreign member of the U.S. National Academy of Sciences.

KUHN'S "NORMAL SCIENCE"

A mark of an initial plateau in the rapid rise in popularity of the dance language hypothesis during those early years was the award of the American Philosophical Society's 1956 Magellanic Premium Award to von Frisch (as first announced in their 1955 yearbook). Magellanic Premium Awards are not given every year, and apparently only for especially notable discoveries or inventions. As stated, that award is given "to the author of the best discovery or most useful invention relating to navigation, astronomy, or natural philosophy (mere natural history only excepted)."

A brief announcement of the award was contained in the 1955 yearbook of the society, as follows: "On motion, the Society voted to approve the recommendation of the Committee [composed of Bronk, Foote, Hunsaker, and Shapley] that the Prize for 1956 be awarded to Karl von Frisch, Professor of Zoology, University of Munich, in recognition of his rather sensational work on the 'mathematics' and navigation of bees."

On April 20, 1956, formal notice of the award was made. As a part of the award, recipients normally attend a meeting of the society and present a paper. Von Frisch could not attend. His paper (von Frisch 1956) was read instead by none other than Donald Griffin, then at Harvard.

One of the final stages in the evolution of the dance language hypothesis to a "paradigm" status was marked by an invitation from the editors of *Scientific American;* they requested von Frisch to write an article for that publication, which he did (von Frisch 1962).

Between 1950 and 1965, then, research on the dance language hypothesis evolved into and prospered in a manner characteristic of research in the "normal science" sense. That is, the hypothesis functioned during that period as a true "paradigm," as defined by Kuhn: "One or more past scientific achievements, achievements that some particular scientific community acknowledges for a time as supplying the foundation for its further practice" (1962:10).

All of the acceptance and endorsement by prominent members of the biological community sparked the imagination of those in other research fields as well, especially since this was the first documented case suggesting that a nonhuman species had a "language." A wide spectrum of research was begun in the fields of linguistics, psychology, and sociology. Various scientists in those fields searched for the presence of "language" in other species and pondered the implications of von Frisch's "find." Kuhn had also commented about the significance of this type of activity: "When the individual scientist can take a paradigm for granted, he need no longer, in his major works, attempt to build his field anew, starting from first principles and justifying the use of each concept introduced" (1962:19–20).

Those caught up in the paradigm fared well. Martin Lindauer and other students and protégés of von Frisch published a series of articles on the communication and navigation of bees, all of them dealing with the presumed use of their "dance language" capabilities. Harald Esch and Adrian Wenner were the first to hear and report the nature of sounds produced by bees during their "waggle dance" (see chapter 7) and were in great demand for lectures and as symposium speakers.

Grants were readily available for supportive research, and journals accepted manuscripts without undue hesitation. Esch obtained a professorship at Notre Dame, and Wenner was invited to submit an article to *Scientific American* (Wenner 1964).

THE OTHER SIDE OF THE MATTHEW EFFECT

Merton's treatment of the Matthew effect emphasized the first portion of the biblical passage quoted above: "Put in less stately language, the Matthew effect consists of the accruing of greater increments of recognition for particular scientific contributions to scientists of considerable repute and with withholding of such recognition from scientists who have not yet made their mark" (1968:58).

The second part of the biblical passage, "but from him that hath not shall be taken away even that which he hath," can also be interpreted as a reference to the inhibition of criticism, as well as to the denigration of those who would "presume" to question the authority vested in the chosen few. Silverman expressed that notion as follows: "When the Matthew Effect transforms fallible men and women into idols of authority, it serves to curb the advancement of knowledge by discouraging criticism" (1986:387).

Thus, whereas kudos go to those who support existing paradigms, quite the opposite reception may await those who would challenge existing dogma (e.g., see Bennett 1968; Merton 1968; Blissett 1972; Mahoney 1976; Veldink 1976, 1989: Gilbert and Mulkay 1984; Cohen 1985). Even though scientists might well argue that they welcome challenge of existing ideas, they do so only when the issues at hand do not threaten existing theoretical and/or sociological frameworks.

The resistance scientists exhibit toward substantive challenge of prevailing theory falls in line with the second portion of the quotation from Matthew (above). Considerable pressure can be exerted on those who begin to propose alternative hypotheses to accepted thought— the human side of the scientist rises to the fore. During the early stages of our challenge of the dance language hypothesis, for example, it was just this sort of social conformity that led Dawkins to write: "Wenner and his colleagues presume to challenge findings of a great biologist" (1969:751).

Pressure to conform thus can come in a variety of forms, even though scientists may deny the existence of such pressures (as indicated above); the result is that crisis develops with the introduction of new and adverse experimental evidence, at least within a small circle of scientists at the time. Thomas Kuhn (chapters 7 and 8 in 1962) fully treated the matter of crises, crises that arise with any recognition that anomalies might alter thinking. He wrote: "Discovery commences with the awareness of anomaly, i.e., with the recognition that nature has somehow violated the paradigm-induced expectations that govern normal science" (1962:52).

In many ways, however, Kuhn was preempted on the matter of "normal science" and "crises" by Robert Merton, author of the Matthew effect. For example, Merton wrote in 1942:

> The ethos of science is that affectively toned complex of values and norms which is held to be binding on the man of science. The norms are expressed in the form of prescriptions, proscriptions, preferences, and permissions. They are legitimatized in terms of institutional values. These imperatives, transmitted by precept and ex-

ample and reenforced by sanctions, are in varying degrees internalized by the scientist, thus fashioning his scientific conscience or, if one prefers the latter-day phrase, his superego. . . . Although the ethos of science has not been codified, it can be inferred from the moral consensus of scientists as expressed in use and [custom], in countless writings on the scientific spirit and in moral indignation directed toward contraventions of the ethos. (1973:268, 269).

Such were the signs of trouble that surfaced when we began to test the dance language hypothesis, to offer an alternative hypothesis for the recruitment of honey bees to food sources, and to make our results known (see chapters 7–10). The first sign of disapproval became evident when we attended scientific meetings and attempted to communicate our findings in that standard manner (e.g., in 1966; see excursus SI). The next evidence we encountered surfaced in the comments of anonymous referees when we submitted papers for publication; others could challenge our work, but we were not permitted space to reply (see excursus EXC).

Shortly thereafter, many correspondents stopped sending reprints (notable exceptions were E. O. Wilson, John Kefuss, and Tom Rinderer). We also no longer received invitations to present seminars at universities or to participate in symposia.

THE EMERGENCE OF CRISIS

A fairly predictable sequence of events occurs during a crisis: 1) emergence of the crisis, 2) progress of the resultant controversy, and 3) eventual resolution of the issue. A satirical statement, dating at least as far back as Louis Agassiz, describes that process: "when a new doctrine is presented, it must go through three stages. First, people say that it isn't true, then that it is against religion [scientific dogma], and, in the third stage, that it has long been known" (Gould and Eldredge 1986:143).

What is normally rarely documented in science, or if documented never stressed, however, is the intensity of debate and the time span required for the resolution of controversies. That is, even though science is "self-correcting," that self-correction is rarely immediate. In fast-moving fields of science the time span for the incorporation of new viewpoints may be quite short; however, that is not always the case even there.

In their book *Opening Pandora's Box*, Gilbert and Mulkay (1984) illustrated the great length of time required (more than ten years) for a majority of biologists in a fast-moving area to become "converted" to a new point of view. Their example was the chemiosmotic coupling hypothesis proposed by Peter Mitchell (see their diagram 6B on page 115 in that book; in that diagram read Mitchell for "Spencer"). In describing the transition, Gilbert and Mulkay wrote:

> The growing consensus about the scientific merits of chemiosmosis . . . is attributed to the gradual accumulation of experimental evidence . . . and to the slow improvement of comprehension. . . . The absence of a complete consensus is linked . . . to reluctance on the part of certain eminent scientists to adopt a theory which they themselves had not originated and which they found rather difficult to understand. (1984:114–115)

After the "conversion" process was complete, some of those same participants summarized the new point of view in Boyer et al. (1977:955–1026). From those writings one gains no impression of the difficulties encountered. It is then that "Nature" seems to have resolved the issue (see Latour 1987, Veldink 1989).

Unfortunately, more is required for "conversion" of the scientific community than a simple passage of time and a reasoned, detached consideration of evidence in the idealistic "tradition" of science. Anyone who "creates" totally new interpretation must actively press the issue, especially in the slower-moving fields. Such forward behavior, however, doesn't sit well with the scientific community. Aronson's statement, "The production of scientific knowledge is simultaneously the production of scientific error" (1986:630) is applicable here as well.

Not even scientists like to admit that their previous "knowledge" was in error.

Michael Polanyi was one who patiently waited for the scientific "climate" to change before attempting to convince other physicists that a new interpretation of his had merit. Polanyi (1958) later pondered over the reasons for the discrepancy he had perceived between the presumed "open-mindedness" of scientists and the reality of what he had experienced. In doing so, he addressed the distinction between what he termed "heuristic passion" and "persuasive passion."

The former of those two terms refers to research of the type Barbara McClintock (Keller 1983) and Polanyi did to "enrich the world." "Persuasive passion," on the other hand, refers to the attempts of scientists to convert others to their interpretation of new results. Polanyi also recognized the resultant (and inevitable) sociological input in science when he wrote:

Scientific controversies never lie altogether within science. For when a new system of thought concerning a whole class of alleged facts is at issue, the question will be whether it should be accepted or rejected in principle, and those who reject it on such comprehensive grounds will inevitably regard it as altogether incompetent and unsound. (1958:150)

Polanyi then continued with language remarkably similar to that expressed by Kuhn four years later and by Atkinson twenty-seven years later:

Proponents of a new system can convince their audience only by first winning their intellectual sympathy for a doctrine they have not yet grasped. Those who listen sympathetically will discover for themselves what they would otherwise never have understood. Such an acceptance is a heuristic process, a self-modifying act, and to this extent a conversion. It produces disciples forming a school, the members of which are separated for the time being by a logical gap from those outside it. (1958:151)

If one exhibits an untoward amount of patience, in the hope that adherents to another paradigm may be converted by evidence, they may well only find themselves contributing to the slowing of scientific progress. Pasteur, for example, not known for such patience, took the opposite tack and forcefully pressed his viewpoints in front of the French Academy of Sciences (Duclaux [1896] 1920). Nowadays, however, general biology textbooks usually provide no hint of the difficulties encountered by Pasteur in both the medical and scientific establishments.

A more usual outcome, for those who persist in pressing the issue and win, despite the discouragement provided by the scientific community, may be a generation of deep resentment by others in that wider community. Blissett provided a relevant quotation to that effect, which he obtained from a scientist who had encountered just such resistance to new interpretation:

To make changes you have to be highly articulate, persuasive, and devastating. You have to go to the heart of the matter. But in doing this you lay yourself open to attack. I've been called fanatical, paranoid, obsessed . . . but I'm going to win. Time is on my side. (1972:141)

Note in that expression the "persuasive passion" element described by Polanyi and practiced by Pasteur. Most scientists, however, lack the necessary persistence to counter the considerable opposition that can develop.

To press forward in the face of opposition, then, one must possess both "heuristic passion" and "persuasive passion." Heuristic passion drives one on to ever more experimentation for the mere pleasure of achieving greater understanding. That effort can incorporate any or all of the various possible scientific approaches (see figure 3.1). The persuasive passion must be exhibited by those scientists who wish their efforts to affect the scientific community at large (hopefully, within a time span that permits them to perceive the "conversion" of others).

Polanyi concluded his section with an expression of the problems recognized later by Kuhn. He also recognized the equivalent of the distinction between Karl Popper's and Thomas Kuhn's "spectacles" (Kuhn 1970b:3). Polanyi wrote:

> The heuristic impulse links our appreciation of scientific value to a vision of reality, which serves as a guide to enquiry. Heuristic passion is also the mainspring of originality—the force which impels us to abandon an accepted framework of interpretation and commit ourselves, by the crossing of a logical gap, to the use of a new framework. (1958:159)

We close this section with a comment by Polanyi on difficulties that may be encountered when one forms radically new ideas: "A hostile audience may in fact deliberately refuse to entertain novel conceptions" (1958:151).

SOCIAL NETWORKS AND THE DANCE LANGUAGE CONTROVERSY

As indicated above, one can never know all that transpires among scientists within the complex set of social webs that prevail in the wider community. Attendance at national meetings, however, can be quite enlightening, particularly if one participates in some of the behind-the-scenes negotiations and "posturing" (as a layperson termed that behavior during one of our meetings).

Although we cannot provide a great deal of information about the private interactions that certainly occurred among proponents of the dance language hypothesis (since we were no longer privy to such conversations), we can provide a sketch of some encounters on the basis of what we learned subsequently.

As mentioned at the beginning of this chapter, a great many very famous people became involved in the dance language hypothesis in one way or another. Some of the people (Thorpe, Krogh, and Griffin) were mentioned earlier in this chapter as having endorsed the dance language hypothesis without the hypothesis ever having been *tested*. Griffin and others had become convinced by merely repeating the original experiments and obtaining equivalent favorable results, but many other theorists became involved on the false premise that the hypothesis had been tested.

In the case at hand, the inception of the dance language controversy itself can be dated with considerable accuracy, namely to a March 1966 incident at the Salk Institute in La Jolla, California (see excursus SI). The last of the above quotations by Polanyi (see the end of the last section) fit what happened at that occasion perfectly, regardless of the fact that many illustrious scientists were present (e.g., Jacob Bronowski, Theodore Bullock, Francis Crick, Jacques Monod, and Jonas Salk).

An incident that followed that meeting appeared to be inconsequential at the time; however, that incident later developed into a major factor in the dance language controversy, because it apparently led to the start of James Gould's career.

As a start, we note that Seymour Benzer of the California Institute of Technology, in a letter to one of us (Wenner) two months after the Salk Institute episode, wrote: "Unfortunately, I missed your talk at the Salk Institute some time ago." Benzer's note was puzzling in itself, since Wenner had not actually given a talk; he had served only as a "discussant" at that encounter (see excursus SI).

The next telling episode occurred during the August 1966 American Institute of Biological Sciences (AIBS) meetings in Corvallis, Oregon. William P. Stephen of Oregon State University and Burkhardt Schricker of Germany presented a paper on the presumed alteration of the use of "dance language" information by recruited honey bees. They had poisoned bees with the organic pesticide parathion. After poisoning, recruited bees apparently went to sites other than to the ones to which they had been "directed" by the "dance language" information.

For their experiments, they had used the "fan" experimental design originally used by von Frisch. Unfortunately, that experimental design is unacceptable for the reasons described in Wenner (1962) and in excursus PN.

In the meantime, Benzer teamed up with Robert Sinsheimer, also, at the time, of CalTech, for a study of the problem. They did not do the research themselves but sponsored undergraduates; James L. Gould, Michael Henerey, and Michael C. MacLeod. The subsequent lead article in *Science* (Gould, Henerey, and MacLeod 1970) constituted the "dance language" community's first formidable challenge of our research. The editor of *Science*, however, did not permit us to reply to that challenge, even after appeal (see excursus EXC).

Other elements of the arrangement were puzzling, considering the fact that the episode involved no more than research on honey bee behavior. For example, the Gould, Henerey, and MacLeod research was funded by a Public Heath Service grant (Biomedical Sciences Support) awarded to Robert F. Bacher of CalTech. When Gould and co-workers published the results of their experiments in eastern Oregon, they also thanked W. P. Stephen for arranging the donation of a bee hive for their work and acknowledged Sinsheimer for his assistance in obtaining funding for their research (there was no mention of Bacher).

Edward O. Wilson of Harvard University was the next major figure we encountered who disagreed sharply with our interpretation of experimental results. In contrast to virtually all other dance language proponents (such as Benzer and colleagues), however, Wilson maintained an open communication with us; we conducted a lively exchange for years. In fact, Wilson's behavior during the controversy was strikingly different from that of most other dance language proponents.

One apparently insurmountable problem in our efforts to communicate with Wilson was the existence of a "logical gap" (in Polanyi's words) between us. As we interpret it now, Wilson was strongly committed to the verification approach (the Realism school) and was deeply committed to the dance language paradigm (e.g., Wilson 1971). On the other hand, we had crossed over to the inference approach and now worked within the Relativism school; that meant that by that time we wore, in Kuhn's words, different spectacles than Wilson had available.

After the appearance of our paper describing the double-control experiments (see chapter 9), Wilson wrote us and insisted that those experiments did not resolve the issue. Instead, he insisted that we conduct another experiment, one that just happened to be remarkably similar in design to our "crucial" or strong inference experiment (Wenner, Wells, and Johnson 1969). We sent him a copy of the manuscript of that paper, soon to appear in *Science*. In addition, we wrote him a long letter explaining the deficiencies in the original experimental designs of von Frisch and Lindauer, deficiencies that were later acknowledged by others (e.g., Gould 1976).

One of the examples sent to Wilson was a translation of one of Martin Lindauer's papers on experiments with sun compass orientation. We asked him to have some of his graduate students read it with the same critical eye that others were using while reading our papers. Little did we know at the time that Wilson was apparently instrumental in inviting Lindauer to Woods Hole as a guest scientist during the summer of 1969, supported in part by a RAND fellowship at the Marine Biological Laboratory (Lindauer 1971).

During that summer at Woods Hole (and later back in Germany) Lindauer repeated our "crucial" experiments (see our chapter 10), but not in exactly the same way as we had done them (Lindauer 1971). What was evident to us at the time is the fact that, the more closely his experimental protocol matched that which we had used, the more nearly his results matched those we had obtained.

One of the last invitations either of us received to present the results of our research in a public forum came from three psychologists, Lester Krames, Patricia Pliner, and Thomas Alloway of Erindale College at the University of Toronto. (Perhaps they had not yet learned that we had fallen out of favor.) The symposium was held in Toronto in February 1972. Peter Marler, who became a prominent figure later in defense of the dance language hypothesis as a member of James Gould's doctoral committee, was one of the speakers at that same symposium.

The first that one of us (Wenner) knew anything was amiss was during the first evening in the lounge of the hotel where we all stayed. Papi and Pardi in Italy had done research on moon compass orientation of amphipods. However, when a student of Wenner's, Peter Craig, had repeated those experiments (Wenner 1989), he found that the slope of the beach accounted for a good portion of the amphipod directional orientation (Wenner 1989).

When that point was brought up that evening, Marler rose to his feet and exclaimed, "Are you suggesting that Papi and Pardi cheated?" At that, he stalked out of the lounge. He did not remain for the full symposium and missed Wenner's presentation.

At about that same time, Marler and Donald Griffin had moved to the Rockefeller Institute (later Rockefeller University) and established an active research program in animal behavior. After finishing his undergraduate work at CalTech (and spending some additional time with Stephen at Oregon State), James Gould was accepted in the graduate program at Rockefeller University. Griffin was the chair of his committee; Marler and Bert Holldobler of Harvard were other members of the committee. Holldobler, in turn, was a myrmecological colleague of Wilson's.

During the time that Gould was pursuing his graduate work at Rockefeller University, von Frisch (together with Konrad Lorenz and

Niko Tinbergen) was awarded the Nobel Prize in physiology and medicine (1973). After Gould finished his doctoral work at Rockefeller, he took a position at Princeton, replacing Mark Konishi. Konishi, in turn, had been a former graduate student of Marler's while Marler was still at the University of California in Berkeley. Where did Konishi go? He took a position at CalTech in the same department occupied by Seymour Benzer.

A brief exchange in *Science* interrupted the rather smooth sequence of events that took place during the reinforcement of the dance language hypothesis. Ankerl and Pereboom of Switzerland wrote a letter of protest to *Science* in reference to a *Research News* article written by Marler and Griffin (Nov. 2, 1973). In that letter (Ankerl and Pereboom 1974) they chastised Marler and Griffin for their omission of any reference to our research (Wenner, Wells, and Rohlf 1967; Wenner 1971a; Wells and Wenner 1973). Griffin and Marler replied in the same issue, with an appeal to authority and a strong endorsement of the verification approach, as follows: "on balance we agree with Wilson [1971] that 'the communicative function *is decisively supported* by experimental evidence . . .' " (Griffin and Marler 1974; emphasis ours).

SUMMARY

In chapter 4 we documented the fluctuation in belief about honey bee "language," as it has occurred for more than two centuries. During that time span the sequential community of scientists tended to work at any one time either within an odor-search paradigm or within a "language" paradigm. The prolonged commitment to one of those choices through each time interval seems to have been the consequence of a strong social element within science.

George Berkeley (1685–1753), bishop of Coyne, early on recognized the importance of such social input within science. In fact, he may well have been the first person to recognize the concept of the "paradigm hold" when he wrote:

> Men learn the elements of science from others; and every learner hath a deference more or less to authority, especially the young learners, few of that kind caring to dwell long upon principles, but inclining rather to take them upon trust: And things early admitted by repetition become familiar: And this familiarity at length passeth for evidence. ([1735] 1951:117–118)

The two centuries of uncertainty about odor versus language seemed to have ended in the 1940s with the advent of von Frisch's "dance language" hypothesis. At last a seemingly "airtight" set of experiments had been run that provided abundant supportive evidence for a newly formulated "language" hypothesis. Anyone who wished to do so could repeat those experiments and achieve the same supportive results as those obtained by von Frisch, providing additional confirmation by means of the verification approach. The fly in the ointment, so to speak, was the lack of a test of that hypothesis before it evolved into the status of a paradigm.

Upon closer inspection, however, it is clear that the acceptance and promulgation of the dance language hypothesis depended to a great degree upon social factors within the scientific community (e.g., Veldink 1989). This particular episode in the two centuries of uncertainty about odor search versus "language," however, is set apart from earlier swings of the pendulum by the degree to which outsiders became involved in the dance language paradigm.

Philosophers and historians of science have previously largely ignored the sociological component of science. This account of our experience in social interactions among scientists might provide a basis for starting research in that area, before the trail grows colder.

12

REAFFIRMING THE DANCE LANGUAGE HYPOTHESIS: INITIAL ATTEMPTS

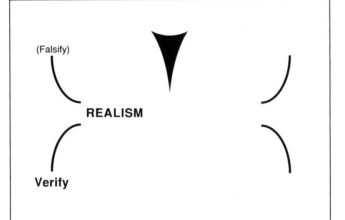

(Falsify)

REALISM

Verify

"By themselves, [scientists] cannot and will not falsify that philosophical theory [which led them into crisis], for its defenders will do what we have already seen scientists doing when confronted by anomaly. They will devise numerous articulations and *ad hoc* modifications of their theory in order to eliminate any apparent conflict."
—*Thomas Kuhn 1962:78*

"This issue of paradigm choice can never be unequivocably settled by logic and experiment alone. . . . As in political revolutions, so in paradigm choice— there is no standard higher than the assent of the relevant community."
—*Thomas Kuhn 1962:94*

"The flaws of a theory never lead to its rejection. . . . Scientists tolerate theories that can easily be demonstrated to be inadequate."
—*Carl Lindegren 1966:6*

"I cannot give any scientist of any age better advice than this: the intensity of the conviction that a hypothesis is true has no bearing on whether it is true or not. The importance of the strength of our conviction is only to provide a proportionately strong incentive to find out if the hypothesis will stand up to critical evaluation."

—*Peter Medawar (1979) 1981:39*

W e published the results of our "crucial experiment" in 1969, the year after James D. Watson published his book, *The Double Helix*. In referring to that book, Merton wrote:

> The stories detailed in *The Double Helix* have evidently gone far to dispel a popular mythology about the complex behavior of scientists. . . . Only in our highly competitive age, allegedly, are appreciable numbers of scientists concerned to "scoop" others at work in the field and so to gain recognition for their accomplishments. (1973:326)

Our experience was just the opposite; we did not have to worry about being "scooped." Soon after the publication of our results it became apparent to the wider "relevant community" that some biologists were willing to accept our contention that something might be amiss with the dance language hypothesis. When that acceptance of our work became apparent, proponents of that hypothesis designed experiments directed toward "resolving" the question of a "dance language" among bees "by logic and experiment."

What few scientists realize is that much of the research conducted by those who belong to the Realism school may be influenced by a deep-seated social control. What Merton had not included in his above comment was the overriding influence of the "reward system" in the scientific community. However, he had made that point elsewhere: "Like other institutions, the institution of science has developed an elaborate system for allocating rewards to those who variously live up to its norms" (1973:297).

There is thus somewhat of a schizophrenia in science. On the one hand, a certain kind of reward (mostly fame and sense of accomplishment) can be forthcoming for someone who succeeds in "scooping" others, as in the case of *The Double Helix* (Watson 1968), or much more slowly in the case of Barbara McClintock (Keller 1983). Note, however, that research by Watson and Crick, as well as that of McClintock, was done in the tradition of the strong inference approach (the Relativism school; see figure 3.1). In fast-moving areas within that school, any deep commitment to a single explanation would only slow progress.

On the other hand, another type of reward (adulation by the scientific community, including referee approval of manuscripts and grant proposals), can be forthcoming to those who "variously live up to [science's] norms" (Merton 1973). Within the Realism school, therefore, there seems to be less of a chance that any challenge of existing doctrine would be considered a "scoop."

For ecologists and sociobiologists, who practice largely within the confines of the Realism school, challenges of hypotheses are never considered "scoops," even if the research meets all scientific criteria with respect to quality or effectiveness, or even if results lead to more intensive research by others. A "scoop" in sociobiology is considered to have occurred when some exotic phenomenon is "proved" to be true or is "discovered" to exist. Ecologists and sociobiologists appear to proceed cautiously, always with an eye to whether they can gain the approval of their peers for their research efforts.

Richard Whitley wrote extensively on the interrelationship between the behavior of scientists and control by the "relevant community," as Kuhn put it. Two quotations from Whitley's work are particularly appropriate here: "Scientists who seek the highest reputations as novelty producers have to convince powerful colleagues of their competence in following standard procedures and applying shared skills and of the significance and relevance of their work for collective goals" (1984:12) and:

> Novelty production is managed by allocating rewards on the basis of how successful a result is in influencing the direction and conduct of others' work so that scientists are constrained by the need to fit in with colleagues' plans and procedures. . . . The "essential tension" between novelty and tradition, or co-operation and competition, is a notable feature of modern scientific work which results in a distinctive kind of work organization being characteristic of scientific fields. (1984:13)

With the above background, it should come as no surprise to those outside of the dance language controversy arena that no biologist published any critique of the actual experimental designs we used in our experiments. As can be seen from comments included in chapter 11, challenges were primarily levied against us for having had the audacity to do our experiments in the first place (attempting to counter "fact"), or for supposed errors in our technique (see, for example, excursus GT). Neither could we get others to repeat our experiments. Lindauer (see below), was the only one who came remotely close to repeating any of our experiments, but that was not at our request (see also chapter 11).

Likewise it should come as no surprise, on the basis of material presented so far in this volume, that various proponents of the dance language hypothesis attempted to shore up that hypothesis (see the Kuhn epigraph, above). If von Frisch had "discovered" the language of bees or if he had "proved" that bees had a language, as so many members of the Realism school had insisted, then it must have been *we* who had erred somehow, in *our* "inability" to get supportive data. At least that line of thinking seems to be the basis for most of the papers published in the early years after we disclosed the results of our experimental tests of the language hypothesis.

It was von Frisch himself who provided one of the best examples of the attitudes described in the above paragraphs. While reviewing two of our publications (Wenner 1971a; Wells and Wenner 1973), von Frisch wrote:

> When basic experiments concerning bee language, which have been proven hundreds of times and generally acknowledged, do not suc- ceed, it may occur, even to the readers who are familiar with the literature, that this may be attributed to errors in the experimen- ter's methods. So is it in this case. (1973:630)

A SEARCH FOR SUPPORT OF THE
DANCE LANGUAGE HYPOTHESIS

A careful perusal of each of the challenges of our work reveals evi- dence of what Kuhn referred to in the opening epigraph. That is, all of those who conducted experiments in order to gain additional sup- port for the dance language hypothesis either 1) had to resort to ad hoc modifications of that hypothesis in their interpretations or 2) had to ignore the fact that their experimental results differed markedly from the claims von Frisch had always made for that hypothesis.

As examples of our assertion, we present next a brief critique of some of the attempts to "reaffirm" the dance language hypothesis, as was done earlier by Wells and Wenner (1973), by Wenner (1974), and in part by Gould (1976). In that critique we illustrate a point we made earlier in connection with Hempel's "affirmation of the consequent," as follows:

> [All previous workers] assumed that, in order to find the food, a recruit must have prior quantitative information about its location. These assumptions lead the authors to interpret arrival of new workers at sites visited by dancing foragers as definitive evidence of linguistic communication. As pointed out earlier they have focused their attention on successful recruits. (Wells and Wenner 1973:173)

However, after the reasoning of Hempel (1966), we continued: "Ex- periments based on these assumptions invariably lead to affirmation of the consequence *[sic]* of the hypothesis (if bees have a language, recruits will reach the food. Some recruits find the food. Therefore, bees have a language). This reasoning is deductively invalid" (1973:173).

As Thomas Kuhn had stated (as in the above epigraph): "this issue of paradigm choice can never be unequivocably settled by logic and experiment alone." Perhaps the meaning of his statement will become more evident as we proceed.

By 1975 the various efforts to re-establish the "truth" of a dance language among honey bees (attempted after our challenge) were already acknowledged as nonconclusive by proponents of that hypothesis. When the results of those experiments first reached print, however, they were all accepted as "definitive" (see Veldink 1989 on this point). What few people realize is that advocates of the dance language hypothesis did not alter their opinion and admit that earlier evidence was unconvincing *until* they were confident that newer experiments *had* yielded "conclusive" evidence (e.g., Gould, Henerey, and MacLeod 1970; Gould 1974, 1975a, 1975b).

GONCALVES (1969)

One can build an enclosed forager system for the laboratory (e.g., Bizetsky 1957; Wenner and Johnson 1966), in which foragers can walk a short distance from their hive to an enclosed feeding station within the laboratory. In the meantime other foragers can leave the hive by another entrance, forage freely outdoors, and thereby maintain colony strength.

Lionel Goncalves of Brazil used such an apparatus. He had a single forager visit the station, walk back to the hive, and execute its waggle dance therein. Presumably, the dance maneuver then indicated a much longer flying distance than that traveled by the forager; a 3- to 4-meter walking distance, according to Bizetsky (1957), would be equivalent to a 50- to 100-meter flight.

Potential recruits in Goncalves' experiments, after contacting the dancer, then left by the outside entrance of the hive rather than traveling back into the laboratory arena visited by the regular forager.

To test the accuracy of the use of direction information by those potential recruits, Goncalves had provided eight stations in a circle around the hive (see figure 12.1). An assistant at each of the stations then counted all visitors, both those that landed and those that circled within 50 centimeters of the dish. The number beside each point in figure 12.1 indicates the total tally for recruit arrivals in eight experiments.

On the basis of information provided in chapters 2 and 3, we can

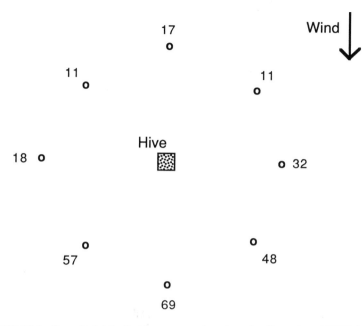

FIGURE 12.1. Recruit distribution for an experiment run by Goncalves (1969), in which foragers presumably indicated a site 50 to 100 meters downwind from the hive (with control stations placed anywhere from 4 to 50 meters away from the hive in different experiments). Recruits ended up at stations in all directions from the hive rather than only in the indicated direction (downwind).

examine Goncalves' results and the interpretations provided under the various scientific approaches possible. Did the results verify the dance language hypothesis? Did the results falsify that hypothesis? Was the experimental design a *test* of the language hypothesis? Was the design a strong inference approach? Were dance language and odor-search hypotheses tested against one another?

First of all, it is obvious that recruits did not arrive at only a few of the stations in one general direction from the hive, as in the von Frisch fan experiments (see chapter 6 and figure PN.2 in excursus PN). Recruits instead arrived at stations located in all directions from the hive. Goncalves thus obtained results that stood in sharp contrast to those obtained by von Frisch at the time he first proposed the dance language hypothesis, as follows: "We see that the majority of searching bees fanning out, moved within an angle deviating not more than 15 degrees each to the left and to the right from the direction leading towards the feeding place" (1948:10).

Von Frisch had apparently erroneously concluded that recruits in his experiments had flown straight out from the hive on the basis of their ultimate distribution at a skewed arrangement of stations in the field (see excursus PN).

Furthermore, in Goncalves' experiments, the wind always blew from the hive toward the site presumably "indicated" by the dancing bee. His experimental design thus did not *test between* two possibilities, a reliance on odor carried by wind and actual "use" of "dance language" information.

Rather than recognize the fact that his results violated expectations of the dance language hypothesis, Goncalves interpreted his results in such a way that the dance language paradigm remained intact, as expected by a member of the Realism school. He apparently assumed the existence of a "dance language" among bees (i.e., that von Frisch had either discovered it or proved it to exist). That attitude apparently prevented him from testing his results against any "expected performance that might have been predicted by the dance language hypothesis.

Goncalves instead statistically tested the deviation he obtained against a heretofore unpostulated "expected" *equal* random distribution of arrivals at stations around the hive. However, no odor-search hypothesis would ever predict an equal distribution of recruits in all directions, because the wind would influence the results when stations were placed all around the hive (see chapter 5 and excursus OS). Goncalves concluded instead: "in Experiments 1–8, 67% of the information the bees used for communication was provided by the scent of the food source and 33% by the dances" (1969:127).

Note here, however, Goncalves' *a priori* assumption that *the* "dance language" existed. He could then conclude that any nonequal distribution of searching bees in the *appropriate* direction not explainable by odor *must* be due to "dance language" use.

Friesen (1973) later conducted experiments in which foragers of two different colors from different hives visited a single station located downwind from one of the hives but upwind from the other (see chapter 8). His results revealed that stations located a short distance downwind from a hive always obtained more recruits than stations located a short distance upwind from the hive, *regardless* of any presumed use of dance language information. Friesen's results thus indicate that there is no need to invoke the dance language hypothesis while interpreting Goncalves' results.

That "focus on the successful," as employed by Goncalves, is a common behavior for those who follow the verification approach. In his review volume E. O. Wilson, for example, considered three lines of experimental evidence, the same three that von Frisch had considered to most firmly establish the dance as a "language."

Wilson then added to that treatment a short account of Goncalves' experiments. In that account he wrote;

> Lionel Goncalves (1969) has recently performed a set of experiments in Brazil that test the waggle dance hypothesis in yet another way. . . . Over the short distances used in the experiments . . . orientation to odors played the major role, but it was also clear that the waggle dance was contributing an important fraction of the information. (1971:267)

Michener later echoed Wilson's nearly unqualified acceptance of Goncalves' interpretation when he wrote; "Another series of recent experiments [by Goncalves] independently supports the communicative function of dances" (1974:175).

Note how Wilson, above, considered the verification approach to be a "test" of the hypothesis. In reference to the three lines of evidence that von Frisch considered conclusive, as well as to the experiments by Goncalves, Wilson also wrote: "Although the communicative function of the waggle dance is firmly established by these experiments, it is still a remarkable and disturbing fact that the sensory modality in which the communication occurs remains to be disclosed" (1971:267).

That passage is most telling; let us consider the two halves separately.

In the first portion Wilson implied that an hypothesis can be established as fact. Note also Wilson's use of the word "test" in his reference to the fact that Goncalves had gained supportive evidence. In doing so, Wilson apparently ignored Karl Popper's assertion that *tests* are not designed to yield supportive evidence. Popper had, in fact, specifically addressed that point, as we pointed out in chapter 2: "It is easy to obtain confirmations, or verifications, for nearly every theory—if we look for confirmations" (1957:159), and: "Confirmations should count only if they are the result of *risky predictions*. . . . Every genuine *test* of a theory is an attempt to falsify it, or to refute it" (1957:159–160).

In the second portion of the above passage written by Wilson ("it is still a remarkable and disturbing fact that the sensory modality . . . remains to be disclosed") one can recognize the "crisis" state referred to by Thomas Kuhn. An inability to find "the sensory modality" could well mean that no such action exists (see this chapter's first epigraph and excursus VGR).

Gould, in referring to the work of Goncalves, followed our lead (Wenner 1974) and disagreed with Wilson's and Michener's assessment of those experiments. Gould wrote: "Another little-known study, again considered conclusive by some, is pointedly ignored by von Frisch and colleagues—perhaps with good reason" (1975b:692, n.9). In that note Gould also briefly mentioned Bizetsky's and Goncalves' protocol, and concluded: "Since recruits seem to have done as well with or without the dance information, this experiment is unconvincing. The preference for the direction of the forager station was probably due to the fact that the wind always blew in that direction."

Gould's treatment of Goncalves' work falls within the realm of what might be expected of one committed to the verification approach. Gould saw the experiment as "unconvincing" with respect to *support* of the language hypothesis. He thereby failed (as Goncalves, Wilson, and Michener had) to recognize the fact Goncalves' results were anomalous and that the dance language hypothesis was in even deeper trouble than it had been before.

Gould later reiterated his dissatisfaction with Goncalves' results in even stronger language. In doing so, he also faulted Goncalves' technique, just as he had done earlier when he criticized our method of training bees (see excursus GT). Gould wrote: "Goncalves' conclusion that there is 'communication of direction by means of dancing' seems wholly unjustified. On the whole, this technique is too inexact to be practical" (1976:234).

Goncalves' experimental results actually quite convincingly countered the expectations of the dance language hypothesis. Indeed, perhaps there was "good reason" for von Frisch and others to have "pointedly ignored" or dismissed Goncalves' contribution.

ESCH AND BASTIAN (1970)

Esch and Bastian restrained experienced foragers that had been feeding at a station near their experimental hive and then released them again after one of the foragers had been retrained to feed at a station located 200 meters away. The behavior of these previously restrained foragers was observed as they attended the dances of that single successful forager. Esch and Bastian also kept track of the success of these rerecruited foragers during their search for the new 200-meter station in the field.

The experiment was repeated seven times, with ten potential foragers involved each time.

According to the dance language hypothesis, these former foragers should have attended the dance and flown directly out. The question, then, was: "Could these attendants *rapidly* find the *new* site, which had the same odor of the food they had visited earlier?" If so, one conclusion could be that foragers had *used* direction and distance information that they presumably could have obtained from the dancing bee in the hive.

It is obvious from the experimental design that Esch and Bastian did not use the strong inference approach but worked within the Realism school. Even so, they were in a position to view their results either: 1) as a test of the hypothesis (the falsification approach) or 2) as a verification of the dance language hypothesis. Their interpretation of results indicated that they chose the latter course.

Even with the strong bias favoring successful rerecruitment inherent in Esch and Bastian's experimental design (such as the presence of a familiar odor), very few foragers provided verification for the dance language hypothesis (see Wells and Wenner 1973; Gould 1976). Only fourteen of the seventy experimental bees attended dances and subsequently found the new location of the station. Twenty others attended dances but failed to arrive at the station. The remaining thirty-six former foragers attended no dances.

Ten of the fourteen "successful" recruits required between two and nine exploratory flights (after repeated contacts with the dances of regular foragers between flights) before they finally located the station. Only four of the fourteen successful recruits, then, located the food on the first flight, and only two of them did so within a minute after leaving the hive. Worse yet, the average time for arrival by successful recruits was 8.5 minutes, compared with the less than a half-minute duration that should have been needed for a "beeline" flight between hive and station (Wenner 1963; see also excursus NEG).

As indicated above, Esch and Bastian could have viewed their results as a "falsification" of the dance language hypothesis; recruit bees (dance attendants) in their experiment did not behave as expected under that hypothesis. That is, recruits obviously did *not* "fly directly out" to the feeding station in the manner claimed by von Frisch (1948:10; see also our chapter 6).

Instead, Esch and Bastian, by following the verification approach, focused on the success of those few recruits that managed to reach the station eventually. They concluded, in part:

> In two cases . . . we were able to see the newcomers approach the food site from a considerable distance. They came straight from the

hive in a zig-zag flight. . . . It was obvious from their behavior that they were *not* searching at random. One had the impression that they knew the location of the food site. (1970:180)

If Esch and Bastian had been working within the strong inference approach (comparing their results to what might be expected under the two competing hypotheses—dance language and odor search), they could have recognized the significance of the "zigzag" flight pattern by those two "successful" recruits. The flight behavior they observed fits in well with the odor-search paradigm ("anemotaxis") for all flying insects (see our chapter 5 and excursus OS).

Furthermore, the wind was very light on the day those two foragers "flew directly out." Under light wind conditions, winds are generally far more variable in direction than when they are stronger. (Esch and Bastian provided information only on the average wind direction during the entire experimental period.)

Even though their experiments were run in the summer of 1969, Esch and Bastian included no mention of our double-control (Johnson 1967a; Wenner 1967) nor of our "crucial" experimental results (Wenner, Wells, and Johnson 1969). We see in that omission, once again, a focus on the successful, as is characteristic of the verification approach. That same attitude was evident in the first sentence of their results: "We performed seven *successful* experiments between June 17 and July 10, 1969" (1970:176; emphasis theirs). They did not indicate the number of "unsuccessful" experiments run.

GOULD, HENEREY, AND MACLEOD (1970)

Earlier enthusiasm for the results of the Gould, Henerey, and Mac-Leod (1970) "definitive" experiments dissipated with time, when it became apparent that the issue had not been resolved by their results after all (e.g., Wells and Wenner 1973; Wenner 1974; Gould 1976). Also, Gould (and his doctoral committee) apparently later recognized the inadequacy of that research, as evidenced by the fact that he continued attempts to conduct other "definitive" experiments for his dissertation project (Gould 1975a, 1975b, 1975c; Gould 1976; see also our chapter 13).

The inclusion of a detailed analysis of all of the early experimental results here would be an empty exercise. Rather than reaffirming the dance language hypothesis, as they thought, Gould and co-workers actually inadvertently negated that hypothesis (see excursus NEG).

However, we include a selection of those earlier results and an accompanying analysis to illustrate further the contrast between the verification, falsification, and strong inference approaches.

In 1965–1970, the intellectual climate surrounding the dance language controversy (see chapter 11) was considerably different than it was ten years later. In the 1960s very few people understood the true nature of our message, which was the need to examine carefully all basic assumptions and to evaluate the *original* experimental evidence that had been gathered in support of the dance language hypothesis. Fewer yet were equipped to appreciate the need for a falsification or (better yet) a strong inference approach rather than a verification approach to the problem.

After the Salk Institute affair in 1966 (see excursus SI), Seymour Benzer and Robert Sinsheimer at the California Institute of Technology became interested in the question of a "language" among bees. Benzer had earlier been a physicist who had moved into phage genetics (Keller 1983). At the time of the Salk Institute affair, he had just moved into research on insects and become intrigued by the dance language issue. In May of that year, he requested reprints of our work, and in July he wrote: "If you are right, it will not be the first time that fairy tales have become part of the gospel of science."

The major question remaining, then, given that the work of Gould, Henerey and MacLeod (1970) is no longer considered "definitive," is not: "Did they resolve the issue?" but: "*Why* did they not resolve the issue?"

From our perspective, the reasons for this failure were threefold: 1) by the summer of 1969, the dance language paradigm was too deeply entrenched to admit any contrary interpretation, 2) Gould and co-workers followed a verification rather than a falsification or strong inference approach in their experiments, and 3) they selected, a priori, an inappropriate "desert" location for their experiments, not realizing that the type of desert they chose for their experiments (eastern Oregon) would have an abundance of very pungent vegetation, the source of many distinctive and extraneous locality odors.

Consider now the following points about those three assertions of ours:

1) *Initial assumptions.* The validity of the first of our three assertions is evident in one of the opening comments in the paper by Gould, Henerey, and MacLeod, as follows: "Simply demonstrating that olfactory cues are sufficient in a particular situation does not mean that *the dance language* is not used under other conditions" (1970:544; emphasis ours). It is clear from their statement that they

began their research with the assumption that bees *had* a language, which had either been "discovered" by von Frisch or been "proven" by him to exist.

2) *The verification approach.* The above quotation also applies to our second assertion. It is evident from the content of the Gould, Henerey, and MacLeod paper that they were seeking confirmation for the language premise; that bias led to an "affirmation of the consequent" as outlined by Hempel (1966). The experiments they ran were thus a return to the single-control design, as employed by von Frisch, and were almost guaranteed to provide supportive evidence. Furthermore, adherence to a verification approach allowed Gould and associates to ignore the extensive set of negative results we had obtained earlier by means of our double-control and "crucial" experiments (see our chapters 9 and 10).

3) *Extraneous odors.* In both their series 1 and series 2 experiments (see their tables 3 and 5), the rate of recruit arrivals actually *increased* after they switched from scented to unscented sugar solution. They apparently did not appreciate the significance of that sudden increase in numbers of recruited bees, even though they had the report of our 1969 "crucial" experiment (Wenner, Wells, and Johnson 1969) in hand before they began their study. In that paper we had published a considerable amount of data (see our table 1), which clearly indicated that lack of odor in the food should result in essentially no recruitment (sucrose in solution has no scent because its vapor pressure is zero). Gould, Henerey, and MacLeod did not mention our extensive results in their paper. (See also our quotation in the discussion of their series 1 experiments, below.)

ANALYSIS OF THE GOULD, HENEREY, AND MACLEOD DATA

To clarify what we mean by the above three points, we provide next an analysis of the two series of experiments run by Gould, Henerey, and MacLeod.

Series 1 Experiments

This series was actually a rather remarkable technical feat. The three of them tagged 5,000 bees with 2,200 distinct markers (duplication meant that two to three bees had the same mark). Gould and co-workers then had foragers trained to visit one or the other of two stations located in opposite directions from the hive, under the assumption that odors in those two localities were identical.

Whenever possible, Gould, Henerey, and MacLeod watched the foragers dance in the hive and kept careful track of the behavior of labeled potential recruits after those marked bees had attended the dance. They measured flight times for searching recruits and also determined the percentage of success.

The distance between hive and feeding station was 120 meters. One-way flight time for that distance by unloaded bees in calm air is only 16 to 18 seconds (Wenner 1963; see excursus NEG; see also the Gould, Henerey, and MacLeod citation no. 16). They wrote: "delays between the recruits' dance attendance and arrival at a feeding station were distributed almost uniformly from < 1 minute to 9 minutes" (1970:551).

However, their statement is apparently not accurate, as data in their table 4 reveals. Actually, more than 40 percent of the bees required more than nine minutes to find one of the two stations, whether it was in the "correct" direction or located in the opposite direction.

The success rate of searching recruits was little better. Less than 14 percent of the marked searching bees found either station, as Gould Henerey, and MacLeod indicated (1970:550): "in the series 1 experiments . . . 277 different bees attended 155 observed dances. Only 37 . . . of these 277 attendants were successfully recruited and later caught at a feeding station" (1970:550).

In addition, of those thirty-seven, only twenty-five recruits ended up in the "correct" direction; the other twelve ended up at a station located in the opposite direction. According to the dance language hypothesis, however, *all thirty-seven* should have arrived at the "correct" station. Gould and co-workers had conducted a real test of the hypothesis without realizing that fact (see excursus NEG).

Finally, searching recruits found the stations even after scent was removed from the food (see their table 3). In fact, the total number of recruit arrivals at the two stations was slightly higher immediately after they had removed odor from the food. For example, they caught 122 recruits after removing odor from the food (their experiment C2), as against the 89 recruits they caught before they removed that odor (their experiment C1).

Those anomalous results thus revealed that locality odors could well have influenced recruitment success in their experiments. We were more fortunate in our experiments, in that we could control against extraneous odors much more effectively in the dry grass fields we used in the Santa Barbara area (see chapter 8).

As is common in the verification approach, Gould and co-workers did not refer in their paper to the fact that no odor leads to no recruitment (Wenner, Wells, and Johnson 1969). Neither did they consider the possibility that their continued success at getting recruitment after odor removal from the food might have been due to extraneous (distinctive locality) odors.

Series 2 Experiments

The series 1 experiments ended abruptly when all of the bees abandoned the experimental hive ("absconded," in beekeepers' terms). As Gould later stated it: "The problem with the Series 1 work was that two different sets of dances were going on simultaneously. Happily, the colony absconded, numbered tags and all, and put an end to this approach" (1976:226).

Thereafter, the format of the series 2 experiments differed considerably from those of series 1 experiments. Even though Gould, Henerey, and MacLeod apparently marked individuals in the new series, they published no data on the performance of individual searching recruits, as they had done for the series 1 experiments. Instead, the experiments had two new design elements.

Ten foragers collected 1.0M sugar solution at one of the stations (the experimental station), and fifteen foragers collected 0.5M solution at the other (the control station). By providing different strengths of sugar solution, foragers visiting the experimental station (with its richer food) would frequently dance after return to the hive, but those from the control station would do so less often. In addition, the Nasanov gland of the foragers (see excursus NG) was sealed shut with a lacquer-based paint.

When Gould, Henerey, and MacLeod ran the experiments in that manner (the single-control design), they found that 96 percent of the 295 recruits caught had ended up at the experimental station (with its richer food), and only 4 percent at the control station. (In earlier experiments they had found that recruits did not arrive at feeding stations unless dances had occurred in the hive, as reported earlier by von Frisch.)

Gould and co-workers attributed this great imbalance of recruitment to the use of direction information obtained by recruits from dancing bees. However, as mentioned above, they failed to entertain the possibility that odor differences in the localities of the stations could have been responsible for the discrepancy (see Wells and Wenner 1973).

Gould, Henerey, and MacLeod also did not address the fact that the results of their series 2 experiments differed markedly from the results of their series 1 experiments. They relied instead on their assumptions, and wrote: "The validity of these results depends upon the success of our efforts to make the stations in every way equivalent" (1970:551).

The pattern of results, however, was similar in some important respects to that of their series 1 experiments, and also revealed anomalies. For example, when they switched from scented to unscented solution (see their table 5), recruitment actually increased (126 recruits after removal compared to the 98 recruit arrivals before scent removal).

According to the results we had published a year earlier (Wenner, Wells, and Johnson 1969), the recruitment rate should have plummeted after scent removal (see our quotation in the above presentation of their series 1 experimental results). The implication is that Gould, Henerey, and MacLeod had *not* been successful at eliminating specific locality odors near each of their stations.

Again, Gould, Henerey, and MacLeod did not mention in their report that their results were anomalous. Under the verification approach, of course, only "successful" results are stressed. Under the falsification or strong inference approaches, however, the negative results they obtained would have to be addressed.

A final point should be made in reference to the experiments done by these three workers. Given the bias they had before they started their experiments (see the quotation at the beginning of this section), Gould, Henerey, and MacLeod should have adopted a double-blind technique for the series 2 experiments. Among other possibilities, the strength of the sugar solution used at each of the two stations should have been unknown to any of them until after all of the results had been tallied.

By contrast, in our double-control and "crucial" experiments, we had no a priori notion of the results we *should* have obtained. We developed our odor-search model only after all the data were in. That is, we were involved with an "exploratory approach" at the time, as may be practiced in the Relativism school (see figure 3.1).

MAUTZ (1971)

Just as Gould, Henerey, and MacLeod had done earlier, Mautz assumed that he could conduct experiments in such a way that his experimental stations did not differ from one another, even with respect to locality odors. Mautz distinctively marked 1,000 bees in a colony of 4,000–5,000 bees. In each of his experiments he had a single forager making round trips between hive and feeding station. The low success rates he obtained for searching recruits were similar to those obtained by Esch and Bastian and by Gould and co-workers.

In an earlier analysis (Wells and Wenner 1973), we stressed that recruits in Mautz's experiments did not do as well as they should have if they had "used" information contained in the dance maneuver. Fewer than half of the marked recruits that attended dances found the feeder. Mautz also found that recruits that spent a longer time attending a dancing bee succeeded more often than those attending a short time.

The average flight time for successful recruits was several times that needed by regular foragers. The flight time for unsuccessful recruits was twice that again.

Gould later concurred with *our* assessment of Mautz's results. He wrote:

> Since the average bee, if it found the source at all, typically took 18 times longer [than the forager's flight time], the statement that recruits "fly rapidly and with certainty" (von Frisch, 1967a) is subject to doubt. The recruits did not find the food rapidly, and since only one feeding station had been set out in both Mautz's and Esch and Bastian's experiments, the "certainty" of the recruits cannot be adequately judged. (1976:228)

Note here also how similar Mautz's results were to those obtained earlier by Gould, Henerey, and MacLeod (1970). Mautz, just like Gould and co-workers, failed to appreciate the "falsification" aspects of such results. Instead, Mautz also focused his attention on the behavior of successful recruits. He stressed, for example, that one bee found a station at 400 meters after following only five waggle cycles of the dance.

Despite the evidence provided by Mautz, Gould and Gould did not hesitate to write in 1988: "[recruit bees] fly directly to the food in the direction indicated by the dances they have attended" (1988:63).

LINDAUER (1971)

As mentioned earlier, Lindauer (1971) was the only one who ever nearly repeated either our double-control or "crucial" experiments; he partially replicated the latter.

The occasion for those experiments, as we understand it, is that Edward O. Wilson from Harvard was instrumental in arranging a trip for Lindauer to the Woods Hole Institution as a guest scientist for the summer of 1969, just months after the publication of the results of our "crucial" experiments in April (see chapter 11). Wilson was also later acknowledged by Lindauer "for critically reading the manuscript," which he later published (Lindauer 1971).

Esch and Bastian did not mention either our double-control or "crucial" experiments nor did they cite those papers. Neither did Gould, Henerey, and MacLeod treat the results we obtained in those experiments. Lindauer, on the other hand, came closer to addressing the issue head on and eventually *nearly* repeated our "crucial" experiments, even though he did not do so while at Woods Hole. Instead, while there his experiments were essentially identical to the series 2 experiments of Gould and co-workers, which were being run during the same season.

Before describing his experiments, Lindauer listed three objections to the design of our "crucial" experiments. In doing so, he revealed that he had somehow missed the reason for our design. In the first point he raised, for example, he wrote: "When the forager group is fed with a scented sucrose solution at sites 1 and 3 [the outside sites] for 2 or 3 days running, the odor still clings to the hairy bodies of the bees on the subsequent days. Thus, on the crucial experimental day, the dances still indicate a food source marked by a [clove] scent. Thus, direction information and odor differ in the same dance, by indicating separate goals" (1971:91).

That statement was precisely the intent of our experimental design! In a mutually exclusive (strong inference) design (Platt 1964), one should permit the recruit bees to use one or the other cue ("language" *or* odor)—but not both. Recall, also, that von Frisch (e.g., 1962) had insisted that the dance directed hivemates "with great precision" to the source of food, that recruits "search only in the neighborhood of the indicated range" and "only in the direction in which the original feeding dish is located."

Lindauer's second objection (also ad hoc) was that we had abruptly terminated our experiments after three hours, and concluded:

> [Any] recruits that had already been alerted at the end of the experiment certainly must have searched unsuccessfully for food . . . long after the experiment had been terminated. Thus, it is understandable that on the next day they first followed the odor signal of the dancers . . . without paying much attention to the direction information in the straight run of the dance. (1971:91)

Unless we are mistaken, however, every experiment ever run on honey bee recruitment has had to be terminated abruptly. In the "Methods" section of his paper, Lindauer provided no indication that he had done otherwise.

Lindauer's third objection to our experiments was his claim that our use of two outside stations would permit recruits to "integrate" the direction information from bees dancing for sites 1 and 3 and fly out in the intermediate direction. A comment on this ad hoc objection will be provided at the end of this section.

In his first series of experiments, Lindauer also assumed, as did Gould and co-workers and as did Mautz, "a perfect symmetry (to bees) of environmental odours at his locations," as we noted later in *Nature* (Wells and Wenner 1973). We continued therein:

> From this [Lindauer] inferred that, "if the recruits followed only the odour signals given by the dancers . . . they should have appeared in equal numbers at (both) sites." In accordance with his assumption Lindauer attributed the asymmetry in recruit arrivals to linguistic communication. Thus, the untested assumption of station symmetry (to bees) is central to the reasoning of Lindauer as well as to the above authors. (1973:172)

Finally, Lindauer could not recognize that it might be the dance language hypothesis itself that was failing; he felt that *we* had done something wrong, and wrote: "In connection with . . . points 2 and 3 [above], the scented site indeed could have misled the recruited bees" (1971:91).

It was only after Lindauer returned to Frankfurt (after encountering severe criticism during his seminar at Woods Hole) that he finally included a third central station in his experimental design and thereby more closely approximated the design of our "crucial" experiment (see chapter 10; figure 10.1; table 10.1; figures 10.2, 10.3).

Even then Lindauer did not follow our lead and conduct the experiment with unscented food at stations 1 and 3 in the first series he ran in Frankfurt. He used scented food at all three stations and thereby avoided the essential "crucial" component of the experimental design, wherein searching recruits would have to choose between odor and any dance language information.

The results Lindauer obtained could thus not strictly be compared to the results we obtained, since searching recruits could cue in on the scented food at the two outside stations, as well as at the intermediate site. Even so, he obtained 146, 91, and 203 recruits at the three stations, respectively; that is, too many arrived at the central station compared to what could be expected from the von Frisch hypothesis.

Lindauer recognized the discrepancy between those results and the expectations of the dance language hypothesis (under which virtually all recruits should have arrived at the two outside stations), and wrote: "Without doubt, direction information had been transmitted for sites 1 and 3. At the same time, the number of recruits which appeared at site 2 is far too high when compared with the statistical results of the fan experiments of von Frisch" (1971:94).

That result clearly bothered Lindauer, but it did not cause him to lose faith in the dance language hypothesis. The next entry in Lindauer's paper (see below) meshes well with a statement by Thomas Kuhn, who indicated that scientists are unwilling to "renounce the paradigm that has led them into crisis" even after severe and prolonged anomalies arise (Kuhn (1962) 1970a:77). Instead, Lindauer continued in his paper:

> This apparent inconsistency [failure to achieve the von Frisch results] was cleared up when the behavior of the recruits was monitored in the observation hive: *novices that were first interested in dancers from site 3 subsequently also followed dancers from site 1. . . .* The most likely conclusion to be drawn from our new result is *that the recruits integrate the directions communicated by other groups of foragers.* (1971:94; emphasis Lindauer's)

Note once again an adoption of an ad hoc auxiliary hypothesis in order to keep intact the original dance language hypothesis. The major problem with Lindauer's new auxiliary hypothesis is that natural nectar sources most often occur in more than one location. Under Lindauer's new hypothesis, recruits would often fly off in the wrong direction when they began their search.

Lindauer tried "a last experiment conducted in this series" (actually two experiments), but still did not duplicate our "crucial" experiment faithfully. Also, even though he used unscented food at the two outside stations, he did not have foragers visiting scented sucrose for several days prior to the test day, as we did.

Instead, Lindauer ran the experiment without odor accumulation in the system and obtained thirty-eight, one, and fifty-four recruits at the three sites, respectively. That result permitted him to conclude that recruits had used direction information obtained from the dance maneuver; he did so, however, only by ignoring the considerable negative evidence he had accumulated by that time.

He then repeated the experiment to see if "odor-accumulation in the hive" would alter those results. To do that, he again did not have bees feed on scented sucrose on the previous day(s), as we did. Instead, he suspended an odor-soaked piece of filter paper in the hive, while regular foragers collected unscented food from the two outside stations.

During the test run he used the same odor at the central station as that placed in the hive, but used no odor in the food at the two end stations. He then collected eighty-three, two, and fifty-two recruits at the three stations, respectively, and concluded that the results were "at least consistent with the [dance language] hypothesis."

However, regular foragers were then not carrying that odor back into the hive; instead, those foragers could have retained distinctive locality odors on their bodies which could have been used by searching recruits. (There would hardly be any reason for recruits to search for an odd odor suspended on filter paper in the hive.)

Gould later also acknowledged that Lindauer's experiments did not resolve the matter and gave several reasons why those experiments were not strictly comparable to ours. He concluded: "Lindauer's results are explained equally well by either the olfaction or the dance-language theory" (1976:230).

In all of the experiments described in this chapter, as well as in accounts of the reactions of scientists to their own negative evidence and to the negative evidence we had uncovered relative to the dance language hypothesis, a common thread can be seen throughout. Medawar covered that point: "It is a common failing—and one that I have myself suffered from—to fall in love with a hypothesis and to be unwilling to take no for an answer. A love affair with a pet hypothesis can waste years of precious time. There is very often no finally decisive yes, though quite often there can be a decisive no" ([1979] 1981:73).

Until 1974, then, the "crisis" (in Kuhn's terms) persisted and caused considerable anxiety in the relevant scientific community (see chapter 11). It was not until Gould did his doctoral research and published the results of that work that the scientific community again "breathed easy." In their minds Gould had "resolved" the honey bee dance language controversy.

Whether Gould actually did so has been thoroughly challenged by Rosin and others; that challenge is the subject of the next chapter.

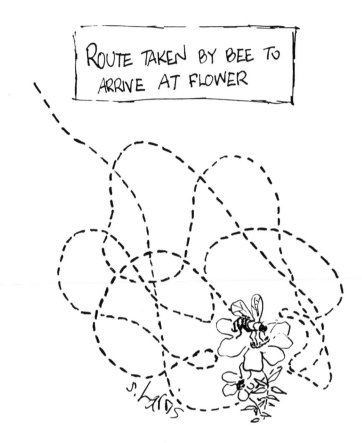

13

THE REALISM SCHOOL AND INTERPRETATION OF BEHAVIOR

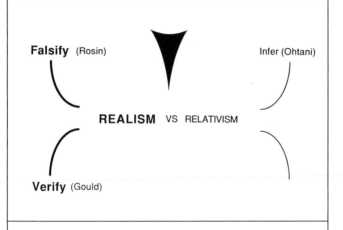

Falsify (Rosin) Infer (Ohtani)

REALISM VS RELATIVISM

Verify (Gould)

"The controversy has now reached a point where, although it is conceded that all previous results are accountable by use of odor, without recourse to 'language,' we are, nonetheless, being offered a 'conclusive' proof that honey bees use a 'language' of abstract symbols, albeit only under 'stress.'
—*R. Rosin 1978:589*

"For Lakatos, a research program ... degenerates if it ceases to make and confirm unexpected predictions and instead accounts for new facts with ad hoc hypotheses unanticipated in its heuristic. (An ad hoc hypothesis predicts only those facts it has been invented to explain; hence it does not promote scientific growth.)
—*George F. Kneller 1978:69*

R esearch done under the verification approach within the Realism school tends to be readily accepted by others working within the same school. That can occur even when hypotheses have not been formalized or really tested and even though work has not been repeated.

As indicated earlier, James Gould emerged from within the social network described in the previous two chapters, became the chief advocate of the dance language hypothesis, and found a willing audience for his reports. A good portion of his success apparently arose out of his focus on evidence he gathered that supported the hypothesis (the verification approach). At the same time he dismissed or failed to stress evidence that contradicted that hypothesis. He did that even though he and/or his co-workers had gathered much of the negative evidence (e.g., see excursus NEG).

The dance language paradigm hold in the scientific community (in ethology and sociobiology, in particular) was so profound that the weakness of results and discrepancies in interpretation went unnoticed. That happened even when the results Gould obtained in some of his experiments contradicted interpretations that he proposed for the results of other experiments (Rosin 1978, 1980a, 1980b.)

In some cases the omission of negative evidence by other proponents of the dance language hypothesis was extreme. In his book *Animal Thinking*, for example, Donald Griffin provided the reader with no hint that all was not right with the dance language hypothesis as originally conceived. He wrote:

> Another example of versatile communication among social insects . . . is the so-called dance language of honeybees, which was discovered by the remarkably brilliant and original experiments of Karl von Frisch. . . . These communicative dances are so astonishingly different from other animal communication that they seem discordant with everything else we know about animal behavior, to the point that they have not been adequately integrated into scientists' understanding of ethology. (1984:176)

Whereas one can dismiss Griffin's omission of contrary evidence because his was a "popular book," that can hardly be the case regarding the treatment of honey bee recruitment afforded in another book, *Honeybee Ecology* (Seeley 1985:83–88). Seeley omitted essentially all evidence, references, and implications not in agreement with the dance language hypothesis, and wrote:

> Our understanding of this remarkable communication system is due largely to the work of Karl von Frisch and his colleagues, whose

investigations now span seven decades. The vast literature on the subject has been summarized in several excellent reviews (von Frisch 1967; Lindauer 1967; Gould 1976; Dyer and Gould 1983). (1985:84)

Winston (1987) followed suit:

[The dance language] studies largely originated with the brilliant work of Karl von Frisch and his students and have involved some of the most refined, extensive, and carefully designed research in all of science. This work has been most thoroughly reviewed in von Frisch's classic book. . . . Other recent reviews have been done by Lindauer (1961); von Frisch (1967b); Michener (1974); Gould (1976); and Dyer and Gould (1983). (1987:150, 151)

The lists of reviews by Seeley and Winston include only publications written by scientists committed to the verification approach and supportive of the dance language hypothesis. Conspicuous by their absence are other reviews and analyses, notably one by Wells and Wenner (1973), one by Wenner (1974), and several by Rosin (1978, 1980a, 1980b, 1984).

Griffin's, Seeley's, and Winston's omissions are telling, in that one learns in general biology courses that opposing viewpoints are welcomed by scientists, an attitude we illustrated in chapter 1 by a quotation from Kneller: "The scientist generally tries harder than the layman to screen out personal prejudice and check for possible error. He seeks to make his assumptions explicit and *attends to the work of others in his field*" (1978:117; emphasis ours). In the case at hand, dance language proponents not only rejected our alternative *interpretation;* they dismissed our experimental *results* as well.

Within the context of the verification approach in the Realism school, on the other hand, Seeley's omissions (and those of others) become quite understandable. Wilson earlier expressed a similar attitude when he wrote: "The evidence . . . is overwhelmingly in favor of a communicative function for the waggle dance. A long series is now published of remarkable experimental results that have not been reasonably explained in any other way" (1972:6).

The depth of commitment in the relevant scientific community was evident also in the fact that Griffin, Seeley, and Winston omitted many pertinent qualifying statements by *proponents* of the dance language hypothesis, such as the following statement by Gould: "Von Frisch's controls do not exclude the possibility of olfactory recruitment alone, and Wenner is certainly correct in saying that an endless repetition of ambiguous experiments does not add anything to the evidence" (1976:241).

Perhaps the most significant omission from virtually all publications dealing with the dance language hypothesis, however, is the absence of any mention of a series of analyses published by Rosin (1978, 1980a, 1980b, 1984). According to tradition in science, one may consider Rosin's comments valid, since they survived the referee process, appeared in reputable journals, and have never been challenged in print.

In the previous chapter we analyzed the material published by Gould, Henerey, and MacLeod in 1970. Rosin went much further and analyzed in depth later publications by Gould, especially material included in his dissertation (1975a) and those contributions emanating from that dissertation research (1974, 1975b, 1975c, 1976).

Many of Gould's experiments relied upon the success of "misdirecting" waggle dances in the hive, as well as on the premise that single-control experiments were adequate. His experiments also relied heavily on the effectiveness of blocking the ocelli with black paint. (The three ocelli are simple eyes located between the two large compound eyes.)

Rosin treated the results of Gould and those of Schricker (e.g., Rosin 1980a, 1980b) in light of the contradictions inherent both with predictions of the dance language hypothesis and in terms of the lack of consistency between different sets of experimental results.

We feel that Rosin's contributions are actually quite pertinent and significant; they deserve special consideration with respect to our schematic diagram (see figure 3.1). We therefore treat portions of those contributions in depth in this chapter, one publication at a time. We follow the treatment of Rosin's work with a brief mention of pertinent contributions by Ohtani (1983), who also analyzed Gould's evidence. Finally, we examine the ocelli-blocking experiment that Renner and Heinzeller (1979) conducted; they had inadvertently (and apparently unwittingly) undermined the experimental design Gould used in his dissertation research.

ROSIN (1978): INSECT-LEVEL VERSUS HUMAN-LEVEL EXPLANATIONS

Those scientists who operate within the Realism school and who emphasize verification in their experimental protocol may fail to recognize flaws in their basic hypotheses and/or assumptions. Rosin, neither an adherent to that school nor a member of the community committed to the dance language hypothesis, on the other hand, did recognize such flaws.

In this first of several articles Rosin dealt with a number of factors related to the question "What might one expect insects to be able to do?" This question was addressed within the context of James Gould's experimental designs, and is treated here one point at a time.

1) *The basic hypothesis.* Gould and his supporters failed to recognize, from their perspective within the verification approach, a flaw in reasoning that did not escape Rosin; that is, one can neither design experiments on the basis of an untested hypothesis nor use that untested hypothesis to explain experimental results.

Gould had already admitted that earlier experimental results had not established the existence of a "dance language." He did so, however, only after he himself had obtained what he felt was sufficient supportive evidence (verification) for the hypothesis; it was then that he became trapped in circular reasoning.

As Rosin pointed out, the very design of Gould's experiments rested upon the assumption that bees had a language (paradigm hold); Rosin wrote:

> In the "Distance experiments" the whole array of experimental stations were restricted only to the direction presumably indicated to dance attendants by dances of the ocelli-treated foragers. . . . In the "Direction experiments" the whole experimental array was restricted to the distance presumably indicated to dance-attendants by dances of the ocelli-treated foragers, i.e. assuming, *a priori,* that potential-recruits use the distance information from dances. (1978:590)

Rosin continued:

> However, since [Gould] conceded that all previous results are accountable without recourse to "language," this basic hypothesis remains nonproven, and one cannot base any experiments on it, without a proper test for the validity of this basic hypothesis. (1978:590)

Unfortunately, Rosin wore a "different pair of spectacles" than those worn by the intended audience. Rosin assumed that the dance language hypothesis should be tested, but the relevant scientific community accepted the hypothesis as fact and focused only on supportive evidence. The paradigm hold prevailed; the assumption that bees already had a "language" was not open to question.

2) *Proper controls.* Rosin recognized that proper controls were lacking in Gould's experiments. However, that point was apparently missed by virtually everyone else who focused only on the evidence Gould

managed to obtain that supported the dance language hypothesis. Among other considerations, Rosin wrote:

> It is obvious that spatial design must have an effect on the distribution of new-arrivals, because it affects the spatial distribution of the air-borne odor-plumes from the food-stations. In fact, the author's "Wenner controls," where the results are attributed by [Gould] to use of odor alone by most new-arrivals, in spite of the fact that it is not proven that even a single [bee] used "language," suffice to demonstrate that the specific spatial design *per se*, results in a majority of new-arrivals at the array. (1978:591)

In the same section Rosin questioned the validity of the "fan experiment" design, as had been done earlier (see our chapter 5; Wenner 1962; Wenner 1971a). The array design itself can alter the distribution of recruits, especially when any wind is present (see excursus PN). Rosin wrote: "In these experiments, a symmetrical arrangement of stations about the axis connecting the hive with the forager-station yielded a distribution of new-arrivals which was also symmetrical about the same axis. This is also to be expected according to the olfactory hypothesis, which views arrival of recruits as a probability matter" (1978:593).

In other words (as described in chapter 5), the very experimental design Gould used could provide the results he obtained. Rosin recognized that failing of the Gould experimental design, and suggested another control that should have been used: "Adding to the original spatial design, a second array in a symmetrical position on the other side of the axis connecting the hive with the forager-station, can therefore serve as a proper control" (1978:593). To date no one has run an experiment with this additional control.

3) *Secondary (ad hoc) hypotheses.* Gould's technique of freely using ad hoc hypotheses to explain away unfavorable results did not escape Rosin's attention:

> The dismissal of the possibility that [recruits] could have arrived, through odor alone, at any station of the array, including the right "language" station, by claiming that the conditions of the experiments create a "stress" situation which elicits use of "language," is an arbitrary contention. Dismissal of new-arrivals at the "language"-wrong stations of the array, by claiming that they used "language," but they use "language" with errors, is another arbitrary contention. Dismissal of new-arrivals at the forager-station, i.e., "language"-wrong, but right locale-odor station, by claiming that . . . some bees, nonetheless, use odor-alone is yet another arbitrary contention. (1978:594)

238 THE REALISM SCHOOL

It was clear in Rosin's mind that Gould could have done much better and designed experiments that would not have necessitated the employment of so many ad hoc dismissals of "unfavorable" results once those results had been obtained (see the epigraph), as warned against by Popper, Lakatos, and many others. Rosin wrote: "All these arbitrary contentions, are, in fact, no more than secondary hypotheses conjured in order to prop [up] the primary 'language' hypothesis" (1978:594)

4) *Results not compatible with the use of "language."* There is probably not a scientist alive who has not *wanted* (at one time or another) a given set of results to emerge from an experiment, as mentioned by Medawar (1979:73). That is because each of us tends to form a "parental affection" (Chamberlin's term) for an hypothesis, even if we do not do so when first beginning experimentation. That parental attachment can lead one to focus only on *some* of the results, particularly results from "successful" experiments or from experiments where results came out "as expected."

Rosin perceived the spell that supportive evidence could hold when considering Gould's results, and wrote: "The results of the studies which led to the presumably conclusive proof that honey bees use a 'language' of abstract symbols, are impressive in that in the majority of cases presented, under 'stress' the distributions of new-arrivals indeed have a maximum at the array-station presumably indicated by 'language'" (1978:595).

However, Rosin also recognized that proponents of a hypothesis who work within the verification emphasis (such as in the case of Gould) may well focus only on experiments that "succeeded." Rosin wrote: "the results seem less impressive when it is realized that they are presented for only four 'Direction experiments' . . . at 390–400 m, out of thirty-nine such experiments mentioned in the text. They become even less impressive when a detailed comparison of arrival-ratios for specific stations is carried out" (1978:595).

After a detailed analysis of Gould's treatment of arrival ratios in his data, Rosin concluded:

Thus, the author ignores the need to view arrivals by odor alone as a probability matter, in spite of the fact that his own concession regarding all previous results requires accepting such a view. He also ignores the effects of spatial design and of changes in this design, in spite of the fact that his own results demonstrate the effect. (1978:597)

An additional problem is that Gould had apparently not realized that bees supposedly using *direction* information with great accuracy

in one set of experiments had failed to use *distance* information correctly in the same experiments, and vice versa. In other words, Gould
overlooked the same anomaly that von Frisch had overlooked earlier
in his original 1946 presentation of the dance language hypothesis
(see our chapter 6).

5) *"Language efficiency.* In this section Rosin recognized an additional point that seems to have escaped the attention of most dance
language proponents. Gould, Henerey, and MacLeod, in their 1970
paper, reported *direct evidence* on: a) the small percentage of recruited
bees that found the feeding station, b) the long time in flight for
successful recruits, and c) the many flights made out from the hive
before recruits found a feeding station (see chapter 12 and excursus
NEG).

Rosin perceived, quite astutely, that Gould's assumptions and
interpretation in his later publications did not correspond with what
was possible on the basis of the results that he and his co-workers had
obtained earlier. Rosin wrote:

> The invalidation of high-efficiency for the presumed use of "lan-
> guage," removes the basic rationale behind the claim that "lan-
> guage" is at all necessary, when honey bees can use odor alone with
> no lesser efficiency. . . . why, with the possession of such a sophisti-
> cated and efficient "language" mechanism, would honey bees not
> use it regularly? (1978:598)

Gould thus apparently did not feel the need to reconcile his experimental protocol with the results he had published earlier (see excursus NEG).

According to earlier results (Gould, Henerey, and MacLeod 1970),
then, recruits had to attend many dances, make repeated trips out
from the hive before being successful, and spend a considerable amount
of time in flight before finding a feeding station (40 percent required
more than ten *minutes* for a sixteen *second* flight; see excursus NEG).

Gould's practice of moving his test stations every twenty minutes
in later experiments (with only a five-minute interval between experimental runs) failed to take into account these earlier results obtained
by his coworkers and himself. Rosin, on the other hand, recognized
that each move of a station would inevitably leave in the air a great
many searching bees supposedly using the "incorrect" dance language information denoting the old station. Earlier departees from
the hive would then be mixed up with those presumably searching for
the new food location.

Rosin concluded that an odor-search hypothesis meshed quite well with what one could expect of an insect, and that a supposed "language" capability would require "no less than a human-level ability," and wrote:

> Although it might have seemed at first glance, that the ability of honey bees to use a "language" of abstract symbols, at least under highly specific conditions, has finally been conclusively proven, a detailed analysis of the theoretical process underlying the design of experiments and interpretation of results, demonstrates that the proof so far remains as inconclusive and non-valid as ever. This maintains honey bees at the state of ordinary insects, which may be somewhat disappointing. But then, it also retains our old-fashioned phylogenetic system in a relatively intact state, which is no small consolation. (1978:600)

Rosin's objections to Gould's handling of his own data can also be viewed in the context of teleology and anthropomorphism. Those committed to the dance language hypothesis are convinced that the dance maneuver "must be good for something, otherwise the bees would not expend all that energy producing it" (see excursus TE).

That teleological assertion is often followed immediately by an unacceptable (and unsubstantiated) anthropomorphic explanation: "It has to be good for what we human beings think it would be used for."

ROSIN (1980A): PARADOXES OF THE DANCE LANGUAGE HYPOTHESIS

With respect to the material presented in the previous section one might ask, "How is it that scientists can live with such serious discrepancies?" One answer to that question was provided by Thomas Kuhn, when he wrote: "Normal science does and must continually strive to bring theory and fact into closer agreement. . . . its object is to solve a puzzle for whose very existence the validity of the paradigm must be assumed" (1970a:80).

"Normal science" was a term Kuhn coined to explain research done under a generally accepted set of assumptions. In another sense, this behavior can come under the heading of "concept-driven" research (Wenner 1989), in which the actual behavior of the organism becomes less important to the scientist than the theories or paradigms under which the scientific community operates. Coupled with that adherence to the paradigm itself, of course, is a need for researchers to mesh in well with their scientific community (see chapter 11). Kuhn also recognized that need to conform when he stressed that there was "no standard higher than the assent of the relevant community" (1970a:94).

The official reaction to Rosin's 1978 paper was a perhaps predictable silence (i.e., if ignored, Rosin might be forgotten). Rosin, however, did not "go away" but persisted and published additional analyses. The 1980a publication provided a treatment of various "reaffirmations" of the language hypothesis (e.g., Brines and Gould 1979; Esch and Bastian 1970; Gould 1974; 1975b, 1975c, 1976; Gould, Henerey, and MacLeod 1970; Mautz 1971; Schricker 1974; Stephen and Schricker 1970). Rosin's treatment had thus earlier covered much the same ground as presented in our chapter 12.

Rosin first treated various problems associated with the odor-search model for honey bee recruitment (see chapter 5 and excursus OS), concluding with the statement:

> Paradoxically, the "dance language" hypothesis could not account for the facts which v. Frisch had discovered in his attempts to support his olfactory hypothesis. It could not account for new arrivals at various distances, up to 1 km from the hive, when foragers foraged [only] 16 m from the hive. In the strain he used dances begin to turn directional at 25 m and are completely so at 100 m. Thus, when foragers forage 16 m from the hive, their dances indicate that the source is at the most 100 m from the hive. (1980a: 777)

(Von Frisch, of course, recognized the existence of a few bees that performed with great error, but he labelled them "outsiders"). Rosin then continued treating objections to an earlier version of our odor-search model, and concluded:

> Nonetheless, it must be stressed that, irrespective of the details of Wenner's model, the ability of new honey-bees to locate a distant food source, by use of no other information from foragers, except odor information, is amply proven. It was initially proven by no other than v. Frisch himself ... long before the inception of the "dance language" hypothesis. It was later proven again by Johnson (1967), Wenner (1967), Wenner et al. (1969), Wells & Wenner (1973), as well as [by] Gould (1975a, b). (1980a:780)

Rosin then dealt with "Wenner's major claim that honey-bees do not use 'dance language' information" (as has been covered in earlier chapters in this book) and continued with "New Paradoxes," which had arisen out of further attempts to verify the dance language hypothesis. In particular, Rosin focused on experimental results and interpretation published by Schricker (1974) and by Gould (1974, 1975a, 1975b). The following text covers the points raised.

1) *Schricker's forager-poisoning technique.* Schricker had poisoned foraging bees with the insecticide parathion in order to get them to provide "misleading" distance information to potential recruits. That is, the recruitment dance of a poisoned forager has a shorter duration time (presumably indicating a shorter distance) than one conducted by a normal forager. Rosin recognized a paradoxical situation that emerged from that approach and from the results obtained:

> There were new arrivals after poisoning, also at the intermediate and furthest stations [in addition to that indicated]. Moreover, before poisoning, the majority of new arrivals arrived not at all at the distance of the forager station (as they should have done, had they used "dance language" information), but at the intermediate stations. Thus we have a paradoxical situation. The "dance language" hypothesis now cannot at all account for facts which gave rise to [the hypothesis] in the first place. (1980a:783)

Rosin also recognized another inconsistency in Schricker's results and interpretation, one that fits in well with what might be expected from those who only attempt to verify their hypothesis: "Incidentally, Schricker himself completely overlooked the fact that his pre-poisoning results are totally incompatible with the 'dance language' hypothesis" (1980a:783).

2) *Gould's "irrefutable" proof.* In his "misdirection" experiments, Gould shined a light into the hive, thereby altering the path of dancing foragers and presumably "misdirecting" potential recruits. Rosin recognized a series of discrepancies in the results Gould obtained (and in the resultant interpretation), discrepancies not reconcilable with the dance language hypothesis. Rosin summarized them:

> The "dance language" hypothesis, as we have seen, originated for the purpose of explaining new arrivals under natural conditions (when the information is not misleading), at the exact source visited by the foragers. Gould claims to have proven use of "dance language" information under "stress." Nonetheless, he managed to prove that all his new arrivals at the forager station always used odor alone. Again, paradoxically, so far the "dance language" hypothesis is presumably needed only to account for new arrivals when the information is misleading. (1980a:784)

As we note elsewhere in this volume (see excursus PN), the fan design used by Gould does not constitute an effective arrangement of stations for *testing* the use of dance maneuver information, since each of them is not identical to the others (e.g., some stations do not have stations on either side of them). In order to use the fan experiment design, Gould had to overlook the fact that such an experimental design had been challenged earlier (e.g., Wenner 1962, 1971a, 1974).

Rosin recognized the overriding appeal of the verification approach (wherein challenge and negative evidence may be ignored in the face of supportive evidence) in Gould's experimental designs, and wrote: "As expected in the case of a scientific revolution (Kuhn 1970) Gould's point of view is incommensurable with that of opponents of the 'dance language' hypothesis. He carried [out] the experiments mentioned above for his own specific purposes" (1980a:786).

Rosin then continued with an analysis of other problems in the presumed proofs of Schricker and Gould. Additional control stations could have been provided in both of Schricker's and Gould's experiments in areas where neither "misdirected" nor "nonmisdirected" recruits should have been searching. (To that we might add that such control sites should be placed upwind from all of the experimental sites; such a placement would constitute a truer *test* of their hypothesis—see chapters 8 and 10).

3) *Resolution of the paradoxes.* In this section of the 1980a paper Rosin recognized incompatibilities in reasoning by Schricker and Gould (and von Frisch before them), as they attempted to dismiss unfavorable results pertinent to the predictions of the dance language hypothesis. We thus again have an example of the "affirmation of the consequent" (Hempel 1966). Each of the three researchers merely provided interpretations consistent with the a priori assumption of a "dance language" among bees. That point did not escape Rosin.

Regarding Schricker, Rosin wrote:

> I could not even imagine that Schricker, in fact, stated here that the majority of new arrivals, who in the pre-poisoning experiment . . . arrived at the intermediate stations, intended to fly to the furthest stations, but were stopped on their way there. . . . A similar suggestion had been earlier invoked by v. Frisch . . . to handle similar problems. Schricker's statement means that he presumes to know what the bees had in mind (which no one can know), and this knowledge takes precedence over what we see, i.e. over the simplest, most obvious conclusion. (1980a:787)

However, within the context of the Realism school, concepts often have precedence over the actual biology of organisms (Wenner 1989). Rosin should not have been surprised by the ad hoc explanation provided by Schricker to explain away the "unfavorable" results he obtained in his experiments.

Rosin also recognized Gould's addiction to supportive evidence and his exclusion of the various sets of negative evidence he obtained during experimentation, evidence counter to the prevailing dance language hypothesis.

Among other considerations, Rosin focused on Gould's ad hoc "locale odor" hypothesis, which he employed to explain how bees could be searching in a location other than that supposedly indicated by dance language information. In doing so, Gould apparently failed to realize that expectations from one of his hypotheses often contradicted expectations from other hypotheses, and vice versa. Rosin wrote:

> Gould's forced concession that his own "nonstress" results are due to use of odor alone by most, or even all, new arrivals, already refutes his "locale odor" hypothesis. . . . Gould's "stress" experiments constitute a proper, though not the best, test of the two hypotheses against one another, and the results refute the "dance language" hypothesis. (1980a:790–791)

Following the treatment of Schricker and Gould, Rosin continued the analysis by documenting the inconsistencies present in von Frisch's writings over time:

> If honeybees have a sophisticated and efficient device like the "dance language", why resort to a crude and inefficient use of odor alone? By [the mid-1970s] practically everyone managed to overlook the fact that v. Frisch had already proven that new arrivals can use odor alone to locate food sources . . . (1923, 1939). Moreover, he had already proven that many of these new arrivals could not have used "dance language" information. (1980a:792)

In that same section Rosin reviewed reasons for von Frisch's early adherence to an olfactory hypothesis and the evidence that he had gathered in support of that hypothesis. By "creating the image" (Atkinson 1985) that bees had a "dance language" and "converting" others to that hypothesis in 1946, von Frisch had to go through a reversal of attitude on the matter of odor perception.

On the basis of early work, von Frisch had concluded that bees did not have a keen sense of odor perception (i.e., it was not different from that of humans). The lack of keen perception, of course, fit in well with the notion that a "dance language" would be "useful."

Ribbands (1953:43, 1955b), on the other hand, conducted much the same type of experiment as those conducted by von Frisch and found bees to be highly sensitive to small odor concentrations. Since the language hypothesis was already deeply entrenched, Ribbands' results had little impact. Neither did other indications that bees might be using odor rather than "language." Rosin wrote: "Ever since its inception, the 'dance language' hypothesis, although it gained general acceptance, has been constantly struggling through numerous additional *ad hoc* revisions" (1980a:794).

Rosin then outlined how von Frisch's objections to the olfactory hypothesis countered some of his own earlier claims, and concluded: "We have seen that the 'dance language' hypothesis was paradoxical from the start, because it could not explain results obtained by v. Frisch in support of his olfactory hypothesis. . . . Because of its great success in gaining fast general acceptance, it presumably did not have to become very precise" (1980a:797).

This last point underscores a weakness in any biological research that relies primarily on gaining confirming evidence (verification), rather than on the testing of hypotheses. Both Schricker and Gould apparently felt that they were "testing" the dance language hypothesis against an olfactory hypothesis. Actually, however, they were seeking supportive evidence for the former (as is evident in many of the statements made by both of them). Rosin summarized the difficulty posed by that approach:

> The ability of honey-bees to use "dance language" information under any circumstances, has, of course, never been proven yet. All the concessions resorted to by supporters of the "dance language" hypothesis so far, are *ad hoc* revisions. As such they can never provide a valid proof, because an *ad hoc* revision at best yields a revised hypothesis for testing. Supporters of the hypothesis seemed to have missed this point too. (1980a:799)

Whereas some staunch supporters of the dance language hypothesis remain convinced that they or that someone has "proven" that bees really do have a language, other known supporters of the dance language hypothesis do not seem to accept those experiments as definitive. Taber, for example, wrote: "You would think that with all the interest in von Frisch's work and the very impressive work of his many students over the past 50 years that the hypothesis could be verified, but to my knowledge it has not" (1986:538).

In this paper (1980a), then, Rosin quite thoroughly outlined the various paradoxes that had emerged during reaffirmation of the dance language hypothesis. For Rosin the process was a demonstration of "the ability of scientists to avoid seeing that which they do not wish to see." For us it has been an example of the weakness of "concept-driven" research as opposed to "organism-driven" research (Wenner 1989).

One can now ask, "Just what is the dance language hypothesis?" As indicated in chapter 1, dance language proponents would likely be hard pressed to agree on a statement. Rosin wrote: "The truth of the matter is that the fast acceptance of an imprecise hypothesis resulted in the passage of twenty years before the challenge of the hypothesis even began" (1980a:798).

With the emergence of so many paradoxes and qualifications, a true test of whatever the modern dance language hypothesis might be becomes ever more difficult to conduct.

ROSIN (1980B): THE FOUNDATIONS OF BIOLOGY AND BEHAVIOR

General biology textbooks often contain mention of "Occam's razor" or the "law of parsimony," whereas psychology texts generally refer to an application of that principle as "Morgan's canon." Simply put, that means that we should not entertain a complex explanation (more forces or causes than are necessary) for a phenomenon, when a simple explanation would suffice. In his 1976 review article Gould challenged that rule in the following manner: "the application of Morgan's Canon and other such 'simplicity filters' has *overcorrected* an earlier tendency to anthropomorphize animals. Too much skepticism may become a blinding bias against yet-undiscovered sensory modalities and processes in animals" (1976:241).

In doing so, Gould followed Donald Griffin's lead. From the approach used in his book *Animal Thinking*, it is obvious that Griffin (1984) wished to become free of the restraints accepted by others of us who are opposed to the use of anthropomorphism and teleology in studies of animal behavior.

Rosin challenged Griffin's and Gould's questioning of the validity of Morgan's canon in a series of scholarly arguments.

1) *The "Dance language" opposition: A counterrevolution?* Rosin viewed the original dance language hypothesis of von Frisch as a "revolution" in the Kuhnian sense. Our challenge of that hypothesis thus became a "counterrevolution," an attempt to convince the scientific community to return to an earlier olfactory hypothesis (see chapter 5 and excursus OS). Rosin wrote: "The quick success of the 'dance language' hypothesis is due, no doubt, to the fact that it offered an answer to two major problems simultaneously. It explained the recruitment of new bees, and also the survival values of the complex dances performed by foragers" (1980b:459).

The dance language hypothesis also proved instrumental in legitimizing what had previously been a purely descriptive science. Before that time, the study of animal behavior involved little more than watching and "objectively" describing behavioral patterns. Investigations into the mechanism of "the dance language" helped to elevate that field to a status on a par with other fields where complex sequences could be unraveled with the application of modern experimental techniques.

Rosin, while recognizing that our challenge of the dance language hypothesis was a counterrevolution, still viewed the new challenge as a revolution in its own right. Rosin's viewpoint rested on the fact that our challenge received such an adverse reception in the established scientific community:

> The counter-revolution, however, has fared as revolutions are expected to fare. The ruling "dance language" paradigm won the endorsement of the Nobel Committee by the end of the same year which saw, at its beginning, the publication by Wells & Wenner (1973) of a proof that recruitment of new bees to distant sources is not at all hampered by the absence of "dance language" information. (Rosin 1980b:460)

2) *The Consequences of the "dance language" revolution.* Rosin perceived what Kuhn had predicted:

> Kuhn (1970) states that a crisis in a ruling paradigm often leads to a period of confusion and to the questioning of fundamental premises. . . . supporters [of the language hypothesis] . . . are already reexamining basic premises. . . . This leads them into a state of confusion, due to a questioning of fundamentals accepted prior to the "dance language" revolution. (1980b:460)

One of the most important questions, according to Rosin, is whether it is even possible for an insect to have a human-type language (in contrast to Griffin's attitude). Under the dance language hypothesis, that possibility was treated as an operational assumption.

With our demonstration that odor could be used by bees during recruitment to crops in the absence of dance language information (Wells and Wenner 1971, 1973; See also our chapters 5, 9, and 10), in much the same manner that other insects find food sources (see excursus OS), the principle of parsimony (Occam's razor) or Morgan's canon could be applied to the competing hypotheses, olfaction and language. Rosin wrote:

> Morgan stressed that his Canon only prohibits imputing to any
> animal a higher psychic faculty than is necessitated by the evidence

at hand. The Canon is thus not dogmatic, and assumes nothing *a priori*. It applies to the evidence only *a posteriori*, and it must be reapplied in view of new evidence. (1980b:463)

As for those in any walk of life, a scientist has several options when evidence emerges that conflicts with preconceived notions (see chapter 3). The evidence can be considered or ignored. Just as one can recognize the limitations imposed by the application of Morgan's canon, so also can one decide to reject Morgan's canon as inapplicable to the situation at hand if such an application would force a change in attitude or interpretation. That is because science has no rules dictating the avenue one should follow when conflicting evidence becomes available.

Moreover, when new evidence threatens the fundamental scientific approach one uses, there is an understandably strong temptation to ignore or dismiss the new evidence rather than reevaluate one's former approach. That is apparently why Griffin (1984:176) rejected all negative evidence while writing about the dance language hypothesis, even while recognizing that such a behavioral trait was not in accord with the known behavior of other animals (see the early part of this chapter). That rejection of negative evidence by Griffin permitted him to retain the highest tone of optimism with respect to what animals might be able to do. It apparently did not occur to him to question the original assumption.

As examples to illustrate problems with Morgan's canon and parsimony, Rosin treated the subjects of chimpanzee mastery of sign language and Griffin's study of bat echolocation. Neither process actually requires a "higher psychic level" on the part of those animals than other activities. Rosin felt that the use of a "language" by honey bees was quite another matter: "A honey-bee can presumably use, and interpret, symbols which stand for any specific value out of a whole continuum such as distance, or direction. The chimpanzee that can do that has not been born yet" (1980b:468).

After treating the results of Schricker and Gould in light of what one might expect of Morgan's canon, Rosin concluded:

> Supporters of the "dance language" hypothesis are, obviously, quite prepared to discard Morgan's Canon. They might be loath to tamper with the theory of evolution. They could, however, perhaps live with a few isolated exceptions to the theory of evolution. Perhaps the genes responsible for very complex responses which reduce survival value, just accumulated by accident. Perhaps the aberrant responses have some, not yet known, positive survival value. (1980b:472)

Rosin was thus disturbed that proponents of the dance language hypothesis could remain comfortable with that hypothesis, when that presumed behavior differed so much from what other animals could do and when so many contradictions existed, and wrote:

> I demonstrate elsewhere (Rosin 1978) that the claims of Gould's presumed proof constitute no more than his own hypothetical interpretation of his results, and a totally [unacceptable] one at that. I therefore challenge supporters to provide an acceptable interpretation of Gould's "stress" results by recourse to "dance language" information. (1980b:473)

The answer provided to Rosin was obvious in the writings of people such as Griffin (1984), Seeley (1985), and Winston (1987), who simply did not mention any of the inconsistencies in the results and interpretation of Schricker, Gould, and others. Griffin, Seeley, and Winston also did not either mention or cite Rosin; neither did they provide their readers with any information about the alternative odor-search hypothesis elucidated by Friesen, Johnson, Wells, and Wenner (as summarized in chapters 5 and 8).

But Rosin did not consider that all was lost when it became obvious that challenges of the dance language hypothesis were not welcome and that no one was about to either repeat Gould's experiments or to test his interpretations. That is because Rosin found that Gould and co-workers had already conducted a proper control experiment (Gould, Henerey, and MacLeod) that actually refuted Gould's presumed "conclusive resolution" of the dance language controversy (Gould 1976:234; see also excursus NEG).

The particular experiments referred to by Rosin were the "series 1" experiments of Gould, Henerey, and MacLeod (1970). In those experiments "dance language" information was not misleading, and "stress" was present at all times. Rosin wrote: "The expectation from the claims of Gould's presumed proof, that not one single new arrival should occur at the opposite station in that series 1, is totally valid. ... In effect there were quite a number of new arrivals at the opposite station in that series. ... Such new arrivals refute the claims of the presumed irrefutable proof" (1980b:477).

Rosin concluded:

> The results of series 1 [experiments] thus include new arrivals (about a third of the total) under "stress," who contradict the claims of Gould's presumed irrefutable proof. Moreover, unless we discredit those claims, such new arrivals must remain a complete mystery.

. . . All new arrivals in that series can, of course, be easily accounted [for] by use of odor alone (Wells & Wenner, 1973). (1980b:480)

However, Rosin overlooked the abovementioned importance of one of Kuhn's comments: "there is no standard higher than the assent of the relevant community." Since the "relevant community" of ethologists and sociobiologists focused only on supportive evidence under the verification approach in the Realism school, all of Rosin's arguments fell on deaf ears. The ad hoc explanations provided by Gould for totally contradictory sets of results and interpretation remained acceptable to the scientific community.

OHTANI (1983): IS THE HONEY BEE "DANCE LANGUAGE" REALLY A FACT?

Ohtani's analysis of Gould's research constituted a truly independent assessment of the evidence and interpretation published by Gould, for two reasons. Ohtani was neither a member of the dance language proponents' "social network" (see chapter 11) nor in any way acquainted with those of us who challenged the dance language hypothesis.

Under those circumstances, according to scientific custom, one would think that his arguments would have been recognized as just such an independent assessment. At least two factors prevented this from happening: 1) Ohtani's article was in Japanese, and 2) those who follow the verification approach are apparently not receptive to critiques of accepted theory.

For clarification of Ohtani's position, we address some of his major points here by reference to a translation of his paper now on file with the International Bee Research Association (IBRA).

1) *The need for a counterexperiment.* Ohtani recognized that Gould conducted only a portion of the experiments that should have been run, and wrote:

Although Gould experimented with dancers having covered ocelli and dance followers with open eyes, he did not experiment with dancers with open eyes and dance followers with ocelli covered with black enamel. Because of this another interpretation cannot be denied. For example, it is possible to think that the open-eyed foragers sensed the light being bent to the left from the opposite direction of gravity and flew to the righthand direction of feeder 1 with the same angle, as compensation for the bent light. In that case dance information would become insignificant. (1983)

2) *"Wenner's" condition*. Ohtani next described the conditions that Gould had claimed represented "Wenner's training method," and stated: "Gould interpreted this result that the bees used mainly the scent information and not the dance information. Why didn't the bees visit the 'right' model feeders using the dance information, even when the area was filled with the same scent?" (1983).

After providing an example of what is known about honey bee foraging behavior in nature, Ohtani further noted: "Regarding the facts above, Wenner's experimental condition is more similar to the natural condition, in which the dance information is not necessary" (1983).

3) *Von Frisch's condition*. Ohtani treated the problem of scent trails left in the air by regular foragers, which von Frisch had not considered. Ohtani then discussed the experiments conducted by Gould that should have negated this problem, and wrote: "Although [Gould's] explanation is that the result in [Gould's] Figure 4C is emphasized, fewer bees arrived at the model feeders shown by the wrong information of [Gould's] D. Even so, it is possible to conclude that the bees arrived in response to the wrong information" (1983).

4) *Information about distance*. Here Ohtani first criticized an interpretation by von Frisch. That interpretation concerned the number of dance cycles per unit time as supposedly indicating the distance from hive to feeding place. Ohtani recognized that dances performed for distances further than 400 meters did not differ from one another and thus could not serve for communication.

Ohtani then analyzed Gould's experiments with reference to other work done by Esch and by Wenner as well as work done by von Frisch; he concluded that experiments purportedly demonstrating the use of direction information yielded data contradictory to the hypothesis that recruited bees could use distance information. As we have seen before, the converse was also true; experiments designed to demonstrate the use of distance information often yielded results negating the hypothesis that recruited bees could use direction information (see our chapter 6).

From his analysis Ohtani concluded:

I hope it is clear now that the "theory of dance language" which is cited as a fact in school text books and won [the] Nobel prize in 1973 while it was still under challenge is not totally proved. . . .

Gould (1975a) argued that evolution never selected for any act unless it had a function and that dance should be a language. (1983)

Ohtani thus stressed the dance language proponents' reliance on teleology, as advocated by Gould (1976) and by Griffin (1984). He also perceived the problems one encounters whenever only correlations are relied upon for drawing conclusions, a common evident weakness of the verification approach. Ohtani wrote:

> I think, however, the information about direction and distance that von Frisch found is a result of too keen a sense by man. When I see my dog running toward me, I may be able to figure out the distance and the direction he [has run], by his habit of sitting with his face towards the opposite direction and how tired he is, but I cannot conclude that my dog communicated to me by his body language. (1983)

Ohtani thus remained unconvinced by the body of circumstantial evidence invoked by dance language proponents.

RENNER AND HEINZELLER (1979): FORAGERS WITH BLINDED OCELLI

One more striking example of the extent to which a paradigm hold can shape interpretation should not go unmentioned. That case concerns an inadvertent undermining of an experimental technique employed by Gould—a blackening of the ocelli of forager bees in order to "misdirect" the straight-run portion of their dance maneuver in the hive.

The results of Renner and Heinzeller's experiments revealed that such ocelli blackening drastically interfered with the flight orientation of foragers. Their commitment to the Realism school, however, prevented them from recognizing the fact that Gould's experiments might be other than convincing.

Just what did Gould do? Besides the two very obvious compound eyes, bees (and many other insects) have three ocelli located in a triangular arrangment on the fore part of the head between the compound eyes. Although considerable research has been done on these three simple eyes, little is known about their possible function.

Gould (1975a, 1975b, 1975c) blackened these ocelli in what he claimed were his "conclusive" experiments. By so doing, he had hoped to manipulate directional information transmitted between forager and recruit and "misdirect" potential recruits to feeding stations placed in the field. The success of that effort is open to question, as indicated above by reference to analyses by Rosin and Ohtani.

Renner and Heinzeller conducted a series of experiments to clarify contradictory claims published earlier about the flight ability of bees and other insects that had had their ocelli blackened. By using different types of blackening agents, they found that not all paints were equally effective at achieving complete blockage of light. It was obvious, however, that when blockage was complete, foragers did not return to the hive. They wrote: "Of the 16 bees that could be regarded as totally blinded *with a black shield*, only 3 ever came to the feeding site; they did so outside the feeding time, and all 16 died within 3 days" (1979:227).

The results they obtained obviously relate to the significance of Gould's experiments, since the success of his experiments relied upon the effective blackening of worker ocelli. If we accept Renner and Heinzeller's results, complete blockage resulted in bees no longer being able to orient. What then, is the reliability of Gould's experimental design? We can also ask, "How did Renner and Heinzeller react to the results of their own experiment in light of Gould's earlier results and interpretation?"

Those familiar with the literature know that Renner and Heinzeller were already proponents of the dance language hypothesis. It is thus no surprise that they perceived no contradiction between their results (i.e., bees with blinded ocelli could not orient) and those of Gould (who relied on bees with blinded ocelli being able to orient and give "misdirection" information). They wrote:

> In the case of the ocelli-painted foragers which Gould (1974) used elegantly for his distance and direction experiments, we suggest that the covering was incomplete enough to allow further flight, but sufficient to reduce sensitivity to the simulated sunlight from the lamp in the hive. (1979:227)

Paradigm hold permitted the dance language hypothesis to survive yet another crisis.

One of the major points Rosin was trying to make in those various contributions was treated more than one hundred years earlier by Claude Bernard, who wrote:

> Yes, the experimenter doubtless forces nature to unveil herself by attacking her with all manner of questions; he must never answer for her nor listen partially to her answers by taking, from the results

of an experiment, only those which support or confirm his hypothesis. We shall see later that this is one of the great stumbling blocks of the experimental method. . . . [An experimenter] must submit his idea to nature and be ready to abandon, to alter or to supplant it, in accordance with what he learns from observing the phenomena which he has induced. ([1865] 1957:23)

14

THE DANCE LANGUAGE CONTROVERSY: CONFLICTS BETWEEN PARADIGMS

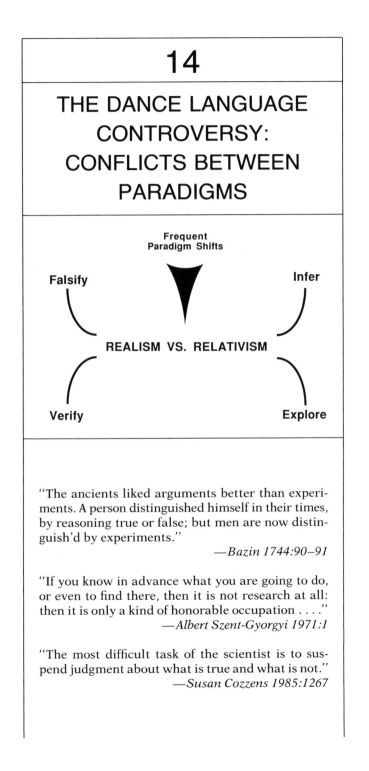

Frequent
Paradigm Shifts

Falsify

Infer

REALISM VS. RELATIVISM

Verify

Explore

"The ancients liked arguments better than experiments. A person distinguished himself in their times, by reasoning true or false; but men are now distinguish'd by experiments."

—Bazin 1744:90–91

"If you know in advance what you are going to do, or even to find there, then it is not research at all: then it is only a kind of honorable occupation . . . ."

—Albert Szent-Gyorgyi 1971:1

"The most difficult task of the scientist is to suspend judgment about what is true and what is not."

—Susan Cozzens 1985:1267

More than twenty years after Kuhn published his popular book and described the important role of paradigm hold in scientific activity, Sternberg published a similar message: "Scientists are sometimes unaware of the exact nature of the model underlying their research, and may even be unclear about the particular and limited set of questions that their model generates" (1985:1111).

In the early days of the honey bee dance language controversy, we did not know that we had a philosophy nor that we followed a restrictive approach in our research. That awareness emerged as we developed a deepening curiosity about the reasons for the intense rejection of both our interpretation *and* of our experimental results (see e.g., excursuses SI and EXC). That curiosity, in turn, led us into a two-decade-long "great adventure," as we learned ever more about the philosophy, sociology, and psychology of science, their role in the conduct of scientific research, and their application to life in general.

Among other concepts, we learned that every scientist operates within the confines of one or another philosophical approach, consciously or not. An interesting exercise in that connection is to ask a biologist a question that should not be embarrassing, but all too often is, namely: "Which of the available philosophical approaches do you use in your research?" Chances are great that the underlying approach has not been formalized and/or is not known.

On that matter, we found Thomas Kuhn more correct in his assessment of how scientists function than were conventional philosophers of science. His message was therefore "useful," which accounts for the continued favorable reception of his message during these past three decades. Paradigm holds and tradition are coupled with reward systems, which in turn are highly socialized; experimental protocol must conform primarily to a prevailing methodology within each scientific subcommunity.

In some cases, methodology may have become rigid to the point of stifling creative research, without biologists being consciously aware of the underlying philosophical rationale of the methodology; such is too often the case, for example, with the "null hypothesis" approach. Unfortunately, a biologist who delves too deeply into philosophical matters, or one who advocates philosophical approaches counter to those commonly used, may soon be outside the mainstream of that scientific community.

OUR EXPERIENCE IN THE WORLD OF SCIENCE

At the beginning of our research program, as indicated above, we could not claim to have had *a* philosophy of science. Instead, a chronicle of our experience (see chapters 7–10) corresponds with our emerging concept of how science operates. The adventure began with the "discovery" of sounds made during the waggle dance of honey bees. We then "created the image" that the sounds made during that dance maneuver could be the actual means by which "*the* dance language information" was transmitted between forager and recruit bee (especially since it is normally dark within a hive).

We next adopted the "verification" approach and sought confirmation of the possibility that honey bees used sound in "their dance language" (see chapter 7). Attempts to build an imitation dancing bee to direct recruits out to food sources (see excursus VGR) provided us only with anomalous results. We pursued those anomalies and found, to our dismay at the time, that bees could be conditioned readily in the classic sense. That find led, in turn, to the realization that much of what had been considered evidence that bees had *used* "dance language information" was actually no more than evidence of conditioned-response capability.

A series of events led us rather quickly through a "falsification" approach (see excursus SI and chapter 9) and over to an "inference" approach (see chapter 10). We thereby came to be the first scientists to *test* the dance language hypothesis (in the Karl Popper falsification sense) since its inception twenty years earlier. Unfortunately, none of the relevant scientific community followed suit—they remained comfortable with the philosophical approaches adhered to earlier. They continued to further "verify" and to pseudo-test the dance language hypothesis (see chapters 12 and 13) in attempts to prove its validity.

During that entire process, we had unintentionally traveled full circle around our theme diagram (see figures 3.1 and 14.0). First, we began by "creating an image" that dancing bees were capable of communication by means of sound waves; then we moved over into the Realism school in order to "prove" that we had an important contribution to make. Later we were forced by our results to use the double-control experimental approach commonly employed in fields such as psychology and to test the dance language hypothesis for the first time ever. Finally, we turned to the inference approach as used in genetics and microbiology, as we came to realize the power of that experimental method.

Our last move into the Relativism school was an awakening, in the same way that it seems to be a one-way path for many who become aware of that philosophical attitude. The transition permitted us to no longer focus on a search for "truth" or "proof"; we were free to explore and to revert to the more restrictive Realism school approaches far less often than before and usually for only a short time.

A parallel can be seen in the transition from typewriter to word processor; one who has become skilled in the use of word processors reverts to use of a typewriter only rarely.

THE COMPLEXITY OF THE DANCE
LANGUAGE CONTROVERSY

The dance language controversy seems to be far more complex than other scientific controversies we have studied, and Sternberg's words come to mind here: "Scientists are sometimes unaware of the exact nature of the model underlying their research." In that connection, we doubt that various proponents of the dance language hypothesis could now even agree among themselves about exactly what that hypothesis is or what its expectations and/or predictions are. Consequently, it is unlikely that proponents could even agree on which assumptions are essential for a *test* of the validity of that hypothesis, or even that tests are necessary in science.

The complexity of the controversy appears to hinge primarily on the fact that there are at least five competing sets of paradigms relevant to the dance language hypothesis. At the same time, it is highly unlikely that any two dance language proponents are committed to the same combination of those paradigms. We list here those five sets of two paradigms and summarize the difficulties that each might pose for the issue at hand.

1) *The Realism and Relativism schools.* Statements in print by dance language proponents (as summarized in this volume) indicate that most dance language proponents belong to the Realism school and believe that the dance language hypothesis "is no longer open to question." That attitude leans heavily on teleological explanations for observed action (e.g., "The information contained in the dance maneuver has to be good for something or it would have been selected against").

However, other dance language proponents may well be staunch members of the Relativism school. In that case, they may merely feel that sufficient negative evidence does not yet exist relative to the dance language hypothesis. It is possible that they may be unaware of the negative evidence that has accumulated already or of the inconsistencies present within von Frisch's own experimental results (von Frisch 1947; see also our chapter 6). They may also be unaware of the contradictions inherent in the experiments conducted and the approaches exploited by James Gould (see our chapter 13) or of the power of relativism-type experiments (as described in chapters 9 and 10).

2) *Supporting and testing hypotheses.* Repeatedly we have heard and read that there is sufficient *supportive* evidence for the dance language hypothesis. Obviously many proponents of it may subscribe to the verification approach of the Realism school. Some of those proponents may also feel that successful repetition of the von Frisch type experiments suffices as a *test* of the hypothesis; for others the mere presence of direction and distance information in the dance maneuver suffices as "evidence" (see above).

However, we found others of this group who erroneously assumed, as we did initially, that the hypothesis had actually been *tested* by von Frisch and/or others (in the null hypothesis sense) before it was accepted as "fact." Upon further discussion with these scientists, however, it has become apparent to us that some of them had relied on the validity of secondary sources (including the popular literature) for their opinions. We now recognize that secondary sources can mislead one badly; only the results contained in primary sources should be consulted when designing experiments.

3) *Dance language and odor-search possibilities.* The discrepancy that exists in this dichotomy is perhaps the most puzzling of all. Many biologists teach about and/or study behavior of flying moths and other insects as these animals mechanistically search for the source of an odor (anemotaxis; see chapter 5 and excursus OS). These same scientists may also subscribe to and teach students about the dance language hypothesis. They may thus unwittingly exhibit a compartmentalization of thought (i.e., searching honey bees are immune from the rules that govern the odor-search behavior of other insects).

On the other hand, we have found others who work within the odor-search paradigm. They may not subscribe to the dance language paradigm, but remain silent. Eventually we would hope that these students of odor-search behavior may realize just how appropriate honey bees are as research material for this type of study.

4) *Insect versus human characteristics.* Rosin (see our chapter 13) was uncomfortable with even the notion that honey bees could *have* a "language."

There are those, on the one hand, who do believe that honey bees can have humanlike characteristics (e.g., Griffin 1984; Gould and Gould 1988). On the other hand, there probably are dance language proponents who do not believe that honey bees can be very different from other insects but who simply may have never pondered the philosophical issue at stake. On that score they are in good company; apparently neither did Karl Popper ([1977] 1985) dwell much on the problems inherent in the belief in a "language" among bees in his essay "The Mind-Body Problem."

Herein lies one of the problems with research on honey bees—one can easily become emotionally attached to the subjects, consider them superior creatures "second only to humans," and imbue them with humanlike capabilities. When such an anthropomorphic attitude is coupled with teleological thinking (point 1, above), detached research becomes almost impossible to conduct. An almost religious fervor sets in, a fervor that, unfortunately, is easy to "sell" to the public at large.

Microbiologists do not fall in love with their microbes; neither should honey bee researchers become too attached to their subjects. Presumed "functions" of a behavioral act should remain just that and not be considered "discoveries" of something *nature* has "designed."

5) *Individual versus population considerations.* We suspect that the vast majority of those who endorse the dance language hypothesis focus primarily on encounters between individual bees within the hive and/or in the field. However, there are others who would not hesitate to treat the recruitment process as a population phenomenon, as we do now. Whereas the behavior of any individual searching bee may appear to be random, the collective performance may well fit into one or another mathematical model (see, e.g., excursus NEG).

It is the above set of opposing paradigms (and perhaps more) that makes the honey bee dance language controversy so complex and, at the same time, so fascinating. An individual scientist can be at one extreme or the other, or somewhere in between, with regard to each of those sets of paradigms.

OUR VIEW OF THE CREATIVE PROCESS

We now advocate a multiple approach to scientific research, one that agrees somewhat with the Feyerabend notion that "anything goes" (Feyerabend 1975). In many ways we have found the scientific process to be quite analogous to skillful detective work, and we suggest that several approaches, not merely the one that may be traditional, can and should be applied in the effort to gain fuller understanding of nature.

First off, we recognize that the scientific process, as applied by scientists in the past, has ordinarily used only one of four well-defined approaches at a time: image creation (discovery), verification, support by failure to falsify, and inference (see chapters 2 and 3 and figure 3.1). We summarize these approaches here in a few paragraphs with reference to the theme diagram at the beginning of this chapter.

Image Creation

The creative process in science involves first and foremost a flash of insight or a novel explanation of observed events—one not perceived earlier by the scientific community. Alternatively, there may be a "personal rediscovery" ("re-creation") of a "dormant" interpretation (as with the odor-search hypothesis in honey bees).

If one thereby recognizes a newly emerging hypothesis (or the possibility of one), then one is a member (at least momentarily) of the Relativism school. The enthusiastic scientist then attempts to "convert" others to the same point of view (Kuhn 1962; Atkinson 1985).

The word *discover* is prominent in this approach. The difficulty one encounters, however, is that one does not discover "truth" in the real world; one merely discovers interpretation.

Verification

The verification of early finds is an essential element in scientific progress. It is here that we recognize the importance of "replication," presumably before other scientists accept the original set of results as valid. In some fields, only a small percentage of scientists seem to appreciate that the successful replication of an inadequately controlled experiment will not provide critically important "confirmation" of a hypothesis.

It is also here that one most often encounters the word *proof*. However, it is easy to gain supportive evidence (e.g., Popper 1957), particularly if one ignores relevant negative evidence.

Falsification

The notion that a persistent failure to falsify hypotheses could lead one ever closer to "truth" (the Realism school) gained prominence after Karl Popper formalized that idea in the early part of this century. Within the past two decades, however, the null hypothesis approach has come under increasing attack (e.g., Mahoney 1976).

The weakness of the null hypothesis approach stems from the fact that paradigm holds can influence the design of experiments; the result can be that an apparent "test" of a hypothesis may not be a test of the target hypothesis after all but may only have the appearance of such a test ("the Snark was a Boojum"—Lewis Carroll). It may also be true that, when the mathematics used in the project (or in the statistical evaluation) becomes too sophisticated, weakness in the experimental design becomes more difficult to spot. False confidence in the outcome can then lead one to believe that a closer perception of "reality" has been attained.

Inference

When the strong inference or multiple inference approach is routinely applied in a laboratory situation (indoor or outdoor), one often finds a nonreligious fervor in the research group. Leads are pursued vigorously; alternative explanations emerge rapidly. In fact, any person who becomes fully aware of how to exploit both the verification and falsification methods as stepping stones during research is often propelled over to the Relativism school.

The inference approach, but a short step away, is no cure-all. However, if results bear out one hypothesis while simultaneously negating an alternative hypothesis, a giant stride has been made toward further understanding.

In short, within collective science the most creative effort involves an application of all four philosophical approaches and attitudes. Each approach has strong points that can and should be exploited. Exploration and image creation (discovery) provide excitement but must be followed by adequate verification (replication) in the Realism sense. The hypothesis so generated should not languish in a pool of further verification ad nauseum and thereby gain the status of a "ruling theory." Rather, attempts to falsify that hypothesis should be instituted as soon as possible after adequate verification has been obtained.

Neither should later failure to falsify the hypothesis by construed as "proof" of the theory. If that happens, one once again may end up with no more than a "ruling theory" (e.g., Chamberlin [1890] 1965).

It is better to immediately assume the relativist role, which involves first an image creation process (exploration), as one attempts to generate alternative explanations for hypotheses previously verified and not negated.

A later step includes experimentation in the strong inference or multiple inference tradition; that is, testing hypotheses against one another with a mutually exclusive design (any result obtained in support of one hypothesis automatically negates the predictions of the other).

The development of an ability to move repeatedly and rapidly from the use of one (or both) of the Realism school approaches to the use of the exploration and inference approaches in the Relativism school strikes us as a characteristic of scientific maturity. John V. Thompson, Claude Bernard, Louis Pasteur, Charles Darwin, Maurice Maeterlinck, and Barbara McClintock (among many others) succeeded in their scientific endeavors through their ability to entertain alternative explanations for "conventional wisdom."

In every such case, however, controversy emerged, as those subscribing to the Realism school rushed to the defense of the prevailing paradigms of the day.

CONTROVERSIES AND THE CONDUCT OF SCIENCE

Controversies often erupt when "conventional wisdom" becomes challenged, but controversies are the real fuel of scientific progress; most "definitive" experiments remain as such for only a few years. Also, as indicated above, scientists should both agree and act on policy, as follows:

1. Hypotheses and expectations are to be stated clearly.
2. Experiments are repeated faithfully by others before results are *tentatively* accepted.
3. *Replication* of an experiment does not constitute a challenge to the credibility of the originator of an hypothesis (e.g., Broad and Wade 1982:77).
4. Proponents of an hypothesis announce what they believe will constitute an adequate test of the hypothesis.
5. The hypothesis is then tested carefully by the originator and others.
6. As in point 3, above, *testing* an hypothesis is a necessary func-

tion in science and does not represent an insult to the originator of that hypothesis.
7. Negative evidence is accommodated rather than dismissed.

One or another of these seemingly obvious points were repeatedly
violated by the scientific community during the dance language controversy. For example, in all of his extensive writings, von Frisch
never indicated what flight times or percentage of success should be
expected for honey bees supposedly using dance language information
after leaving the hive; he used "mushy" phrases such as "fly directly
out," which could later be interpreted in a variety of ways.

One must also keep in mind that controversies are almost unavoid-
able because of the human component present in each scientist. A
truly revolutionary idea that could result in the "conversion" of a
number of scientists can easily threaten the security of many others.
That is partly because entire careers and the self-images of innumer-
able scientists may appear to be undermined, especially if they had
worked much of their lives within a paradigm that would later be
found to be inadequate. The longer an hypothesis is considered "established fact," the more difficult it becomes to accept another test of
it.

By contrast, as scientists in the more rapidly advancing areas of
biology (e.g., microbiology and genetics) tend to become more fully
aware of the pivotal role controversies play in scientific progress,
controversy has become a topic worthy of consideration in its own
right. For example, the 1987 Marine Biological Laboratory History of
Science series was entitled "Controversies in Science: When the Experts Disagree." At that time Judith Anderson wrote:

> Controversy is not necessarily damaging; some say it is the soul of
> growth. . . . To end controversies, scientists must first understand
> them; but scientists would rather do science than discuss it. Too
> often debates about what science is and how it works are left to
> scholars sequestered in humanities departments, or relegated to the
> pages of arcane scholarly journals. (1988:18)

Controversies get resolved in science in much the same way that
they get resolved in other areas of human endeavor. Those scientists
closely involved with the controversy are most often not in a position
to resolve the issue. Someone from outside the field, usually one who
has a clearer perception of appropriate methodology, is a more likely
candidate to resolve a nagging problem (e.g., Moore 1988).

A common misconception is that controversial issues will be resolved eventually by "younger" scientists, presumably those who come into the field unhampered by preconceptions about the "truth" of any matter under consideration.

We feel that younger scientists, or those who enter from another field, are not likely to be instrumental in resolving a controversy, for at least three reasons: 1) A person with no formal training or experience in the sociology of science would lack necessary understanding about the importance of interpersonal relationships; 2) Young people are as likely as anyone else to develop an "investment" in the scientific establishment and often rather quickly adopt the prevailing paradigms that seem to "deserve" the most support; and 3) Scientists too often dare not be "wrong"; they must come up with "appropriate" results and interpretation as they climb the ladder toward scientific respectability.

Neither is evidence the most important factor in the resolution of controversies, contrary to standard belief in science. Adequate evidence, as obtained from crucial experiments, cannot immediately override emotional attachment to "pet theories." That is because paradigm holds dictate to the participants how that evidence shall be viewed. Thus it is that adequate evidence, while absolutely essential in the resolution of controversies, is necessary although not sufficient during that resolution.

Neither does "nature" ultimately resolve controversies (Latour 1987; Veldink 1989). The actual behavior of searching bees, as documented by the proponents of the dance language hypothesis, for example, did not correspond with the tenets of the hypothesis. However, the resultant discrepancy "passed over the heads" of the proponents of that hypothesis (see excursus NEG).

If controversies could be resolved by one or another of the above factors, they would/could be resolved quickly. Instead, hypotheses ultimately last only as long as they remain "useful" (Schram 1979; Wenner and Wells 1987). On the other hand, support of an hypothesis can benefit one in the sociopolitical arena long after that hypothesis itself had outlived its usefulness in the scientific arena. An hypothesis may thus persist long beyond its scientific life span, especially if it is backed by strong emotional investment. That prevailing hypothesis, though no longer necessarily valid, may continue to provide the basis for experiments and spawn offspring hypotheses that ultimately count for very little. When that happens, there may be no real progress, and practical (useful) application may be wanting.

Just how much erroneous material in science continues to be believed to be true is anybody's guess (see Wenner 1989). A more serious question, however, is the extent to which erroneous science has been promulgated, funded, and perpetuated in the past because it has the approval of a "consensus" of experts. Witness the hypotheses of "polywater," as described by Franks (1981), and of the magnetic navigation by pigeons, as analyzed by Moore (1988). The resultant research activity was a waste of time and effort, while far more progressive research could have been funded with that grant money (see Muller 1980).

We should seriously try to reverse Feyerabend's assessment:

> Popular science books . . . spread the basic postulates of the theory; applications are made in distant fields, money is given to the orthodox and is withheld from the rebels. More than ever the theory seems to possess tremendous empirical support. (1975:43)

One would hope that the present granting system could begin to shrug off enough of its bureaucracy to support creative and revolutionary science "done" by those outside the mainstream. As a start, certainly, participants on *both* sides of a controversy should be able to get funding and be able to publish their results and interpretations in scientific journals, not just whichever side supports prevailing opinion.

Can the *process*, instead of the method, of science be taught? We believe that it can; a nearly uniform lack of formal training in the process itself at all academic levels in biology, from elementary through graduate school, can be reversed.

As a start, at the faculty level we should heed John Platt's admonition (1964:350): "[Chamberlin's 1890] paper . . . could be required reading for every graduate student—and for every professor" (1964:350). We can follow with Richard Muller's thought: "Innovative science, like a small child, can be guided and encouraged, but well-meaning attempts to force it in preconceived directions can be counterproductive" (1980:883).

Science should be exciting and dynamic; when treated as a "thing," science constantly seems to need "sugar coating" and embellishment for public consumption. Maeterlinck addressed that point in reference to the study of honey bee biology when he wrote: "The fact that the hive contains so much that is wonderful does not warrant our seeking to add to its wonders" (1901:4).

By contrast, science as a *process* is exciting in its own right. Fortunately, "the scientific method," as taught in past decades, seems to have disappeared from most college biology textbooks. On the other hand, that omission of an unrealistic perception of the scientific method has not been replaced by material illustrating some of the advantages of the Relativism school approaches, namely exploration and inference. Neither is the scientific community very often receptive to true innovation and creativity in the teaching laboratory. Whether or not experiments "work" continues to be a major reason why they are chosen for classroom exercises. Why not interject an occasional experiment that yields an anomalous result, and help students learn how to handle such real situations in science?

Finally, we have to get across the point at all levels that we are scientists because it is fun, and that the interjection of humor and tolerance of disparate viewpoints in our scientific controversies is a part of the fun, and is a part of life itself.

EXCURSUSES

Excursus AR: Aristotle and Honey Bee Recruitment?

Quotations from Aristotle are commonly used in historical treatments to illustrate progress in biology, but those passages often become modified in translation and/or transcription. Rarely do scholars return to the original Aristotle passage in order to seek out *intended* meaning. Aristotle's passage about what transpires when bees return to the hive after a successful foraging trip is a case in point, even though it appears that there are only two sentences in his writings that apply to honey bee interaction in the hive during the recruitment of new foragers:

Καθ' ἑκάστην δὲ πτῆσιν οὐ βαδίζει ἡ μέλιττα ἐφ' ἕτερα τῶ εἴδει ἄνθη, οιον ιἀπὸ ἴου ἐπιὸν, καὶ οὐ θιγγάνει ἄλλου γε, ἕως ἅιεὶς τὸ σμῆνος εἰσπε τασθῇ. Ὅταν δ' εἰς τὸ σμῆνος ἀφίκωνται, ἀποσείονται, καὶ παρακολο υθοῦσιν ἑκάστῃ τρεῖς ἢ τέτταρες.

As translated by David Young (classics professor at the University of California, Santa Barbara, in a personal communication) those two sentences read:

> On any one flight the bee does not go about to flowers which are different in type; [rather, she travels] for example from violet to violet, and does not touch any other to that point where she flies into the hive. When they arrive in the hive, they shake themselves off, and three or four [other bees] follow each one closely. (Aristotle [330 B.C.] 1931: book 9 passage 40)

Professor Young, on the basis of what he feels is usually intended in such ancient Greek phrases, interprets the above passage to mean that the three or four bees actually "follow" each forager bee back out to the gathering place. Virgil apparently recognized the same behavior three hundred years later, and described the recruitment of honey bees with the words: *"Some lead their youth abroad*, while some condense their liquid store, and some in cells dispense" (Virgil [30 B.C.]1937:88; emphasis ours).

Later, one finds a reminiscence of Aristotle's passage in writings of Pliny the Elder, who lived from A.D. 23 to 79; the meaning by then had become quite different: "[Bees] when fully loaded return bulging with their burden. Each is received by three or four others who relieve him of his load" (Book 11, section 10, passage 22; translated by H. Rackham 1967:447).

In an 1862 English translation of Aristotle, Cresswell provided this version: "During each flight the bee does not settle upon flowers of different kinds, but as it were from violet to violet, and touches no other species till it returns to the hive. There they are unloaded, and two or three bees follow every one on its return to the hive" (1862:262). Note here the implication that other bees unload the returning forager. Also note how the last three words, "to the hive," have been added to the second sentence; those words properly belong only at the end of the first sentence.

Apparently J. B. S. Haldane was the first to direct von Frisch's attention to the Aristotle passage (von Frisch [1965] 1967a). In his review book, von Frisch quoted the von P. Gohlke 1949 version (a version that seems to match Aristotle's intent very closely), as follows:

> Bei jedem Ausflug setzt sich die Biene nie auf artverschiedene, sondern nur artgleiche Bluten, fliegt z. B. von Veilchen zu Veilchen und ruhrt keine andere an, bis sie in den Stock zuruck-geflogen ist. Sobald sie in den Stock kommen, schutteln sie ihre Last ab, und einer jeden folgen drei odor vier andere. (von Frisch 1965:6)

In translation, that text reads as follows:

> Each time the bee takes off, it doesn't sit down on different kinds of blossoms but only on the same kind. It flies, for example, from violet to violet and doesn't touch a different sort before it returns to the hive. As soon as they return into their hive, they shake off their load, and after each one three or four others follow. (translation by Manfred Stader and Kurt Wenner)

When Leigh Chadwick translated von Frisch's 1965 book into English, he did not use a direct translation of the German version of Aristotle's sentences. Instead, he used a translation of Aristotle's passage that was published by Thompson in 1910:

> On each trip the bee does not fly from a flower of one kind to a flower of another, but flies from one violet, say, to another violet, and never meddles with another flower until it has got back to the hive; on reaching the hive they throw off their load, and each bee on her return is followed by three or four companions. (von Frisch 1967a:6)

The phrase "on her return," in the above quotation is not in the original Greek version, but that phrase does not mislead if one recognizes that it refers to the return of the experienced bee to the foraging place (David Young, personal communication).

Despite minor differences, each of those passages reveals little more than that 1) bees are faithful to one type of food source in the field, and 2) successful bees are "followed," apparently as they return to the food source after leaving the hive.

Two exceptions to the relative uniformity of translation and/or meaning of Aristotle's passage have appeared. One is in a recent French version:

A chacun de ses vols l'abeille ne passe pas d'une fleur d'une espèce à une fleur d'une autre espèce, elle va, par exemple, de violette en violette, sans toucher à aucune autre fleur, jusqu'à ce que son vol la ramène à la ruche. Une fois de retour dans la ruche, elles se secouent et chacune est assistée de deux ou trois compagnes. (Louis 1969:116)

Yann Ricard translated that passage to read as follows:

On each of its flights the bee does not go from one flower species to a flower of another species; it goes, for instance, from violet to violet, without touching any other flower, until its flight brings it back to the hive. Once back in the hive, they shake [themselves] off and each is attended by two or three companions. (Yann Ricard, personal communication)

Note both that the number of bees involved has changed and that the forager bee is no longer "followed" by other bees. The meaning of the second sentence is now closer to what one finds in Pliny the Elder (see above) than it is to the original Greek version.

A more significant alteration of substance was published by Gould:

More than 2000 years ago, Aristotle noticed that when a dish of honey is set out near a hive, it may take hours or even days for a forager honey bee to find it. Once the food is discovered by even a single bee, however, new bees soon begin to arrive. The forager must, in some way, have "recruited" these new bees. Aristotle thought that the recruit bees simply followed the forager to the food. (1976:211)

Whereas the last sentence of the above text may agree with the intent of the original Aristotle passage (as cited by Gould 1975a), or with one of the various available translations (as provided above), the first three sentences of Gould's paragraph apparently cannot be found in Aristotle. Instead, those three sentences bear a striking resemblance to a passage from von Frisch:

When I wish to attract some bees for training experiments I usually place upon a small table several sheets of paper which have been smeared with honey. Then I am often obliged to wait for many hours, sometimes for several days, until finally a bee discovers the feeding place. But as soon as one bee has found the honey many more will appear within a short time—perhaps as many as several hundred. They have all come from the same hive as the first forager; evidently this bee must have announced its discovery at home. (1950:53)

However, even here we find a puzzling question of priority, since von Frisch did not use the method described above while training bees. (That method does not work; see excursus GT and von Frisch 1967a:17ff). Furthermore, the 1950 von Frisch passage resembles the last two sentences of a 1788 description of events· by the German Ernst Spitzner, as follows:

When a bee finds a good source of honey somewhere, after her return home she makes this known to the others in a remarkable way. Full of joy, she waltzes around among them in circles, without doubt in order that they shall notice the smell of honey which has attached itself to her; then when she goes out again they soon follow her in crowds. I noticed this in a glass-walled hive when I put some honey not far away on the grass and brought to it only two bees from the hive. Within a few minutes, these two made this known to the others in this way, and they came to the place in a crowd. (Ribbands 1953:147; also in von Frisch 1967a:6)

Notice also how Spitzner's first two sentences parallel the original two sentences of Aristotle. Furthermore, the training technique described by Spitzner works no better than the method described by von Frisch in 1950 (Wenner 1961).

In summary, it is not completely clear what Aristotle meant when he wrote the original passage, partly because the Greek itself is not a clear statement (David Young, personal communication). With the passage of time, the same description of interchange within the hive cropped up in other writings. Pliny's description reminds one of Aristotle's statement, and Spitzner's 1877 passage could have been derived, at least in part, from the earlier Aristotle statement. Part of the 1950 expression by von Frisch, in turn, closely resembles Spitzner's passage. Finally, a portion of Gould's account matches a 1950 von Frisch account or perhaps the original Spitzner account more closely than anything Aristotle wrote.

Excursus EXC: Exchange with the Journal *Science*

> "[The] development becomes known to the public. Popular science books ... spread the basic postulates of the theory; applications are made in distant fields, money is given to the orthodox and is withheld from the rebels. More than ever the theory seems to possess tremendous empirical support."
>
> —Paul Feyerabend 1975:43

Scientists reputedly welcome challenge and readily adopt new interpretation whenever evidence no longer conforms to observed phenomena (Kneller 1978). Both Mahoney (1976) and Veldink (1989) found otherwise. Some comments can clarify why this discrepancy in attitudes about scientific objectivity exists.

Collectively, and over varying time spans, Kneller's assessment appears to be correct; scientific interpretation changes constantly and *relatively* rapidly. That change in commitment to interpretation is one feature that distinguishes science from religion.

When new evidence arises that conflicts with "conventional wisdom" on relatively important issues in science, however, *individual* scientists may momentarily rush to the defense of an existing paradigm with religious fervor. Feyerabend deplored this defensive behavior of scientists, and wrote: "To sum up: *Unanimity of opinion may be fitting for a church. ... Variety of opinion is necessary for objective knowledge*" (1975:46; emphasis Feyerabend's).

Something akin to religious fervor was what we encountered when we challenged the dance language hypothesis. That was because that hypothesis had already evolved into a full-fledged paradigm spanning several fields. As might be expected, some felt that our impression — that the defense of the dance language hypothesis was extreme — was a gross exaggeration, since "everyone knows that" scientists shun "censorship" and suppression of new ideas. We were even considered by some scientists to be "paranoid" (Veldink 1989).

Prior to our challenge, and while we were still respected members of the animal language research community, our manuscripts received favorable reviews and were published without undue delay. Subsequent to that challenge, we encountered increasing hostility (as noted in excursus SI). Within a very few years, our chance of getting material into print or obtaining grant support went from difficult to nearly impossible. The negative evidence we had gathered relative to the dance language hypothesis seemed to be accorded little significance in this development (e.g., Veldink 1989).

Due to the extreme adverse reaction we encountered, we feel that this volume would not be complete—dealing as it does with the human side of scientists—unless we included some documentation for the comments made above. Accordingly, we provide here a chronological sequence of some pertinent material spanning those first few critical years.

ATTEMPTED REBUTTAL TO A LETTER BY RICHARD DAWKINS IN THE JOURNAL *SCIENCE*

Richard Dawkins, in a letter to *Science,* exemplified the confusion existing among some ethologists on the significance of our crucial experiment (Wenner, Wells, and Johnson 1969; see also our chapter 10). He objected to the interpretation we provided for the results of that experiment, in part, as follows:

> Suppose a man tells me there is a bar three blocks down the street on the right. I set off thirsty, but on the way a strong smell of beer distracts me to another bar hidden up a side alley. Does this prove that human language does not communicate information? . . . it is entirely reasonable to suppose that bees have alternative ways of finding food—among them, the dance, smell, and the presence of other bees—and that each of these cues may predominate under different circumstances. For example, the artificial use of strong scent might cause olfactory cues to prevail. (1969:751)

Dawkins concluded his letter: "In brief, bees are easily distracted. This modest and uncontroversial conclusion is all that can be drawn from the experiments purporting to disprove von Frisch's classic work" (1969:751).

Dawkins thereby adhered close to the "party line" of those committed to the dance language paradigm. From our perspective, on the other hand, Dawkins' ad hoc rationalization merely confused the issue, because he ignored the potential influence of wind direction, an essential element when one considers odor movement and resultant insect flight (see chapter 5 and excursus OS). Furthermore, Dawkins contradicted von Frisch's earlier assertions that recruit bees would *not* be distracted during their outgoing flight. For example, von Frisch had written:

> There is no doubt that the bees understand the message of the dance. When they fly out, they search only in the neighborhood of

the indicated range, ignoring dishes set closer in or farther away. Not only that, they search only in the direction in which the original feeding dish is located. (1962:78; see also our chapter 9)

Scent (notice in the above passage Dawkins' use of the word *strong*), strong or otherwise, *if* of the right kind, *can* "distract" searching bees (see chapter 8), but *only if* searching bees are already downwind from such a source. In that sense odors are quite a different stimulus than either sound or light stimuli.

Dawkins, for example, could have been distracted by the smell of beer during his tavern hunt *only if* the second tavern had been upwind of his original path. But he could have been distracted by the sound or sight of the tavern, *regardless* of its direction from his original path. It is unlikely that that Dawkins would have been distracted by the odor of a bakery under the circumstances of his example.

Other dance language proponents began citing Dawkins' letter as refutation of our work, even though it was obviously nothing more than an expression of opinion, faulted at that by Dawkins' failure to consider wind direction in his polemical statement. This curious turn of events led one of us (Wells) to draft a reply to that Dawkins letter. We present that short draft here in its entirety so that the referee's comments, which follow and which formed the basis for rejection by *Science,* will fall into perspective.

Reply to Dawkins

Subsequent to our comparison of the predictive values of the "olfaction" and "language" hypotheses of honey bee forager recruitment [Wenner, Wells, and Johnson 1969], Richard Dawkins generated a challenge [Dawkins 1969] which confuses key issues. I am surprised to find that some ethologists have [now] accepted Dawkins' discussion as an excuse for disregarding our experimental work. It is necessary, therefore, to reply to his three objections to our paper.

First, Dawkins asserted that we "presume to challenge the findings of a great biologist" (Karl von Frisch). To this we plead guilty; but, the charge isn't serious enough. In so doing we also presume to challenge a host of subsequent investigators who have uncritically accepted any and all of von Frisch's *interpretations* of available data; and who have used these interpretations as a foundation on which their own work is based. This may account for the emotion occasionally engendered by our papers.

Next, he objected to our citing (in our paper's introductory paragraphs) earlier studies which yielded data inconsistent with the hypothesis that bees use linguistic communication [Wenner, Wells, and Rohlf 1967; Wenner and Johnson 1966; Johnson 1967a; Lopatina 1964; Wells and Giacchino 1968; Wenner 1967] on grounds that the failure of bees to use language does not prove they have none. With this we heartily agree! Experimentation does not "prove" or "disprove" hypotheses, for formally this can never be done. Rather, it tests their *usefulness* in the *a priori* prediction of events. Usually one retains as his working hypotheses those with high predictive success under the most rigorously controlled conditions.

Rather than "purporting to disprove von Frisch's classic work" (Dawkins' misinterpretation of the intent of our experiments) our experimental results show that, under well controlled conditions, the olfactory hypothesis is successful while the language hypothesis fails to predict the distribution of recruit foragers in the field.

As a substantive objection to our paper, Dawkins suggested in an eloquent but anthropomorphic analogy that crowds of bees or strong scent might distract recruits just as "the smell of beer distracts me" from a prior destination. We purposely inserted controls against these possibilities in our experiments. These controls preclude his interpretation. As the legend to our Fig. 2 [in Wenner, Wells, and Johnson 1969] indicates, one experimental feeding station always was upwind and the other one downwind from a control station visited by *no* bees.

According to Dawkins' line of reasoning, bees would have had to be simultaneously distracted to the scent at that control site both upwind and downwind from their "intended" destinations. Either that, or recruited bees would have failed to verify von Frisch's contention that "if no clues are provided by scent the bees use information conveyed by the dance" [von Frisch 1968:532].

Furthermore, on days nine and fourteen of our experimental series [table 1 of Wenner, Wells, and Johnson 1969] no scent was placed at the control station. In the absence of "distracting" odor cues, recruit bees still failed to find the unscented experimental stations about which they might have been linguistically informed, even though "crowds of bees" were there.

But back to Richard Dawkins' delightful analogy. I feel confident that he and I would agree that scientific questions are more likely to be resolved by experimentation than by polemics such as our exchange of letters in *Science*. If I am right, and we can avoid being distracted from that one key point of agreement, next time he is in Los Angeles, I'll buy!

The letter by Wells attempting to reply to Dawkins was rejected by the editor of *Science*. The rejection was accompanied by a set of comments by an anonymous referee. We include that text, also in its entirety.

Referee's Comments

> This paper is uncomplimentary to all scientists who do not accept the author's theory. Specifically the author accuses ethologists of accepting Dawkins' discussion as "an *excuse* for disregarding our experimental work." Can't he accept the thought that they reject his work because after critical study they do not consider it irrefutable?
>
> And if that were not infuriating enough he accuses a "host of investigators for uncritically accepting any and all of von Frisch's interpretations." How can he presume to know that? Is any new theory accepted without critical study? Perhaps if his own work were as thorough, complete and convincing as that of von Frisch he would not need to berate other scientists for not accepting it. The use of polemics is a poor substitute for irrefutable facts.

THE FIRST ATTEMPT TO REBUT THE GOULD, HENEREY, AND MACLEOD 1970 ARTICLE

In 1970 Gould, Henerey, and MacLeod, three undergraduate students at the California Institute of Technology, published their ten-page lead article in *Science* (see chapter 12). By then we were becoming aware of the sociological implications of the dance language controversy. Nevertheless, we were still ill prepared for what transpired next.

A study of the paper by Gould and co-workers revealed that these undergraduates had gathered data for only a few hours at the end of the summer in 1969, just after the publication of our crucial experiment paper (Wenner, Wells, and Johnson 1969). It was immediately apparent to us that the results they had obtained were completely at variance with the expectations of the dance language hypothesis (see chapters 1 and 13). At the same time their results supported our interpetation (see excursus NEG).

One of us (Wenner) submitted a letter to *Science* that stressed the fact that their results, in fact, supported our position. In the cover letter to that manuscript Wenner included the following comments:

> After carefully studying that article, I have concluded that it is not really a challenge of our work but a substantiation of our earlier findings. Unfortunately, this aspect of their study is clouded by the investigators' efforts to discredit our earlier work and by their conclusion which does not necessarily follow from their data [see our chapter 12].

I think that your readers should have an opportunity to read this divergent opinion. Toward this end I have written the enclosed comment, "A Divergence from the Expected," and hope you will publish it. I have kept my statement short and in the nature of opinion so that it can appear as a Letter in your journal.

Wenner also included a list of names of reputable people who could serve as referees, as follows: Bernard Abbott, Kenneth Armitage, Vincent Dethier, Jerry Downhower, W. George Evans, and Edward Glassman. We do not know if any of them were used.

The manuscript was rejected, and comments from only a single referee were appended, with the last portion of those comments removed. Furthermore, the number 2 circled at the top of the page (in the manner of *Science* editors in those days) indicated that the comments of referee number 1 were not furnished to us. We reproduce that one referee's comments verbatim:

Dr. Wenner should read the paper he is criticizing! The average time spent by successful recruit bees was 3 to 4 minutes as clearly stated in the second paragraph on p. 551 of Gould *et al* and in their *Table 2*. It can only be perversity which led Wenner to utilize, instead, the data in Table 7, which contains *(clearly stated!)* data on delay between *dance attendance* and arrival at a feeding site. To repeat, Gould *et al.* clearly show the successful recruit takes 3 to 4 minutes to fly to the feeding site not "40 times the usual flight time."

Contrary to Dr. Wenner's incredible "interpretation" of Gould et al. all 225 recruits arrived at a station. Only 37 were marked, the 188 not listed in Table 4 were unmarked recruits, *not* unsuccessful recruits! Thus, we have 25 marked bees that arrived at the "correct" station and 12 that arrived at a station ± 180° from the correct direction. *No* marked recruits arrived at stations ± 90° from the correct direction. This may be an interesting comment on bee language. I have performed bee-language experiments with my animal behavior classes and we have occasionally seen: (a) foragers which indicated both the training direction and the opposite direction in a single bout of dancing, (b) foragers which indicated only the opposite to the training direction *[sic]*. In both of these cases, it has been my impression that these errors were the result of interference in the dances by too many attendants to the dance. However, occasional bees may be misled by such errors, or as some of our data also suggest, there may be some ambiguity or confusion in the dance which can lead recruits to seek food in a direction 180° from the dance direction. If the editors of *Science* would like such a comment on the excellent paper by Gould et al. I should be happy to write one. (unpublished comments by an anonymous referee; emphasis his)

THE FATE OF AN APPEAL TO REBUT THE SAME ARTICLE

When Wenner showed the above comments to Larry Friesen, Friesen replied, "But virtually everything the referee wrote is wrong in point of fact!" We then sat down and listed some of the errors in the referee's comments as follows:

1. The "3 to 4 minutes as clearly stated" applied to forager bees, not recruits.
2. There are no data on flight times in table 2.
3. There is no table 7 in the Gould, Henerey, and MacLeod paper.
4. From page 550 one can conclude that 225 recruits arrived, but on page 552 Gould and co-workers clearly stated: "Only 37 (that is, 13 percent) of these 277 attendants were successfully recruited and later caught at a feeding station. . . ."
5. There were no stations at locations 90° from the correct direction.
6. The original dance language hypothesis does not permit recruits to arrive at a station located 180 degrees from the "correct" direction.

At that point Friesen insisted to Wenner, "if you point out the errors made by the referee, they will *have* to publish your letter." Wenner replied, "Larry, you don't know what's going on, do you?"

Nevertheless, Wenner wrote a detailed comparison of the comments made by the referee to the actual facts in the case, revised the manuscript slightly, and resubmitted it with a cover letter. Some of the points made in the cover letter are as follows:

Normally I would not appeal such a decision on your part (This is the third consecutive rejection of such a manuscript by *Science* [on this issue]); but in this latest case I feel the referee has done both *Science* and me a disservice. The referee has made some serious errors in fact, a point which will undoubtedly make a difference to you as editor. (Attached herewith please find documentation for this claim.)

Even if the referee had been correct, my opinion should be printed in *Science*. In this regard I have always admired *Science's* stated policy:

"*Science* serves its readers as a forum for the presentation and discussion of important issues related to the advancement of science, including the presentation of minority or conflicting points of view, rather than by publishing only material on which a consensus has been reached."

I would hope that this particular controversy does not fall outside that general policy. That is, if *Science* can print a 10-page challenge of our work, surely space can be provided for a few paragraphs of divergent opinion. Even if my facts had been wrong (which they are not), I do not see why the referee should object to an airing of my opinion. If I had been as incorrect as he implied, supporters of the language hypothesis should be pleased to see such gross errors on my part in print.

On the positive side, the referee's comments did help reveal two minor errors in my manuscript (neither of which he pinpointed and neither of which makes any difference in my argument). For purposes of clarification, however, I have modified the manuscript slightly. The revised manuscript is enclosed.

I trust you will pass favorably on my manuscript this time around. Thank you for considering the topic once again.

We provide here the entire manuscript, as submitted the second time to *Science*.

A Divergence from the Expected

A recent article in *Science*, "Communication of direction by the honey bee," is of more than incidental interest, as it contains an extensive amount of data not available earlier. However, some important aspects of their data do not fall into line with what one might expect from the classic honey bee "dance language" hypothesis. The series 1 experiments were especially pertinent in this regard, since they were: "... designed to examine the behavior of individual recruits as each attended a dance and subsequently arrived at a feeding station."

The first item of interest is that approximately a third of those marked recruits which succeeded in finding a station arrived at one in a direction opposite to that "indicated" in the dance maneuver. This result clearly contradicts the expectations of the classic hypothesis [von Frisch 1947, 1950; Wenner, Wells, and Johnson 1969]. All 37 of the successful bees should have arrived at the "correct" station.

In their study these investigators also found that successful recruit bees spend a considerable amount of time in flight, on the average, before reaching a food source. The direct line flight time between hive and feeding stations in their experiments would normally be only about 24 sec [Wenner 1963]; and recruited bees generally fly from the hive within a minute and a half after leaving a dancing bee (50% leave within 30 sec) [Wenner 1963]. With these facts in mind, an examination of the data in Table 4 of the Gould, et al. paper reveals that the 25 bees which arrived at the "correct" station flew an average of about 30 times longer than necessary if they were to "fly directly out" to the food source. (Interestingly enough, the 12 bees which ended up at a station in the opposite direction averaged only 36 times as long as necessary.)

Clearly the above results do not match the expectation that ". . . recruits alarmed by these dancers . . . find the feeding place with surprising speed and precision" [von Frisch 1967].

Another interesting point is that Gould and co-workers have confirmed earlier findings of my co-workers and myself [Johnson and Wenner 1970; Wenner, Wells, and Rohlf 1967]; that is, that bees which leave the hive are not likely to find a food source, even under the best of circumstances [Note: Some confusion results here because Gould and co-workers apparently define "recruits" as those bees which succeed in reaching a station. I prefer to consider recruits as those bees which leave the hive after contact with a successful forager]. [For example, they stated]: "Only 37 of 277 attendants were successfully recruited and later caught at a feeding station, even though the high molarity of the sucrose used reportedly produces maximum dancing and recruitment. . . ."

If one works in unscented localities, rather than in the highly pungent area such as that chosen by the authors, the recruitment efficiency becomes even worse. As we reported earlier in *Science*, while working with unscented sucrose in a relatively odor-free locality, ". . . in the absence of a major nectar source for the colony, we received only five recruits from a hive of approximately 60,000 bees after ten bees had foraged at each of four stations for a total of 1374 round trips during a 3-hour period" [Wenner, Wells, and Johnson 1969]. This result is especially interesting since we have subsequently found that ever smaller amounts of odor in the food and in the locality result in an ever higher frequency of dancing, all other factors being equal [unpublished data, available upon request].

In summary, these workers have obtained results which generally agree with what we have published earlier and which differ markedly from those obtained earlier by von Frisch and co-workers or with those expected on the basis of the classic language hypothesis [von Frisch 1967]. And, in contradistinction to the authors' conclusion, the results are generally in excellent agreement with what we would expect under the circumstances. The final distribution of successful recruits does differ significantly from what one might obtain if these animals had flown at random about the countryside, it is true, but there is no compelling reason for assuming that the dance language hypothesis is a necessary explanation for this divergence from randomness [Wenner, Wells, and Johnson 1969]. I feel that a slight difference in composite location odor near the experimental sites, perceptible to bees but not to investigators, could have been responsible [Johnson and Wenner 1970].

This second time around, the manuscript was again rejected. The comments of only one referee were enclosed, as follows:

> As one of the referees who urged *Science* to publish earlier research reports by Dr. Wenner and his associates, I now recommend that you do not publish this particular critique of the article by Gould, Henery, and MacLeod. Enough is enough! His critique, the referee's criticism of the critique, and his countercritique of the referee's criticism, have become labyrinthine. It is conceivable that the Gould *et al.* paper should not have been published; however, you would require a jury discussing all this material for hours to decide. I no longer believe it is worth the effort, because Dr. Wenner's own criticisms of the von Frisch explanation are mostly beside the point, and they consistently fail to mention a growing body of positive evidence strongly favoring the von Frisch explanation. To publish an increasingly complex and ambiguous debate on but one aspect of negative evidence is an inefficient—and misleading—use of space in *Science*. If and when Dr. Wenner comes up with solid evidence to support his views, he will find an interested and sympathetic audience waiting.

(Note in the above referee comments the reliance on the verification approach.)

REBUFF OF THE ATTEMPT TO REBUT THE 1975 GOULD *SCIENCE* ARTICLE

Five years after the Gould, Henerey, and MacLeod lead article, *Science* published an eight-page lead article by Gould, based upon work he did for his doctoral dissertation (see our chapter 12). Again, this article was a challenge of our work. Once again, Wenner "tested the water" to see if *Science* was by now receptive to the publication of a rebuttal of the paper by Gould (actually a clarification). The letter of inquiry included the following statements:

> Anyone well-versed in the work of my colleagues and myself who carefully reads the Gould article will certainly recognize a convergence of viewpoints, with Gould now coming very close to our position in the bee language controversy. Unfortunately, he does not mention the existence of that convergence, and those not overly familiar with our work will likely miss that important point.

As evidence of the foregoing, Wenner provided some appendices to the letter, documentation that juxtaposed quotations from our earlier work and quotations from the Gould paper so that the editor could compare the statements. Wenner continued:

> Dr. Wells and I would like to know whether *Science* might publish something similar to that which is enclosed. While it is true that there is a normal process which should be followed (submitting a manuscript), our recent attempts at getting material into print in *Science* have failed because of an intensely hostile peer review. . . . Dr. Wells and I eventually got our message into *Nature* ([1973] 241:171–175), but only after a considerable delay. Ironically, Gould has now gotten that same message into print in *Science*—See the two starred items in the enclosed Appendix *A*.
>
> Gould's publication of the same train of thought as we have expressed earlier would indicate that the climate has now changed at *Science*. Is this true? Do our comments now have a chance of getting into print? We realize that space is at a premium and would be happy to have only the cover statement considered [two manuscript pages], provided some reference would be made to the availability of the two appendixes for those who might wish to obtain them directly from us.

The cover statement included two quotations from the Gould paper, as follows:

> Excepting the experiments reported here, the locale-odor hypothesis can effectively account for all the results achieved to date [including those of von Frisch] without recourse to the dance-language theory. . . . recruitment to odors alone might be the usual system in honey bee colonies not under stress. (1975b:686, 691)

The same assistant editor again rebuffed our attempt, and wrote:

> When you have an experimental paper we would be glad to consider it. However, we would not be interested in publishing your cover statement, with or without the appendices. . . . As for the circumstances that prevail here, bee classes *[sic]* are not among the controversies on which we have a position.

In the years that followed, however, *Science* continued to publish papers supportive of the dance language hypothesis and peripheral research areas, but one finds no research papers reporting results that do not fit within the dance language paradigm.

Excursus GT: The Method of Training Bees

"Some genuinely testable theories, when found to
be false, are still upheld by their admirers—for
example, by introducing *ad hoc* some auxiliary assumption"
—*Karl Popper 1919–1920 (reformulated in
1957:159)*

"*Excess of Hubris.* Success has sometimes a bad
effect in young scientists. Quite suddenly it turns
out that everyone else's work is slovenly in design
or incompetently carried out. . . ."
—*Peter Medawar (1979) 1981:51*

One of the surprises we encountered during the controversy was
the insistence by others that we had followed an improper procedure
during our training of bees to visit a feeding station. The implication
from those objections was that we could somehow get anomalous
results during our experiments even though two to three weeks had
passed since bees were first trained out.

We knew such charges to be false for more than one reason: 1) the
controls we had inserted into our experimental designs precluded any
error due to training method; 2) the training method we had used was
actually virtually identical to that used by von Frisch (Boch, personal
communication; see below); and 3) bees involved in the initial training were no longer present when data were gathered, due to the
gradual turnover of experienced foragers.

Under those circumstances, one wonders how something so trivial
as a "training method" could be exaggerated far out of proportion to
the significance of the experimental results themselves. The answer,
as we see it, lies in the power of paradigm holds within the Realism
school; that is, bees "obviously" have a language under that paradigm.

No one ever found flaws in our experimental designs; therefore,
according to that reasoning, perhaps it had been our lack of technical
competence that somehow yielded our "bad" results. An ad hoc argument that assumed that an inability on our part to handle bees properly would serve as well as any other explanation for those who
wished to hold on to the dance language hypothesis.

Anyone interested in the process of science might well wonder,

285

however: "What tales lurk behind the scenes on this matter?" Several items apply to this intriguing question, as covered below.

SIMILARITY OF METHODS

In commenting about the experimental results we had obtained from our double-control experiments, von Frisch (1967b) used a number of ad hoc arguments to dismiss our results (just as he had done earlier when discussing Francon's experiments; see our chapter 4). Among those arguments was a criticism of the method by which we trained our bees. Von Frisch wrote:

> Both Wenner and Johnson refer to Wenner's training method. When gradually bringing the bees to the goal, he offers a strong sucrose solution from the very beginning. Consequently newcomers are continuously aroused; many of them, judging from our own experience, may loose [sic] contact with the group while it is moved along. During the next days of testing when food is offered, these bees can be rearoused by feeding, and they go searching all over the surroundings, so providing a serious source of error to the experiments. (1967b:1073–1074)

In his doctoral thesis research James Gould (1975a) also obtained results contradictory to the expectations of the dance language hypothesis. He labeled the experiments that yielded those results "Wenner type controls," and echoed von Frisch's ad hoc claim, as follows: "The difference between the training techniques of von Frisch and Wenner appear to be crucial to the way by which recruitment is accomplished" (1975a:168).

Gould was far more positive about his claim in the 1976 review paper, when he wrote in the abstract of that paper: "The apparently contradictory results of [von Frisch] and Wenner and his colleagues are *shown* to be due to their techniques for training bees" (1976:211; emphasis ours).

Let us next consider the evidence and ask, "Are the above claims valid?" For a start, we can turn to another statement by Gould, as follows: "Von Frisch (1967a:17–20) trains foragers on a *dilute* solution of sucrose in order to prevent dancing and recruitment until the beginning of the experiment. Wenner (1961), on the other hand, trains foragers on a *concentrated* solution" (1975c:169).

The problem with this last statement is that it is simply not true. Compare the following two excerpts upon which it is based. From the above-cited von Frisch reference we read: "At the beginning of the experiment and during movement of the feeding table the sugar water should be a 2M solution (near saturation) of cane sugar (C.P. sucrose or commercial sugar)" (von Frisch 1967a:19). Furthermore, in Wenner we find: "the hive was opened and the top bars and bees were liberally sprinkled with a 2-molar solution of peppermint-flavoured sugar syrup" (Wenner 1961:9).

That is, the sugar concentrations mentioned in both of Gould's citations were *identical;* one was *not* dilute and the other concentrated, as insisted upon by Gould.

Besides the inaccuracy of Gould's above mentioned passages, there are several other objections to Gould's claims, as follows:

1. Our odor-switch protocol on days 15, 16, and 17 of our "crucial design experiment" (table G.T.1; see also Wenner, Wells, and Johnson 1969; chapter 10, above) negates Gould's claim that the training method was at fault. Gould, in fact, admitted as much in his doctoral thesis, when he referred to that experimental series: "Recruitment in the hive on the basis of odor alone is a distinct possibility. This is especially likely, since on one day when the foragers were fed peppermint, 44 recruits nevertheless went to the clove station and only 2 to the forager stations" (1975a:47). Since we had trained the bees for that experimental series several weeks before we began the twenty-four-day sequence, Gould knew that an ad hoc "training difference" argument could not possibly apply. Although he thus recognized the implications of those results of ours in his unpublished thesis, he failed to do so in his published accounts.

TABLE GT.1. Total number of recruits received per day and the experimental procedure at the three sites on three of the experimental days.

Day	Procedure	Recruit Arrivals		
		Site 1	Site 2	Site 3
15	First scent at 1 and 3	93		87
16	Second scent at 1 and 3, first scent at 2	2	44	0
17	First scent at 1 and 3	71		29

SOURCE: Portion of table 1 in Wenner, Wells, and Johnson 1969.

NOTE: Foragers never visited the control site (site 2), and ten bees made a relatively constant number of trips per unit time to the experimental sites (sites 1 and 3).

2. Gould's (and von Frisch's) claim that we had improperly trained our bees contradicts other statements by von Frisch. For example, in 1950 and 1954 von Frisch indicated that he used honey for training bees (see his quotation on that matter, below). Honey is far more concentrated than saturated sugar solution (much greater than 2.5 molar sucrose).

3. The results published in our 1967 papers (see chapter 9) indicate very clearly that we *could* obtain von Frisch's results whenever we used his single-control experimental design. However, we *did not obtain* his results when we inserted additional controls. (That is how a scientist determines that the additional controls inserted are, in fact, necessary.) Neither did we "train out" (i.e., introduce bees to a feeding site not currently visited by their hivemates) the bees in between each of our experiments.

4. Bees were always trained out at least two weeks before the start of *any* of our experiments. It is unlikely that any "lost" bees would be searching the terrain after so much time had elapsed, as claimed by von Frisch and Gould.

5. In our "crucial design" paper (Wenner, Wells, and Johnson 1969), we published data gathered on twenty-four consecutive days. During the course of that series, we killed thousands of recruits as we gathered our data. That number was at least an order of magnitude greater than the total number of bees involved in the training process several weeks earlier.

6. The training technique described on pages 72 and 77 in Gould's thesis (Gould 1975a) was essentially identical to ours and to that published by von Frisch (Wenner 1961; von Frisch 1967a:17–20).

7. We found that 2M sugar solution, although acceptable for experiments in the high-humidity environment of Michigan (Wenner 1961), was too concentrated in California, where humidity is low. Most of our experiments in Santa Barbara were done with 1.0M or 1.5M sucrose solution (e.g., Wenner, Wells, and Johnson 1969; Friesen 1973).

8. The claim that we used too strong an odor in our experiments (Gould 1975a:47) is also an ad hoc, spurious argument. Each type of odor has its own vapor pressure; there is no way one can directly cross-compare the "strength" of various types of odor cues (different scents) on the basis of the amount of extract used per liter of solution.

In summary, by claiming that the results we had obtained in our double-control and strong inference experiments were due to the use of an improper method of training bees, Gould diverted the attention of the scientific community away from the significance of our results. Claude Bernard apparently encountered the same sort of experience during his career, and wrote:

> Among the artifices of criticism, many do not concern us because they are extra-scientific; one of them . . . consists in considering in a piece of work only what is [presumably] defective and open to attack, while neglecting or concealing what is valid and important. ([1865] 1957:189)

Those discrepancies between Gould's (and von Frisch's) claims and the actual facts as published earlier should have been recognized for what they were by the referees and the editors of the journals to which the manuscripts were submitted. The referee system, unfortunately, suffers from a serious bias, particularly among those who operate within the Realism school (Mahoney 1976; Broad and Wade 1982). Any reviewer of the Gould or von Frisch manuscripts who felt that a "dance language" among bees was a "fact" would be in no position to evaluate their claims about the presumed inappropriate use of methodology on our part.

THE PERSONAL EXPERIENCE OF WENNER

The above treatment omits some of the more interesting personal aspects of the case. As I indicated in my 1961 paper, the training method as published was in part supplemented by information gained from Rolf Boch, who assisted von Frisch in his experiments. That item requires further clarification.

During the initial stages of my doctoral research, I initially could not train bees to visit a feeding station. One method I tried to use was described by von Frisch (1939:427, 1950:53, 1954:100), exemplified as follows:

> When I wish to attract some bees for training experiments I usually place upon a small table several sheets of paper which have been smeared with honey. Then I am often obliged to wait for many hours, sometimes for several days, until finally a bee discovers the feeding place. But as soon as one bee has found the honey many more will appear within a short time—perhaps as many as several hundred (1950:53).

Neither that method nor other methods that von Frisch described before 1967 were sufficient for my successful training of bees, so it was necessary to develop independently a method that would work. Fortunately I had worked for large-scale commercial beekeepers for several years and could rather quickly devise a satisfactory method. That resultant training method was the basis for a paper on a method by which one can train bees to visit a feeding station (Wenner 1961).

While reporting the results of my experiments on sound production by dancing bees at the 1959 American Association for the Advancement of Science meetings in Cleveland, Ohio, I met Rolf Boch, who was also attending those meetings. After my talk we discussed this type of research, and I had the opportunity to tell him that I was not able to train bees according to the methods von Frisch had published. Boch smiled and said, "No, those methods won't work." He then indicated that he had trained bees for von Frisch while employed as a technician. The method he described was remarkably similar to that which I had devised on my own.

After publishing that technique paper, I remember receiving a note of protest from von Frisch, that read somewhat like the following (in translation): "There was no need for you to have published that method; it was all to have appeared in my memoirs."

When von Frisch finally published his method (1967a:17–20), it closely matched both Boch's earlier description and the method we used (Wenner 1961). However, in the 1967 von Frisch account, the 1961 Wenner publication was not included in the list of references cited.

A few years after the 1961 paper appeared, a colleague from Iowa State University stressed to me the difficulty he had had in attempting to employ von Frisch's stated training method. When that method didn't work for him either, he had to abandon the experiments he had planned.

Nobel laureate Peter Medawar commented on this problem, as follows: "It is a discreditable—indeed, an unforgivable—trick of scientmanship that withholds from a published paper some details of technique to prevent someone else from taking up the story where its author left off" (1979:44).

Excursus JNR: Edward Jenner and the Cowpox-Smallpox Connection

Prior to 1800, pus containing the smallpox virus taken from people having mild cases was injected into healthy people (an "inoculation" process), with the hope that the "less virulent" inoculum would produce a similar mild form of disease in the recipient. That technique was only partially successful; many deaths occurred as a consequence. Edward Jenner changed all that, admittedly with reliance on anecdote and the use of untested methodology. Both would be frowned upon today.

Jenner published a short paper in 1798: "An inquiry into the causes and effects of the variolae vaccinae, a disease discovered in some of the western counties of England, particularly Gloucestershire, and known by the name of the cow-pox." In that paper he described how men working with horses sometimes came into contact with a pus (known then as "grease") on the heels of horses. These men later infected cows while milking them without having washed their hands after handling the horses. Milkmaids with any cuts on their hands, in turn, developed cowpox by milking infected cows. Thereafter milkmaids were apparently immune from infection by the dreaded smallpox virus.

The research described by Jenner was *not* an example of a scientist setting up an hypothesis and testing it in a manner that would be considered acceptable today. According to Camac ([1909] 1959), Jenner gained the notion that smallpox immunity was possible on the basis of an anecdote provided by a young countrywoman, who had come to him for medical advice while he was an apprentice physician. Camac wrote: "In questioning her regarding smallpox she observed, 'I cannot take that disease for I have had the cow-pox'" ([1909] 1959:207).

Jenner apparently took her words seriously and gathered circumstantial evidence relating to that possibility (the exploration and verification approaches; see figure 3:1 in chapter 3). In his 1798 paper Jenner provided seventeen case histories in support of the tentative conclusion he had reached. His account provides an excellent example of how a single anecdote, one that might be dismissed by others, can lead to compelling evidence when augmented by concrete experiences.

The important point here is that Jenner responded positively to whoever had initially "created the image" (see chapter 3) that cowpox

infection conferred immunity against smallpox. He himself then became "converted" to that viewpoint when exposed to a sufficient
number of incidents, and proceeded to verify what he had observed.
We do not know how many experiments were sufficient to "convert"
Jenner, but that process necessarily preceded his design of further
experiments.

Jenner described his experiments in his classic paper and in other
papers, experiments that would be considered totally unacceptable
under today's research guidelines (e.g., rules for experimentation with
human subjects). One experiment he described yielded "direct evidence," as against many experiments that only yield indirect evidence.

Jenner inoculated with the smallpox virus a boy who had earlier
had cowpox. The boy exhibited no ill effects, except for the characteristic pustule at the site of inoculation. Jenner then described a sequential inoculation involving five people who had already had cowpox.
Pus from the first boy's developed pustule was used to inoculate one
of the five subjects. When a pustule developed in that person, pus
from it was used to inoculate the next person, etc. None of the five
subjects contracted smallpox.

As a final test, the virus from the incision of the last person in the
series was then used to inoculate a healthy person who had never had
cowpox; that last person in the series then became ill with smallpox
(direct evidence). Jenner wrote: "These experiments afforded me much
satisfaction; they proved that the matter [i.e., the virus], in passing
from one human subject to another, through five gradations, lost none
of its original properties" (in Camac [1909] 1959:229).

Jenner also addressed the problems of attitude in experimentation.
He wrote:

> They who are not in the habit of conducting experiments may not
> be aware of the coincidence of circumstances necessary for their
> being managed so as to prove perfectly decisive; nor how often men
> engaged in professional pursuits are liable to interruptions that
> disappoint them almost at the instant of their being accomplished.
> (Camac [1909] 1959:230)

One might think that either the partial success provided by inoculation with the smallpox virus or Jenner's more complete success,
through immunization by inoculation with the cowpox virus (vaccination), would have led to a rapid acceptance of vaccination as a
means of staving off subsequent smallpox affliction. The acceptance

was not as rapid as it would be today, due in large part to a public resistance to inoculation in general.

In his thorough 1895 treatment, "A History of the Warfare of Science with Theology in Christendom," Andrew D. White documented the resistance to inoculation encountered among the clergy. White wrote: "As late as 1803 the Rev. Dr. Ramsden thundered against vaccination in a sermon before the University of Cambridge, mingling texts of Scripture with calumnies against Jenner" ([1895] 1955 2:58).

Despite resistance, Jenner's technique prevailed, largely because it was based on direct evidence ("One fact may be worth a thousand arguments") and because it was useful (by providing the necessary immunization against the smallpox scourge). His success today is evident by the apparent total eradication of naturally occurring smallpox from the earth. However, cultures still exist in American, British, and Russian high-security research laboratories.

Excursus MM: Maurice Maeterlinck's Alleged Plagiarism

A shadow was cast on Maurice Maeterlinck's character in 1927 after he published *The Life of the White Ant*, a sequel to his 1901 work, *The Life of the Bee*. Maeterlinck's 1927 book deeply upset Eugene Marais, a South African naturalist, who had himself published a series of articles on termites in an Afrikaans periodical *Die Huisgenoot* (1923–1926, in the Afrikaans language). Some of these Marais termite articles also appeared later as translations in European periodicals.

Because of similarities in text and in ideas (and perhaps since Africaans and Flemish are similar languages), Marais concluded that Maeterlinck had used the Africaans material without proper acknowledgment. In a Johannesburg newspaper article Marais wrote: "When I got a copy of his work it became at once evident that the great Belgian had done me the honour of using my writings without the customary courtesy of acknowledgment" (photocopy inserted by Robert Ardrey in Marais 1969).

Robert Ardrey championed Marais' cause many years after the death of both principals. In his book *African Genesis*, Ardrey included quotations written by Winifred de Kok, the translator of Marais' 1933 book, *Die Siel van die Mier* (see Ardrey 1963). Those quotations had appeared in the 1936 English version of *The Soul of the White Ant*.

In much stronger language than that used by de Kok, Ardrey insisted that Marais had priority in the notion that a social insect colony functions as a "super-organism." Ardrey wrote: "Marais, indeed, had sued the Nobel prize-winner, alleging that page after literal page had been taken from his writings and that Maeterlinck's scientific naivete had been such that he had even used terminology invented by Marais under the impression that it was common scientific language" (1963:62).

Marais' distress was understandable, given the limited information available to him at that time. In her preface to Marais' book, Winifred de Kok wrote:

> About six years after [Marais'] articles appeared, Maurice Maeterlinck published his book, *The Life of the White Ant*, in which he describes this organic unity of the termitary and compares it with the human body. This theory aroused great interest at the time and was generally accepted as an original one formulated by Maeterlinck. The fact that an unknown South African observer had devel-

oped the theory after many years of indefatigable labour was not generally known in Europe. Excerpts from Marais' articles had, however, appeared in both the Belgian and the French press at the time of their publication in South Africa. Indeed, the original Afrikaans articles would have been intelligible to any Fleming, for Afrikaans and Flemish are very similar. (Marais 1937:vi)

Ardrey pressed the case even more fervently in an introduction he wrote for the 1969 posthumous publication of Marais' book, *The Soul of the Ape:*

> How a man of such stature could in later years commit such a crime, I do not know. But in 1926, the year after the appearance of Marais' article, Maurice Maeterlinck published in French a book that by the following year appeared in English and in several other languages. In that book, without acknowledgment, Maeterlinck took half of Marais' life work and published it as his own. *The Life of the White Ant* stands even today on many a library shelf, but the name on its cover is that of a plagiarist. (Ardrey in Marais 1969:16, 17)

E. O. Wilson (1971:318) concluded that Ardrey had reacted "melodramatically," and labeled the entire episode "just a tempest in a teapot." (In his book Wilson indicated that the plagiarism charge was in Ardrey's book, *The Territorial Imperative*. However, Ardrey's claim actually appeared in one form in his 1963 book, *African Genesis*, and in another form in his introduction to the 1969 Marais book, *The Soul of the Ape*.) The case becomes more interesting when one examines the actual passages under consideration.

As indicated above, Ardrey published a photocopy of the 1927 newspaper article presumably written by Marais, in which Marais compared exerpts from Maeterlinck's book and from Marais' own 1925 article in *De Huisgenoot*. From a review of that article and other material, we conclude that Maeterlinck did not plagiarize Marais. If anything, the converse could have occurred; Marais could have obtained the essence of his original idea from the earlier publication of Maeterlinck on bees (1901) or from one by Wheeler (1910) without having been aware of that circumstance. Elaboration follows.

In the 1927 version of Maeterlinck's book from which Marais obtained his quotations, one finds that Maeterlinck had actually devoted the third section of his chapter 9 to the "superorganism" concept. Marais (or a reporter), in the newspaper article of that same year, had selected only a few noncontiguous sentences, or fragments of sentences, from that Maeterlinck passage. The total for the comparison was less than a quarter of its entirety, that is, 30 short lines out of

131. It is hard to fathom how that much material could be interpreted as being "half of Marais' life work," as Ardrey claimed.

In addition, in the newspaper article Marais (or the author of the article) had omitted a crucial paragraph from Maeterlinck's 1927 book. That paragraph had preceded the passage that Marais claimed Maeterlinck had used without acknowledgment; it began with the sentence: "In *The Life of the Bee* I attributed the occult, provident government and administration of the community to the 'spirit of the hive'—for lack of a better explanation" (1927:151; see also Maeterlinck 1901:ch. 2, sec. 9).

Maeterlinck had then continued, as quoted by Marais in the 1927 newspaper article: "Another hypothesis might consider the hive, the ant-hill and the termitary as a single individual, with its parts scattered abroad; a single living creature, that had not yet become, or that had ceased to be, combined or consolidated" (1927:151).

There is actually a considerable body of scattered reference to "the spirit of the hive" in the first chapter of Maeterlinck's classic book, with one of the concluding passages reading:

> From the crowd, from the city, [the bee] derives an invisible aliment that is as necessary to her as honey. This craving will help to explain the spirit of the laws of the hive. For in them the individual is nothing, her existence conditional only, and herself, for one indifferent moment, a winged organ of the race. Her whole life is an entire sacrifice to the manifold, everlasting being whereof she forms part. (1901:23)

From Maeterlinck's *complete* statement, it is evident that his concept of the colony as a superorganism had roots in his 1901 book, *The Life of the Bee*. However, the idea could perhaps be traced even further back. Pliny the Elder (23–79 A.D.), for example, wrote: "What men, I protest, can we rank in rationality with these [bees], which unquestionably excel mankind in this, that they recognize only the common interest" (Rackham 1967:441).

The foregoing Maeterlinck passage (or one by Pliny or Wheeler) could, in fact, have served as a basis for the later expression of Marais, when he wrote: "One of my theses was that the termitary is a separate and perfect animal, which lacks only the power of moving from place to place. I will give you my proofs of this little by little, and the explanation will make clear at the same time the beginning and development of the group soul" (1937:59).

Furthermore, before 1925 there was a considerable amount of information published on termites; by then information about termite community organization had indeed become common scientific knowledge. Maeterlinck provided fifty-six references in his bibliography (Marais provided none), and wrote in his introduction:

> It would have been easy, in regard to every statement, to allow the text to bristle with footnotes and references. In some chapters there is not a sentence but would have clamoured for these; and the letter press would have been swallowed up by vast masses of comment, like one of those dreadful books we hated so much at school. (1927:5)

Maeterlinck (1901), by his early use of the expression, "spirit of the hive," already had some notion of a "superorganism" concept by the time he published his book. Shortly thereafter, Wheeler expressed a similar concept when he wrote:

> There is thus a striking analogy, which has not escaped the philosophical biologist [such as perhaps Maeterlinck, above], between the ant colony and the cell colony which constitutes the body of a Metazoan animal; and many of the laws that control the cellular origin, development, growth, reproduction and decay of the Metazoan, are seen to hold good also of the ant society regarded as an individual of a higher order. (1910:7)

Maeterlinck's priority in the notion of a social insect colony as a superorganism was recognized by the renowned naturalist John Burroughs, in the expression: "Maeterlinck's conception of the Spirit of the Hive was an inspiration, and furnishes us with the key to all that happens in the hive" (1921:158).

Finally, in the same year (1923) in which Marais first published his notion that a termite colony could be considered a "self-contained animal in a certain stage of development," Wheeler had become far more explicit in his book *Social Life Among the Insects*, when he wrote:

> For the relations between parents and offspring tend to become so increasingly intimate and interdependent that we are confronted with a new organic unit, or biological entity—a super-organism, in fact, in which through physiological division of labor the component individuals specialize in diverse ways and become necessary to one another's welfare or very existence. (1923:10, 11)

Marais certainly should have known of Wheeler's priority to his expression on the matter of a superorganism concept. One wonders, then, why he should have leveled the charge of plagiarism against Maeterlinck at all.

How did Maeterlinck respond to this "tempest in a teapot"? Marais himself perhaps expressed it best in a letter to Winifred de Kok, the translator of his termite book, when he wrote: "In any case, Maeterlinck, like other great ones on Olympus, maintained a mighty and dignified silence" (Ardrey in Marais 1969:18).

Wilson concluded his treatment of the Marais and Maeterlinck incident with the statement: "Wheeler was clearly the architect of the idea, for what it was worth, and neither Marais nor Maeterlinck had any claim for priority or visible effect on later students of social insects" (1971:318).

The negative tone of that statement by Wilson clarifies, somewhat, the significance of an earlier comment by him in that same passage, in which he had credited Maeterlinck with priority in the use of the expression "spirit of the hive." Wilson wrote: "Later, in *The Life of the White Ant* (1927) and *The Life of the Ant* (1930), Maeterlinck brought this pretty nonsense in line with Wheeler's concept, to which he was openly indebted, and gave it a more scientific veneer (1971:318)."

Here we also may well be encountering a relatively common phenomenon among scientists, expressed by Whitley as follows: "In the modern sciences research objectives and procedures are controlled by insisting that only contributions which have been published in collegiate journals constitute scientific knowledge" (1984:26).

In summary, after Pliny, Maeterlinck was perhaps one of the first people to popularize the concept of a "superorganism," by his use of the phrase "spirit of the hive"; Wheeler formalized it further, and Marais could have independently hit upon the same idea. By then, however, the superorganism concept may well have already been "general scientific knowledge."

How does all of this relate to the honey bee dance language controversy and the theme of this book? Actually, it has considerable application. Maeterlinck had, after all, executed a strong inference experiment (see our chapter 3), which has yet to be repeated. Given the climate that prevailed at the time, it is doubtful that anyone could have successfully resurrected Maeterlinck's experiment during the 1960s and 1970s. The popularity of the dance language hypothesis, coupled with Ardrey's claim that Maeterlinck was a plagiarist, would surely have diverted attention away from *The Life of the Bee* and the implications of the crucial experiment described therein.

Excursus NEG: Negation of the Dance
Language Hypothesis

"To cling rigidly to familiar ideas is in essence the
same as blocking the mind from engaging in creative free play."
— David Bohm and F. David Peat 1987:51

Bohm and Peat wrote of "creative free play" (above), Keller (1983)
used the expression, "a feeling for the organism," and Atkinson (1985)
recognized "image creation." These writers thereby perceived the
value of reentry into the exploration approach (see chapter 3 and
figure 3.1) whenever new observations or experimental results provide insight not in accord with preconceived notions.

Early in the dance language controversy, the results of our own
double-control experiments (see chapter 9) revealed to us that a population of searching recruits ultimately distributed itself at four feeding stations with mathematical regularity. The pattern corresponded
with a binomial or multinomial distribution (Johnson 1967a; Wenner
1967), a repeatable result corresponding with the distance of each
station from the center of them all.

Those results are somewhat astonishing on the face of it, since
searching honey bees are constantly exposed to varying winds, vegetation obstructions, and extraneous odors. We were then forced into
an exploration approach; we recognized that the same mathematics
that had been applied to the random assortment of genetic alleles
suited our data on a population of flying bees as well. That insight
facilitated the development of an odor-search model for honey bee
recruitment (see excursus OS).

The mathematical correspondence between station placement and
recruit arrival frequency reinforced an impression we had gained
earlier—that the behavior of a population of animals can often be
expressed in simple mathematical terms, even though the behavior of
individuals within that population may appear random. Unfortunately, in animal behavior studies the emphasis has usually been on
the performance of individuals, not on populations. Not surprisingly,
our new attitude about the behavior of populations of searching bees
was not shared by others in the ethology community.

Gould, Henerey, and MacLeod (1970) missed a similar exciting
opportunity. They had gathered some of the most direct and meaningful data available on the behavior of searching recruits by actually

measuring the individual flight times of thirty-seven recruits that had left the hive after contacting a dancing bee. However, their commitment to the dance language hypothesis prevented them from analyzing those data from a population perspective.

If they had worked within the intellectual climate of a previous era, when the odor-search paradigm prevailed (prior to 1940), they would have been in a position to exploit the mathematical implications of the excellent data they had gathered relative to the *pattern* of recruit search times (as against the performance of one individual). During the 1930s classical genetics was thriving; the parallel between assortment of genetic alleles and assortment of searching recruits may have been obvious.

Exactly what we mean by all of the above requires a step-by-step treatment of the issue. The following reanalysis of the Gould, Henerey, and MacLeod data may be somewhat complicated, in that it involves the notion of lognormal distributions. However, a clear statement of the problem and a simplified presentation of the actual results Gould and co-workers obtained, combined with the implications of those results, should clarify the relevance of mathematics to the issue.

THE PROBLEM

When Gould and co-workers published their challenge of our work in *Science*, they actually provided results that *completely undermined* the honey bee dance language hypothesis. However, the scientific community, being locked into the dance language paradigm, was not prepared to consider any alternative interpretations at that time. As an example, one of us (Wenner) was rebuffed in an attempt to get a short letter published in *Science* as a reply to that challenge of our work (see excursus SCI).

Although the editor and referees of *Science* would not permit a reply to the Gould, Henerey, and MacLeod paper, the journal *Nature* did so a few years later (Wells and Wenner 1973:173). At that time we were able to reiterate a point we had made earlier—Gould and co-workers could conclude that all recruit arrivals had "used" information obtained from a dance maneuver only by focusing on "successful" recruit performance and by ignoring evidence to the contrary.

In a series of papers, Rosin (1978, 1980a, 1980b) expanded on that theme. More recently, Rosin stated the problem quite succinctly, in both one statement: "Wenner & Wells (1987) have already noted my refutation of Gould's version of the 'dance language' hypothesis, on the basis of earlier results by Gould et al. (1970)" (1988a:267) and in another: "Gould managed to prove that no matter what he did to his bees, they still invariably, that is irrespective of training conditions, arrived at his *forager-station* without use of 'dance language' information" (Rosin 1988a:267; emphasis ours).

That is, the particular group of recruits referred to by Rosin was supposed to be arriving at Gould's *experimental* station and not at the forager station, because the dance directions in the hive had been altered experimentally. Rosin continued in the same vein as we had done in our *Nature* paper: "Gould apparently presents the results for only a very small portion of the experiments he actually carried out" (1988a:267).

Exactly what Rosin meant by the above statements can be clarified by means of a close examination of the data published by Gould, Henerey, and MacLeod in 1970. Ironically, those workers inadvertently provided the most direct set of evidence anyone has gathered *against* the notion that recruited bees might be able to *use* direction and distance information contained in the celebrated waggle dance.

Gould and his associates appeared instead to have been channeled by their paradigm hold. Neither they nor any other language proponents (later including the members of Gould's doctoral committee; see chapter 11) recognized the negative implications of those earlier results. In fact, there is no published indication that any language proponent carefully studied the Gould and co-worker 1970 data during the twenty years following publication of those results.

A "SHUTOUT" FOR ALMOST ALL SEARCHING BEES

Our assertion deserves further elaboration, since the matter is not likely to be obvious even to a discerning reader. Consider first the following Gould, Henerey, and MacLeod statement: "Only 37 (that is, 13 percent) of [the] 277 [dance] attendants were successfully recruited and later caught at a feeding station, even though the high molarity (2.5M) of the sucrose used reportedly produces maximum dancing and recruitment" (1970:552).

Two points can be made at the outset. First, as low as that percentage of recruitment success appears to be (and as much as it undermines the dance language hypothesis), the actual success for searching recruits is far less than stated. Second, the distinctive flight performance of the thirty-seven recruits that finally reached a station weighs even more heavily against invoking the language hypothesis to explain the results they obtained. Clarification follows.

Of the thirty-seven "successful" recruits, twelve (one-third) actually ended up at a station located in *a direction opposite from* that indicated by the dancing bee. That result is an unacceptable departure from the expected; von Frisch had insisted that the flight direction for most recruits did not deviate more than 15° from the line of flight used by foragers (e.g., von Frisch 1954:124).

The results that Gould and co-workers obtained thus actually eliminate most of the original 277 searching bees from consideration. However, Gould and co-workers then mistakenly concluded that all remaining 25 recruits (only 9 percent of those that left the hive) had arrived at the "correct" station by *use* of direction information obtained from dancing bees.

In applying their arithmetic, they failed to recognize that one-half of the thirty-seven arrivals could have arrived at each of the stations by chance alone *without* use of "dance language" (*even if* search had been "random" and the stations and wind conditions had been identical). That means that only seven or eight recruits ($25 - 37/2$, or less than 3 percent of the 277) actually remained as viable candidates for the concept that information from the dance maneuver had been *used*.

If those results are not enough to lead one to question the "dance language" interpretation, we can ask a penetrating question about the flight times that Gould and co-workers obtained: "Did the search pattern of those twenty-five bees that had performed "correctly" differ from that of the twelve bees that ended up in the opposite direction?"

EXPECTED VERSUS OBSERVED FLIGHT PATTERNS OF SEARCHING BEES

The results obtained by Gould and co-workers provide an unequivocal negative answer to that question as well; the composite flight time patterns for those 25 recruits and for the 12 recruits that ended up in the opposite direction (from the last two columns of their table 4) also negated the dance language hypothesis. We thus need deal no further with the less than 3 percent of the 277 recruits that left the hive and that *may* have used direction information.

However, the flight pattern of searching bees is interesting in its own right and requires more elaboration. As a start, we can ask:

"What can one expect a flight pattern to be for a number of bees searching for a point source to which they have presumably been directed by dancing bees?" A reasonable assumption is that some searching bees should find the station rather quickly and some should take more time, with an average time of flight prevailing for most of them. That is, there should be a normal "bell-shaped" distribution of flight times during the search, with a measurable mean and standard deviation.

Can one estimate such expected search times on the basis of known information about honey bee flight speed? Fortunately, the flight speed of both loaded and unloaded honey bees has been measured (Wenner 1963), permitting reasonable estimates of what might be expected for searching bees "heading directly out" to the food place.

We analyze the Gould, Henerey, and MacLeod flight time data here in a three-stage process: first in terms of the normal flight speed of experienced foragers, second in terms of what might be expected for recruits using dance maneuver information in a normal distribution manner, and third in terms of the actual flight performance documented by Gould and co-workers.

Forager Flight Speeds

As indicated above, the flight speed of forager honey bees is known (e.g., Wenner 1963). Experienced bees travel in a straight line (a "beeline") out from their hive at about 7.5 meters per second to a feeding station. In doing so, those foragers are influenced relatively little by wind speed and/or direction (see figure NEG.1); they merely fly closer to the ground in stronger winds.

In the series 1 experiments of Gould and co-workers, conducted at wind speeds equivalent to those in the Wenner flight speed study, foragers traveled a distance of only 120 meters. At normal flight speeds for outgoing foragers, the outward travel time for a representative set of foragers (derived from the data shown in figure NEG.1) would be about 16 seconds (16.1 ± 2.2 sec; n = 51) at that distance.

Expected Search Times

From flight speed data provided by Wenner (see figure 1 in Wenner 1963) one can also derive a family of curves for *expected* search times for a representative set of searching recruits under different assumptions. That is because each of the points shown in the original data

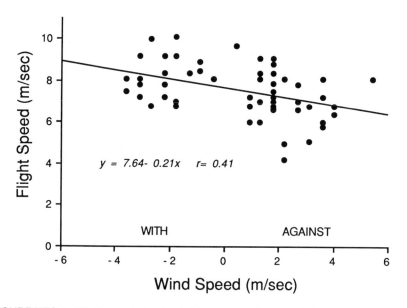

FIGURE NEG 1. Flight speed of unloaded foragers as they traveled from their hive to a feeding station (after figure 1 in Wenner 1963). Wind (measured at 2 meters above ground) influenced their net speed only slightly, because bees normally fly nearer the ground in stronger winds and thereby exploit drag.

represents an actual flight speed for an individual bee; data on variation is accordingly available.

One can then estimate the time each of those bees would need to cover the 120-meter distance used in the Gould, Henerey, and MacLeod study under different assumptions of efficiency (e.g., five times as long as a forager, ten times as long as a forager, etc.). In each case the extracted flight times can be represented as a mean and standard deviation, as indicated in the previous section.

The flight pattern of a *population* of searching recruits can also be represented by ranking each bee's performance in a manner similar to that used in presenting percentile rankings for SAT, MCAT, and GRE test scores. That is, the estimated and/or derived recruit mean search times can be viewed as a function of the cumulative success of all recruits. Furthermore, normal distribution results can be displayed as straight lines on normal paper (probability graph paper), with the location and slope of each line representing a mean and standard deviation for search times.

To illustrate the above, consider the estimated flight times of the unloaded foragers, as derived from figure NEG.1. In figure NEG.2

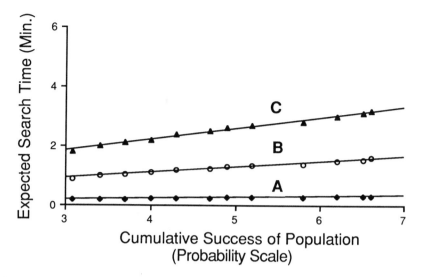

FIGURE NEG 2. Three models for expected normal distributions of search times for recruited honey bees. These are based upon the flight speed of unloaded foragers and the length of time those experienced foragers need to travel 120 meters from hive to feeding station. (Estimates are plotted as "normal" rather than as linear plots; each line thus represents a bell-shaped curve. The value at 5 is the mean; values at 4 and at 6 are one standard deviation away from the mean.)

A) Average time spent by experienced foragers in their "beeline" flight out from the hive (derived from figure NEG. 1). B) Expected flight time for recruits that would require five times the amount of time expended by foragers. C) Expected flight time for recruits requiring ten times that necessary for foragers.

those times are represented by line A as a function of the cumulative success of the total number of bees involved. Rather than use percentiles (which would range from 0 to 100 on a nonlinear scale), we have converted the percentiles to probits in order to make that scale linear. The mean search time then can be read at the 5 mark on the abscissa; the 4 and 6 marks are each one standard deviation away from the mean.

Since no one expects recruits to travel quite as fast as foragers, we provide two other lines on that same plot. Line B represents the cumulative behavior pattern for a population of searching recruits that would have required an average of five times the flight time of experienced foragers; line C represents the pattern for a body of recruits searching ten times as long as necessary for a flight by a group of regular foragers.

The assumption thus rests on a reasonable premise. If recruits were following instructions about direction and distance information obtained from a dancing bee, one should expect a population of them to be searching in a normal distribution manner (e.g., searching for an average time, with standard deviation). The 5X and 10X figures do for initial assumptions in a family of curves; one can use other multiples of forager flight time, if so desired, in keeping with what one should expect of recruits "flying directly out" in response to the "use" of information obtained from the dance maneuver before leaving the hive.

Observed Flight Patterns

We can now turn our attention to a comparison of the flight performances of the two groups of "successful" searching recruits in the series 1 experiments of Gould and co-workers. In doing so, we can separate the data into the performance of those that had arrived at a station in the "correct" direction (twenty-five bees) and those that had arrived at a station in the opposite direction (twelve bees).

For that comparison, we provide two plots on the same graph (figure NEG.3). To accommodate the extreme range of search times Gould and co-workers obtained, however, we had to expand the ordinate scale by ten times for figure NEG.3 compared to that used in figure NEG.2. (Line C of figure NEG.2 is included for comparison in figure NEG.3).

The data gathered by Gould and co-workers then clearly reveal two additional problems with respect to applying the dance language hypothesis to the interpretation of results. In the first place, there was no difference in search pattern for those recruits that ended up in the "correct" direction from their hive compared to those that ended in an opposite direction from their hive ($r = 0.99$ in each case).

In addition, the flight time pattern for the population of searching bees formed a logarithmic function on normal paper (a near perfect lognormal correlation, in fact) as opposed to the normal distribution one might expect from a simple "reading" and execution of dance maneuver information (i.e., as in lines B and C of figure NEG.2). Those Gould, Henerey, and MacLeod data indicate instead that recruits may have been using some other search mode during their search for the feeding stations (see chapter 5 and excursus OS).

In summary, only a small percentage of the recruits in the Gould, Henerey, and MacLeod experiments managed to find either of the two stations; a third of them actually ended up in a direction opposite from that "intended." One can deduce that only 7 or 8 of the 37 that

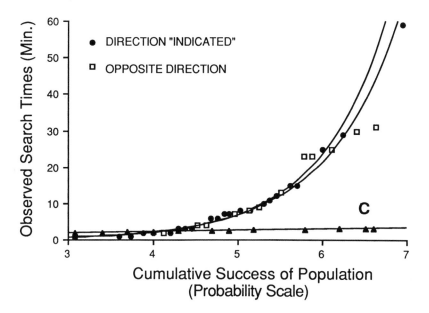

FIGURE NEG. 3. Observed flight time patterns for the relatively few recruited honey bees that were "successful" in the Gould, Henerey, and MacLeod (1970) experiments. Closed symbols represent bees that arrived in the "intended" direction; open symbols represent data for bees arriving at a station in the opposite direction. Line C from figure NEG. 2 is included for comparison; note also the greatly increased ordinate scale compared to that used in figure NEG. 2.

The 75-minute search time in the Gould, Henerey, and MacLeod table was omitted for this graph, since that value would be considerably off scale and would require too great a changing of scales for the comparison intended here.

The observed search flight patterns differed markedly from the normal distribution pattern (figure NEG. 2) one would expect under expectations of the dance language hypothesis. Furthermore, the flight pattern of bees that arrived at the "intended" station did not differ from that of bees that landed at a station in a direction opposite from that "intended." The results thus negated the dance language hypothesis. Searching recruits were clearly using some other search behavior.

arrived at a station (out of 277 that left the hive) differed from what one would expect by chance (25 – 38/2; see above). Even with those few successes, differences in wind or other environmental factors could have altered the results.

Furthermore, the flight pattern for the group of bees that found any station at all differed markedly from expectations of the dance language hypothesis, in that:

1. The flight pattern times followed the laws of logarithmic probability rather than an anticipated simple normal distri-

bution of search times based upon distance from the hive, and

2. The search pattern for bees supposedly using dance maneuver information did not differ from that of the search pattern for bees that had ended up at a station located in the opposite direction from the hive.

HOW A PARADIGM HOLD CAN LIMIT OPTIONS

The excellent data gathered by Gould and co-workers on the search times of recruited honey bees (their series 1 experiments) thus provided *no* evidence in support of the notion that recruits can use dance maneuver information; those results actually *negated* the language hypotheses. How was it, then, that they and others could conclude that their results *supported* the dance language hypothesis?

Dance language proponents could accept the Gould, Henerey, and MacLeod results as supportive of the dance language hypothesis only by believing that any recruit arrivals at their stations that was different from random arrival would be evidence of "language" use. By doing so, they failed to perceive the need to subtract the eighteen or nineteen recruits (half of the thirty-seven) that could have arrived by chance alone at either station (all conditions equal) from the twenty-five that apparently arrived at the "correct" station, before they interpreted their results.

Eventually Gould himself (1976:241) realized that this 1970 article had not settled the issue. That new awareness on Gould's part, however, was apparently not sufficient to shake the hold of that paradigm. He could admit that his earlier work was not conclusive only after he believed that his newer evidence had verified the dance language hypothesis. Even though he was by then acquainted with the writings of Thomas Kuhn (Gould 1976:241), Gould apparently did not grasp the significance of one of Kuhn's often-quoted statements: "Though they may begin to lose faith and then to consider alternatives, they do not renounce the paradigm that has led them into crisis" (1970a:77). Instead, Gould pursued the matter from within the dance language paradigm during his doctoral studies and insisted, on the basis of that work, that: "A conclusive resolution of the dance-language controversy seems finally to have been achieved (Gould 1974, 1975a,b,c)" (1976:234).

ROSIN'S OBJECTIONS

By now it should also be more evident what Rosin (1988a) intended by the statements quoted near the beginning of this excursus. We cover Rosin's two points here one at a time.

> 1. Wenner and Wells (1987) have already noted my refutation of Gould's version of the "dance language" hypothesis on the basis of earlier results by Gould et al (1970). (Rosin 1988a:267)

Gould's practice of moving his test stations every twenty minutes in his later experiments (Gould 1974, 1975a, 1975b, 1975c), with only a five-minute "grace" period between sites to accommodate those recruits still searching, obviously failed to take into account results published in the 1970 paper. Most of the recruits in that earlier study searched longer than that.

If we accept the search times published in the 1970 publication (see Table 4 in Gould, Henerey, and MacLeod 1970), each move of a station would inevitably result in a great many recruits being left in the air and (by now) using "incorrect" dance maneuver information. That is, bees supposedly recruited to the station at the location used before the move would still be in the air searching for the location of the feeding station at that earlier site rather than using any updated indication about the new food place location.

> 2. Gould apparently presents the results for only a very small portion of the experiments he actually carried out [in 1973–1974]. (Rosin 1988a:267)

Gould's later results (e.g., figure 4A in Gould 1975b), for example, suggested great precision in the use of dance maneuver information. However, since we are not provided with the results of the numerous other similar experiments run that same summer, we cannot judge how representative those published results were. Also, the experimental protocol used is inconsistent with what we know of recruit bee search times (see Figure NEG.3). One point we recognize is that we have here another example of the "affirmation of the consequent" by the apparent selection of supportive results.

This case thus becomes a good example of how those who work within the verification approach may focus only on the "successful" outcomes of experiments, firm in the belief that they are merely providing documentation (hopefully irrefutable) for what is already known to be true (the Realism school).

As indicated, Rosin seems to be the only one (besides us; see excursus EXC) who has recognized the severe contradictions inherent in the experimental analyses and interpretation provided by Gould (see our chapter 13). Perhaps it is that inability (or unwillingness) of the dance language proponents to perceive those contradictions that led Rosin to write:

> A theoretical analysis of claims vs. experimental results demonstrates that the "dance language" hypothesis has gradually become ever more paradoxical. The analysis also demonstrates a most perturbing phenomenon, i.e. the ability of scientists to avoid seeing that which they do not wish to see. (1980b:775)

A more interesting question will likely now arise in the minds of some readers: "How could the journal referees fail to recognize the perfectly viable alternative interpretation for the Gould, Henerey, and MacLeod results?" Some of Feyerabend's comments on theory acceptance may apply here: "Next, the development becomes known to the public. Popular science books . . . spread the basic postulates of the theory; applications are made in distant fields. . . . More than ever the theory seems to possess tremendous empirical support" (1975:43).

We feel that some thoughts from Walter Weimer also apply: "one cannot bridge the gap between *empirical* content and *truth* content. There is no way to *know* that one can arrive at truth content from empirical consequences; the appraisal of a theory and its truth are not related in any straightforward manner" (1979:69).

WHAT MIGHT HAVE BEEN

Others may agree with us that this episode has important implications for those interested in the sociology, psychology, and philosophy of science. Consider what could have happened.

It is clear to us that Gould and co-workers failed to recognize the value of the data they had gathered in terms of how those results actually negated the dance language hypothesis. To paraphrase one of Thomas Kuhn's statements (1970:3), with their verification spectacles firmly in place (the Realism school), Gould and co-workers could not perceive that they had actually conducted a strong inference experiment (the Relativism school).

From their Realism perspective, Gould, Henerey, and MacLeod could not appreciate the fact that they had obtained data on the existence of a lognormal distribution in cumulative search times for searching recruit bees. From our current vantage point, we view this failure on their part as a missed opportunity; the behavioral pattern of searching bees had provided a clue to them about what stimuli searching recruits might be using; recognition of that fact could have led them into a fruitful area of research.

Now to the sociological and psychological aspects of the case.

What if Gould and co-workers *had* recognized the fact that their recruits *had not* performed as expected under the expectations of the dance language hypothesis? What if they had then pursued that new line of research? Would Gould's career have been the same? Would the scientific community have welcomed the results regardless of the emerging interpretation? Those are the type of questions now being pursued by investigators interested in the psychology (e.g., Mahoney 1976) and sociology (e.g., Veldink 1989) of science.

Excursus NG: The Scent Gland (Nasanov Gland) of Honey Bees

The scent gland of worker honey bees is usually called the Nasanov (or Nassanoff) gland, after the Russian anatomist who first described it. That gland is located on the upper surface of the abdomen, between the last and next-to-last segments (see plate 7A in Ribbands 1953 and figure 7 in Wenner 1971a). When a bee raises its abdomen and flexes the last segment down, a fragrance exudes from a pouch opened by that motion.

Fragrant components emanating from that gland include the alcohols geraniol (*trans*-3,7-Dimethyl-2,6-octadien-1-ol) and nerol (the *cis*-isomer of geraniol). The oxidation products of those components, citral (two isomers), geranic acid, and nerolic acids, are also present (Boch and Shearer 1962; Shearer and Boch 1966; Pickett et al. 1980, 1981). The mixture has a pleasant floral smell to human beings, as do its individual components.

These fragrances are not unique to bees; they also occur in some plants, such as in the herb "lemon balm" (*Melissa officianalis;* see Burgett 1980), and in leaves of the exotic lemon-scented gum tree (*Eucalyptus citriodora*). The principal volatile component of the latter is geraniol (results from an unpublished gas chromatographic analysis).

In field experiments one cannot help but notice the exposure of the Nasanov gland when bees feed at dishes of sugar solution, particularly if scent levels are low (Wells and Wenner 1971). Bees apparently do not expose that gland while they feed on flowers (Free 1968), even though von Frisch and Rosch (1926) had reported earlier that they did.

Researchers have sometimes gone to elaborate lengths to exclude the presence of that odor during bee "language" experiments (e.g., von Frisch 1923). Gould, Henerey, and MacLeod (1970) also took pains to seal off the gland, despite the fact that considerable data had already existed that indicated that Nasanov glands were apparently not a factor in recruitment (e.g., data in von Frisch 1947; Wenner, Wells, and Johnson 1969; see also Wells and Wenner 1971, 1973).

In chapter 6 we noted that von Frisch's 1923 conclusion, that Nasanov gland exudate attracted recruits, was not supported by his later and more extensive experimental results in 1947. However, since that 1947 paper dealt mainly with other important issues (the generation of the dance language hypothesis), we and most other readers paid scant attention to discrepancies in the scent gland data he published therein. Indeed, we were not sensitized to von Frisch's difficulties in this area until our own observations of Nasanov gland exposure failed to correspond with existing interpretation.

The Nasanov gland attractant problem has interesting application to the relationship between paradigm hold and experimental procedure in science. We pursue that topic here.

HOW SHOULD AN ANIMAL BEHAVE TOWARD AN ATTRACTANT?

The "attractiveness" of a pheromonal mixture, as the honey bee Nasanov gland secretion was presumed to be, can only be assessed biologically. Baker, Meyer, and Roelfos defined *attraction* as "net within-plume displacement toward the [chemical] source" (1981:269; see also our chapter 5 and excursus OS). An example of an attractant that meets this definition is that of methyl eugenol in the case of the Oriental fruit fly, *Dacus dorsalis*. Steiner reported a series of experimental tests in Hawaii, in which the movement of Oriental fruit flies toward that chemical was well documented. For example, he wrote: "In one experiment some 1300 flies were attracted a half-mile to a muslin screen that had been treated with methyl eugenol and exposed to daylight for 5 hours. None appeared until after 15 minutes had elapsed, but 30 appeared during the next hour and 67 during the first 100 minutes" (1952:242).

In addition, catches of flies in areas downwind of such traps declined, and times of first arrivals of flies were correlated with the distances of those populations from the traps. Steiner noted: "The area influenced by methyl eugenol is triangular in shape with the base downwind and the width of the base regulated by wind velocity and directional stability" (1952:242).

Steiner's experimental results, a "net within-plume displacement [of *Dacus dorasalis*] toward the [methyl eugenol] source," clearly fit within the above definition of "attraction."

HOW DO BEES BEHAVE TOWARD NASANOV GLAND SECRETIONS?

Von Frisch was not the first to suggest an attraction of honey bees to Nasanov gland secretions. In 1901 Sladen concluded that the Nasanov gland attracted disoriented swarm bees, as well as bees returning to the entrance of their hive (in Ribbands 1953:172, 173). However, von Frisch may have been the first to suggest the hypothesis that Nasanov gland exudate was responsible for attracting searching bees to feeding dishes. In 1923, for example, he reported that he had obtained ten times as many new arrivals at stations where Nasanov glands were exposed than at stations where glands were sealed.

Those early von Frisch results seemed to verify Sladen's earlier conclusion that Nasanov gland secretions attract bees. Indeed, von Frisch's 1920s results had so increased his confidence in the "truth" of his hypothesis (that Nasanov gland secretions attract recruits to feeding dishes) that he dismissed anomalous data he gathered during the 1940s, at which time he wrote: "there is no doubt about the existence of an attraction exerted by the scent organ, (c.f. v. Frisch, 1923. p. 155 ff) which has also been confirmed in further experiments into which I do not want to go here" (1947:22).

An analysis of his 1940s data may reveal why he had to dismiss those later results if he was to keep the Nasanov gland attraction hypothesis alive. We reproduce here table 6.2 (as table NG.1) from the body of our text for ready reference (from Wenner 1971a:95).

Compare the results von Frisch obtained in his experiments 1 and 3 (September 17 and 19). Whether the scent gland was open or closed

TABLE NG.1. Summary of results from four experiments, showing the number of recruits arriving at a feeding station and at a test station a short lateral distance from it.

Date	Food in One Direction from Hive		Food in Opposite Direction from Hive	
	Food Place at 300m	Station 30m from Food Place	Food Place at 250m	Station 25m from Food Place
Scent Gland Open				
Sept. 17	178	257	—	—
Sept. 18	—	—	362	39
Scent Gland Closed				
Sept. 19	190	228	—	—
Sept. 20	—	—	80	25

SOURCE: Adapted from information on pp. 21 and 22 of von Frisch 1947.

NOTE: On two days regular foragers had their scent glands open; on the other two days the glands were sealed out.

made no difference in the pattern of recruitment at the two stations —at the feeding station compared to a station 30 meters away from that station. Furthermore, the station 30 meters distant from the feeding station received more recruits than the feeding station itself. That result contradicts expectations, both of the Nasanov gland attraction hypothesis and of the dance language hypothesis.

Results from von Frisch's experiments 2 and 4 reveal further discrepancies. On both of those days (September 18 and 20) the results agreed with predictions that one might make on the basis of the dance language hypothesis, but they contradicted results obtained on the other two days (September 17 and 19). Note also that these September 18 and 20 experiments were run with the feeding station in the opposite direction from the hive. A difference in influences of wind could have been responsible, perhaps, for the discrepancies noted (see our chapter 8).

Many subsequent attempts to verify an attraction "function" of the Nasanov gland secretion have yielded equally puzzling results. Woodrow et al. (1965), for example, tested 195 natural and synthetic odorous compounds on bees in a modified olfactometer. Only four non-Nasanov compounds were "weak to moderate" attractants, and a larger number were repellents. The Nasanov constituents themselves, citral, geraniol, and geraniol acetate, were neither.

Waller (1970) reported the results of field tests with Nasanov components sprayed on an alfalfa field. He used citral, geraniol, and anise (a non-Nasanov component) in attempts to attract recruits to that crop. None of these fragrances regularly increased bee populations in experimental alfalfa plots when applied in water, but each of them singly or in mixtures did so when applied in sucrose solutions. Apparently these odors had thereby merely served as marker stimuli when coupled with a food reward in a conditioned response situation (see our chapter 7).

Preference tests, with dishes placed at several feeding stations, as exemplified by experiments run by Free (1962, 1968), provided another experimental approach by which the attractiveness of Nasanov gland chemicals could be assessed. In one such test (1968) nine dishes were set 90 centimeters apart on a lawn near an apiary. Free had placed excised Nasanov glands near three dishes, three other dishes had whatever residual scent recent foragers might have left, and three dishes were clean and empty. "Inspection" visits and landings of "scout" bees were recorded.

In the ten tests run in Free's experiment, 158 inspections occurred at the three Nasanov-containing dishes, and twenty-five landings were recorded. On the other hand, 227 bees inspected the six non-Nasanov dishes, with twenty-four landing thereon.

Earlier experiments by Free (1962), using geraniol-scented dishes, an alternative non-Nasanov scent, and unscented dishes (three of each) yielded similar results. There were 577 inspections or landings on the three geraniol-containing dishes and 772 on the six nongeraniol dishes. Under the verification approach, one can focus on the slightly greater frequency of success at the dishes marked by geraniol or Nasanov glands, as Free did (1962, 1968). For example, Free wrote: "Experiments are described which show that geraniol, the principal volatile component of honeybee scent-gland secretion, is attractive to foragers, but that it is not nearly as attractive as scent-gland odour itself" (1962:52).

Alternatively, it is conceivable that the experimental results could reflect no more than a difference in odor intensity. If the Nasanov odor were a true attractant, according to the Baker, Mayer, and Roelfos (1981) definition, nearly all 158 approaches to the Nasanov dishes in Free's 1968 study should have resulted in landings, instead of the less than 14 percent that did so. Also, a large majority of the observed bees not landing at the control stations should have moved over into the odor plume emanating from the dishes marked by Nasanov gland odors (see excursus OS).

It is clear that these and similar dish preference tests failed to qualify Nasanov gland secretions as attractant pheromones according to the usual definition.

THE USEFULNESS OF NASANOV SECRETIONS

All of the above is not to say that Nasanov pheromones may not be *useful* somehow in honey bee studies. Free and co-workers found that traps baited with synthetic Nasanov "lures" were more effective than unscented traps for catching stray honey bees. Also, synthetic lures at in-hive feeders encouraged bees to consume more water or to forage more at pollen substitute sources (Free, Ferguson, and Pickett 1983), or they may facilitate the trapping of stray honey bees (Free, Ferguson, and Simpkins 1984). Useful as Nasanov lures may be, however, preference for that scent over no scent at all does not characterize the glandular secretion as an "attractant."

It is also well documented that dispersal of the Nasanov odors by fanning and scenting workers apparently help disoriented bees to find their hive entrance (Sladen 1901; Ribbands and Speirs 1953). If one shakes bees off a comb onto the ground in front of a hive, workers at the entrance begin fanning and expose their Nasanov glands. Disoriented bees then walk toward the hive entrance. However, nondisoriented bees from adjacent hives are unaffected by the pheromone at the time.

Beekeepers have also observed heavy use of the Nasanov gland during the settling of a newly emerged swarm, a phenomenon reported as early as 1901 by Sladen and later by Witherell (1985:828). According to Morse and Boch (1971), disoriented bees in a swarm may be induced to land by Nasanov gland exposure. Again, nonswarming bees from nearby hives are not attracted to that aggregation.

OUR EXPERIMENTS AND CONCLUSIONS

Our own disillusionment with the established doctrine of Nasanov gland attractance arose during our "crucial" test of the dance language hypothesis (Wenner, Wells, and Johnson 1969; see also our chapter 10). We noted that we had minimal recruitment of new bees on days when we used little or no odor at the feeding station. However, we also noticed heavy exposure of the Nasanov glands by foragers at the dishes whenever odor level was low. On high recruitment days, when we used scent at the stations, there was little Nasanov gland exposure. These observations contradicted what we expected from the Nasanov gland attraction hypothesis.

Eventually we found that we could control Nasanov gland exposure levels to some degree by altering the amount of scent in the food (Wells and Wenner 1971). A similar inverse correlation was obtained in results on experiments with dance frequency; with less odor at the feeding station, dance frequency increased in the hive. The following table (from Wenner 1971a:94) summarizes that information:

TABLE NG.2. Experimental results when using either scented or unscented food.

Station Condition	Trips	Nasanov Use	Number of Dances	Recruits
Scented food	239	19	49	35
Unscented food	242	169	114	4

SOURCE: Wenner 1971a: 94.

NOTE: The less scent in the food, the more frequently bees danced in the hive. Nevertheless, recruit arrivals plummeted, despite a marked increase in use of the Nasanov glands at the feeding station by foragers.

It was *as though* foragers were *attempting* to attract recruits when odor was not present. (Note the anthropomorphic and teleological implications here.) However, recruitment rate increased neither with increased dancing nor with increased Nasanov gland exposure. Therefore, Nasanov glands can hardly be considered to produce an "attractant" according to the accepted definition of that term.

Two other anecdotes apply here. In midsummer of one year, when hives had little nectar to forage on, we opened a bottle of geraniol 200 meters upwind from a strong colony. During a three-hour period, only one bee flew close to the bottle. The second observation is that lemon-scented gum trees are common on the University of California (Santa Barbara) campus. A gas chromatographic analysis of their leaves (mentioned above) revealed that their strong odor was largely due to the geraniol component of those leaves. Near those trees, the fallen leaves exude a pungent odor of geraniol, but honey bees are never seen inspecting the area.

After all of our experimentation and review of the literature, we had to conclude: "None of the evidence [we] obtained supports the hypothesis that Nasanov secretion contains an attractant pheromone. . . . The Nasanov scent appears to provide a point of orientation for confused bees, but bees engaged in normal activity are not attracted to it" (Wells and Wenner 1971:208).

REACTION TO OUR FINDINGS

Even though the question of Nasanov gland function may appear to some to be peripheral to the dance language controversy, this episode provides another example of the application of different scientific approaches during the course of research on a specific problem. Von Frisch's initial "exploration" approach yielded evidence in support of an "attraction function" for the Nasanov gland exudate. During subsequent years he continued his verification approach with regard to that attraction hypothesis (as indicated above), and others followed suit.

When von Frisch and others obtained negative results with respect to the Nasanov gland attraction hypothesis during the mid-1940s and later, it was apparently too late for them to recognize the implications of such negative evidence. They had passed the point of commitment (see figure 3.2), moved into a paradigm hold, and dismissed those negative results.

Most subsequent researchers followed the verification approach as well. Any positive bias in the data obtained from experimentation was seized upon as support of the hypothesis; negative results were either dismissed or ignored. Even at this time, the Nasanov gland exudate is still sometimes considered an "attractant" by proponents of that hypothesis, as expressed by Witherell: "The scent from [the Nasanov] gland is used to attract other bees" (1985:827).

That attitude was also exemplified by Seeley's comments: "If the recruit target lacks significant odor . . . bees will mark the site with scent from their Nasonov glands (Free 1968, Free and Williams 1970)" (1985:86).

In the tradition of the verification approach to science, neither Witherell nor Seeley made reference to studies that produced data in conflict with that hypothesis. It is noteworthy, however, that the frequency with which Nasanov gland exudate is mentioned as an "attraction" pheromone has decreased in recent years. Careful reading of the above quotation reveals that even Seeley did not claim an attractive "function" for the exudate, and he published little more on the subject than the above brief comment in his book on honey bee ecology.

The "function" of the Nasanov gland thus remains largely a mystery, but it is becoming apparent that the bee research community has been "backing away" from the von Frisch interpretation that emanations from that gland attract searching recruits. Note, however, that publications on this subject do not directly challenge von Frisch's interpretation.

Instead, what we seem to have here is a gradual (subdued) paradigm shift, wherein both positive and negative evidence are simultaneously deemphasized. In addition, it is evident that no one is credited with refuting the former prevailing hypothesis. We thus have here a category apparently unrecognized earlier by either Kuhn or subsequent sociologists of science; paradigm shifts may occur and remain unrecognized as such when issues and/or personalities are relatively unimportant.

Excursus OS: Odor Search by Flying Insects

An odor-search hypothesis of some sort or another has persisted through centuries, as indicated in the chapter 5 epigraphs; von Frisch himself embraced that explanation for honey bee recruitment in the 1920s and 1930s (von Frisch 1939; Rosin 1980a). Even though we were only vaguely aware of an earlier odor-search hypothesis for recruit flight behavior, the performance of searching recruits in our experiments finally led us to that explanation for what we observed.

However, our first attempt to formulate an odor-search model for honey bee recruitment to food sources (Wenner 1974) was not warmly embraced by the scientific community. Even Rosin (see our chapter 14), who has strongly argued against "presumed proofs" of the language hypothesis, objected to certain features of our odor-search model for recruitment. Rosin wrote:

> Many details in Wenner's model are not yet proven, or even tested, and some are problematic. One such problem is posed by the proposed effect of hive odor. If potential recruits were to be affected by any attractive odors from the start, they would be attracted first and foremost to the hive, and would not be able to depart at all. Wenner (1974) suggests that potential recruits first drop downwind until they escape hive odor. This, however, contradicts the suggestion of an upwind flight under the effect of an attractive odor. It is also questionable that honey-bees can ignore the attractiveness of a specific odor at will, when they leave the hive, and respond to it later. Moreover, if they can ignore the attractiveness of hive odor at will, they need not escape it [etc.]. (1980b:778)

In proposing the model earlier, we had assumed that others would be quite familiar with the orientation of bees in flight and with the relationship of that flight behavior to other research on insect anemotaxis, as summarized more recently by Kennedy (1983) and Carde (1984). Apparently that was not the case. The following treatment will place our earlier odor-search model more fully within the context of known information about flying insects in general. We will also include some description of honey bee behavior not mentioned in the earlier model and not normally investigated by students of insect flight orientation.

THE ELEMENTS OF ANEMOTACTIC SEARCH

In chapter 5 we suggested that zigzagging, casting, circling orientation, and looping flights could all contribute to the effective orientation of recruit bees to odor sources. In fact, a description of insect flight patterns, a perusal of some diagrams, and an elementary consideration of wind behavior in nature all contribute to the model without much additional elaboration.

Zigzagging and Casting

Since we first proposed that recruited honey bees use odor and not "dance language" information while orienting to food sources in the field, considerable additional research has been done on the orientation of flying insects in wind streams. The contributions by J. S. Kennedy, particularly "Zigzagging and casting as a programmed response to wind-borne odour: A review" (1983), and R. T. Carde, "Chemo-orientation in flying insects" (1984), place the description of insect odor-search flight behavior squarely in a mechanistic context reminiscent of Fraenkel and Gunn ([1940] 1961).

The term "zigzagging" refers to a behavior we mentioned in the text (see figure 5.1). It is easy to observe newly arriving honey bee recruits behaving in that manner when they are downwind from a feeding station. Their "zigzagging" approach does not differ from that of other flying insects searching for odor. Such a flight is back and forth and progressively upwind against an odor plume.

One can appreciate how a bee might experience a lowering of rate of odor perception (the number of molecules perceived per unit time by antennal receptors) while traveling away from the center of the odor plume. That decrease in stimulation could result in a near reversal (with an upwind bias) in its flight direction. The bee would then travel in that nearly opposite direction during the next leg of its zigzag flight pattern.

The term "casting" applies to a commonly observed behavior exhibited by flying insects that have lost track of a familiar odor while zigzagging toward it from downwind. A flying insect may begin casting whenever a marked wind change occurs, as is often the case in nature, and the plume moves away from the vicinity of the insect in flight. The insect then suddenly ceases its customary and rather slow zigzagging flight upwind. It instead travels rather rapidly perpendicular to the former wind plume direction, reverses a full 180° after flying a considerable distance, and travels back on the same path past the original point at which it had lost the odor stimulus.

Such a casting behavior thus increases the probability that the searching recruit will again enter the lost odor plume and contact the familiar odor. When it perceives the familiar odor once again, the insect will resume its zigzagging flight and rather slowly work its way upwind toward the odor source.

Orientation Flights

Earlier in this volume we used a quotation by Root and co-authors that contained the phrase "[recruits] increase the circles of flight until the coveted sweets are located" (Root et al. 1947:49). Beekeepers have long known about such types of "orientation flights" by bees (Ribbands 1953; Butler 1962), which actually consist of different categories of "circling" flight.

The first and rather short flight in the life of a young bee is known by some as a "play flight." It is then that a bee flies out from the hive and expels the first fecal pellet that it has produced as an adult (e.g., Butler 1962). The young bee also circles about in the immediate vicinity of the hive; it may become acquainted with nearby landmarks at that time.

Honey bees have another behavior, known as an "orientation flight." That flight behavior presumably familiarizes older worker bees with nearby landmarks and is often described in books that include descriptions of bee behavior. The first written record of such a flight pattern appears to be that of the poet Virgil, who lived between 70 and 19 B.C.; he wrote: "let out one of the bees in the box: which, when she hath cast a ring to know where she is . . ." (in Butler 1609:ch. 6, passage 53).

Throughout the ages, others have noticed the same behavior. For example, in the *ABC and XYZ of Beekeeping* Root et al. wrote:

> The bees of a colony moved from their old location to a new place will, on their first flight, mark the location. As the bees fly out they will apparently take a survey of all the surroundings adjoining their home. The circles become larger and larger until they are lost to sight. . . . There is no marking of the location thereafter except by young bees that go out for their first flight, and then their behavior is very much the same. (1947:52)

In addition to close-in orientation flights, those bees that have been newly recruited to a food source apparently make an expanding circular flight (a spiral path) after leaving the hive, as credited above to Root. Buzzard described the same behavior as follows, "those that found no honey would circle in ever-increasing circles in an attempt to find it" (1946:166). Ribbands described those orientation flights more succinctly, as follows; "The departure flight is usually referred to as the orientation flight" (1953:98). Perhaps that type of flight behavior is what von Frisch referred to when he wrote: "Flying out in all directions, they find out in the shortest time the plant which has commenced to bloom, wherever it is in the entire flying district" (1939:430).

From all of the above, we feel confident that a considerable body of information on "orientation flights" was common knowledge prior to the time von Frisch generated his dance language hypothesis.

Looping Flight

A "looping" flight by recruit bees approaching our feeding stations occurred frequently; that flight was reminiscent of what is known as "hill-topping" by lepidopterists. That is, we could observe an approaching recruit in its characteristic zigzag flight coming in from downwind. If it overshot and suddenly found itself outside the odor plume while still heading upwind, it quite often rose straight up in the air and allowed itself to be carried downwind once again. Presumably the searching bee later dropped back down closer to the ground, where it would once again pick up the scent trail in an area where the odor plume was wider.

1:3:3:1—A CLUE TO ODOR-SEARCH BEHAVIOR

Anyone who has ever had a course in elementary Mendelian genetics has been exposed to the 1:2:1 and 1:3:3:1 ratios (binomial expansions). It was for that reason that we were very surprised by the results of our double-control experiments (compare figures 9.4 and 9.5 in chapter 9). In those experiments we had a number of foraging bees visiting an array of four presumably identical stations located along a straight line (Wenner 1967).

We had expected an equal number of recruits to arrive at each station, because we had made the stations as identical to one another as we could, including the provision of forager visitation at each station. Instead, the distribution of arrivals was very close to a 1:3:3:1

ratio (Wenner 1967). That recruit behavior thus indicated to us something about the search pattern of recruits.

Eventually we realized that the binomial distribution we had obtained was what one would expect if recruits had arrived at the four stations in inverse proportion to the distance of each station from the center of all stations. As Johnson wrote:

> Under the circumstances of these experiments, the middle station always lay closer to the geometric center of all sites (center of moments) than did any other station. . . . Just as the center of moments remains near the middle control station, so also were most recruits collected at the middle site when all stations became more similar in attractiveness. (1967:847)

What was most important to us at that time was that we recognized an important implication about the results von Frisch had obtained in his "precision" experiments (the classic step and fan experiments). It became obvious to us that his results could be explained by the same mathematical analysis without invoking an explanation about "dance language" use (Wenner 1971a, 1974; see also figures 6.4 and 6.5 in our chapter 6).

However, our failure to specify exactly what we meant by the flight behavior of recruits "searching for the center of odor" later led to some confusion. Rosin wrote:

> Since the opposition [to Wenner's hypothesis] began the "dance language" hypothesis has also been endorsed as fact by the Nobel Committee. . . . v. Frisch was then well aware of the opposition, but rebutted it successfully. . . . (The success was based on pointing out what is, in fact, a minor error in Wenner's hypothesis, i.e. flight to an odor center which potential recruits cannot know.) (1980b:458)

Both von Frisch and Rosin were correct in their assertions that a recruit bee cannot "knowingly" head toward "the center of an odor field." What their assertions overlooked is the fact that our model for a probabilistic search pattern, based upon the placement of an *array* of stations and a *population* of searching recruits, was not intended to apply to the searching behavior of an *individual* recruit bee.

The expected distribution we proposed was instead a net distribution for many individuals. Our model was thus developed with the same intent found in considerations of the genetic sorting of alleles. For example, geneticists do not concern themselves with the ultimate destination of any particular individual gene during a Mendelian sorting in a genetics experiment. Geneticists concern themselves only with the *proportional distribution* of alleles prior to a number of fertilization events.

A diagram (figure OS.1) may help to illustrate our concept of the importance of an "odor center" in determining the ultimate distribution of searching recruit bees according to our odor-search model. To keep it simple at first, we consider an experiment with a single hive and four stations in a straight-line array, as used earlier by Wenner (1967).

When winds are light, they continually vary somewhat but still have a prevailing direction. In the Santa Barbara area during the summer, winds are very light from the southeast in the morning and slightly stronger from the southwest during the afternoon. We nearly always did our experiments in the morning to take advantage of the lower wind velocity at that time of day.

Winds move odor molecules downwind from each of the stations, not as a single line but as a plume. Each plume wavers about downwind from the station array as winds shift back and forth; that variability in direction is not shown in the diagram, in order to keep the presentation simple. Odor molecules from the bodies of forager bees also move downwind from their flight line (the "beeline") between hive and feeding stations.

It is here that we see a serious weakness in understanding by proponents of the dance language hypothesis. The consistent focus on the one-to-one encounter between forager and recruit has blinded investigators to the population aspect of recruitment to food sources. In experiments, one does not work only with a single forager making round trips between hive and food source. Usually several bees are involved, and the flight line becomes a virtual aerial pathway (Wenner 1974). Those frequent flights provide a considerable odor input to the system (Friesen 1973) downwind from that flight path (Lineburg 1924).

As first indicated in the 1960s (Wenner 1962) and elucidated a decade later (Wenner 1971a), an array of stations is inappropriate for these types of experiments. As a matter of simple logic, it is evident that the stations are not "identical" to one another, as they are supposed to be if one wishes to conduct a controlled experiment.

In the example shown, the two central stations have at least one station on either side of them, but that is not true for the two end stations. The four stations are thus not "equal" and cannot serve as true "control" stations. As a result of that nonequality, the composite odor plume downwind also becomes nonuniform (see figure OS.1). In

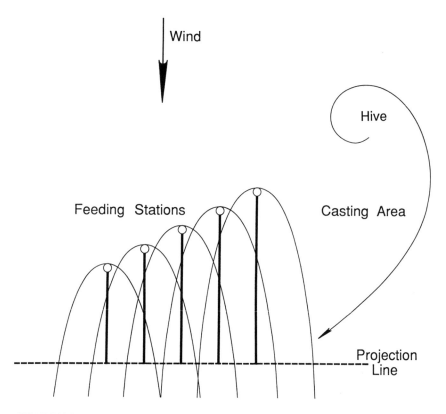

Wind

Hive

Feeding Stations

Casting Area

Projection
Line

FIGURE OS. 1. Foraging bees fly in a "beeline" between the hive and any stations to which they have been trained. Odor plumes emanate from each of the indicated stations and overlap downwind from those sources.

A newly recruited honey bee leaves the hive in a spiral flight (e.g., Buzzard 1946); sooner or later it may enter the odor plume area, aided by occasional molecules it has encountered from the many foragers traveling on their "aerial pathway" between hive and feeding stations. Once the appropriate odor combination has been perceived, the recruit begins its zigzagging flight upwind toward one of the odor sources (as in figure 5.1). The bee cannot perceive the number of sources available; it can only proceed upwind. If no molecules are perceived for a time, it begins a casting flight.

The highest concentration of molecules per unit area is necessarily downwind from the geometric center of all stations (Johnson 1967a). However, some recruits are likely to pass through most of the odor field before they begin their zigzagging flight upwind. A few others may perceive such molecules soon after they enter the downwind odor field. Most will orient upwind toward the center of the odor field due to the higher concentration of molecules in that area. Successful recruits thus most often end up at one of the central stations (Wenner 1967).

The downwind projection of odor molecules from a number of stations arranged in a straight line reflects that uniform spacing. That uniformity is not true for a set of stations in an arc (see figure OS. 2).

an ideal situation and far enough downwind, the resultant plume would have a predictably greater concentration of odor molecules toward its center. A line drawn parallel to the stations and downwind from them, in fact, reveals a binomial distribution of odor concentration along that projected line in that model.

The same objection exists for all experiments that have used an array of stations—for example, Gould (1974, 1975) and Shricker (1974).

THE REVISED ODOR-SEARCH MODEL

Consider now all aspects of the flight behavior of recruit bees. After obtaining the scent of food from a dancing forager, a recruit leaves the hive and executes a *circling orientation* flight (rather than "dropping downwind," as postulated earlier). That bee is already habituated to the multiplicity of odors drifting downwind from its hive (an "adaptation to hive odor"; see Rosin 1980a:779) and thereby ignores that composite set of odors in its circling flight.

That ever-expanding circling flight, regardless of initial spiral direction, eventually places the recruit bee downwind from both the "aerial pathway" of foragers and from the odor plume(s) of the sought-after food. Immediately upon the perception of specific odor molecules traveling downwind from those four sources, the recruit begins *zigzagging* and works its way upwind toward the odor sources. If a bee zigzags too far in the wrong direction, it may leave the odor plume. In that case, it begins *casting* and enjoys a high probability of once again entering the odor plume.

For single odor sources, then, the model as published earlier (Wenner 1974) needs only the inclusion of a expanding circling flight for the initial orientation of recruit bees after they leave the hive (as a replacement for the "dropping downwind" notion).

In the case of several odor sources, a high probability exists that the searching recruit can move into an area of greater concentration during its zigzagging flight behavior (see figure OS.1), particularly if it continues its flight away from the hive area. After it enters a region of higher odor concentration, it will continue its zigzagging in this new area; it may then enter the next higher region of odor concentration, etc. This continual "testing of the wind," as it were, eventually results in the "average" searching recruit working its way *toward* the center of the composite odor field.

As searching recruits move upwind, however, the overlapping of odor plumes becomes less pronounced. The body of searching bees then becomes separated, with the highest number of searchers remaining nearest the center of the composite odor plume. Any searching recruits that overshoot the stations *loop* up and are carried back downwind. They then drop down nearer the ground, perceive the appropriate odor molecules, and begin their zigzag flight upwind once again.

This looping behavior would be particularly important for those recruits that have been relying primarily on odors drifting downwind from the "aerial pathway" of regular foragers on their beeline flight (Friesen 1973; Wenner 1974), that is, before they have gone far enough from the hive to enter the plume(s) itself. Eventually, a portion of them should end up within the odor plume drifting downwind from the stations (Lineburg 1924). Many obviously do not, however, which explains the rather small percentage of potential recruits that succeed after their first contact with a dancing forager in the hive (Esch and Bastian 1970; Gould, Henerey, and MacLeod 1970)

FURTHER PROBLEMS WITH THE ARC ARRAY

With a little imagination, one can recognize that a change in the wind direction will not alter the relative spacing of the downwind projection of odors with respect to the ratio of distances between stations in a straight-line array (see figure OS.1). The exception is that of a highly unlikely straight-on and invariant wind direction.

The above reasoning, however, does not apply if one places the stations in an arc, as von Frisch did for his "fan experiments," or as Schricker (1974) and Gould (1975a, 1975b) did later in their attempted tests of the "accuracy" in use of direction information by searching recruits. On one hand, if the wind blew either straight from or straight onto the line of stations in an arc, the odor distribution would project an approximate binomial distribution.

However, whenever wind comes from an angle, the apparent distribution (when perceived from downwind) would be greatly skewed to one end or the other (see figure OS.2). The downwind projection would provide a clustering of odor molecules downwind from one end of the array *as if* the upwind stations at that end were relatively close to one another. A composite set of plumes downwind from an arc array would thus project a set of ratios other than a binomial distribution at some distance downwind from that source under most wind conditions.

Since winds continually vary somewhat in direction, the "ex-

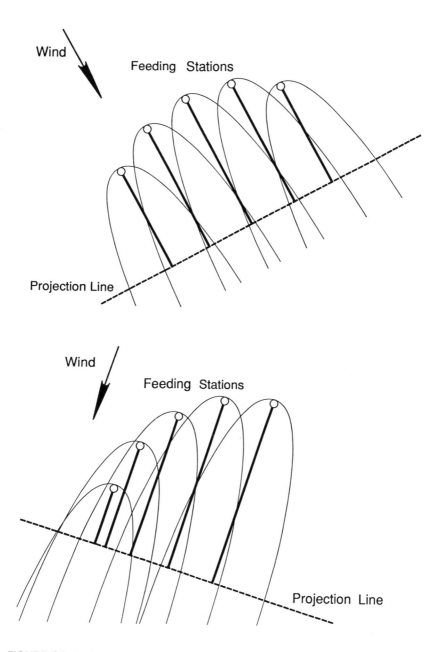

FIGURE OS. 2. Placing a set of experimental stations in an arc introduces a bias into the downwind projection of odor molecules. Any change in wind direction alters the relationship between concentration of odor molecules in the area downwind from all stations. Searching recruit bees in that area are more likely to end up at stations that *appear* to be closer to one another along the downwind projection. Any slight shift in wind direction can thus alter the distribution of recruited bees.

pected" distribution of searching recruits in an arc array design would likewise change with time in our model. Different sets of results could be obtained even between different contiguous half-hour periods (as in Gould's experiments), depending on whatever wind direction prevailed during that short period of time. The arc array is thus inappropriate for any experiments purporting to test "precision" in the supposed recruit bee use of any direction information contained in forager dances. These objections prevail in addition to the disparity in equality of stations, as treated in the previous section.

Slight differences in locality odor between station sites would additionally complicate the characterization of odors that potential recruits could exploit as they searched for a food source. That is, if foragers visited only one of the several stations in an array, specific odors of vegetation near that site, as well as the odors of the foragers themselves, would provide additional stimuli that could serve as orientation markers for searching recruits (see chapter 8). Furthermore, the last site in an array would also be the terminal point for odors emanating from the aerial pathway produced by regular foragers.

One of the main points we have stressed in this excursus is that honey bees apparently do not differ from other flying insects in the means by which they find odor sources. At the same time we cannot help but wonder how much longer honey bee researchers will ignore the applicable research done by other scientists on odor location by flying insects.

We also wonder how much longer dance language proponents will turn to the flawed arc array design in their attempts to obtain supporting evidence for the presumed use of "dance language" information (see excursus PN).

Excursus PN: Experiments on the Precision of "Language" Use

> "Thus, we have had to infer what is going on in the unmolested system, an inference often difficult or impossible because we do not know to what extent the experimental intervention disturbed the system under study. Nor can we ever know except by further experiment, and this involves a further dislocation of the phenomenon of unknown and unknowable extent. The interactions we are producing are thus *obstacles* in the quest for certainty. This source of uncertainty is of momentous importance in biology."
>
> —William Beck 1961:86

Early on, von Frisch became convinced (and had convinced others) that recruited bees actually *used* the distance and direction information contained in the dances of successful foragers. In doing so, he did not realize that the various sets of results from his earliest experiments contained contradictions (see our chapter 6; see also von Frisch 1947). That is, when recruits appeared to be *using* direction information in von Frisch's early experiments, they at the same time appeared to be ignoring distance information. The converse was also true.

Neither von Frisch nor others treated those discrepancies. Instead, von Frisch began all of his later experiments with the assumption that the "dance language" use was real and set out to determine the *precision* with which recruited bees could "follow" the information contained in the dance.

PROBLEMS WITH THE STEP AND FAN EXPERIMENTS

Two types of experiments were involved. One was the "step" experimental design, in which an array of stations was placed in a straight line leading out from the hive. The other, the "fan" arrangement, included an array of stations equidistant from the hive, with a feeding station directly behind the central control station.

Both types of experiments included fundamental weaknesses in design; in fact, the very design could have dictated the pattern of recruit arrivals (Wenner 1962, 1971). When von Frisch (e.g., 1947, 1950) published his initial results, apparently no one recognized the

fact that substantive qualitative differences existed between his experimental and control stations. (Control stations must be as nearly
identical to the experimental station and to each other as possible, if
they are to serve as effective controls; his were not.)

Eventually we realized the implications of that fact, but only after
we had already found that searching bees behaved other than as
expected from the dance language hypothesis (see chapters 7–10). It
soon became apparent to us that an alternative explanation had existed all along for von Frisch's results. Searching recruits could be
treating the entire set of stations as one system and would approach
the system of stations from downwind. (See figure OS.1 in excursus
OS: the odors emanating from the stations would overlap downwind).

Some searching recruits would therefore arrive closer to the center
of the system than others merely as a consequence of a probability
pattern of search behavior (Wenner 1971a; see also our chapters 5 and
8 and excursus OS). The two types of experimental designs will be
treated separately here.

Step Experiments

The first clue that something could be amiss in the step experiments of von Frisch was uncovered inadvertently during a doctoral
research project (Wenner 1962). A comparison of the variation in
distance information present in the dance maneuver to the actual
distribution of successful recruits in the field revealed a discrepancy;
the performance of successful recruit bees was far more accurate than
the distance information present in that waggle dance.

Wenner then reanalyzed von Frisch's results and concluded: "The
unique shape of the graph is in part due to the peculiar arrangement
of the unequally spaced stations" (1962:93).

A summary analysis of one of von Frisch's step experiments will
illustrate how a biased result could be obtained. Marked foragers
visiting a feeding station at 750 meters made round trips between
hive and feeding station, and recruitment of other bees occurred.
Observers were stationed at each of the control stations that had been
placed in the same direction but at varying distances from the hive.

Each of these observers then tallied but did not kill the unmarked
bees that came close to the scent posts. All unmarked bees arriving at
the feeding place itself were killed but not included in the overall data
set.

The arrangement of scent posts and the number of bees tallied at

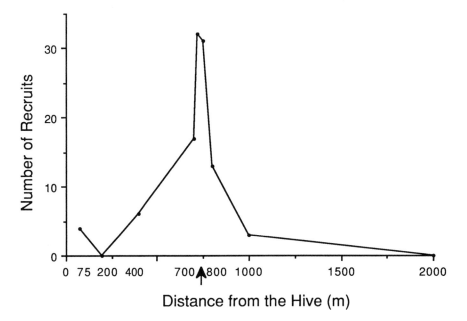

FIGURE PN. 1. Results of a "step experiment" conducted by von Frisch and Jander (1957). Foragers collected sugar solution at a station placed 750 meters from their hive. Recruits arrived in largest numbers at the station indicated in the waggle dance. However, the nonuniform placement of stations apparently dictated the distribution of searchers (Wenner 1962).

each of the scent posts during the 750-meter step experiment (data from von Frisch and Jander 1957) are shown in figure PN.1. The shape of the line in that figure suggests great precision in the orientation of searching recruits, bees that had presumably been using the distance information contained in waggle dances performed by foraging bees.

However, both von Frisch and Jander (1957) and Wenner (1962) had also provided data on the variability present in the distance information of dance maneuvers for each of several distances. They found that the variability of distance information in the dance maneuver itself was far greater than the actual performance of searching recruits. These results thus constituted an anomaly: one would not predict that recruited bees would be able to perform far better than would be expected from the information provided by foragers dancing in the hive.

Fan Experiments

Unfortunately, von Frisch nearly always conducted his fan experiments with a single basic design: the feeding station was *behind* the center of the array of control stations. The center of all stations was thus also in the same direction as the feeding station. The results were remarkable, as indicated by von Frisch: "Fanwise experiments reveal how precisely the newcomers swarming out follow the dancers' indications of direction. The majority of newcomers fly out in the direction of the goal or within a few degrees to one side" (1967a:231).

A better design would have been an arrangement in which the forager station *competed* with the theoretical center of all stations located in a different direction, and one in which bees were feeding at

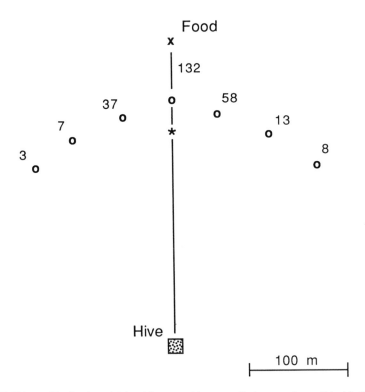

FIGURE PN. 2. Distribution obtained for searching recruits in one of von Frisch's "fan" experiments. Recruits appeared to fly out in the correct direction. An asterisk indicates the geometric center of all stations.

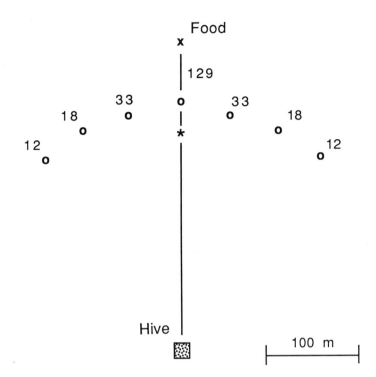

FIGURE PN. 3. Mathematical multinomial model for expected distribution of searching bees ending up at each station in inverse proportion to the distance of each station from the center of all stations (asterisk). The design of von Frisch's experiment thus did not permit a distinction between recruits searching for a center of odor or *using* direction information.

each of the stations rather than only at one (e.g., Johnson 1967; see also our chapter 9).

To illustrate the nature of the problem, we include one such analysis as an example here in figures PN.2 (observed) and PN.3 (expected). The former is based upon figure 45 of von Frisch (1950); the latter is what one might expect from a probability distribution (see excursus OS and chapter 9).

As mentioned earlier, in any experiment, experimental and control stations should be as nearly identical to one another as possible. That was clearly not the case in this type of design. Some stations had several others on either side, while those at each end of the array had other stations only on one side. Furthermore, regular foragers always traveled in a "beeline" between hive and feeding place, thereby introducing a complicating factor (other stations did not have a "beeline" between them and the hive). Some of the stations were thus closer to that "aerial pathway" than others, as well as closer to the station at which foragers were landing and feeding (thereby providing an odor of bees that could drift downwind).

ACCOMMODATION OF THE ANOMALY

A question arises: How does a member of the Realism school treat the anomaly uncovered? For Karl Popper (the falsification approach), such an anomaly would have constituted a negative result in what could be construed as a test of the dance language hypothesis. According to Popper: "Every 'good' theory is one which forbids certain things to happen; the more a theory forbids, the better it is" (1957:159).

Recruited bees should not have been able to perform better than could be predicted from information provided in the dance. Indeed, one should expect *inefficiency* in the use of any information, as occurs in other natural systems.

Von Frisch and Jander (1957), on the other hand, were members of the Carnap "verification" wing of the Realism school (see chapter 3; figure 3.1). Although they recognized that they found a discrepancy in the apparent use of distance information, they could not recognize the potential damage it could do to the dance language hypothesis. Instead, they concluded that the excellent behavior of recruited bees must have been due to the recruit bee's ability to "average" distance information from several runs of the waggle dance. They concluded that bees could thereby obtain a more accurate perception of the actual distance than we human observers.

However, Wenner (1962), even though still a Realist at the time (and still an advocate of the dance language hypothesis), stressed that, while such an "averaging" could perhaps reduce *within-bee* error, it could not correct for *between-bee* variation in the dances. An averaging out of the *within-bee* error, by itself, could not explain the too-excellent performance of searching bees.

In later years dance language proponents exploited this notion of the presumed "averaging" ability on the part of recruit bees whenever results differed from those expected on the basis of dance language hypothesis predictions. Von Frisch led the way by reasoning from only within the dance language paradigm; he wrote: "[Recruits] come in more precisely than conforms with the degree of scatter of the individual determinations of the duration of waggling. From this we may conclude that they average together several waggling runs" (1967a:106).

Von Frisch was not alone. Lindauer (1971) similarly dismissed anomalous results (see our chapter 12), and Wilson wrote:

> A surprising aspect of the communication is that the precision of the newcomers in achieving the goal is greater than that of dances from which they received the information. . . . This difference may well be due to the flaws in von Frisch's experimental design, which I pointed out earlier. But it might also be explained in the following way. The newcomers typically follow more than one dance of each dancer and even more than one dancer before leaving the nest in search of the food site. By averaging the information, they are able to obtain a more precise estimate than is available in many individual dances. There is nothing remarkable about such a calculation. (1971:268)

By so doing, however, von Frisch, Lindauer, and Wilson ignored an earlier analysis by Wenner (1962), in which he proposed an alternative explanation that required no special ability on the part of bees. Wenner noted that, since unmarked bees inspecting scent posts were not killed by the observers in the early von Frisch and co-workers' experiments, they could be tallied more than once during the course of the experiment. Wenner calculated the distribution that could be obtained if the bees tallied had "then visited another scent post (i.e., if they had searched at random and came to the next closest one proportionately but did not travel more than 500 m from the first post they had visited)" and were tallied again. This theoretical model (Wenner 1962) closely approximated the results von Frisch and Jander had obtained.

Von Frisch later acknowledged that bees could have been counted repeatedly but dismissed that as a problem, as follows:

> Since [recruits] are not captured and are unmarked, whether the same bee repeats its approach several times of course remains unknown. When the bee has disappeared from the observer's field of view, she is counted again [as a new bee] on a new approach. That is no disadvantage, for the persistent searching of a given insect at a definite distance shows that it is just here that she is expecting something. (1967a:85–86)

Wenner did not appreciate at the time the fact that the very arrangement of stations could dictate the *entire* subsequent distribution of searching bees, even if they had not "used" *any* of the information present in the dance maneuver. That realization came later in an analysis of the results from the "fan experiments." A summary of that analysis follows; a more extensive treatment can be found in excursus OS.

The above considerations led to the proposal of a model that could explain the results obtained from von Frisch's fan experiments without any need to invoke the "dance language" hypothesis (Wenner 1962, 1971a:47). According to the revised model provided in excursus OS (see also chapter 9), the *population* of searching bees could well be distributed according to the distance of each site from the center of all sites.

When that model was applied to the total number of recruit arrivals, as shown in figure PN.3, a theoretical distribution emerged that was nearly identical to that obtained by von Frisch in his field experiments (see figure PN.2). The dance language hypothesis then no longer provided an *exclusive* interpretation of the results; an older odor-search model sufficed. (Despite the fundamental weakness in this type of experimental design, both Schricker and Gould returned to it again during the mid-1970s; see our chapter 12).

However, long before the above critical evaluation of the design in the step and fan experiments revealed the weaknesses outlined here, the scientific community had ceased questioning basic assumptions on the matter of a "dance language" among honey bees. Established researchers had moved beyond the point of commitment to the dance language hypothesis and had become thoroughly locked into the paradigm hold (see figure 3.2). The "method of the ruling theory" (Chamberlin [1890] 1965) had become the sanctioned approach.

Excursus RE: Realism Versus Relativism

Proof—Inference
Security—Insecurity
Realism—Antirealism
Persuasion—Heuristics
Innovation—Creativity
Certainty—Uncertainty
Discovery—Exploration
Objectivism—*Relativism*
Objectivity—Subjectivity
Rationality—Irrationality
Authoritarianism—Skepticism

Dichotomies in thought seem to be the rule in Western culture. Science (which is mostly Western in practice) is no exception in that regard; one can find the above terms applied in one way or another throughout the scientific literature, as well as in other scholarly work.

Those who write about the philosophy of science may settle on one or another of the above descriptive sets of terms to delineate the opposing schools. While some have written of realism and antirealism, Bernstein contrasted objectivism and relativism and wrote:

> Confusion is compounded not only by the complexity of the issues involved and the shifting meanings of such key concepts as rationality, objectivity, realism, and norms but [also] by the different fundamental attitudes of philosophers toward opposing positions. (1983:4)

In our chapter 3 (and throughout the volume) we singled out the terms *realism* and *relativism* for the schematic diagram to represent the opposing schools of thought in the philosophy of science. We also used those terms for reference because we felt that they provided the most intuitive contrast for the general reader.

KARL POPPER AND REALISM (LOGICAL EMPIRICISM)

Karl Popper remains the undisputed "leader" of the Realism school (the "logical empiricism" of others). Ian Hacking somewhat face-

339

tiously summarized the scientific realist's view of the world as follows: "science at least aims at the truth, and the truth is how the world is" (1983:27).

We recognize in Hacking's statement three implicit assumptions made by the scientific realist:

1. *Nature is real.* An essential ingredient of all science is that objects and phenomena related to them have a real existence independent of our observation or thought about them. This concept implies not only that observed objects really do exist; it also implies that there may exist a set of real objects not yet observed, of which some may never be observed (i.e., there is always science still to be done).

2. *Nature is orderly.* The second assumption rests on the notion that similar sets of objects and conditions will produce similar phenomena, because nature follows "laws." As a corollary of such orderliness, multiple observers (people or instruments) of a given thing or phenomenon will record similar data.

3. *Nature is knowable.* By sensory and/or instrumental *observation*, by experimental *manipulation*, and by *rational interpretation* of the data obtained thereby, we may gain or approach *true knowledge* of the objects and phenomena of nature. Furthermore, our theories (hypotheses) and explanations about natural objects and events can become part of true knowledge when they agree with reality.

The degree to which the "nature is knowable" assumption is valid and applicable has often been the subject of discussion among both philosophers and scientists. Popper, realism's persistent champion, unabashedly accepted "realism as the only sensible hypothesis—as a conjecture to which no sensible alternative has been offered" (in Miller 1985:223). He both *advocated* that view and *perceived* it as the way science actually operates.

Popper insisted: "there are excellent reasons for saying that *what we attempt in science is to describe and (so far as possible) explain reality*" (in Miller 1985:222; emphasis Popper's). Popper also felt that critical rationalism (hypothetico-deductive procedures) was the method of choice for finding reality: "We do so with the help of conjectural theories; that is, theories that we hope are true (or near the truth)" (in Miller 1985:222).

It was here that Popper interjected his ad hoc qualifier relative to our assumption number three, above: "but (there are theories) that we cannot establish as certain . . . even though they are the best theories that we are able to produce, and [they] may therefore be called 'probable' " (in Miller 1985:222).

Elsewhere, Popper defined "best theory": "from a rational point of view . . . we should *prefer* the best tested theory as a basis for action" (in Miller 1985:114; emphasis Popper's). Note here, however, how perilously close Popper skated toward relativism in that attitude (see below).

Among competing philosophies, "idealism" (not dwelt upon here) rejects assumption number one and is therefore not conducive to science; "pragmatism" substitutes the word "useful" for the word "true" as the modifier of knowledge, curiously bringing it closer to relativism (see Schram 1979). Other philosophies modify or limit assumption number three, a limitation based usually on the indirectness of observation (the object is external to the observer—only energy of some kind, not the object itself, travels from object to observer). However, Popper rejected all of those alternatives, as follows:

> But I think I know all the epistemological arguments—they are mainly subjectivist—which have been offered in favour of alternatives to realism, such as positivism, idealism, phenomenalism, phenomenology, and so on, and . . . I regard all the philosophical *arguments* which (to my knowledge) have ever been offered in favour of [those] *isms* as clearly mistaken. (In Miller 1985:223–224; emphases and parentheses Popper's)

Popper believed, instead, that such philosophies lead to a kind of undesirable or untenable "antirealism" (in Miller 1985:106). Thus, in the Realism school's view of science, one can approach "true knowledge" asymptotically by "objective, pure description" (see our figure 3.2), coupled with conjecture and attempted verification (Carnap) or refutation (Popper) of theories. Popper stated his position clearly:

> The procedure we adopt may lead (as long as it does not break down, for example, because of antirational attitudes) to success, in the sense that our conjectural theories tend progressively to come nearer to the truth; that is, to true descriptions of certain facts, or aspects of reality. (In Miller 1985:222; parenthetical phrase Popper's)

Hacking (1983) retained and expanded the use of the "antirealism" label. However, we have chosen the less disparaging label of "relativism" in our discussions (as indicated above, and in figure 3.1 and in the theme diagrams) to identify any philosophy that is in some way opposite to or that does not conform to realism's basic assumptions or its implications.

KUHN'S BREAK WITH REALISM: OPENING THE DOOR TO RELATIVISM

It is exactly in Popper's parenthetical qualifer about "antirational attitudes" that we find the basis for the very great interest (and controversy) generated by Thomas Kuhn's book, *The Structure of Scientific Revolutions*. While not itself a new "ism," Kuhn's position led to a recognition of the existence and importance of human factors in scientific research (points related to the third assumption of realism).

Kuhn did not *advocate* irrationality; rather, he *perceived* irrationality as a common occurrence in the scientific process. With respect to ordinary or "normal" science, Kuhn noted:

> The coherence displayed by the research tradition in which (scientists) participate may not imply even the existence of an underlying body of rules and assumptions. . . . Paradigms may be prior to, more binding, and more complete than any set of rules for research (1970a:45). . . . As in political revolutions, so in paradigm choice— there is no standard higher than the assent of the relevant community. To discover how scientific revolutions are effected, we shall therefore have to examine not only the impact of nature and of logic, but also the techniques of persuasive argumentation effective within the quite special groups that constitute the community of scientists. (1962:94)

Elsewhere Kuhn stated: "the transition between competing paradigms cannot be made a step at a time, forced by logic and neutral experience. Like the gestalt switch, it must occur all at once . . . or not at all. . . . The transfer of allegiance from paradigm to paradigm is a conversion experience" (1962:150–151).

Thus, for Kuhn, the rationality of science was limited by the dominance of paradigm holds over logical rules and assumptions of research during normal times, as well as by the social, psychological, and even quasi-religious aspects of the paradigm shift. Imre Lakatos summarized his perception of Kuhn's position quite succinctly and perhaps somewhat pejoratively: "The change is a bandwagon effect. Thus, *in Kuhn's view scientific revolution is irrational, a matter for mob psychology*" (1970:178; emphasis Lakatos').

The essence of this entire matter appears to us to revolve around the question of which raw materials are available to the philosophers of science. Those philosophers of science who attempt to assess the progress of science by relying upon the printed accounts of what may have transpired in the far distant past (e.g., with Galileo or Pasteur) may well conclude that such progress conforms to the tenets of the "Realism" school.

Those same philosophers, however, seem to have lacked input on what is happening today and what *may* have happened in the past during scientific controversies. Instead, they have apparently relied too often on elements that "giants" in various fields felt were responsible for progress in their fields.

Kuhn's insight apparently also applies to intellectual fields other than science. We can ask, "Why are there so many schools in the philosophy of science?" Kuhn might reply that students interested in the philosophy of science will likely study under whichever philosopher has impressed them the most. In doing so, they will come under the influence of that particular paradigm hold (see Masterson 1970).

In summary, Realism school philosophers insist that we can know the "truth" and have advocated means by which that "real truth" can be "discovered" by means of verification and/or falsification. (For further treatment of scientific realism, see Jeplin 1984.)

On the other hand, Kuhn seems to have perceived and interjected a critical element in the process: that is, the notion that social and political factors can intervene and alter the course of scientific progress. The wedge that Kuhn inserted in the rather solid front of philosophical thinking before that time permitted the relativist position to gain expression. In regard to that point Bernstein wrote:

> The relativist not only denies the positive claims of the objectivist but goes further. In its strongest form, relativism is the basic conviction that when we turn to the examination of those concepts that philosophers have taken to be the most fundamental . . . we are forced to recognize that in the final analysis all such concepts must be understood as relative to a specific conceptual scheme, theoretical framework, paradigm, form of life, society, or culture. (1983:8)

Bernstein continued, in the same manner as expressed in our opening comments: "The *agon* between objectivists [realists] and relativists has been with us ever since the origins of Western philosophy, or at least from the time of Plato's attack on the Sophists and on Protagoras's alleged relativism" (1983:8).

We are now in a position to address the question, "How does science differ from other areas of human endeavor?" Nonscientific pursuits tend to become locked into the realism frame of mind. The substance of a presidential debate, for instance, is not likely to alter the minds of those committed to one candidate or another (although the performance of participants might). So also is it with religion.

Science, on the other hand, occasionally experiences a fundamental paradigm shift, in which some participants momentarily become members of the Relativism school on a particular issue. If that alternative view ultimately proves more "useful" (Schram 1979) during subsequent studies, the remainder of the relevant scientific community also shifts over. Any such shift, however, may take decades; the "self-correcting" element in science is certainly not a phenomenon that occurs immediately whenever new evidence comes to bear on a problem (see Veldink 1989).

© 1985 Sidney Harris—*American Scientist Magazine*

Excursus SCI: The Evolution and Status of The "Scientific Method"

> "The hapless student is inevitably left to his or her own devices to pick up casually and randomly, from here and there, unorganized bits of the scientific method, as well as bits of *un*scientific methods."
> —T. Theocharis and M. Psimopoulos 1987:597

> "Today, virtually no one believes that there is a purely formal scientific method."
> —Hilary Putnam 1981:125

In the past few centuries, some scientists in some disciplines have been remarkably productive. That selective productivity, in turn, led to considerable speculation about the reasons for such success. As time passed, various philosophers and scientists credited one methodology or another for the success enjoyed by creative scientists.

The most extreme adherence to methodology has persisted within the Realism school, especially among the "logical positivists" (the followers of Rudolph Carnap and Karl Popper). These philosophers and the scientists adhering to their philosophy had become convinced that the application of rationality and logic could provide convincing arguments in support of hypotheses, or, alternatively, decisive indirect support of a view by a failure to negate hypotheses. Putnam phrased that attitude as follows: "Statements testable by the methods in the list (the methods of mathematics, logic, and the empirical sciences) would count as meaningful; all other statements, the positivists maintained, are 'pseudo-statements,' or disguised nonsense" (1981:105).

The influence of the logical positivists became ever more important during the first half of this century; general textbooks in biology contained a section describing a fairly standardized "Scientific Method." Most were variations on a theme, that is, formal statements that had arisen out of deliberations by scientists and philosophers of science. The influence of the verificationists (see chapter 2 and figure 3.1) was particularly pervasive in some of the "softer" areas of biology.

More recently, philosophers of science have begun to recognize the artificiality of some of the methodology and have been able to phrase their comments accordingly. Putnam, for example, wrote:

From the publication of Mill's *Logic* in the 1840s until the publication of Carnap's *Logical Foundations of Probability*, influential philosophers of science continued to believe that something like a formal method *("inductive Logic")* underlies empirical science, and that continued work might result in an explicit statement of this method, a formalization of inductive logic that was achieved starting with the work of Frege in 1879. (1981:189)

There have been other attempts to further formalize what was considered successful scientific method and to apply that methodology to research efforts in slow-moving fields. This was done in the expectation that such fields could then suddenly progress more rapidly. (An outgrowth of that movement was the institutionalization of the "null hypothesis" approach in ecology.)

The security engendered by a rather universal acceptance of the "scientific method" eroded steadily in the 1960s, 1970s, and 1980s (e.g., Mahoney 1976; McIntosh 1987). It became ever more apparent that striking advances in science had not arisen out of rigid adherence to one or another scientific method. Concurrently, descriptions of the "scientific method" began to disappear from science textbooks.

What few laypeople realize is that attitudes in science reflect attitudes of the populace as a whole. Scientists' adherence to the "scientific method" closely parallels the public's image of "objective" scientific activity (e.g., Kneller 1978). Putnam wrote:

The forms which have been *institutionalized* by the logical positivists are forms which have been *institutionalized* by modern society. What can be "verified" in the positivist sense can be verified to be correct (in a non-philosophical or prephilosophical sense of "correct"), or to be probably correct, or to be highly successful science, as the case may be; and the public recognition of the correctness, or the probable correctness, or the "highly successful scientific theory" status, exemplifies, celebrates, and reinforces images of knowledge and norms of reasonableness maintained by our culture. (1981:106)

A little historical treatment can illustrate just how these attitudes in both the scientific and lay communities developed through several centuries.

THE EVOLUTION OF LOGICAL POSITIVISM

The origin of the modern "scientific method" can be traced to the fifteenth century. Putnam wrote:

Starting in the fifteenth century, and reaching a kind of peak in the seventeenth century, scientists and philosophers began to put forward a new set of methodological maxims. These maxims are not rigorous formal rules; they do require informal rationality, i.e., intelligence and common sense to apply; but nevertheless they did and do shape scientific inquiry. (1981:195)

Francis Bacon (1561–1626) was one of the first of the early philosophers to have a lasting effect on our contemporary culture. He legitimized the concept of inductive reasoning, whereby one collects facts and generates hypotheses that fit that body of facts. His approach survives today in the approach we termed "verification" in chapter 3 (see figure 3.1).

A contemporary of Bacon, Rene Descartes (1596–1650), might be considered responsible for the injection of formal deductive reasoning into our culture. He felt that one could build on self-evident truths, step by small step, and eventually attain certainty. His approach, which might be considered a forerunner to the "falsification" approach (see figure 3.1) worked quite well in the development of analytical geometry and in the mechanistic physiology of William Harvey. (Descartes also achieved some degree of fame for "proving" the existence of God by the same logical process.)

Shortly after Bacon and Descartes, John Locke (1632–1704) and Robert Boyle (1627–1691) emphasized the need to rely on experience (the empirical approach) instead of relying too heavily on scientific principles; they thereby became some of the first relativists (Boyle wrote *The Sceptical Chymist*). Putnam recounted one of Boyle's major contributions:

> Prior to the seventeenth century, physicists did not sharply distinguish between actually performing experiments and simply describing thought experiments which would confirm theories that they believed on more or less a priori grounds. Moreover, physicists did not see the need to publish descriptions of experiments which failed. In short, experiments were conceived of largely as *illustrations* for doctrines believed on deductive and a priori grounds. . . . the specific instructions given by Boyle may have been more important or as important in shaping the course of physical inquiry as the more abstract and schematic defense of inductive procedure given by Bacon. (1981:195,196)

David Hume (1711–1776), a British empiricist, went further and insisted that we cannot generalize from a few experiences. In that regard he preempted later relativists by insisting that our ideas come from mere impressions (sensations, passions, emotions). Immanuel Kant (1724–1804), a contemporary of Hume, added to that notion by stressing that we should refuse to claim absolute knowledge.

The essential elements of both the Realism and Relativism schools thus existed before 1800. In the Realism school one can approach "truth" by use of one or another well-defined method that may include inductive and/or deductive reasoning. In the Relativism school (at the risk of oversimplifying), one is not sure what will emerge during experimentation; the outcome dictates what should be done next (nature provides the guide).

Despite this rich heritage of diverse viewpoints (and approaches) from the eighteenth century and before, a new movement began with the increasing dominance of the "Vienna school" in the early 1900s. Putnam wrote:

> In the past fifty years the clearest manifestation of the tendency to think of the methods of "rational justification" as given by something like a list or canon . . . was the movement known as Logical Positivism. . . . the list or canon . . . [was] supposed to exhaustively describe the "scientific method" (1981:105). . . . according to the watered-down operationism which seems to have become the working philosophy of most scientists, the content of the scientific theory consists in testable consequences, and these can be expressed by statements of the form *if we perform such and such actions, then we will get such and such observable results.* (1981:178)

By the 1940s, 1950s, and 1960s logical positivism dominated thought in many subfields of biology; *the* scientific method could be stated very clearly. We summarize here one of the more complete published descriptions of the standard scientific method (Silvernale 1965), one that matches very closely that taught to us during our undergraduate biology training.

THE SCIENTIFIC METHOD

Silvernale believed that the scientific method of thought originated among Greek philosophers and that social scientists laid down its foundations before the natural sciences adopted that approach. He listed nine of the "several steps" needed to proceed "scientifically" and commented upon each one, as follows:

1. *Observation.* At one point Silvernale wrote: "Not all people make accurate observers because they do not know how or

what to look for. Likewise, many people only see what they want to see rather than what they really see, because the untrained, unscientific observer is often unconsciously prejudiced in making his judgments" (1965:4).

2. *Defining the problem.* Silvernale recognized that "how" or "what" questions are valid in science but that "why" questions "are usually unsolvable." He thereby implicitly dismissed teleology.

3. *Gathering data.* The point made here was that research should first be done "to determine whether or not the problem has been solved before."

4. *Organization of the data.*

5. *Formulation of an hypothesis.* Silvernale felt that this step permitted a scientist to arrive at a temporary solution or "scientific guess" about which might be the logical answer to a problem, and wrote:

> A competent scientist may have a foregone conclusion of what the solution to the problem might be as soon as he conceives the problem. This "hunch" or "intuition" is often the mark of a true scientist, and once again sets him apart from the layman who would not be likely to arrive at a workable hypothesis. . . . The scientist deliberately sets out to disprove his hypothesis in every conceivable way, whereas the layman has a tendency to try to prove his hypothesis because his personal pride unconsciously causes him to come to the defense of his assumption in a desperate attempt to prove it to be correct. (1965:5)

6. *Controlled experimentation.* Experiments would next be designed and conducted "in order to prove that the results would not have occurred accidentally."

7. *Solution.* Here we see Silvernale's strong verificationist bent. He wrote: "The solution is the answer to the problem and constitutes a verification of the hypothesis. If the controlled experiment proves the hypothesis to be correct, the solution is passed on to other scientists; if it does not, the hypothesis is discarded" (1965:5).

8. *Scientific verification or repeatability.* The linear sequence inherent in this description of "the scientific method" led Silvernale to write: "If [the results of other scientists] are essentially the same as those of the original experimenter, the hypothesis is then considered to be valid and may assume the status of a *theory*" (1965:5).

9. *Publication and application.* As a conclusion for the process,

Silvernale wrote: "The results of the study can now be submitted to the public as scientific facts and can be used in solving similar problems" (1965:5).

THE EROSION OF LOGICAL POSITIVISM

At about the same time that biologists were becoming most comfortable with their notions of the scientific method (1940–1980), serious doubts were developing relative to the underlying premises of that stated method, including one by Putnam:

> It is, perhaps, not surprising that the Logical Empiricist tendency began to disintegrate by 1950. . . . When the phenomenalism was given up, and the philosophical *defense* of the claim was replaced by the bare claim, and even more when the bare claim was made more "reasonable" by allowing exceptions, modifications, etc., the whole cutting power of the movement disappeared. (1981:187)

A swing toward relativism was already under way. Polanyi (e.g., 1958) was one of the first prominent scientists to speak out; Kuhn (1962) followed soon thereafter (see our chapter 3 and figure 3.1). Those biologists committed to the Realism school, however, remained largely unaware of these developments.

McIntosh expressed the problem facing ecologists in this way: "Historically, however, philosophy of science has not been notably relevant or helpful to biology, and philosophers have paid little attention to specific problems of ecology, preferring to focus on genetics and evolution" (1987:324).

The important point to remember is that several generations of biologists had been exposed to a quite limited impression of the *process* of science. That means that those who practice biology today were likely to have been taught only one standard version of the "scientific method" (the Realism school). Breaking away from that mold would be possible only if one encountered a different philosophy of science in graduate school or shortly thereafter. Breaking away is also possible for those who are especially receptive to anomalous results as they arise and who may exploit new leads when a research program runs into trouble.

SCIENCE AS A COLLECTIVE PROCESS

The scientific community has too long been restricted by a lack of awareness of how it operates. Even on so simple a matter as a "test" of a hypothesis, for example, there is no agreement about what constitutes such a test. For one biologist, the ability to repeat an experiment and get the same results suffices. For another, conducting a similar experiment under different circumstances and getting "acceptable results" constitutes a test. Others feel that any subsequent experiment that yields "predictable results" provides an adequate test of the hypothesis. Some biologists hold out and insist that a test should be a real attempt at falsification (Popperian falsification). The inference approach, on the other hand, is virtually unknown in several biological disciplines.

In addition to the difficulties on agreement about protocol, such as what constitutes a "test," there is ignorance about fundamental methods. Each of the approaches that can be used by scientists (see figure 3.1) has limited application, according to circumstances prevailing at the time (see chapter 14). Currently, however, some fields of biology function largely within the restrictions of the Realism school and are back where physics was in the seventeenth century. Bohm and Peat commented about the status of physics after that time:

> When science won its battle with the Church for the freedom to entertain its own hypotheses, it in turn became the principal repository of the idea that particular forms of knowledge could either be absolute truths or at least could approach absolute truths. Such a belief in the ultimate power of scientific knowledge evoked strong feelings of comforting security in many people, almost comparable with the feelings experienced by those who have an absolute faith in the truths of religion. (1987:24)

Progress in science, on the other hand, occurs as a consequence of the collective activity of scientists; the more rapidly someone in the community can shift from one approach to another, when necessary, the more rapid the progress. On the other hand, the more strongly established ideas are defended in the face of serious anomalies, the deeper the certain-to-appear controversy when new results emerge. The result is a slower progress toward better understanding in science.

Increasingly, interested parties are recognizing the pervasive influence of the human factor in scientific research, a factor earlier considered trivial. Putnam wrote:

> To put the matter somewhat more abstractly, we might say that the "method" fetishist assumes that rationality is *inseparable*. But Bayes' theorem indicates that this is not the case; that we can separate rationality, even in the area of science ... into two parts: a *formal*

part, which can be schematized mathematically and programmed on a computer, and an *informal* part which cannot be so schematized and which depends on the actual changing beliefs of scientists. ... a scientist will only assign degrees of support to hypotheses that look "reasonable" if he starts out with a "reasonable" prior probability function. ... but [if] his prior probability function is extremely "unreasonable," then his judgments of the extent to which various hypotheses are supported by the evidence will be ... wildly "irrational." ... Formal rationality, [that is,] commitment to the formal part of the scientific method, does not guarantee real and actual rationality. (1981:191, 192)

The very foundation of science, the "scientific method," has thus been opened to question (see Burk 1986), but biologists remain largely unaware of the changes that have taken place. Questions remain. Will philosophers of science continue to focus on relatively narrow views of how science functions? Will biologists recognize recent developments in the philosophy, sociology, and psychology of science? Will scientists in general recognize the fact that application of the scientific method by only one person at one time is merely a part of a much larger picture of the *process* of science?

A final question: In what way will the "scientific method" evolve next?

Excursis SI: The Salk Institute Stimulus

> "We have to understand first how many elements
> can be brought to bear on a controversy; once this
> is understood, the other problems will be easier to
> solve."
>
> —*Bruno Latour 1987:62*

Interviewing successful scientists is a technique often used by sociologists and philosophers of science when they wish to ascertain the reasons for scientific achievement. On the other hand, many mistakes are made in projects that are begun with the best of intentions; projects started may fail early in the planning stages due to faulty assumptions. Such attempts are rarely the subjects of discussion. One can be certain in any event that the interview technique is unlikely to reveal many truly embarrassing episodes.

What propels a research project forward? Sometimes the desire to know suffices. At other times adversity plays an important role; the desire to prove oneself correct and others wrong can be quite an incentive. One might even say that controversy fuels important scientific progress. However, a great many such incidents in science go unreported and thereby completely escape the attention of sociologists, psychologists, historians, and philosophers of science.

Under the current anonymous peer review grant system, unfortunately, adversity can lead to the early termination of a project. Another social factor prevails, despite claims to the contrary; the scientific community is uncomfortable with controversy, unless the issue is rather unimportant (see chapter 14). All of this means that discussion of only a very small portion of conflict resolution actually reaches print.

Our volume would not be complete without a recounting of one such experience Wenner had at the Salk Institute during the mid-1960s. It was an incident that led to the first real test of the dance language hypothesis.

The first question one might ask is, "Why should a bee researcher be involved with the Salk Institute?" The occasion appears to have been the intended launching of a major research project spawned by Jacob Bronowski. He had apparently convinced the Salk Institute leadership that they could unravel brain function by conducting research on the "dance language" of bees. A "kickoff" seminar was to be given by Harald Esch of Notre Dame University.

The following account of that experience is necessarily written in the first person singular by Wenner. The accuracy of the account was verified by one of the participants, the renowned honey bee geneticist Harry Laidlaw of the University of California at Davis. When he read the account, he remained silent for a long while and then commented, "Yes, that's how it was." After a brief pause he added, "But are you sure you should publish it?" Wenner's account follows.

THE HARALD ESCH SEMINAR

Jacob Bronowski telephoned in 1965 and invited me to serve as a "discussant" immediately following a talk to be given at the Salk Institute by Harald Esch of Notre Dame University. Esch and I, who had never met before then, had independently recorded sounds made by forager bees (see chapter 6) during their dance maneuver within the hive. Both of us had also appreciated the potential significance of those sounds in terms of the purported "dance language" (see Esch 1961; Wenner 1959, 1962, 1964). We both reasoned at that time that bees maybe used sound rather than the dance configuration during communication.

The invitation was quite puzzling for at least two reasons. First of all, the Salk Institute is not known for its interest in natural history studies. Secondly, the formal use of a "discussant" after scientific seminars is a rather rare event. In that arrangement, one person or a group of people give presentations. Then a designated "discussant" provides pro and/or con arguments about the material presented. This procedure seems to be a means by which some notion or other can be "legitimized" in the minds of those present.

Since this invitation came when all of us still worked within the dance language paradigm, it would appear that the occasion was expected to proceed smoothly. Esch would give his presentation, and I would discuss the material and give a "stamp of approval" on the idea that the "dance language" hypothesis of bees was valid.

By the time that Bronowski extended his invitation, however, my colleagues and I had already succeeded in conditioning honey bees to respond as if to a language upon the presentation of a stimulus (see chapter 7). We had also already recognized the implications of that conditioned-response behavior during the rerecruitment of foragers in nature. That is, we knew that *experienced* bees did not need to "use" information contained in the dance (see Wenner 1974) as they once again traveled to food sources that they had visited earlier.

Those conditioning experiments had thus revealed to us what von Frisch (1950) and Ribbands (1954) had meant when they reported that experienced bees could be rerecruited to food sources "without the need for a dance." As indicated in chapter 7, at any one time virtually all foraging bees are experienced. That means that foragers would rarely be recruited to food sources by means of the presumed "dance language."

At the time of the invitation from the Salk Institute, we had already perceived that the "dance language" of bees, if it existed (and we were no longer certain of that), would be useful primarily for the recruitment of naive bees. Once those naive recruits learned the location of nectar, however, they could very well spend much of their remaining life visiting that one source. Rerecruitment each day could be by means of conditioned-response behavior.

While inviting me, Bronowski asked if I knew of a good bee geneticist, which I did. Harry Laidlaw of the University of California at Davis had had a long-term association with my beekeeper relatives in Northern California and was perhaps the world's leading bee geneticist at the time. Subsequently he was also invited to the Salk Institute at the time of Esch's seminar.

Another factor entered in. When Bronowski invited me to be a discussant for Esch's talk at the Salk Institute, we had already completed and submitted two manuscripts to journals. Those papers described the results of our experiments on simple conditioning (Wenner and Johnson 1966) and communication by means of conditioned response (Johnson and Wenner 1966). I therefore felt it my professional responsibility to provide the results of these experiments to both Esch and Bronowski before the forthcoming event, even though I was unaware at the time of the reason for Esch's forthcoming talk at the Salk Institute (see below). Bronowski acknowledged receipt of the manuscript but encouraged me to come despite that new development and despite any possible implications of those results to the question of honey bee recruitment.

PRECIPITATION OF A CRISIS

The seminar setting at the Salk Institute totally surprised me. I was expecting a small, relatively informal seminar, as is customary at academic institutions. Instead, perhaps three hundred people were in attendance, as well as television crews and reporters for major news outlets. This was obviously not a routine academic seminar, but no one had informed me of that fact.

Just before Esch began his talk, Bronowski requested that I not mention any of our latest experimental results on honey bee learning (the content of the manuscripts sent earlier) during my "discussion" of Esch's seminar at its conclusion. He said, "That matter can be handled tonight at the dinner."

Bronowski's request caught me unawares, because scientists pride themselves on being open and receptive to new ideas and information. Why then, I wondered, the sudden insistence on even a temporary suppression of new results? Claude Bernard had criticized such action, as follows: "True science suppresses nothing, but goes on searching, and is undisturbed in looking straight at things that it does not yet understand" ([1865] 1957:223).

Esch's talk was, to me, a quite elementary treatment of the presumed evolution of the honey bee "dance language." He outlined a scheme whereby the intricate "recruitment dance" pattern of European bees (which contains information on the distance and direction of food sources; see chapter 6) could have evolved from the behavioral patterns found in related genera of bees living in tropical and subtropical countries.

Esch failed to mention an important point; one could argue equally convincingly that evolution could have proceeded the other way. For example, stingless bees may be considered more "advanced" than European bees, *because* they have secondarily lost their sting. That is because the sting is a modified ovipositor found in most bees, wasps, and ants.

Taxonomists now recognize that honey bees are not as closely related to stingless bees (Kimsey 1984) as once thought (Michener 1974). Rather, stingless bees are in another (earlier) branch of the family Apidae. Honey bees are thus more closely related to the bumble bees and euglossine bees, which have no dances, than they are to the stingless bees.

During Esch's presentation my thoughts were in turmoil. How could Bronowski, a renowned scholar, mathematician, and philosopher, insist on suppressing results, even if only temporarily? Furthermore, how could I "discuss" Esch's exposition on the "evolution of bee language" in front of three hundred people and reporters, when our experimental results on learning had the potential of relegating the entire "dance language" hypothesis into, at most, a minor facet of honey bee recruitment?

I found myself in a position that was probably incomprehensible to the rest of the audience. I had already undergone a "paradigm shift" in the Kuhnian sense and had resolved the "crisis" state in my own mind. It had been evident to my colleagues and to me that our experimental results on conditioned responses had matched almost perfectly the earlier experimental results described by von Frisch (1950) as evidence of "dance language" use.

However, von Frisch had not addressed the importance of learning during recruitment and had insisted that the rerecruitment of experienced bees (which we now recognized as conditioned responses) was "proof" that bees had a "language." By contrast, we now realized that two interpretations existed that could both fit that *same* set of experimental results.

The circumstance we were in was remarkably similar to that encountered by Thomas Kuhn when he was able to perceive that scientists behaved differently from the pattern perceived or advocated by Karl Popper (the "wearing of a new set of spectacles"). How could I then discuss the "evolution of bee language" in front of the audience at the Salk Institute when the very foundation of that hypothesis had been shaken to its roots in our minds? We had undergone a "gestalt switch" and viewed the same results from the vantage point of a new paradigm (see chapter 5 and excursus OS). Once that happens, there is no going back.

Eventually there came the moment of truth. Esch ended his seminar to resounding applause. Then it was my turn to say something to that same audience, an audience that was content with the dance language hypothesis and that was totally unaware of our experimental results and the implications of those results for that hypothesis.

A LACK OF ADEQUATE CONTROLS

As I walked to the front of the room, my dilemma became resolved. For the very first time, I realized that von Frisch's original experiments had lacked adequate controls against forager flight paths and extraneous odor cues. I had "created the image" at that instant, on the way to the front of the room, in the sense meant by Atkinson (1985) and Wenner (1989) (see also figure 3.1).

The idea that von Frisch's original experiments lacked adequate controls was conceded later even by proponents of the dance language hypothesis (e.g., Seymour Benzer in 1966; in a personal communication; Gould 1976). As Gould wrote at that time: "Throughout the dance-language controversy, Wenner has made perceptive and valuable contributions. Von Frisch's controls do not exclude the possibility of olfactory recruitment alone" (1976:241).

However, that open and tolerant attitude did not prevail at the Salk Institute that day. Nevertheless, I had to address the issue as I saw it with my "new spectacles," as Kuhn phrased it. If a "dance language" had never really been established as "fact," there was little need to address, at that time, the points made by Esch in his seminar. Any discussion of evolution of "the dance language" (in the teleological sense) would be pointless.

Instead, I strode to the blackboard and drew sketches of the experimental design and the results of von Frisch's classic "step" and "fan" experiments. I then highlighted the missing controls and described how those same results fit an odor-search model (e.g., Wenner 1971a, 1974; see also our chapter 5 and excursus OS). The consequence was that I ended up questioning the entire honey bee dance language hypothesis.

The audience reaction immediately turned from what might best be termed one of euphoria to one of intense hostility. It was certainly not the reaction one would have expected from an audience of scientists. The reaction of Theodore Bullock, an eminent physiologist, was fairly typical; he shouted: "What's the matter, don't you believe anything unless you have done it yourself?"

Shortly thereafter the seminar ended. As far as I know, nothing appeared in either the newspapers or on television, despite the presence of all the media and the extensive film footage taken.

THE DINNER CONFERENCE

Bronowski had earlier informed me that a small group would have dinner together and exchange views on honey bee dance language research. That dinner party included several luminaries, including Jonas Salk, Francis Crick, Jacques Monod, Jacob Bronowski, and Theodore Bullock. Harald Esch, Irving Bengelsdorf (the *Los Angeles Times* science editor), Harry Laidlaw, and a few others were also present. After the dinner itself, the dishes were cleared away and a rather intensive discussion of honey bee communication began.

Eventually (by now unfettered by Bronowski's request that our new experimental results not be presented), I began to describe our conditioned-response experiments. I presented the results of those experiments and indicated the significance of the experimental results in terms of their importance to recruitment efficiency in honey bees.

At one point I said, "One must consider the ecology of the whole system, not just whatever behavior may occur between two individual bees." At that point Bullock came forth with another outburst, "Ecologists be damned, there's not a scientist among the lot of them!"

The discussion became quite heated at that point, and many others joined in. Bengelsdorf, who had remained quiet until that point, finally said, "Wenner's correct; von Frisch's experiments were not well enough controlled." (Bengelsdorf had a doctorate in chemistry.) Shortly after that, Francis Crick leaned over to Jonas Salk and said quietly (I was close enough to hear), "Perhaps we had better not go ahead." The dinner engagement was over shortly thereafter.

HARRY LAIDLAW'S INPUT

After returning to the hotel, I could not relax. Clearly something had been transpiring about which I had not been informed. The last comment directed to Salk by Crick indicated that something big had been in the offing. Since Laidlaw had been a longtime friend, I felt free to telephone him in his room and ask if he knew what had been going on during dinner. He replied, "Yes, didn't they tell you?"

He then came to my room and told me all he knew of what had been planned. As he understood it, the Salk Institute, under Bronowski's prompting, was interested primarily in the functioning of the brain. The "instinctual signaling system" of bees appeared to be an appropriate material for the investigation of brain function. After all, that would be true if, as von Frisch had said: "The astoundingly precise adherence to the direction indicated, regarded from the viewpoint of sensory physiology and psychology, stands as a great accomplishment in reception and evaluation of information" (1967a:231).

Apparently, Bronowski's "brainchild" was to quick-freeze a foraging bee while it was engaged in its dance maneuver; then neural pathways could be traced. Other races of bees could be used as well, and hybrids of those various races could be bred. More freezing and slicing of brains could then be done at the time of communication, and brain function could be elucidated eventually.

What was the role of Esch in all of this activity? As we later surmised, it appears that he was to have performed the field experiments with the bees during their "bee language" dance. The seminar was apparently what is known as a "recruitment" seminar. Apparently my role as "discussant" was to "legitimize" that activity and the project. In retrospect, I concluded that it probably had eventually dawned on those present at the dinner conference that the honey bee dance language hypothesis may not have been on as solid a foundation as was stated by proponents of that hypothesis.

THE STIMULUS FOR BETTER EXPERIMENTAL DESIGN

The Salk Institute experience provided an additional strong stimulus for our further research on honey bee recruitment. Better experimental designs were obviously needed for investigating honey bee recruitment to food sources. We then gradually developed the more rigorous double-control and "crucial" experimental designs (see chapters 9 and 10). (It is also noteworthy that Gould and co-workers later reverted to single-control experimental designs in their "verification" approach; see chapter 13.)

Esch's seminar at the Salk Institute occurred in March 1966; that very summer we set out to repeat von Frisch's original experiments. Our eyes had been opened wider by now (we suddenly had new "spectacles"). We moved back to the "exploration" approach (Atkinson 1985; see also our figure 3.1) and away from our former "verification" approach of attempting to "prove" that bees used sound signals as part of their "dance language."

We already knew that we could obtain at will results similar to those obtained by von Frisch. We also knew that several controls were missing from von Frisch's experimental designs. The question then became, "Were any *essential* controls missing from von Frisch's experiments?"

That summer we repeated von Frisch's experiments many times and with many variations. During that process we realized that his single-control experimental design did not exclude the possibility that searching recruit bees could exploit odors and the flight paths of other bees during their search. While watching newly recruited bees approach our feeding stations, we could clearly see that they always approached from far downwind (the use of binoculars helped). They obviously were *not* flying directly out from the hive.

Through a trial-and-error process, we slowly came to the realization that we could conduct a double-control experiment (a design rarely used in field behavior experiments). That realization was facilitated by the fact that we just happened to have another hive in the area with its different color of bees. The experiments described in chapter 9 were the outcome of all of those deliberations.

The trauma resulting from the Salk Institute encounter cannot be described adequately; it is something that has to be experienced to be believed (but not something one would wish on others). However, sometimes it is an encounter of that sort that enables one to appreciate fully some of the human elements involved in the conduct of science. The Salk Institute affair may account for the surprisingly confrontational attitude we encountered at the Twenty-First International Apicultural Congress a few months later and at subsequent national meetings.

The Salk Institute episode also apparently precipitated events that led to experiments conducted by James Gould and co-workers (see chapter 11).

Excursus TEL: Teleology

"Teleological explanations, then, are essential to biology. They imply that the parts, processes, and behavior patterns of living things are organized so as to attain specific goals, which contribute as a rule to the ultimate goal of reproductive fitness."

—*George F. Kneller 1978:146*

"The nature of our mind leads us to seek the essense or the *why* of things. . . . experience soon teaches us that we cannot get beyond the *how*, i.e., beyond the immediate cause or necessary conditions of phenomena."

—*Claude Bernard (1865) 1957:80*

"But the greatest fallacy in, or rather the greatest objection to, teleological thinking is in connection with the emotional content, the belief. People get to believing and even to professing the apparent answers thus arrived at, suffering mental constrictions by emotionally closing their minds to any of the further and possibly opposite 'answers' which might otherwise be unearthed by honest effort."

—*John Steinbeck (1941) 1962:143*

Most nonscientists and many contemporary biologists, particularly students of animal behavior, are quite comfortable with Kneller's position on the issue of teleology. They want to know "why" an animal does this thing or that in a given situation.

For example, one can ask, "Why do geese fly south for the winter?" "To keep warm" is a disarmingly satisfying answer! This explanation of biological phenomena in terms of purposeful or goal-directed behavior has wide appeal, but it leads nowhere in scientific investigation. Claude Bernard (see the epigraph) early on recognized that severe limitation in teleological approaches.

We often encountered a teleological pattern of thinking when we offered an "odor-search" answer to the question: *"How* do naive bees find a food source to which they have been recruited?" Our audiences appeared to be uncomfortable not so much with our answer as with our question! "But *why* then," they wanted to know, "do they dance?" Indeed, von Frisch himself objected, as follows: "The reason why these complicated and ingenious behavioural patterns could evolve and be a functionless repertoire remains undiscussed [by Wenner and Wells]" (1973:626).

Martin Lindauer even more forcefully articulated the teleological argument in the opening sentences of his challenge of our work. He wrote: "each morphological structure and behavioral act is associated with a special function" (1971:89). Although his assertion is open to question, it is not necessarily teleological; if true, it could be merely descriptive.

However, Lindauer continued that passage with a teleological non sequitur: "On this basis alone, it would seem highly unlikely that information contained in the waggle dance of a honeybee is not transmitted to her nest mates" (1971:89). Lindauer implied by that reasoning that design or purpose was inherent in the system and that such purpose would mesh with what human beings would do in like circumstances (an anthropomorphic conclusion).

We later cited Hempel (1966) and Popper (1957) when we replied to Lindauer's use of: "Aristotelian (Darwinian) teleology as an argument in favour of language." We did that "in part by discussing the relevant data in terms of philosophy of science which we consider to be more powerful" (Wells and Wenner 1973:175).

We also offered a disproof by counterexample of the notion that "each behavioral act" is necessarily adaptive. We described Steiner's (1952) use of methyl eugenol as an attractant for Oriental fruit flies in Hawaii, and noted:

> [Methyl eugenol] is not a component of the natural food of this fly and probably has no nutritional value. Yet male oriental fruit flies are irresistibly attracted to it and "apparently cannot stop feeding when they have free access to it, and they kill themselves with overindulgence." (Wells and Wenner 1973:175)

We could have added that the flash rate of fireflies (family Lampyridae) contains ambient temperature information; however, that fact does not lead to the conclusion that fireflies are communicating information about temperature to one another.

We further indicated that this example reveals "a weakness in the teleology argument. The mere presence of a characteristic behavioural pattern in an animal cannot be construed as purposeful, adaptive or 'associated with a special function'" (Wells and Wenner 1973:175).

That particular debate might have ended there, but Anthony Ferguson (1975) took exception and came to the defense of von Frisch and Lindauer. Ferguson, in turn, was challenged by Jack Hailman (1977), who was then rebutted by Ferguson (1977). Elaboration follows.

First, Ferguson transformed von Frisch's "why" into "what for?" (a semantic disguise), posed a question, and gave his own answer: "Question: what is bee dance information for? Answer: To find food more efficiently. Even expressed in these terms, teleology is not involved. . . . [Such] 'what for?' questions are merely a convenient verbal shorthand," Ferguson argued. He then continued, "While the linguistic form . . . is teleological, its conceptual content is not" (Ferguson 1975:369).

Hailman replied that we (Wells and Wenner 1973) had actually addressed the points raised by Lindauer (1971), since von Frisch's 1973 article had not yet been published when we wrote our paper. Hailman argued that Lindauer's position was vulnerable to several epistemological points inherent in our comments, as follows:

1. Wells and Wenner (1973) are denying that just because information is encoded in dances it must be transmitted, as implied by Lindauer.
2. [Wells and Wenner] are also arguing that it is teleological to see communicative design "apparent" in dancing.
3. It is irrelevant whether the teleology is naively Aristotelian or framed in Darwinian language—it is still incorrect to "see" communicative design apparent in dancing. (Hailman 1977:187)

Ferguson (1975) had continued by challenging our "disproof by counterexample." He argued that, since Steiner's fruit flies had never encountered methyl eugenol in nature, their reaction to it need not be considered "nonadaptive." He felt that fruit flies may react to methyl eugenol (as do "mammals to saccharine") because they *perceive* it to be similar to a relevant environmental stimulus. Ferguson wrote, "The *foundations* of the response could thus ultimately be adaptive."

This last argument by Ferguson, however, fell to the next point in Hailman's discussion, the citing of a naturally occurring counterexample:

4. Yet Blest (1960) discovered that the postflight rocking movements of saturniid moths also contain information concerning the locus from which they have flown. The adaptive significance, if any, of this behavior is unclear, and no one has suggested that the inherent information is transmitted to other moths. (Hailman 1977:187, 188)

Thus, Hailman (1977) refuted Ferguson's objections largely with arguments we had offered in the first place—but much more clearly stated and with a far better example of nonadaptive (in this case, neutral) behavior.

The remainder of Hailman's article dealt with two questions: 1) whether von Frisch's statement (quoted above) really was teleological, and 2) whether we were obliged to offer an alternative answer to Ferguson's "why" question. He concluded both that "it was" and "we weren't." Ferguson's (1977) rebuttal relied largely on semantic arguments dealing with what we had said (or presumably had meant to say) and included an attempt to trivialize Hailman's "moth" counterexample.

Apparently neither author succeeded in "converting" the other in the sense of Atkinson (1985). Neither did the inconclusive debates between Lindauer and us, then by Ferguson and Hailman, and later by Rosin (1988a, 1988b) and Walls (1988), below, settle the issues. The conceptual foundations of the disagreement both preceded and survived those published discussions.

As noted by Michael Ruse (1973), teleological explanations are a carry-over from pre-Darwinian times, "when the dominant biological paradigm was the Argument from Design (for God's existence)." Ruse continued:

> Thus, [philosopher William] Whewell could write that "each member and organ not merely produces a certain effect [but] was *intended* to produce the effect. . . . each organ is designed for its appropriate function. . . . each portion of the whole arrangement has its *final cause;* an end to which it is adapted, and in this end, the reason that it is where and what it is. . . . Here it is clear that things are being explained in terms of what we would call their effects—modern evolutionists can and do do the same thing, . . . because of the quasi-Design effect selection has. (See Young 1971, for a discussion of how pre-Darwinian thought found its way into the *Origin* and later biological works.) (Ruse 1973:196; see also Whewell 1840:2:79–80)

James Gould, writing at about the same time as Ferguson, approached the teleological argument more carefully. "It has been argued that the dance correlations *must* be useful, or they would not exist," he wrote (1975b:686). He then suggested: "In the case of *the dance language* [emphasis ours], the evolutionary argument appears particularly persuasive."

However, Gould recognized the significance of "disproof by counterexample" and included several relevant instances in addition to those cited by Hailman and by us. By then, however, he had unwittingly implied that *"the* dance language" was a "fact."

The pragmatic argument that teleological thinking may actually *inhibit* research was at the root of Steinbeck's thinking earlier (see the epigraph). Gould also advocated caution "lest we glibly explain away phenomena and inhibit research," and forcefully articulated: "Used as a basis of proof or as an article of faith [the teleological argument] can merely reinforce our predispositions, stifling research by making further work seem unnecessary" (1976:238).

Did *any* of the above debates and arguments make a lasting difference in the dance language controversy? Perhaps a little, but the teleology argument is still raised by proponents of the dance language hypothesis—by Roland Walls, for instance, who wrote: "One has to assume that in the competitive world of the honey bee there is survival value to all patterned energy expenditure. Karl von Frisch and his colleagues showed that there was meaning and predictability in those gyrations bees do" (1988:576).

In spite of Rosin's observation (1988b:576) that "this [teleological] argument is probably the one most important cause for the quick success of the 'dance language' revolution" (see also our chapter 6), that argument has lost some of its force. Rosin continued:

> By now both staunch opponents of the "dance language" hypothesis (Wenner et al. 1967; Wenner 1971; Wells & Wenner 1973; Wenner 1974), as well as staunch supporters (Gould 1975[b], 1976) have, for good reasons, invalidated the Teleological argument, and concluded that the dances may have a yet unknown adaptive value, or no adaptive value at all. (1988b:576, 577)

Thus it is that, to this day, the issue of teleology remains an important one in the dance language controversy, in behavioral ecology, and in other important fields of biology. Perhaps that is why Hailman (after expressing confidence that bees had a "language" after all) ended his article with the observation that "the underlying epistemological issues ... in some respects transcend in importance [the] scientific [dance language] controversy" (1977:188).

We agree with this last assessment, of course; that is why we wrote this book. We further suspect that the current devotion to teleological explanations by some biologists is but one more episode of a pendulum swing between adoption and rejection of that type of explanation.

Excursus VGR: The Efficacy of "Artificial Bee" Experiments

THE VERIFICATION APPROACH

One of the best ways to verify an hypothesis in behavioral studies is to determine which individual elements of a complex stimulus will produce a predictable response. Much of the early research along that line involved "dissecting" the observed behavior and then using models and/or imitations of specific stimuli to alter behavior. Animals are thus subjected to one component of a complex stimulus at a time in attempts to elicite ("release") the appropriate response.

Tinbergen, among others, exploited that technique in his research, and wrote: "an animal does not react to all the changes in the environment which its sense organs can receive, but only to a small part of them. This is a basic property of instinctive behaviour, the importance of which cannot be stressed too much" (1951:25).

One example of success obtained by Tinbergen included the use of a stick with a red dot painted on its underside. The painted dot simulated the red dot on the underside of a gull's beak; when held over the nest, the stick elicited a begging behavior in young gull chicks (Tinbergen and Perdeck 1950). An earlier classic example was that of female crickets moving toward a loudspeaker as it broadcasted male chirps (see Ewing 1984:230–234).

The complex waggle dance of bees initially seemed to us to be an excellent candidate for the same sort of experiment. The dance maneuver appeared to be a well-defined behavioral sequence that could be analyzed and broken down into component parts. If bees had had a "dance language," it should have been possible to analyze carefully all components of the dance and construct an imitation bee.

Under the verification approach, success in that attempt would have been evident if naive bees would "fly directly out" *only* to the "specified" food site location after contact with the dancing model. Selective and successive removal of a single stimulus at a time from the entire repertoire would have helped elucidate which of the elements present in the dance were necessary for successful recruitment.

At that time (the early 1960s) we conducted research primarily within the verification approach, and thought that we should employ a model bee that vibrated (played sound) with the same characteristics as that of a dancing bee (see figure 7.1) or use a model that produced no sound. Under that approach, success while sound was included in the dance maneuver but lack of success while sound was omitted from the dance would implicate sound as an important component during the recruitment of naive bees.

While still working within the dance language paradigm, then, we set about to construct such a model bee. We recognized that, while building such a model bee, it would be necessary to observe very carefully *all* that happens during that dance. However, we also recognized that what we saw (or heard) during our observations of the waggle dance might not be the component(s) that elicits an appropriate behavior in potential recruit bees.

To learn as much as we could, we studied the dance intensively in ways that had never been done before. For example, we photographed (using time exposure) marked dancers in the hive while they were illuminated by flashing strobe lights. That process enabled us to trace the precise track taken by dancing bees.

We also altered the sugar concentration in the food provided and analyzed the dance maneuver sounds made by foragers after their return to the hive (e.g., Wenner 1962; Wenner, Wells, and Rohlf 1967). By seeking correlations between sound elements and sugar concentration, we had hoped to ascertain what von Frisch might have meant by his use of the term "vigor" when he wrote: "The sweeter the sugar, the more vigorous are the dances" (von Frisch 1950:65).

THE QUESTION OF "VIGOR" IN THE HONEY BEE WAGGLE DANCE

Despite our efforts during a four-year period of research, we were not able to obtain reliable data on a presumed relationship between sugar concentration and a consistent variation in any element (sounds or otherwise) of the dance that bees later executed in their hive. The paradox inherent in the notion of a "nonmeasurable" quantitative variable was dismissed by von Frisch, who wrote: "That these [dances] become more vivacious with increasing sugar content is very conspicuous to the observer, but is not to be defined quantitatively" (1967a:237).

Continued reference to the "vigor" of the dance up to the present time suggests that some investigators still perceive vigor as a verified phenomenon, despite the fact that it has never been quantified. For example, Michener did not question von Frisch's account, and wrote: "Vigor or liveliness of the dance is not easy to measure, . . . but according to [von] Frisch it increases with sugar concentration and is easily recognized by an observer" (1974:162).

Waddington (1982) was another who unqualifiedly accepted von Frisch's assertion, and wrote: "Once the concentration threshold for dancing has been reached, further increase in concentration results in: 1) increased 'liveliness' of the dance, 2) increased duration of the dancing, and 3) increased frequency of acoustic burst during the straight waggling run" (1982:297). However, Waddington missed the point of our earlier paper, which indicated that we could not find such correlations (Wenner, Wells, and Rohlf 1967). Nor, apparently, has anyone else.

DIFFICULTIES WITH ATTEMPTS TO EXPERIMENT WITH AN "IMITATION BEE"

There have apparently been several such attempts to direct naive recruits out to a point source in the field by use of a model bee in the hive, but experimental results have been interpreted in large part through the "eye of the beholder," namely those who continue to seek verification of the dance language hypothesis. For example, von Frisch provided some encouraging words about the Harald Esch experiments, as follows:

> Unfortunately the outcome is still unknown. . . . As yet it has been possible to carry out only one such experiment, and because of the [circumstance of a] single dancer only a few newcomers appeared. Repetitions were ruined by unusually unfavorable weather, and hitherto other circumstances have prevented Esch from continuing with this work. (1967a:106)

For us, however, the anomalous experimental results and observations we obtained on recruitment efficiency only led us further away from an earlier conviction that bees had a "dance language." We also realized that correlations (the mainstay of animal behavior research) are inadequate when one searches for causalities (Wenner, Wells, and Rohlf 1967). Instead of answers, we found ever more anomalies.

Among other anomalies, it had become apparent to us that potential recruits did not "follow" the dancer (see figure 7.3). The famous "figure-eight" configuration (as in figure 6.1) is perceived as such only if one has had the maneuver described in that manner before viewing it for the first time. Instead of proceeding further with our experiments, we concluded that fundamental difficulties inherent in at-tempts to experiment with an artificial bee precluded the effective-ness of that technique. We list here the problems we recognize in those attempts to use a model bee to verify the dance language hy-pothesis.

1. The construction of a model bee must be based on an implicit dismissal of all of the negative evidence that has accumulated during the last two decades with respect to the dance language hypothesis. For example, Gould, Henerey, and MacLeod found that only a very small percentage of bees contacting the dancing bee actually found *any* station in the field. Furthermore, each of those few successful recruits had obviously searched a large area before finally arriving at one of their experimental stations (see chapter 12 and excursus NEG).

One cannot avoid the question: "What is to prevent those searching recruits from happening upon any or all of the stations during that extensive search time?" The results published by Gould and co-work-ers clearly indicate that foragers, even if they "intended" to recruit naive bees, perform remarkably poorly in that capacity, and recruits obviously do not "fly directly out" (Gould, Henerey, and MacLeod; see also excursus NEG). A model bee would necessarily be even less efficient, as von Frisch suggested Esch had found (above).

2. One who experiments with a model bee must also nearly com-pletely disregard the alternative odor-search hypothesis (see chapter 5 and excursus OS). Searching bees are apparently very perceptive to the odors of the food, of the environment, and even of the assistants who help run the experiment. How can an investigator using a model bee be certain that all extraneous odor cues have been eliminated as factors in recruitment? Also, scent must be employed or there will be no recruitment (Wenner, Wells, and Johnson 1969). How can one control against undue influence of that scent?

3. One would have to guard against sensationalistic reporting of the results of any experiment with an artificial bee. Any naive bee that reached (even by chance) the desired location could be inter-preted as having *used* "dance language" information (see chapter 12) and would be considered "news." Negative results of any kind would tend not to catch the interest of science reporters.

That is why, if by chance some "positive" results were obtained by the use of a model bee, we suspect that there would be a rush to have an account of that success printed in the popular media. As indicated throughout our text, we know that there would be a large and willing audience for the news.

4. As with "polywater" (see chapter 3) or "desk-top cold fusion,"

any report of linguistic communication by an artificial bee would require, first of all, independent replication of the experiment and later rigorous tests by a detached scientist or scientists. Unfortunately, the construction of a mechanical bee can be quite expensive; it is unlikely to be accomplished by a detached person who is aware of the considerable body of negative evidence relative to the dance language hypothesis and/or who is familiar with the powerful alternative odor-search hypothesis (see chapter 5).

5. The experimental protocol would also require some kind of *test* of the dance language hypothesis with a "successful" model as the next step. Perhaps an attempt could be made to falsify the dance language hypothesis; better yet, one could design a mutually exclusive or "crucial" experiment. The important point here is that adequate controls must be incorporated into the experimental design to counter the inherent positivistic bias that is so much a part of the verification approach.

6. One would need to avoid the use of the von Frisch experimental "fan" design for any of these experiments, or any modification of that experimental design (see excursus PN). That is because, all factors being equal, recruits tend to end up near the center of all feeding stations (Johnson 1967a; Wenner 1967).

It would also be necessary to attend to the work of Friesen (1973), who found that recruitment any distance downwind from the hive was an unlikely occurrence whenever only a few bees traveled between hive and feeding station. If one felt that a model bee had been successful and that bees could recruit one another by means of the dance maneuver, for example, it should be possible to test the model by attempting to send recruits 500, 1,000, and 1,500 meters and so on *downwind*, with appropriate control stations located *upwind* from the hive.

The advantage of using such a downwind station, of course, should be obvious. Any of the odor marking that station would be traveling *away* from the hive and could not serve as a cue for searching recruits in the early stages of their search pattern (see excursus OS).

Above all, we suspect that the honey bee dance language controversy will not be resolved through experimentation involving a model bee executing the dance maneuver in the hive. A model can only be as strong as its assumptions, and one must be *very* committed to the dance language paradigm before expending an inordinate amount of time and effort in the construction of such a model, which leads to a severe problem of circular reasoning. The fundamental issues at stake are far more profound than can be resolved by simplistic attempts to direct bees out to food sources in the field; that is why we wrote this book.

We hope that the text of our book adequately illustrates why we could no longer attempt to construct an "imitation bee" and attempt to have recruits "fly directly out" to experimental stations. That is why, in our own research program, we quit trying to *verify* the dance language hypothesis and turned instead to the basic question of how newly recruited bees find a food source exploited by their hivemates (see chapter 5 and excursus OS).

Note

In 1989, A. Michelsen, B. B. Andersen, W. H. Kirchner, and M. Lindauer (*Naturwissenschaften* 76:277–280) claimed success in attempts to recruit hive bees to point sources in the field with the aid of a computer-driven mechanical bee ("electronic" or "robot" bee, as variously named). It appears that they did not take into account the six problems listed above, thereby failing to provide adequate controls against the possibility that odor cues could have dictated the results they obtained (distribution of recruit bees in the field). Those results differed little from a recruitment pattern expected of a population of searching bees flying upwind toward the center of an odor field (Wenner 1962, 1971, 1974; see also our excursus PN). However, an intense media presentation followed, ranging from an illustrated article in the January 1990 issue of *National Geographic* to a clip in the March 19, 1990 issue of the Jehovah's Witness magazine, *Awake*. A reply by Rick Weiss to our challenge of that work (*Science News*, 1990: Vol 137, pp. 19, 31) both called on authority (Roger Morse at Cornell University) and ignored the negative evidence provided him relative to the dance language hypothesis. Morse, in turn, remained committed to the verification approach in his support of Weiss.

REFERENCES CITED

Anderson, J., ed. 1988. Controversies in science: When the experts disagree. *MBL Science* (Woods Hole), 3:18.

Ankerl, G. and D. Pereboom. 1974. Scientific methods in ethology (letter). *Science* 185:814.

Ardrey, R. 1963. *African Genesis*. London: Readers Union, Collins.

Aristotle. (330 B.C.) 1931. *Historia Animalium*. Book 9.40 (vol. 3; vol. 4). London: Oxford University Press.

Aronson, N. 1986. The discovery of resistance: Historical accounts and scientific careers. *Isis* 77:630–646.

Atkinson, J. W. 1985. Models and myths of science: Views of the elephant. *American Zoologist* 25:727–736.

Bacon, Sir F. (1620) 1952. Novum organum. In R. M. Hutchins, *Great Books of the Western World*, pp. 103–195. Chicago, Ill.: Encyclopedia Britannica.

Baker, T. C., W. Meyer, and W. L. Roelfos. 1981. Sex pheromone dosage and blend specificity of response by oriental fruit moth males. *Entomologica Experimentalis et Applicata* 30:269–279.

Bate, C. S. 1878. Report on the present state of our knowledge of the

Crustacea. *Report. British Association for the Advancement of Science* 4:193–209.

Bazin. 1744. *The Natural History of Bees.* London: J. and P. Knapton. (Translated from the French).

Beck, W. S. 1961. *Modern Science and the Nature of Life.* Garden City, N.Y.: Doubleday (Anchor Books).

Bennett, A. M. 1968. Science: The antithesis of creativity. *Perspectives in Biology and Medicine* 11:233–245.

Berkeley, G. (1735) 1951. The defence of freethinking in mathematics. In A. Luce and T. Jesson, *The Works of George Berkeley, Bishop of Cloyne,* pp. 103–141. London: Thomas Nelson.

Bernard, C. (1865) 1957. *An Introduction to the Study of Experimental Medicine.* New York: Dover.

Bernstein, R. J. 1983. *Beyond Objectivism and Relativism: Science, Hermeneutics, and Praxis.* Philadelphia: University of Pennsylvania Press.

Bizetsky, A. R. 1957. Die Tanze der Bienen nach einem Fussweg zum Futterplatz. *Zeitschrift fuer vergleichende Physiologie* 40:264–288.

Blest, A. D. 1960. The evolution, ontogeny and quantitative control of the settling movements of some New World Saturniid moths, with some comments on distance communication by honey-bees. *Behaviour* 16:188–253.

Blissett, M. 1972. *Politics in Science.* Boston, Mass.: Little, Brown.

Boch, R. and D. A. Shearer. 1962. Identification of geraniol as the active component in the pheromone of the honey bee. *Nature* 194:704–706.

Bohm, D. and F. D. Peat. 1987. *Science, Order, and Creativity.* New York: Bantam Books.

Bonnier, G. 1906. Sur la division du travail chez les abeilles. *Comptes Rendus. Academie des Sciences* (Paris) 143:941–946. (Cited in Ribbands 1953.)

Boyer, P. D., B. Chance, L. Ernster, P. Mitchell, E. Racker, and E. C. Slater. 1977. Oxidative phosphorylation and photophosphorylation. *Annual Review of Biochemistry* 46:955–1026.

Brines, M. L. and J. L. Gould. 1979. Bees have rules. *Science* 206:571–216.

Broad, W. and N. Wade. 1982. *Betrayers of the Truth.* New York: Simon and Schuster.

Bruner, J. S. and L. Postman. 1949. On the perception of incongruity: A paradigm. *Journal of Personality* 18:106–223.

Burgett, M. 1980. The use of lemon balm (*Melissa officinalis*) for attracting honeybee swarms. *Bee World* 61:44–46.

Burghardt, G. M. 1970. Defining "communication." In J. W. Johnston, Jr., D. G. Moulton, and A. Turk, eds., *Communication by Chemical Signals,* pp. 5–18. New York: Appleton.

Burk, M. 1986. The scientific method (letter). *Science* 231:659.

Burkhardt, R. W., Jr. 1988. Charles Otis Whitman, Wallace Craig, and the biological study of animal behavior in the United States. In R. Rainger,

K. R. Benson, and J. Mainenschein, eds., *The American Development of Biology*, pp. 185–218. Philadelphia: University of Pennsylvania Press.

Burroughs, J. 1875. *Birds and Bees and Other Studies in Nature*. New York: Houghton Mifflin.

Burroughs, J. 1921. *Under the Maples*. New York: Houghton Mifflin.

Butler, C. (1609) 1969. *The Feminine Monarchie*. New York: Da Capo Press.

Butler, C. G. 1962. *The World of the Honeybee*. St. James's Place, London: Collins.

Buzzard, C. N. 1946. *Shining Hours*. St. James's Place, London: Collins.

Camac, C. N. B. (1909) 1959. *Classics of Medicine and Surgery*. New York: Dover.

Carde, R. T. 1984. Chemo-orientation in flying insects. In W. J. Bell and R. T. Carde, *Chemical Ecology of Insects*, pp. 111–124. New York: Chapman and Hall.

Carde, R. T. and R. E. Charlton. 1984. Olfactory sexual communication in Lepidoptera: Strategy, sensitivity and selectivity. In T. Lewis, ed., *Insect Communication*, pp. 241–265. New York: Academic Press.

Chamberlin, T. C. (1890) 1965. The method of multiple working hypotheses. *Science* 148:754–759.

Coffin, H. G. 1960. The ovulation, embryology, and developmental stages of the hermit crab *Pagurus samuelis* (Stimpson). College Place, Washington: Walla Walla College Publication 25:1–28.

Cohen, I. B. 1985. *Revolution in Science*. Cambridge: Harvard University Press (Belknap Press).

Cozzens, S. E. 1985. The character of science. *Science*, December 11, 1985. Book review of Collins, H. M. 1985. *Replication and Induction in Scientific Practice*. Beverly Hills, Calif.: Sage.

Cresswell, R. 1862. *Aristotle's History of Animals*. London: Henry G. Bohn.

Dawkins, R. 1969. Bees are easily distracted. *Science* 165:751.

Dixon, B. 1973. *What Is Science For?* London: Collins.

Dubos, R. J. 1950. *Louis Pasteur: Free Lance of Science*. Boston: Little, Brown.

Duclaux, E. (1896) 1920. *Pasteur: The History of a Mind*. Trans. E. F. Smith and F. Hedges. Philadelphia, Pa.: W. B. Saunders.

Dujardin, F. 1852. Quelques observations sur les abeilles, et particulierement sur les actes qui, chez les insectes peuvent etre rapportes a l'intelligence. *Annales des Sciences Naturelles (B) Zoologie*, 3d series, 18:231–240. (Cited in Ribbands, 1953.)

Dyer, F. C. and J. L. Gould. 1983. Honey bee navigation. *American Scientist* 71:587–597.

Emery, J. 1875. Ants and bees. *Nature* (London) 12:25–26.

Esch, H. 1961. Uber die Schallerzeugung beim Werbetanz der Honigbiene. *Zeitschrift fuer vergleichende Physiologie* 45:1–11.

Esch, H. and J. A. Bastian. 1970. How do newly recruited honey bees approach a food site? *Zeitschrift fuer vergleichende Physiologie* 68:175–181.

Ewing, A. W. 1984. Acoustic signals in insect behavior. In T. Lewis, ed., *Insect Communication*, pp. 223–240. New York: Academic Press.

Ferguson, A. 1975. Evolution, von Frisch, and teleology (letter). *American Naturalist* 109:369–370.

Ferguson, A. 1977. Reply to Hailman (letter). *American Naturalist* 111:189–191.

Feyerabend, P. K. 1970. Consolations for the specialist. In I. Lakatos and A. Musgrave, eds., *Criticism and the Growth of Knowledge*, pp. 197–230. London: Cambridge University Press.

Feyerabend, P. K. 1975. *Against Method: Outline of an Anarchistic Theory of Knowledge*. London: New Left Books.

Feyerabend, P. K. 1978. *Science in a Free Society*. London: New Left Books.

Fraenkel, G. S. and D. L. Gunn. (1940) 1961. *The Orientation of Animals: Kineses, Taxes and Compass Reactions*. New York: Dover.

Francon, J. (1938) 1939. *The Mind of the Bees*. London: Methuen.

Franks, F. 1981. *Polywater*. Cambridge, Mass.: MIT Press.

Free, J. B. 1962. The attractiveness of geraniol to foraging honeybees. *Journal of Apicultural Research* 1:52–54.

Free, J. B. 1968. The conditions under which foraging honeybees expose their Nasonov gland. *Journal of Apicultural Research* 7:139–145.

Free, J. B., A. W. Ferguson, and J. A. Pickett. 1983. A synthetic pheromone lure to induce worker honeybees to consume water and artificial forage. *Journal of Apicultural Research* 22:224–228.

Free, J. B., A. W. Ferguson, and J. R. Simpkins. 1984. A synthetic pheromone lure useful for trapping stray honeybees. *Journal of Apicultural Research* 23:88–89.

Free, J. B. and I. H. Williams. 1970. Exposure of the Nasonov gland by honeybees (*Apis mellifera*) collecting water. *Behaviour* 37:286–290.

Friesen, L. J. 1973. The search dynamics of recruited honeybees, *Apis mellifera ligustica* Spinola. *Biological Bulletin* 144:107–131.

Frisch, K. von. 1915. Ueber den Geruchsinn der Biene und seine Bedeutung fuer den Blumenbesuch. *Verhandlungen: Zoologische-Botanische Gesellschaft in Wien* 65:26–35.

Frisch, K. von. 1920. Uber die "Sprache" der Bienen, 1. *Muenchener Medizinische Wochenschrift* 20:566–569.

Frisch, K. von. 1923. Uber die "Sprache" der Bienen, eine tierpsychologische Untersuchung. *Zoologische Jahrbuecher: Abteilung fuer Allgemeine Zoologie und Physiologie der Tiere* 40:1–186.

Frisch, K. von. 1939. The language of bees. In *Annual Report of the Smithsonian Institution for the Year Ended June 30, 1938*, pp. 423–431. Publication 3491. Washington, D.C.: U.S. Government Printing Office.

Frisch, K. von. 1947. The dances of the honey bee. *Bulletin of Animal*

Behaviour 5:1–32. (Translated from: 1946. Die Tanze der Bienen. *Oesterreiche Zoologie Zeitschrift* 1:1–48.)

Frisch, K. von. 1948. Solved and unsolved problems of bee language. *Bulletin of Animal Behaviour* 9:2–25.

Frisch, K. von. 1950. *Bees: Their Vision, Chemical Senses, and Language.* Ithaca, N.Y.: Cornell University Press.

Frisch, K. von. 1954. *The Dancing Bees: An Account of the Life and Senses of the Honey Bee.* London: Methuen. (Translated from: 1953. *Aus dem Leben der Bienen.* Berlin: Springer Verlag.)

Frisch, K. von. 1956. The "language" and orientation of the bees. *Proceedings of the American Philosophical Society* 100:515–519.

Frisch, K. von. 1962. Dialects in the language of the bees. *Scientific American* 207:78–87.

Frisch, K. von. 1965. *Tanzsprache und Orientierung der Bienen.* Berlin: Springer-Verlag.

Frisch, K. von. 1967a. *The Dance Language and Orientation of Bees* (Translated from the 1965 German edition by Leigh E. Chadwick). Cambridge: Harvard University Press.

Frisch, K. von. 1967b. Honeybees: Do they use direction and distance information provided by their dancers? *Science* 158:1072–1076. (See also the reply by A. M. Wenner and D. L. Johnson. *Science* 158:1076–1077.)

Frisch, K. von. 1968. The role of dances in recruiting bees to familiar sites. *Animal Behaviour* 16:531–533.

Frisch, K. von. 1973. Book review and postscript (*The Bee Language Controversy: An Experience in Science,* by Adrian M. Wenner). *Animal Behaviour* 21:628–630.

Frisch, K. von and R. Jander. 1957. Uber den Schwanzeltanz der Bienen. *Zeitschrift fuer vergleichende Physiologie* 40:239–263.

Frisch, K. von and G. A. Rosch. 1926. Neue Versuche ueber die Bedeutung von Duftorgan und Pollenduft fuer die Verstaendigung im Bienenvolk. *Zeitschrift fuer Vergleichende Physiologie* 4:1–21.

Gilbert, G. N. and M. Mulkay. 1984. *Opening Pandora's Box.* New York: Cambridge University Press.

Gohlke, P., ed. 1949. Aristotle, *Tierkunde* IX, passage 624b:423. Paderborn.

Goncalves, L. 1969. A study of orientation information given by one trained bee by dancing. *Journal of Apicultural Research* 8:113–132.

Gould, J. L. 1974. Honey bee communication. *Nature* 252:300–301.

Gould, J. L. 1975a. *Honey Bee Communication: The Dance-Language Controversy.* Ph.D. dissertation, Rockefeller University, New York. (Xerox, University Microfilms no. 77–17,289)

Gould, J. L. 1975b. Honey bee recruitment: The dance-language controversy. *Science* 189:685–693.

Gould, J. L. 1975c. Communication of distance information by honey bees. *Journal of Comparative Physiology* 104:161–173.

Gould, J. L. 1976. The dance-language controversy. *Quarterly Review of Biology* 51:211–244.

Gould, J. L. and C. G. Gould. 1988. *The Honey Bee*. New York: Scientific American Library, Freeman.

Gould, J. L., M. Henerey, and M. C. MacLeod. 1970. Communication of direction by the honey bee. *Science* 169:544–554.

Gould, S. J. and N. Eldredge. 1986. Punctuated equilibrium at the third stage. *Systematic Zoology* 35:143–148.

Griffin, D. R. 1984. *Animal Thinking*. Cambridge: Harvard University Press.

Griffin, D. R. and P. Marler. 1974. Reply to Ankerl and Pereboom (letter). *Science* 185:814.

Griffith, B. C. and N. C. Mullins. 1972. Coherent social groups in scientific change. *Science* 177:959–964.

Grinnell, F. 1987. *The Scientific Attitude*. Boulder, Colo.: Westview Press.

Gutting, G. 1980. Introduction: Appraisals and applications of Thomas Kuhn's philosophy of science. In G. Gutting, *Paradigms and Revolutions*, pp. 1–21. Notre Dame, Ind.: University of Notre Dame Press.

Hacking, I. 1983. *Representing and Intervening: Introductory Topics in the Philosophy of Natural Science*. New York: Cambridge University Press.

Hailman, J. P. 1977. Bee dancing and evolutionary epistemology (challenge of a letter by Ferguson). *American Naturalist* 11:187–189.

Hardin, G. 1967. Pop research and the seismic market. *Per/Se* 2(3):19–24.

Harding, S. 1986. *The Science Question in Feminism*. Ithaca, N.Y.: Cornell University Press.

Hempel, C. G. 1966. *Philosophy of Natural Science*. Englewood Cliffs, N.J.: Prentice-Hall.

Henkel, C. 1938. *Unterscheiden die Bienen Tanze?* Doctoral Dissertation, Bonn. (Cited in von Frisch 1947.)

Hull, D. L. 1988. *Science as a Process: An Evolutionary Account of the Social and Conceptual Development of Science*. Chicago; University of Chicago Press.

Jenner, E. (1798) 1959. An inquiry into the causes and effects of the variolae vaccinae, a disease discovered in some of the western counties of England, particularly Gloucestershire, and known by the name of the cowpox. In C. N. B. Camac, ed., *Classics of Medicine and Surgery*, pp. 206–242. New York: Dover.

Jeplin, J., ed. 1984. *Scientific Realism*. Berkeley: University of California Press.

Johnson, D. L. 1967a. Honeybees: Do they use the direction information contained in their dance maneuver? *Science* 155:847–849.

Johnson, D. L. 1967b. Communication among honeybees with field experience. *Animal Behaviour* 15:487–492.

Johnson, D. L. and A. M. Wenner. 1966. A relationship between conditioning and communication in honeybees. *Animal Behaviour* 14:261–265.

Johnson, D. L. and A. M. Wenner. 1970. Recruitment efficiency in honeybees: Studies on the role of olfaction. *Journal of Apicultural Research* 9:13–18.

Kalmus, H. 1960. Training bees to smells and exciting bees in a hive. In *101 Simple Experiments with Insects*, pp. 96–97. Garden City, N.Y.: Doubleday.

Keller, E. F. 1983. *A Feeling for the Organism: The Life and Work of Barbara McClintock*. New York: Freeman.

Kennedy, J. S. 1983. Zigzagging and casting as a programmed response to wind-borne odour: A review. *Physiological Entomology* 8:109–120.

Kimsey, L. S. 1984. A re-evaluation of the phylogenetic relationships in the Apidae (Hymenoptera). *Systematic Entomology* 9:435–441.

Kneller, G. F. 1978. *Science as a Human Endeavor*. New York: Columbia University Press.

Kroeber, A. L. 1952. Sign and symbol in bee communications. *Proceedings of the National Academy of Sciences* 38:753–757.

Krogh, A. 1948. The language of the bees. *Scientific American* 179:18–21.

Kuhn, T. (1962) 1970a. *The Structure of Scientific Revolutions*, 2d edition, enlarged. Chicago; University of Chicago Press. (Foundations of the Unity of Science, vol. 2, no. 2.)

Kuhn, T. 1970b. Logic of discovery or psychology of research. In I. Lakatos and A. Musgrave, eds., *Criticism and the Growth of Knowledge*. Cambridge: Cambridge University Press.

Lakatos, I. 1970. Falsification and the methodology of scientific research programmes. In I. Lakatos and A. Musgrave, *Criticism and the Growth of Knowledge*, pp. 91–195. London: Proceedings of the International Colloquium in the Philosophy of Science (1965), vol. 4.

Lakatos, I. and A. Musgrave, eds. 1970. *Criticism and the Growth of Knowledge*. London: Proceedings of the International Colloquium in the Philosophy of Science (1965), vol. 4.

Latour, B. 1987. *Science in Action: How To Follow Scientists and Engineers Through Society*. Milton Keynes, England: Open University Press.

Latreille, P. A. 1830. *Cuvier's le regne animal, distribue d'apres son organization, pour servir de base a l'histoire naturelle des animaux et d'introduction a l'anatomie comparee*. 2d ed., 5 vols. Paris.

Leppik, E. E. 1953. The language of bees and its practical application. *American Bee Journal* 93:434–435, 470–471.

Lewis, T. 1984. The elements and frontiers of insect communication. In T. Lewis, *Insect Communication*, pp. 1–27. New York: Academic Press.

Lindauer, M. 1961. *Communication Among Social Bees*. Cambridge, Mass.: Harvard University Press.

Lindauer, M. 1967. Recent advances in bee communication and orientation. *Annual Review of Entomology* 12:439–470.

Lindauer, M. 1971. The functional significance of the honeybee waggle dance. *American Naturalist* 105:89–96.

Lindauer, M. 1985. The dance language of honeybees: The history of a discovery. In B. Holldobler and M. Lindauer, *Experimental Behavioral*

Ecology and Sociobiology, pp. 129–140. Sunderland, Mass.: Sinauer Associates.

Lindergren, C. C. 1966. *Cold War in Biology*. Ann Arbor, Mich.: Planarian Press.

Lineburg, B. 1924. Communication by scent in the honeybee: A theory. *American Naturalist* 58:530–537.

Loeb, J. (1918) 1973. *Forced Movements, Tropisms, and Animal Conduct.* New York: Dover.

Lopatina, N. G. 1964. Physiology of the recruiting activity of bees (in Russian). *Pchelovodstvo* 84:34–36.

Louis, P., ed. and trans. 1969. *Aristotle: Histoire des Animaux*, book 3. Paris: Bude, Societé d' Edition "Les Belles Lettres."

Lubbock, J. 1874. Observations on bees and wasps, 1. *Journal of the Linnean Society* (Zool.) 12:110–139. (Cited in Ribbands 1953.)

Lubbock, J. 1882. *Ants, Bees, and Wasps.* London: Kegan Paul, Trench.

Maeterlinck, M. 1901. *The Life of the Bee.* Trans. Alfred Sutro. New York: Dodd, Mead.

Maeterlinck, M. (1901) 1939. *La Vie des Abeilles.* Paris: Bibliotheque-Charpentier, Fasquelle Editeurs.

Maeterlinck, M. 1927. *The Life of the White Ant.* New York: Dodd, Mead.

Maeterlinck, M. 1930. *The Life of the Ant.* London: Allen and Unwin.

Mahoney, M. J. 1976. *Scientist as Subject: The Psychological Imperative.* Cambridge, Mass.: Ballinger (Lippincott).

Marais, E. 1937. *The Soul of the White Ant.* Trans. Winifred de Kok. London: Methuen.

Marais, E. 1969. *The Soul of the Ape.* Introduction by Robert Ardrey. New York: Athenaeum.

Masterson, M. 1970. The nature of a paradigm. In I. Lakatos and A. Musgrave, eds., *Criticism and the Growth of Knowledge*, pp. 59–88. London: Proceedings of the International Colloquium in the Philosophy of Science (1965), vol. 4.

Mautz, D. 1971. Der Kommunikationeffekt der Schwanzeltanze bei *Apis mellifica carnica* (Pollm.) 72:197–220.

Mayr, E. 1982. *The Growth of Biological Thought, Diversity, Evolution, and Inheritance.* Cambridge, Mass.: Belknap (Harvard University Press).

McIntosh, R. P. 1987. Pluralism in ecology. *Annual Review of Ecological Systematics* 18:321–341.

Medawar, P. B. (1979) 1981. *Advice to a Young Scientist.* New York: Harper and Row.

Merton, R. K. 1968. The Matthew effect in science. *Science* 159:56–63.

Merton, R. K. 1973. *The Sociology of Science: Theoretical and Empirical Investigations.* Chicago; University of Chicago Press.

Mervis, J. 1988. Erich Bloch's campaign to transform NSF. *American Scientist* 76:557–561.

Michener, C. D. 1974. *The Social Behavior of the Bees: A Comparative Study.* Cambridge; Harvard University Press.

Miller, D., ed. 1985. *Popper Selections.* Princeton, N.J.: Princeton University Press.

Milne-Edwards, H. 1830. Description des Genres Glaucothoe, Sicyonia, Sergeste et Acete, de l'ordre des Crustaces Decapodes. *Annales des Sciences Naturelles (B) Zoologie,* 1st series, 19:333–352.

Moore, B. R. 1988. Magnetic fields and orientation in homing pigeons: Experiments of the late W. T. Keeton. *Proceedings of the National Academy of Sciences* 85:4907–4909.

Morse, R. A. and R. Boch. 1971. Pheromone concert in swarming honey bees (Hymenoptera: Apidae). *Annals of the Entomological Society of America* 64:1414–1417.

Muller, R. A. 1980. Innovation and scientific funding. *Science* 209:880–883.

Mullins, N. C. 1968. The distribution of social and cultural properties in informal communication networks among biological sciences. *American Sociological Review* 33:786–797.

Ohtani, T. 1983. Is honeybee's "dance language" really fact? A criticism of Gould's work (in Japanese). *Honeybee Science* 4:97–104. (Translation by Keiko Sekiguchi Wells available in the International Bee Research Association Library, 18 North Road, Cardiff CF1 3DY, United Kingdom.)

Panem, S. 1987. Image makers. *Science* 236:973–974. Book review of Nelkin, D. 1987. *How the Press Covers Science and Technology.* New York: Freeman.

Park, O. W. 1929. Time factors in relation to the acquisition of food by the honeybee. *Research Bulletin of the Iowa Agricultural Experiment Station* 108:181–226.

Peters, D. P. and S. J. Ceci. 1982. Peer-review practices of psychological journals: The fate of published articles, submitted again. *Behavioral and Brain Sciences* 5:187–255.

Pickett, J. A., I. H. Williams, A. P. Martin, and M. C. Smith. 1980. Nasonov pheromone of the honey bee, *Apis mellifera* L. (Hymenoptera: Apidae), part 1: Chemical characterization. *Journal of Chemical Ecology* 6:425–434.

Picket, J. A., I. H. Williams, M. C. Smith, and A. P. Martin. 1981. Nasonov pheromone of the honey bee, *Apis mellifera* L. (Hymenoptera: Apidae), part 3: Regulation of pheromone composition and production. *Journal of Chemical Ecology* 7:543–554.

Platt, J. R. 1964. Strong inference. *Science* 146:347–353.

Polanyi, M. 1958. *Personal Knowledge: Towards a Post-Critical Philosophy.* Chicago; University of Chicago Press.

Popper, K. R. 1957. Philosophy of science: A personal report. In C. A. Mace, ed. *British Philosophy in the Mid-Century,* pp. 155–191. New York: Macmillan.

Popper, K. R. 1968. *Conjectures and Refutations: The Growth of Scientific Knowledge.* New York: Harper and Row.

Popper, K. R. 1970. Normal science and its dangers. In I. Lakatos and A. Musgrave, eds., *Criticism and the Growth of Knowledge*, pp. 51–58. London: Proceedings of the International Colloquium in the Philosophy of Science (1965).

Popper, K. R. (1977) 1985. The mind-body problem. In D. Miller, ed., *Popper Selections*, pp. 265–275. Princeton, N.J.: Princeton University Press.

Putnam, H. 1981. *Reason, Truth and History*. New York: Cambridge University Press.

Rackham, H. 1967. *Pliny's Natural History*. Vol. 3, Loeb Library Series. Cambridge; Harvard University Press.

Renner, M. and T. Heinzeller. 1979. Do trained honeybees with reliably blinded ocelli really return to the feeding site? *Journal of Apicultural Research* 18:225–229.

Ribbands, C. R. 1953. *The Behaviour and Social Life of Honeybees*. London: Bee Research Association.

Ribbands, C. R. 1954. Communication between honeybees, part 1: The response of crop-attached bees to the scent of their crop. *Proceedings of the Royal Entomological Society of London (A)* 29:10–12.

Ribbands, C. R. 1955a. Communication between honeybees, part 2: The recruitment of trained bees, and their response to the improvement of the crop. *Proceedings of the Royal Society, London* (A) 30:26–32.

Ribbands, C. R. 1955b. The scent perception of the honeybee. *Proceedings of the Royal Society, London (B)* 143:367–377.

Ribbands, C. R. and N. Speirs. 1953. The adaptability of the homecoming honey bee. *British Journal of Animal Behaviour* 1:59–66.

Root, A. I., E. R. Root, H. H. Root, and M. J. Deyell. 1947. *The ABC and XYZ of Bee Culture*. Medina, Ohio: A. I. Root.

Root, E. R. 1908. (No title.) *Gleanings in Bee Culture* 36:830, 868. (Cited in Ribbands 1953.)

Rosin, R. 1978. The honey bee "language" controversy. *Journal of Theoretical Biology* 72:589–602.

Rosin, R. 1980a. The honey-bee "dance language" hypothesis and the foundations of biology and behavior. *Journal of Theoretical Biology* 87:457–481.

Rosin, R. 1980b. Paradoxes of the honey-bee "dance language" hypothesis. *Journal of Theoretical Biology* 84:775–800.

Rosin, R. 1984. Further analysis of the honey bee "dance language" controversy, part 1: Presumed proofs for the "dance language" hypothesis, by Soviet scientists. *Journal of Theoretical Biology* 107:417–442.

Rosin, R. 1988a. Do honey bees still have a "dance language"? *American Bee Journal* 128:267–268.

Rosin, R. 1988b. Questioning von Frisch's honey-bee dance language (response to a letter by Walls). *American Bee Journal* 128:576–578.

Ruse, M. 1973. *The Philosophy of Biology.* London: Hutchinson University Library.

Schram, F. R. 1979. *The Myth of Science or the Fantasy of Truth.* New York: Vantage Press.

Schricker, B. 1974. Der Einfluss subletaler Dosen von Parathion (E 605) auf die Entfernungsweisung bei der Honigbiene. *Apidologie* 5:149–175.

Seeley, T. D. 1985. *Honeybee Ecology: A Study of Adaptation in Social Life.* Princeton, N.J.: Princeton University Press.

Shearer, D. A. and R. Boch. 1966. Citral in the Nassanoff pheromone of the honey bee. *Journal of Insect Physiology* 12:1513–1521.

Sigma Xi study. 1987. *A New Agenda for Science.* New Haven, Conn.: Sigma Xi.

Silverman, W. A. 1986. Subversion as a constructive activity in medicine. *Perspectives in Biology and Medicine* 29:385–391.

Silvernale, M. N. 1965. *Zoology.* New York: Macmillan.

Singer, C. 1959. *A Short History of Scientific Ideas to 1900.* New York: Oxford University Press.

Sladen, F. W. L. 1901. A scent-producing organ in the abdomen of the bee. *Gleanings in Bee Culture* 29:639.

Smith, B. H. 1988. Book review. (*Neurobiology and Behavior of Honeybees,* R. Menzel and A. Mercer, eds.). *Quarterly Review of Biology* 63:250.

Spitzner, M. J. E. 1788. *Ausfuehrliche Beschreibung der Korbbienenzucht im sachsischen Churkreise, ihrer Dauer und ihres Nutzens, ohne kunstliche Vermehrung nach den Grunden der Naturgeschichte und nach eigener langer Erfahrung.* Leipzig: (Reference as in von Frisch 1967.)

Steinbeck, J. (1941) 1962. *The Log from the Sea of Cortez.* New York: Viking.

Steiner, L. F. 1952. Methyl eugenol as an attractant for oriental fruit fly. *Journal of Economic Entomology* 45:241–248.

Stephen, W. P. and B. Schricker. 1970. The effect of sublethal doses of parathion, part 2: Site of parathion activity, and signal integration. *Journal of Apicultural Research* 9:155–164.

Sternberg, R. J. 1985. Human intelligence: The model is the message. *Science* 230:1111–1118.

Szent-Gyorgyi, A. 1971. Looking back. *Perspectives in Biology and Medicine* 15:1–5.

Taber, S. 1986. The foraging of honey bees. *American Bee Journal* 126:538–541.

Theocharis, T. and M. Psimopoulos. 1987. Where science has gone wrong. *Nature* 329:595–598.

Thompson, D. W. 1910. *The Works of Aristotle.* Oxford, England: Oxford University Press.

Thompson, J. V. 1828. *Zoological researches and illustrations.* No. 1, 36 pp., 4 plates. Cork, England.

Thompson, J. V. 1829. Memoir 3: On the luminosity of the ocean, with descriptions of some remarkable species of luminous animals (*Pyrosoma pigmaea* and *Sapphirina indicator*) and particularly of the four new genera *Noctiluca, Cynthia, Lucifer* and *Podopsis* of the Schizopoda. Pp. 37–61, 4 plates. And addenda to Memoir 1: On the metamorphoses of the Crustacea, pp. 63–66.

Thompson, J. V. 1831. On the metamorphoses of decapodous Crustacea. *Zoological Journal, Linnean Society* 5:383–384.

Thompson, J. V. 1835a. Memoir on the metamorphosis of Porcellana and Portunua. *Entomology Monthly Magazine.* Pp. 275–280, 3 figures.

Thompson, J. V. 1835b. Discovery of the metamorphosis in the second type of the Cirripedes, viz. the Lepades, completing the natural history of these singular animals and confirming their affinity with the Crustacea. *Philosophical Transactions of the Royal Society of London*, part 2, pp. 355–358, plate 5.

Thorpe, W. H. 1949. Orientation and methods of communication of the honey bee and its sensitivity to the polarization of the light. *Nature* (London) 164:11–14.

Thorpe, W. H. 1963. *Learning and Instinct in Animals.* London: Methuen.

Tinbergen, N. 1951. *The Study of Instinct.* Oxford: Oxford University Press.

Tinbergen, N. and A. C. Perdeck. 1950. On the stimulus situation releasing the begging response in the newly-hatched Herring Gull chick (*Larus a. argentatus*). *Behaviour* 3:1–38.

Veldink, C. 1976. *Paradigm Challenges in Modern Science: The Bee Language Controversy.* Ph.D. dissertation, University of California, Santa Barbara.

Veldink, C. 1989. The honey-bee language controversy. *Interdisciplinary Science Reviews* 14:166–175.

Virgil. (30 B.C.) 1937. *Virgil's Aeneid.* Trans. John Dryden. New York: Collier. (The Harvard Classics, C. W. Eliot, ed.)

Vowles, D. M. 1961. In W. H. Thorpe and O. L. Zangwill, eds., *Current Problems in Animal Behaviour*, pp. 5–29. London: Cambridge University Press.

Waddington, K. D. 1982. Honey bee foraging profitability and round dance correlates. *Journal of Comparative Physiology* 148:297–301.

Waller, G. D. 1970. Attracting honeybees to alfalfa with citral, geraniol and anise. *Journal of Apicultural Research* 9:9–12.

Walls, R. K. 1988. Bee language controversy (challenge of a letter by Rosin). *American Bee Journal* 128:576.

Watson, J. D. 1968. *The Double Helix.* New York: New American Library.

Weimer, W. B. 1979. *Notes on the Methodology of Scientific Research.* Hillsdale, N.J.: Lawrence Erlbaum Associates.

Wells, H. and P. H. Wells. 1983. Honey bee foraging ecology: Optimal diet, minimal uncertainty or individual constancy? *Journal of Animal Ecology* 52:829–836.

Wells, H. and P. H. Wells. 1986. Optimal diet, minimal uncertainty and individual constancy in the foraging of honey bees, *Apis mellifera. Journal of Animal Ecology* 55:881–891.

Wells, H., P. H. Wells, and D. Contreras. 1986. Effects of flower-morph frequency and distribution on recruitment and behaviour of honeybees. *Journal of Apicultural Research* 25:139–145.

Wells, H., P. H. Wells, and D. M. Smith. 1983. Ethological isolation of plants, part 1: Colour selection by honeybees. *Journal of Apicultural Research* 22:33–44.

Wells, P. H. 1973. Honey bees. In W. C. Corning, J. A. Dyal, and A. O. D. Willows, eds., *Invertebrate Learning*, vol. 2: Arthropods and Gastropod Mollusks. New York: Plenum Press.

Wells, P. H. and J. Giacchino, Jr. 1968. Relationship between the volume and the sugar concentration of loads carried by honeybees. *Journal of Apicultural Research* 7:77–82.

Wells, P. H. and H. Wells. 1985. Ethological isolation of plants, part 2: Odour selection by honeybees. *Journal of Apicultural Research* 24:86–92.

Wells, P. H. and A. M. Wenner. 1971. The influence of food scent on behavior of foraging honeybees. *Physiological Zoology* 44:191–209.

Wells, P. H. and A. M. Wenner. 1973. Do bees have a language? *Nature* 241:171–174.

Wenner, A. M. 1959. The relationship of sound production during the waggle dance of the honeybee to the distance of the food source. *Bulletin of the Entomological Society of America* 5:142.

Wenner, A. M. 1961. A method of training bees to visit a feeding station. *Bee World* 42:8–11.

Wenner, A. M. 1962. Sound production during the waggle dance of the honeybee. *Animal Behaviour* 10:79–95.

Wenner, A. M. 1963. The flight speed of honeybees: A quantitative approach. *Journal of Apicultural Research* 2:23–32.

Wenner, A. M. 1964. Sound communication in honeybees. *Scientific American* 210:116–124.

Wenner, A. M. 1967. Honeybees: Do they use the distance information contained in their dance maneuver? *Science* 155:847–849.

Wenner, A. M. 1969. The study of animal communication: An overview. In T. Sebeok, ed., *Approaches to Animal Communication*, pp. 232–243. Paris: Mouton.

Wenner, A. M. 1971a. *The Bee Language Controversy: An Experience in Science.* Boulder, Colo.: Educational Programs Improvement Corporation.

Wenner, A. M. 1971b. Animal communication. *McGraw Hill Encyclopedia of Science and Technology,* 1:433–436.

Wenner, A. M. 1974. Information transfer in honeybees: A population approach. In L. Krames, P. Pliner, and T. Alloway, eds., *Nonverbal*

Communication, vol. 1: *Advances in the Study of Communication and Effect*, pp. 133–169. New York: Plenum Press.

Wenner, A. M., ed. 1985. *Larval Growth*. Vol. 2 of *Crustacean Issues*, F. Schram, senior ed. Rotterdam: Balkema.

Wenner, A. M. 1989. Concept-centered vs. organism-centered research. *American Zoologist* 29:1177–1197.

Wenner, A. M. and D. L. Johnson. 1966. Simple conditioning in honeybees. *Animal Behaviour* 14:149–155.

Wenner, A. M. and P. H. Wells. 1987. The honey bee dance language controversy: The search for "truth" vs. the search for useful information. *American Bee Journal* 127:130–131.

Wenner, A. M., P. H. Wells, and D. L. Johnson. 1969. Honeybee recruitment to food sources: Olfaction or language? *Science* 164:84–86.

Wenner, A. M., P. H. Wells, and F. J. Rohlf. 1967. An analysis of the waggle dance and recruitment in honeybees. *Physiological Zoology* 40:317–344.

Westwood, J. O. 1835. On the supposed existence of metamorphoses in the Crustacea. *Philosophical Transactions of the Royal Society of London*, part 2, pp. 311–328, plate 4.

Wheeler, W. M. 1910. *Ants, Their Structure, Development and Behavior.* New York: Columbia University Press.

Wheeler, W. M. 1923. *Social Life Among the Insects.* New York: Harcourt, Brace.

Whewell, W. 1840. *Philosophy of the Inductive Sciences.* London: Parker.

White, A. D. (1895) 1955. *A History of the Warfare of Science with Theology in Christendom.* New York: George Braziller.

Whitley, R. 1984. *The Intellectual and Social Organization of the Sciences.* New York: Clarendon (Oxford University Press).

Wildman, T. 1768. *A Treatise on the Management of Bees; Wherein is Contained the Natural History of those Insects; With the Various Methods of Cultivating Them, both Ancient and Modern, and the Improved Treatment of Them. To which are added, The Natural History of Wasps and Hornets, and the Means of Destroying Them.* London: T. Cadell.

Wilson, E. O. 1971. *The Insect Societies.* Cambridge: Harvard University Press.

Wilson, E. O. 1972. (Letter exchange). *Scientific American* 227:6.

Winkler, K. 1985. Historians fail to explain science to laymen, scholar says. Scholarship: *The Chronicle of Higher Education*, August 7, 1985.

Winsor, M. P. 1969. Barnacle larvae in the nineteenth century: A case study in taxonomic theory. *Journal of the History of Medicine and Allied Sciences* 24:294–309.

Winston, M. L. 1987. *The Biology of the Honey Bee.* Cambridge: Harvard University Press.

Witherell, P. C. 1985. A review of the scientific literature relating to honey bee bait hives and swarm attractants. *American Bee Journal* 125:823–829.

Woodrow, A. W., N. Green, H. Tucker, M. H. Schonhorst, and K. C. Hamilton. 1965. Evaluation of chemicals as honey bee attractants and repellents. *Journal of Economic Entomology* 58:1094–1102.

Zuckerman, H. 1977. *Scientific Elite.* New York: Macmillan (The Free Press).

INDEX

ABC and XYZ of Bee Culture, The (Root et al.), 79, 322

Acceptance, 11; of dance language hypothesis, 60, 65, 91-110; of dance language paradigm, 192, 195; degree of, 32; of hypothesis, 9; of new interpretation, 20; of odor-search paradigm, 79; of theory, 41; of von Frisch olfactory hypothesis, 73; of Wenner, Wells, and Johnson hypothesis, 209

Accountability, 7

Aerial pathway, 78-79, 105, 325-28, 336

"Affirmation of the consequent," 211, 220, 243, 309

African Genesis (Ardrey), 294-95

Agassiz, Louis, 197

Alloway, Thomas, 203

American Bee Journal, 372

American Institute of Biological Sciences (AIBS), 201

American Philosophical Society, 109-10, 194

American Psychological Association, 155

Amphipod directional orientation, 203

Amplitude modulation, 117

Andersen, B. B., 372

Anderson, Judith, 3, 265

Anecdote, 113, 291; significance of, 132

Anemotactic search, 321-23

Anemotaxis, 72, 74-75, 81, 218, 260, 320

Animal behavior, 233, 246-47, 299, 362; toward attractant, 313; human bias and, 75-76; mechanistic approach to, 80; quantitative approach to, 113

Animal Thinking (Griffin), 233, 246

Ankerl, G., 204

Anomalies, 126, 369-70; accommodation of, 336-38; awareness of, 125; basic assumptions and, 31; in Gould, 239; in Gould, Henerey, and MacLeod, 223; importance of, 113, 118; Kuhn and, 227; learning, 111-28; in Nasanov gland attraction, 185-86; odor, 129-49, 131; recruit arrival pattern, 177; significance of, 132

Anthropomorphism, 75-76, 240, 246, 261, 277

Antirealism, *see* Relativism school

Arc array, 328-30

Ardrey, Robert, 44-45, 294-98; *African Genesis*, 294-95

Aristotle, 35; importance of odor and, 87; odor-search paradigm and, 76-77, 81; olfactory sense of bees, 71; translations of, 270-73

Aronson, Naomi, 2, 198

Array design, 237

Artificial bee, 367-72

Assumptions, 219-20, 240; about nature, 340; basic, 26, 31, 153; of Gould, 239; of Gould, Henerey, and MacLeod, 223; hypothesis and, 60-61; *see also* Paradigm hold

Atkinson, James W., 15, 19, 23, 39, 199, 299; image creating, 40, 47-48, 153; philosophy of science and, 50-51; protocol and, 49; science as process and, 131

Attraction hypothesis, 312-19

Authority, 204; questioning of, 196

"Averaging," 336-37

Awake, 372

Bacher, Robert F., 202

Bacon, Sir Francis, 1, 3, 40, 47-48, 347; induction and, 173; null hypothesis and, 156-57

Baker, Meyer, and Roelfos, 313, 316

389

Opening Pandora's Box (Gilbert and Mulkay), 197-98
Orientation flights, 83, 322-23, 327
Osterreichische Zoologische Zeitschrift, 97

Panem, S., 7
Papi and Pardi, 203
Paradigm, 24-26, 29; choice, 207, 212; competing, 66-68; conflicts in, 255-68; as controlling factor, 31-32; dance language hypothesis as, 65; insect-level v. human-level, 67-68; Kuhn and, 66; odor-search v. dance language, 67; peer group pressure and, 28; prevailing, 155; Realism v. Relativism, 68-69; ruling, 247; v. hypothesis, 60, 66-67
Paradigm hold, 24-26, 31, 50, 52, 67, 204, 263, 266, 308; anomalies and, 113; effect on interpretation, 252-54; of Gould, 236; Maeterlinck and, 42; Ribbands and, 126; role of, 257; ruling theory and, 41-42, 47
Paradigm shift, 29, 32, 50, 255, 319, 342, 357; of von Frisch, 64-65, 73-74
"Parental affection" (for hypothesis), 42, 103, 106, 238
Parsimony, law of, 246-48
Pasteur, Louis, viii, 4, 26, 29, 30, 189, 199, 264
Peat, F. D., 31, 60, 299, 351; paradigm concept and, 66
Peer group pressure, 28, 186; *see also* Social considerations; Scientific community
Peer review, 284, 353
Pereboom, D., 204
"Persuasive passion," 198-200
Peters, D. P., 191
Phenomenalism, 350
Pheromones, 312-19
Philosophers, of science, 20, 38, 68
Philosophy, of science, 4, 6, 310, 339-44
"Philosophy of science: A personal report" (Popper), 21-23
Phonotaxis, negative, 80
Phototaxis, positive, 75, 80
Physiology, 80

Plagiarism, 294-98
Platt, John, 37-39, 267; inductive-deductive approach, 40; strong inference and, 44, 47-49, 174-75
Pliner, Patricia, 203
Pliny the Elder, 270, 272-73, 296-98
Polanyi, Michael, 28-29, 50, 198-202, 350; "crossing a logical gap," 29; paradigm holds and, 40
Politics: in controversies, 8; of science, 5-6
Polywater hypothesis, ix, 49-50, 267, 370
Popper, Karl, 13, 15-17, 238, 357; acceptance of new ideas, 20-21; ad hoc assumption and, 285; confirmations and, 215; falsifiability approach, 37, 53, 105, 153; hypothesis testing and, 95; Kuhn view of (diagram), 28; "Mind-Body Problem, The," 261; "null hypothesis approach," 21-23; realism and, 339-42; Realism school and, 39-40, 262-63; self-correcting science and, 30; view v. Kuhn, 26-32, 153-54, 200
"Pop Research," 6
Popular science, 267, 274, 310
Population, v. individual, 261
Positivism, 341
Postman, L., 120
Pragmatic approach, 26; *see also* Relativism school
Pragmatism, 341
Predictions: of dance language hypothesis, 138, 145, 160, 182; risky, 22, 215
Probability, 238
Proof, v. discovery, 47
Protocol, 239, 257, 309, 351; odor-switch, 287
Psimopoulos, M., 345
Psychology, of science, 4, 310-11
Purposefulness, 114
Putnam, Hilary, 131, 345, 346-47, 347-52

Rationalism, 340
Rationality, 23, 345
Realism school, 15, 26, 45; animal behavior research and, 114-15; anoma-

lies and, 155; Carnap and, 39-40; Esch and Bastian and, 217; interpretation of behavior and, 231-54; paradigm hold and, 51; paradigm shift and, 74; Popper and, 39-40; social control and, 209-10; "truth" in, 47; view of progress, 50; von Frisch and, 93-95, 104-6; v. Relativism school, 39, 47, 68-69, 189, 255-68, 259-60, 339-44

Reasoning: circular, 236; deductive, 3, 347-48; inductive, 3, 347-48; objective, 8

Recruit: arrival, binomial distribution, 88; arrival, food scent and, 143; buildup, 135-36, 177-78; search behavior and wind direction, 144

Recruitment: binomial distribution of, 165; dance orientation and, 141; by disoriented dances, 138-41; inefficiency of, 87; mechanism of, 82-83; multinomial distribution of, 166-71; pattern of (diagram), 136; population aspect of, 324-25; as population phenomenon, 87-88; remote interference with, 136-38

Referee system, 289

Refutability, 22

Refutation, 341

Relativism school, 15, 26, 33-53, 40, 67; v. Realism school, 39, 47, 68-69, 189, 255-68, 339-44

Relevant community, 209, 236, 241, 258; assent of, 207, 250, 342; commitment in, 234; control by, 210; endorsement by, 192

Renner, M., 235, 252-54

Replication, 7-8, 43, 63, 262-63, 264

Research: concept-driven, 240, 245; organism-driven, 245; traditional approach to, 131

Respectability, 16

Results, negative, 223

Review practices, 191

Reward, 119, 125

Reward system, 209, 257, 267

Rheotaxis, 81

Ribbands, C. R., 57-58, 244, 323, 355; odor stimulus and, 126-27; Spitzner and, 85-86

Ricard, Yann, 272

Root, A. I., *ABC and XYZ of Bee Culture, The* (with others), 79, 322

Root, E. R., 58, 322

Rosch, G. A., 93, 312

Rosin, R., 33, 231, 235, 253, 320; biology and behavior, 246-50; dance language paradoxes and, 240-46; insect-v. human-level capability, 67-68, 235-40; odor center and, 324; refutation of Gould by, 300-1, 309-10; teleological argument and, 366; use of odor and, 72; von Frisch odor-search paradigm and, 79

Ruling theory, 41-42, 50, 67, 69, 172, 263, 338; Chamberlin and, 46-47, 76; Gould and, 45; von Frisch and, 107

Ruse, Michael, 365

Salk, Jonas, 201, 358-59

Salk Institute, 201, 219, 353-61

Scent, 78; removal of, 221-23; training, in hive, 86, 127

Scent gland, 88-89, 99; attractiveness of, 94-95; von Frisch experiments on, 102; *see also* Nasanov gland

Scent plates, 100

Scent trail, 71, 78

Schneirla-Lehrman school, 68

Schricker, Burkhardt, 201, 235, 242-49, 328, 338

Science, 155, 175, 202, 300; Wenner, Wells, and Johnson exchange with, 274-84

Science: advances in, 24; as collective process, 350-52; erroneous, 266-67; hierarchy in, 16; history of, 15; image of, 5; as inductive process, 129-31; nature of, ix, 3-4; philosophy of, x, 37, 50-51; politics of, 5-6; process of, viii, x, 3-5, 15, 17, 30, 39, 68, 131, 285-86; progress in, 27, 29; public image of, 26; rationality of, 342; reality of, 5; self-correcting, 7, 21, 30, 344; social forces in, 16, 19; sociological aspect of, 49-50, 187-205

Science News, 372

Scientific American, 193, 195

Scientific approach, 47

Scientific community, 241, 257, 265; attitude of, 62; behavior of, 21; con-